10773993

15.70

SERIAL LEARNING
AND
PARALEARNING

WILEY SERIES IN BEHAVIOR

KENNETH MacCORQUODALE, Editor

University of Minnesota

A Temperament Theory of Personality Development
ARNOLD H. BUSS AND ROBERT PLOMIN

Serial Learning and Paralearning
E. RAE HARCUM

SERIAL LEARNING
AND
PARALEARNING

E. RAE HARCUM
The College of William and Mary

A WILEY-INTERSCIENCE PUBLICATION

JOHN WILEY & SONS, New York London Sydney Toronto

To Phoebe, my wife,

to whom I owe the most

Copyright © 1975 by John Wiley & Sons, Inc.

All rights reserved. Published simultaneously in Canada.

No part of this book may be reproduced by any means,
nor transmitted, nor translated into a machine language
without the written permission of the publisher.

Library of Congress Cataloging in Publication Data

Harcum, Eugene Rae, 1927–
    Serial learning and paralearning

    (Wiley series in behavior)
    "A Wiley-Interscience publication."
    Bibliography: p.
    Includes indexes.
    1.   Cognition.   2.   Learning, Psychology of.
3.   Memory.   I.   Title.

BF311.H337   153.1'52   75–5857
ISBN 0–471–35137–7

Printed in the United States of America

10 9 8 7 6 5 4 3 2 1

SERIES PREFACE

Psychology is one of the lively sciences. Its foci of research and theoretical concentration are diverse among us, and always on the move, sometimes into unexploited areas of scholarship, sometimes back for second thoughts about familiar problems, often into other disciplines for problems and for problem-solving techniques. We are always trying to apply what we have learned, and we have had some great successes at it. The Wiley Series in Behavior reflects this liveliness.

The series can accommodate monographic publication of purely theoretical advances, purely empirical ones, or any mixture in between. It welcomes books that span the interfaces within the behavioral sciences and between the behavioral sciences and their neighboring disciplines. The series is, then, a forum for the discussion of those advanced, technical, and innovative developments in the behavioral sciences that keep its frontiers flexible and expanding.

KENNETH MacCORQUODALE

December 1974
Minneapolis, Minnesota

PREFACE

A more complete and accurate title for this book would read "Cognitive Control Processes and Related Mechanisms in Serial Learning and Memory." This is because the book concentrates on the macroprocesses of information assimilation from multiple-element arrays, rather than on the microprocesses (Feigenbaum & Simon, 1962). The term "control processes" follows the usage of Atkinson and Shiffrin (1968). As the reader will note, the present approach is very cognitive in language and orientation. A basic assumption of the book is that the same type of information analysis and encoding processes is involved in the so-called perception of patterns and in serial learning and memory (Harcum, 1967b). These processes, which are intimately related to the actual formation of learned associations but are not actually part of the serial learning per se, are called *paralearning processes.*

My theoretical point of view must ultimately be described as behavioristic and associationistic, although both words carry connotations that do not seem fair. My approach incorporates more emphasis on field or contextual factors than those words imply. Also, I greatly emphasize cognitive organization and strategies of selective attention. Finally, I tend to be a "leveler" of theoretical issues—seeking commonalities and similarities of relationships and phenomena, rather than picking at differences.

The book first examines the serial-position effect of rote learning and then shows how traditional attempts to account for this outcome of serial learning have led many earlier researchers away from an examination of the fundamental mechanisms involved in the learning. The sheer ubiquity of the positional distribution of differential performance within serial learning has made the serial-position curve appear to be indeed a manifestation of very significant general laws of behavior. It seemed to me, and to many others, that it was very important for students of the psychology of learning to understand the origins of this curve.

Explanation of the serial-position outcome was my first interest in experimental psychology; my first research was aimed at understanding this phenomenon—or perhaps epiphenomenon, if the thesis of this book is correct. My first research paper in graduate school was a summary of the literature on serial learning. I suggested an explanation for the serial-position effect in terms of two factors: (1) a set by the subject to learn forward associations, and (2) interference caused by backward and remote associations. Learning was attributed to a reduction of the incorrect interfering tendencies through a process of differentiation, from the use of all available cues. This differentiation was thought to be more difficult for items in the middle of the list because of the smaller number of cues.

The reader will probably conclude that my interpretation of the phenomenon has not changed much in more than 20 years. Indeed, some reviewers agree that general understanding of the problem has not shown appreciable gains from that point over these intervening years. In any case, I was sufficiently satisfied with the above interpretation, and the Deese and Kresse (1952) support of it, that I did not view the serial-position effect as a problem that remained to be solved by psychology. Other psychologists apparently agreed to this general point of view, because there was relatively little published on the problem until Glanzer and Peters (1962) and some others rekindled interest about ten years later. Research programs on the general topic have multiplied since then, although there have been some (e.g., Young, 1968) who suggest that we should return the task to inactive status. Unfortunately, most of the more recent literature has concentrated on the false issue of whether a series is learned by positional or sequential cues—a controversy that seemed to have a clear resolution by as early as 1950—at least in my opinion.

I subsequently decided that the so-called serial-learning effect still overlaid some psychological problems that were worthy of further study. The generally molar cognitive approach (which I adopted along with a frequent molecular, nonstatistical analysis of individual cases) was, however, not in harmony with the prevailing attitudes and space limitations of the psychological journals. Therefore, often I have not been able to publish in sufficient detail what I considered relevant and useful information. I try to describe the acquisition of single items by individual subjects. The present book attempts to justify the type of approach and analysis that I have adopted.

The work that provides the core material for this book was facilitated by PHS grants (HD-00207) from the Institute of Child Welfare and Human Development, Public Health Service. Much of the material was conceived or modified during my tenure as a Visiting Scholar at the Institute of Human Learning, University of California, Berkeley, during the academic year 1967–1968. The advice and assistance of Leo Postman and other members and staff of the Institute are gratefully acknowledged. Some of the material was presented in seminar and discussion at the Institute, but a great deal of new material has been added since those discussions. I am particularly indebted to Harry Bahrick and Arthur Jensen for careful reading and detailed comments on an early version of this material.

Progress on the book was accomplished during a leave from my teaching duties, supported by a grant from the College Science Improvement Program of the National Science Foundation, during the first semester of the 1970–1971 session. I was privileged at that time to present portions of the material to selected groups of faculty and students at the Universities of Bristol, Cambridge, London, Oxford, Reading, and Sussex, England. The kind reception and helpful comments of the many persons involved are warmly acknowledged.

My colleagues, students, and friends at The College of William and Mary have been most patient and helpful in listening to my formal presentations and in responding to frequent requests for feedback and help. I am particularly grateful to Peter Derks, Virgil McKenna, Lynn Schulz, and Stanley Williams for reading and making helpful comments on a previous draft of the substantive arguments. Cynthia Null, of The College of William and Mary, and Adam Alexander, of New York City, graciously gave me their mathematical advice. I also am indebted to Edwin Coppage, now of Furman University, for collaboration on several of the studies that are reported in detail here. My thinking was shaped by rewarding discussions with him about these topics that are discussed.

I am grateful to James Deese, of the University of Virginia, for supporting my early interest in verbal learning. His comments about my general approach were most encouraging and helpful.

These acknowledgments of professional debt do not imply that everyone concurred with my basic approach or arguments. Since, in instances of a difference of opinion, I followed my own judgment, I am responsible for any errors that remain.

I thank Natalie Gillette, who prepared most of the figures and rendered able advice during the early phases of this project. Scott Castle, Diana Murrell, Johanna Ness, and Leslie Slemmer assisted with the preparation of the final manuscript. I also thank all of my research assistants for their dedicated help in many ways. The book could not have been completed without them.

I am especially grateful to the authors and publishers who generously gave permission for their material to be reproduced. Their contributions are identified in the Acknowledgments and also as the material is presented.

Finally, my family made a substantial contribution. My wife, Phoebe, assumed many of the household burdens and allowed me more time for this work. My children, Sally and Payten, paid the price mostly in the form of missed vacations.

E. RAE HARCUM

Williamsburg, Virginia
March 1975

ACKNOWLEDGMENTS

The following materials have been reprinted with the permission of authors and publishers:

Asch, S. E. The doctrinal tyranny of associationism: or what is wrong with rote learning. In T. R. Dixon & D. L. Horton (Eds.), *Verbal Behavior and General Behavior Theory*. Englewood Cliffs, New Jersey: Prentice-Hall, 1968, 214–228. (Chapter 9, pp. 217, 223, 225–226, 227.)

Battig, W. F. Paired-associate learning. In T. R. Dixon & D. L. Horton (Eds.), *Verbal Behavior and General Behavior Theory*. Englewood Cliffs, New Jersey: Prentice-Hall, 1968, 149–171. (Chapter 7, p. 164.)

Brown, C. H. The relation of magnitude of galvanic skin responses and resistance levels to the rate of learning. *Journal of Experimental Psychology*, 1937, **20**, 262–278. (Figure 1.)

Bugelski, B. R. A remote association explanation of the relative difficulty of learning nonsense syllables in a serial list. *Journal of Experimental Psychology*, 1950, **40**, 336–348. (Modification of data in Table 2 and replotting of Figure 1.)

Cofer, C. N. Problems, issues, and implications. In T. R. Dixon & D. L. Horton (Eds.), *Verbal Behavior and General Behavior Theory*. Englewood Cliffs, New Jersey: Prentice-Hall, 1968, 522–537. (Chapter 20, pp. 530, 531.)

Coppage, E. W., & Harcum, E. R. Temporal vs. structural determinants of primacy in strategies of serial learning. *Journal of Verbal Learning and Verbal Behavior*, 1967, **6**, 487–490. (Further analysis of the data.)

Crowder, R. G. Behavioral strategies in immediate memory. *Journal of Verbal Learning and Verbal Behavior*, 1969, **8**, 524–528. (Figure 1.)

Deese, J. *The Psychology of Learning*. New York: McGraw-Hill, 1958. (Use of the data on page 168 to construct three figures.)

Deese, J. Association and memory. In T. R. Dixon & D. L. Horton (Eds.), *Verbal Behavior and General Behavior Theory*. Englewood Cliffs, New Jersey: Prentice-Hall, 1968, 97–108. (Chapter 4, p. 99.)

Deese, J., Lazarus, R. S., & Keenan, J. Anxiety, anxiety-reduction, and stress in learning. *Journal of Experimental Psychology*, 1953, **46**, 55–60. (Modification of Figure 1.)

Dey, M. K. Generalization of position association in rote serial learning. *American Journal of Psychology*, 1970, **83**, 248–255. (Modification of Figure 1.)

Fischer, G. J. & Norton, J. A. A test of alternative hypotheses as to the nature of the serial learning curve. *Journal of General Psychology,* 1961, **64,** 219–224. (Modification of Figure 1.)

Harcum, E. R. Parallel functions of serial learning and tachistoscopic pattern perception. *Psychological Review,* 1967, **74,** 51–62. (Figure 1 and Table 1.)

Harcum, E. R. Cognitive anchoring of different errors in continuous serial learning. *Psychological Reports,* 1969, **25,** 79–82. (Figure 2, p. 81.)

Harcum, E. R. Serial learning with shorter intertrial interval than interstimulus interval. *Psychological Reports,* 1973, **33,** 487–494. (Figures 1, p. 490, and 2, p. 493. Further analysis of data.)

Harcum, E. R. Serial learning of heterogeneous items in ordered and unordered sequences. *Psychological Reports,* 1975, **36,** 3–11. (Modification of Figures 2 and 3.)

Harcum, E. R. & Coppage, E. W. Serial learning without primacy or recency effects. *Psychonomic Science,* 1965, **3,** 571–572. (Figure 1.)

Harcum, E. R. & Coppage, E. W. Serial position curve of verbal learning after prolonged practice. *Psychological Reports,* 1965, **17,** 475–488. (Figures 3, p. 480, and 4, p. 488. Further analysis of data.)

Harcum, E. R. & Coppage, E. W. Explanation of serial learning errors within Deese-Kresse categories. *Journal of Experimental Psychology,* 1969, **81,** 489–496. (Modification of Figures 1 and 2; Figure 4. Further analysis of unpublished data.)

Harcum, E. R., Pschirrer, M. E., & Coppage, E. W. Determinants of primacy for items in continuous serial learning, *Psychological Reports,* 1968, **22,** 965–975. (Figure 1, p. 968. Further analysis of data.)

Hayes, K. J. The backward curve: a method for the study of learning. *Psychological Review,* 1953, **60,** 269–275. (Figure 4.)

Horton, D. L. & Dixon, T. R. Traditions, trends, and innovations. In T. R. Dixon & D. L. Horton (Eds.), *Verbal Behavior and General Behavior Theory.* Englewood Cliffs, New Jersey: Prentice-Hall, 1968, 572–580. (Chapter 23, p. 21.)

Hovland, C. I. Experimental studies in rote-learning theory, III. Distribution of practice with varying speeds of syllable presentation. *Journal of Experimental Psychology,* 1938, **23,** 172–190. (Modification of Figure 3.)

Hovland, C. I. Experimental studies in rote-learning theory, VII. Distribution of practice with varying lengths of list. *Journal of Experimental Psychology,* 1940, **27,** 271–284. (Use of data in Table 4.)

Jensen, A. R. Individual differences in learning: interference factor. *Cooperative Research Project No. 1867,* Institute of Human Learning, University of California, Berkeley, Calif., 1964. (Research supported by Cooperative Research Program of the Office of Education, U. S. Dept. of Health, Education, and Welfare.) (Use of data in Table 13.)

Jensen, A. R. & Postman, L. Unpublished data.

Mandler, G., Mussen, P., Kogan, N., & Wallach, M. A. *New Directions in Psychology III.* & D. L. Horton (Eds.), *Verbal Behavior and General Behavior Theory.* Englewood Cliffs, New Jersey: Prentice-Hall, 1968, 109–119. (Chapter 5, pp. 117, 118.)

Mandler, G., Mussen, P., Kogan, N. & Wallach, M. A. *New Directions in Psychology III.* New York: Holt, Rinehart and Winston, Inc., 1967. (Mandler, Figure 1, p. 23.)

Malmo, R. B. & Amsel, A. Anxiety-produced interference in serial rote learning with observations on rote learning after partial frontal lobectomy. *Journal of Experimental Psychology,* 1948, **38,** 440–454. (Use of data in Table 1.)

McGeoch, J. A. The direction and extent of intra-serial associations at recall. *American*

Journal of Psychology, 1936, **48,** 221–245. (Use of data in Table VI.)

McKenna, V. V. & Harcum, E. R. Strategies in serial learning and tachistoscopic perception by aged subjects. *Virginia Journal of Science,* 1967, **18,** 210. (Further analysis of data.)

Melton, A. W. & Von Lackum, W. J. Retroactive and proactive inhibition in retention: evidence for a two-factor theory of retroactive inhibition. *American Journal of Psychology,* 1941, **54,** 157–173. (Modification of Figure 2.)

Noble, C. E. & Fuchs, J. E. Serial errors in human learning: a test of the McCrary-Hunter hypothesis. *Science,* **129,** 27 February 1959, 570–571. (Table 1.)

Obrist, W. D. Skin resistance and electroencephalographic changes associated with learning. *Unpublished doctoral dissertation, Northwestern University,* 1950. (University Microfilms, Inc., Ann Arbor, Michigan, No. 66–1, 145.) (Figures 1, 2, and 4.)
No. 66–1, 145.) (Figures 1, 2, and 4.)

Pollio, H. R. Associative structure and verbal behavior. In T. R. Dixon & D. L. Horton (Eds.), *Verbal Behavior and General Behavior Theory.* Englewood Cliffs, New Jersey: Prentice-Hall, 1968, 37–66. (Chapter 2, p. 55.)

Postman, L. Association and performance in the analysis of verbal learning. In T. R. Dixon & D. L. Horton (Eds.), *Verbal Behavior and General Behavior Theory.* Englewood Cliffs, New Jersey: Prentice-Hall, 1968, 550–571. (Chapter 22, p. 565.)

Postman, L. & Schwartz, M. Studies of learning to learn: I. Transfer as a function of method of practice and class of verbal materials. *Journal of Verbal Learning and Verbal Behavior,* 1964, **3,** 37–49. (Modification of Figure 2.)

Raskin, E. & Cook, S. W. The strength and direction of associations formed in the learning of nonsense syllables. *Journal of Experimental Psychology,* 1937, **20,** 381–395. (Use of data in Table 3.)

Slamecka, N.J. An inquiry into the doctrine of remote associations. *Psychological Review,* 1964, **71,** 61–76. (Analysis of data in Table 3.)

Tulving, E. Theoretical issues in free recall. In T. R. Dixon & D. L. Horton (Eds.), *Verbal Behavior and General Behavior Theory,* Englewood Cliffs, New Jersey: Prentice-Hall, 1968, 2–36. (Chapter 1, pp. 14, 24.)

Underwood, B. J. & Goad, D. Studies of distributed practice: 1. The influence of intra-list similarity in serial learning. *Journal of Experimental Psychology,* 1951, **42,** 125–134. (Figure 2.)

Young, R. K. Tests of three hypotheses about the effective stimulus in serial learning. *Journal of Experimental Psychology,* 1962, **63,** 307–313. (Figure 6.)

Young, R. K. Serial learning. In T. R. Dixon & D. L. Horton (Eds.), *Verbal Behavior and General Behavior Theory.* Englewood Cliffs, New Jersey: Prentice-Hall, 1968, 122–148. (Chapter 6, p. 142; Figure 1 on p. 138.)

E. R. H.

CONTENTS

PART

1

PROBLEMS
AND
APPROACHES

CHAPTER

$$\boxed{1}$$

ORIENTATION AND PLAN OF THE BOOK

Serial learning with ordered recall is one of the most familiar of the psychological tasks, in daily life as well as in the research laboratory. It occurs whenever a person learns what item follows or is adjacent to another in a spatial or temporal array. The precise conditions of the task vary tremendously, from a simple execution of directions having more than one step, through the brief task of remembering a telephone number long enough to dial it, to the very complex tasks of ordering the words in a sentence or reciting a poem or reading a book. The information processing mechanisms of serial learning and memory apply to all of these informal tasks, as well as to the formal laboratory serial-anticipation task to which psychologists typically constrict the use of the terms.

As every student of serial learning knows, the body of literature on the problem of learning serial ordering is enormous. In order to simplify the task of summarizing this literature, the present book concentrates on tasks in which the individual items are presented successively and the required responses duplicate this serial order. Emphasis will be on studies using the conventional method of serial anticipation, in which the items are presented singly in series for repeated trials, and the sub-

3

jects on succeeding trials must correctly reproduce an item before it appears in its proper position within the temporal series. Studies in which multiple-item stimuli are briefly presented only once, as in the so-called perceptual or attention span and immediate-memory experiments, will not be analyzed extensively. Nevertheless, it is impossible to deny the theoretical relevance of the serial-learning data to the so-called short-term memory tasks. In fact, models of short-term memory are frequently checked against data presented in the form of distributions of errors—known as serial-position curves (Norman, 1970). Any strong attempt to incorporate these results fully into the present formulation would, however, represent too formidable a challenge at the present time.

This book will also not discuss memory, as usually defined in terms of the usual retention tests after an elapsed interval, separately from the learning processes. Retention processes are, of course, relevant to the present subject, because the extended time of acquisition makes it necessary for subjects to retain the items in memory for seconds, or even minutes, from one presentation trial to the next. Obviously, in learning from repeated presentations, the amount and kind of information that is retained from the previous presentations of the material are important. Tulving and Madigan (1970) propose the use of the term "ecphoric processes" in order to avoid the schism that frequently appears in the approaches and theories of researchers on what is frequently discretely categorized as "learning" and "memory."

The present selective basis for choosing studies for inclusion certainly does not deny the commonality or similarity of mechanisms in the nominally different tasks. Many writers have, in fact, explicitly asserted such commonality. For example, Broadbent (1958) concludes that "it seems artificial to distinguish between 'perception' and 'memory for stimuli arriving a second or so previously' " (p. 224). He points out "the difficulties which words such as 'perception' and 'memory' produce when they are used in anything more than a very rough general sense, to indicate a field of interest" (p. 224). Melton (1963b) concurs in this. He argues that the mechanisms of short-term memory and long-term memory are not discretely different. Other researchers (e.g., Garner & Gottwald, 1967; Woodward, 1970) have come to support this argument for continuity, or overlapping mechanisms, in perception and learning and for different types of learning (e.g., Melton, 1963b, 1964; Gruneberg, 1972).

Melton (1964) concludes that there is "a progressive movement of the taxonomy of human learning processes away from a strictly operational base in which inferred processes become the categories" (p. 331).

Melton hopes that such a movement will result in the establishment of newer and fewer categories because of our greater understanding of the similarities of processes. Thus, many nominally different psychological tasks, such as pattern perception, short-term memory, and serial learning, may share the same underlying mechanisms. Neisser (1967) draws an analogy between visual perception and remembering. The primary process in memory is the parallel construction of general thoughts or ideas, like the preattentive processes in vision. The secondary processes are serial, directed, and deliberate, like focal attention in vision.

Asch (1968) also argues for commonality of mechanisms in perception, memory and learning. He points out, however, that one rarely finds mention of perception in the literature of rote learning. Nevertheless, the evidence for the implication of perception in rote learning is most convincing. He concludes:

> The formation of a percept in primary experience is a case of acquisition, and the products of perception form part of the contents of memory. Their relevance to this discussion arises from the fact that many percepts are relationally determined, that they are effects of organization. Indeed, the formation of a unitary percept does not conform to the associative paradigm, which has always referred to a pair of units. At least as instructive are those perceptual facts that depend directly upon the contribution of past experiences. All percepts that are built up over time, such as the perception of motion or of auditory configurations, are instances of organization among immediately past and present stimulations; thus they demonstrate short-term memory effects. What is of consequence in these cases is that the memory traces which participate in the process do not simply add their sensory content to the incoming stimulations; rather they impose a particular structure on a percept (1968, p. 217).

I have argued in other publications that the attention-span task is a miniature process of serial learning (Harcum, 1965a, b, 1966b) and have pointed out certain specific points of similarity (Harcum, 1957a, 1966a, 1967b). An obvious point of similarity is the close parallel between the functions relating performance per stimulus-element according to relative position within a tachistoscopic spatial array and the function relating rate of acquisition for an item to the relative position of that item within the temporal series of the learning task. In this context the term "item" refers to the complete unit to be acquired, rather than the components of that unit. Specifically, in a list of consonant-vowel-consonant (CVC) nonsense syllables, the unit would be the complete trigram and not the letters that compose it.

A striking example of the correspondence of serial-position curves of perception and learning was given in an earlier paper (Harcum, 1967b); it is reproduced as Figure 1-1. The curve labeled "Learning" represents the serial learning of nonsense syllables by the anticipation method (Hovland, 1940b), and the other, labeled "Perception," represents correct reproductions (plotted inversely) of tachistoscopically exposed letter patterns (Wagner, 1918). The reader will surmise that I was lucky to find two curves that were so similar for this comparison, since not all comparisons of similar data produce such close correspondence between the curves. This general correspondence is the rule, however.

Thus, in spite of the gross formal dissimilarities between the two tasks of serial-anticipation learning and tachistoscopic-pattern perception, the critical variables underlying the serial-position distribution of performance seem to be quite similar. Although elements in a tachistoscopic pattern appear simultaneously, the perceptual process can involve temporal components that may persist after the physical pattern has been removed (e.g., Heron, 1957). One "scanning" of a tachistoscopic pattern may be generally equivalent to a single trial in the typical task of serial learning. Similarly, spatial concepts can be important in the serial-learning task (Asch, Hay, & Diamond, 1960).

There are other bases of similarity as well. For example, Houck and Mefferd (1971a, b) have compared relative performance on tachistoscopic recognition, auditory recognition, and serial learning using identical stimulus populations and items that vary in the number of associations that are possible for perceptual categorization. Performance on each task improved monotonically in similar steps on each task. Therefore, the

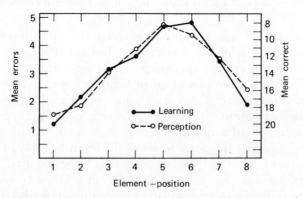

Figure 1-1 Comparison of serial learning and tachistoscopic perception, from Harcum (1967b). Copyright © (1967) by the American Psychological Association. Reprinted by permission.

same type of categorization, or differentiation, process seems to underlie each task.

The changes in theoretical approaches to learning and perception are paralleled by changes in research methods. For example, the experiments in what is called short-term memory now seem to differ from pattern-perception experiments largely in terms of whether the stimuli are presented auditorially or visually. The microgenetic approach to perception (Haber & Hershenson, 1965) looks at the change in perceptual performance as a result of repeated exposures—sometimes even with identical stimulating conditions. It is now well established that the performance of the subject on tachistoscopic pattern perception is influenced strongly by a memory (fading trace) factor (e.g., Sperling, 1960).

The mechanisms that form the overlap of these nominally different tasks are the primary concern of this book. These mechanisms seem to be the ones that are more likely to be under the voluntary control of the subject and thus to represent more molar, cognitive, and attentional factors.

NATURE OF THE TASK

There are those who argue (e.g., Young, 1968) that the conventional serial-learning task, using the anticipation technique, is not a good way to study the mechanisms of learning because that task is too complicated—relative to paired-associate learning, for example. As Melton (1963a) observes, the analysis of a psychological task is rendered extremely difficult when the stimulus is not unambiguously identified. The stimulus for serial learning is, in fact, difficult to identify—obviously more than for paired-associate learning—because of the added positional cue. Nevertheless, the argument that Battig (1965b) makes for not standardizing paired-associate tasks can be similarly extended to argue that learning studies should not be restricted to paired-associate tasks alone.

Restle and Brown (1970a) conclude that the results of serial pattern learning experiments need not necessarily be the same as those of serial-verbal learning, since certain formal characteristics of the two tasks are not the same. In serial-verbal learning the items are usually not related to one another, and the presentation order is random. In serial-pattern learning, on the other hand, the items are mutually related and the sequence is constructed to form patterns. Nevertheless they conclude:

> What *is* implied by the results of the present study is that the conventional theories of serial-verbal learning are inadequate to account for serial

learning *in general* since they do not deal with *S*'s ability to generate abstract and flexible rules to guide his performance (1970a, p. 264).

Two comments should be made at this point: first, some unconventional studies of serial-verbal learning, which employ internal relationships among items, are now being done in increasing numbers (e.g., Bower & Clark, 1969; Harcum, 1975; Simpson, 1967); and, second, these factors that are left out in accounts of serial learning are, in general, the common processes that underlie both "verbal" learning and "pattern" learning.

Underwood (1963) has emphasized the distinction that must be made between the "nominal" and the "functional" stimulus. Many studies have been aimed at discovering the latter, with either a little or a lot of success—depending upon how one defines success. As will be discussed in Chapters 2, 3, and 4, the true stimulus may never be determined exactly. Jensen and Rohwer (1965), for example, raise doubts that the discovery of the actual stimulus is possible. The more Gestalt-like our thinking, the more pessimistic we tend to be about the relevance of artificial, probelike devices and the results of transfer studies.

New techniques of investigating immediate memory (e.g., Peterson & Peterson, 1959; Waugh & Norman, 1965), have been added to the arsenal of techniques to study retention. These techniques, typically involving single presentations of the material, are oriented to answering questions about how information is remembered, rather than how it is learned. The questions about long-term memory are contaminated by effects of extra variables, particularly differences in the time of reproduction for items at the beginning or end of a series. Gruneberg (1972), arguing for the continuity of learning, has questioned the value of examining changes in the serial-position curve of free recall for evidence of a dichotomy between short-term and long-term memory. Factors such as differential time intervals between presentation and recall of first and last items, for example, produce differential performance for these items independent of actual learning mechanisms. Furthermore, one suspects that the experimental tasks are of interest primarily as a test for some model, rather than as representative tasks to be encountered in the real world.

The single-trial approach incorporates the obvious advantage of simplifying the processes to be analyzed. The other side of this coin is, however, that the complexity of the multiple-trial task is consequently absent. Whereas the multiple-trial situation can show the progress of learning a task, the single-trial technique shows an outcome—a result of learning, rather than the acquisition process.

Paralearning

The present book is concerned more with the processes directing the acquisition of items in serial learning, rather than the processes of learning per se. Items become associated to other items, in some way, either directly in dyads, small clusters, or configurations, or indirectly through associations between codes or mediators. The definition of learning is, of course, difficult. For present purposes the one proposed by Bugelski (1956) is satisfactory:

> . . . learning is the process of the formation of relatively permanent neural circuits through the simultaneous activity of the elements of the circuits-to-be; such activity is of the nature of change in cell structures through growth in such a manner as to facilitate the arousal of the entire circuit when a component element is aroused or activated (p. 120). (Footnote deleted which indicates that a circuit might already be formed but it must be used before it can operate in the final way.)

Thus, the empirical concept of the formation of an association between two events is taken here to indicate the learning process per se. Other factors that enter into the total acquisition process will be discussed later.

The commonality of the mechanisms underlying the serial-position curve in nominally serial-learning and pattern-perception tasks means, however, that these mechanisms are not exclusively tied to the paradigms of learning. For example, Tulving and Madigan (1970) suggest that the serial-position curve may reflect "a perceptual-memory phenomenon rather than a learning phenomenon" (p. 454). Others (e.g., Postman, 1964; Harcum, 1967b) point out the factors that control the output of the learning task. Of main concern here is the discovery of factors determining the order in which the items are acquired, and at what rate.

The selection of some stimuli over others to be responded to reflects what Postman (1964) calls performance factors, as opposed to principles of association. This is a traditional distinction, emphasized by Hull (1943). Such factors direct the learning, but they are not part of the learning process per se. Since they affect the priority in which items of a multi-item task are learned, they do, of course, have a large effect on accuracy of performance. Learning, however, is the process by which an association between two items is formed. Since it is operationally defined as a change in performance as a result of experience, it is necessary to distinguish between the processes of learning and what Postman (1964) calls performance factors. The concept of an association, according to Postman (1968a), refers to a disposition toward elicitation of some response as a result of learning, with the likelihood of such elicitation depending upon the conditions of testing performance. It is therefore possible to establish the existence of an association empirically, even if one has doubts about the actual mechanisms of association.

An example of a performance factor would be the process by which the subject selects from an array of stimuli the one to which he will respond. Such factors may set the stage for learning and guide it, but they are not part of the actual process of learning per se. Since they are so closely associated with learning processes, and closer than would be implied by the mere selection of a response, and since other factors are also relevant, here they will be grouped under the rubric of *paralearning* factors.

The derivation of the term *paralearning* should be explained. According to Webster's (1968) dictionary, the term "para" used in combinations means "beside" or "alongside of" and also "closely resembling the true form." Therefore, *paralearning* processes closely resemble learning processes and are, in fact, almost learning processes. A second dictionary meaning, however, emphasized that the words "beside" and "resembling" carry, too, the implication of a difference. "Para" also means "beyond" or "outside." Therefore, the processes grouped under the paralearning label are nevertheless not a central part of the learning process itself, as it has been defined above.

After much hesitation, I suggest some other factors that might also fit into the category of paralearning factors. These factors will not be mutually exclusive, and the list will probably not be exhaustive. I will begin with the easiest, less controversial propositions. First is the broad category of factors that Atkinson and Shiffrin (1968a) have called control processes. Atkinson and Shiffrin emphasize that these control processes are not permanent features of memory, but transient processes under the subject's control. Examples of these are sets manipulated by instructional and task variables, and by the results of the subject's prior experiences, all of which may influence the strategy that the subject adopts for both acquisition and memory. For example, Gardner and Long (1960) have shown that subjects who used a leveling cognitive style made more backward intrusions in serial recall, and that their anticipatory errors tended to be more remote. Thus, individual differences in perceptual-mnemonic processing of information can affect performance in learning and recall.

Retrieval processes are paralearning factors, also. Whether or not an item is recalled influences the possibility of the frequency of associations with a stimulating context and also which contexts will elicit the response.

Nonspecific transfer is perhaps another illustration of a paralearning mechanism, although the author would have to agree with Postman (1969) that the distinction between specific and nonspecific transfer is a matter of degree only. Surely the same principles of learning would be involved in either case. In his discussion of warm up and learning-to-learn mechanisms Postman (1969) suggests that the former may be the result of perceptual-motor adjustments and the latter to learning skills. Both of these mechanisms would have to be considered as paralearning mechanisms according to the present restrictive definition of learning. The warm up would reestablish the context for retention—to set the stage for retention, so to speak—but it would not be part of the retentive mechanism per se.

I agree with Restle (1962) that the selection of cues for responding represents something other than learning per se:

> It seems reasonable to assume that cue learning is not so much a matter of the formation as the selection of responses (Restle, 1962, p. 329).

But I go a bit farther to suggest that the processes of encoding, labeling, and predifferentiation (Ellis, 1973) may also be subsumed under the rubric of paralearning. Certainly this inclusion of encoding and organizational mechanisms would not generate universal agreement.

As I said, the list of paralearning factors is subject to controversy both on empirical and definitional grounds. The distinction is not meant to be fine. Obviously the interaction of learning and paralearning factors is most intricate, and it is difficult to separate them. An attempt will be made in the final chapter of the book to describe the microprocesses of learning in the context of the total acquisition process.

The present argument is, therefore, that what is learned is not completely determined by the mechanisms of learning. This argument is consistent with that of Ebenholtz (1972), who proposes that the factors that produce a serial-position effect may be orthogonal to those involved in the learning of sequences. With respect to the typical serial-learning tasks, therefore, the mechanisms that control the differential distribution of performances on the dependent variable are either more basic, as Harcum (1967b) proposed, or more superficial, as Miller (1963) proposed. Miller (1963, p. 327) based his conclusion on the results of an informal experiment in which the pace of a memory drum was increased to a rate at which the subjects could not copy the stimuli with perfect accuracy on a single presentation. The numbers of trials necessary for each item to be copied correctly described a typical serial-position curve. Therefore, the curve obviously does not require the mechanisms of learning per se. In any case, the origins of the serial-position curve are not central to the learning process itself. Whether or not these mechanisms represent more fundamental behaviors, or less, depends upon the point of view and interests of the theorist. The present position is that a full understanding of the processes involved in serial acquisition will account for the serial-position result as a natural outcome of those processes.

Learnability of Items

Obviously, a part of the problem is that the "learnability" of an item in serial learning is not completely an intrinsic characteristic of the item itself. Cofer (1969) has argued that an important consequence of the controversy of all-or-none versus incremental learning has been to direct attention to the fate of individual items in learning and memory, instead of concern for means of groups of items. Learnability is determined primarily by the learning task itself, by the kind of analysis, and by other fringe or field conditions. For example, the difficulty of individual items seems to be affected by the length of the total series. A list of one or two simple items could doubtless be learned in a single trial by a competent subject, whereas the learning would be difficult for the same items in a list of, for example, 50 items. The number of trials necessary to learn a given word depends upon whether it is embedded in a list of highly meaningful words or words of low meaningfulness (Roberts, 1962).

The physical characteristics of other items in the series are also important, as in the case of a perceptually isolated item. In what is typically called the isolation, or von Restorff (1933) effect, an item that is made to stand out from the others in the series by giving it some different physical characteristic is remembered better than it would be if it had not been so differentiated. There are many examples of this phenomenon, using many different techniques of isolation and measurement of retention. The most frequent method of isolation is to print the critical item in a different color of ink (e.g., Jones & Jones, 1942).

The relative nature of the isolation mechanism is illustrated by a study of Pillsbury and Raush (1943). They varied the proportions of three-digit numbers and trigrams in an eight-item series and found that the least frequent category of item—the most isolated one—was recalled best. This effect increased as the proportions were more unequal. Thus, the saliency of the stimulus is typically determined by various field conditions in the external environment, presumably mediated by a cognition by the subject of a relative difference among items. In a sense, the isolated item becomes a "figure" against the "ground" provided by the remainder of the items within the series.

Subject and Field Effects

Internal factors are also potent. The stimulus falls upon active central processes (e.g., Hebb, 1949; Neisser, 1967)—making individual differences important, as always. Thus, factors such as transitory set or general strategy of the subject are important. These processes can also be controlled by the sensory input (Hebb, 1963), thus producing potentially different psychological states for the different psychological tasks. As will be argued later in this book, these central control processes are particularly important in the learning and memory for multiple-element stimuli.

The results of Young (1968) have seriously weakened the simple associationistic approach to serial learning; this view states that items are learned by associating them to some stimulus cue such as the previous item or a relative position. Asch (1968) charges Young, however, with not doing justice in his conceptualizing to his own results, as follows:

His main concern is to characterize serial learning so as not to disturb the usual S-R conceptualization, which he takes for granted. This commitment determines his treatment of the positional factor in serial learning; it seems clear that he is uncomfortable with the role of position as long as he cannot convert it to the dimensions of a stimulus in the rote learning sense. Accordingly he fails to consider adequately the relational character of position and sacrifices, in my opinion, an important insight. This orientation is also responsible for the negative conclusion he reaches about the value of the serial learning paradigm for the area of rote verbal learning. Young apparently does not realize that this conclusion only tends to narrow further an area that is already unduly restricted (1968, pp. 225–226).

Mandler (1967b) also emphasized the role of organization in memory and argued that we must study the development of organizational schemas in order to understand how the adult subject uses words to organize material into memory. The importance of organizational factors in several types of memory tasks has been shown by Bower (1970). He points out, however, that it is possible to discuss such factors in less emotion-provoking terms, such as the formation of groups, relations, and relational rules. I trust this is not necessary, however. It is in fact possible to discuss organizational mechanisms in associationistic terms. For example, Estes (1972) has shown that an associative theoretical orientation is not incompatible with the concepts of coding and organization in learning and memory. In the same volume, N.F. Johnson (1972) proposes a model in which the associations are between codes for items, rather than between the items themselves.

The theoretical point of view adopted for this book will therefore be called "field associationistic." This is obviously an eclectic term that covers me from all criticism save the one of being too general. By this term, I mean that the view is basically associationistic in that items are hooked together in some way so that one item, or a group of items, can elicit another item, or group of items. This is the definition that Postman (1968a) uses for an association. The qualifications of "field" means that the stimulus may be some emergent property of a total stimulus complex. Similarly, a single, simple stimulus may elicit a complexly organized response of multiple elements. The associations may, of course, be between stimulus, response, and mediator or control elements. In sum, learning must consist of the formation of associations between things, although these associations do not have to be restricted to simple dyads. Depending upon conditions, the association can be between a stimulus-response dyad or, at the other extreme, between emergent properties of a total stimulus field and a complex, integrated response. As Anderson and Bower (1972) point out, the evidence generally points to a simple associationistic view when the material to be learned is meaningless and easily analyzed into parts. On the other hand, a field (Gestalt) approach is generally supported when the material to be learned is meaningful and complexly organized.

The present point of view has much in common with the "neoassociationistic" view of Anderson and Bower (1973), except perhaps to disagree when they deny the possibility of item-to-item associations. If they mean, as they apparently do, that there is no such thing as a literal nonsense syllable, I would then be inclined to agree. Obviously, two items are not associated, but their central representations are. This point is trite. Again, the less meaningful the task of association, the more relevant the question of simple dyadic associations.

Task Differences

Postman (1968b), in his commemorative address honoring Hermann Ebbinghaus, emphasized the fruitfulness—yet the great complexity—of Ebbinghaus' legacies of the nonsense syllable and the serial-learning task.

As Postman pointed out, these tools for the experimental study of learning and memory became all too soon generally standardized instruments, but are now being supplemented by new methods for the study of new problems. In truth, the serial-learning task was often used as just a standardized task in which the primary goal was to study effects on learning of other variables, such as effects of drugs (Burnstein & Dorffman, 1959). Nevertheless, Postman concludes that the classical methods of verbal learning and memory are valuable for students of linguistic skills.

The mechanisms in paired-associate and serial learning are not equivalent, since transfer of principles between the two tasks has proven to be problematic. Therefore, we do not automatically understand one if we comprehend the mechanisms of the other. On the other hand, the principles of ordinal organization, which are so evident in serial learning, have been shown to contribute something to the paired-associate task (e.g., Battig, Brown, & Nelson, 1963).

Jensen and Rohwer (1963) observed that the difference in difficulty of learning by the paired-associate technique relative to the serial-learning technique is greater for color-form stimuli than for verbal stimuli. They argued consequently that verbal mediation plays a greater part in paired-associate learning. They found, using retarded subjects, that instructions to use verbal mediators improved paired-associate performance, but not performance in serial learning. Jensen (1965) later supported the conclusion of Jensen and Rohwer (1963); whereas mediators given to retarded adults and normal subjects of equal mental age facilitated paired-association learning, these mediators did not aid serial learning for either group.

Underwood (1964) proposes that the tasks of rote verbal learning are centrally relevant to all learning theory. As he puts it,

> In any event, the position taken here is that the work in verbal learning—rote verbal learning—may stand squarely in the center of all human learning. Research in verbal learning is shooting out phenomena and theories which are touching, and sometimes in a very fundamental way, areas of human learning from simple conditioning to the study of the thought processes (Underwood, 1964, p. 52).

He goes on to point out, as does Postman (1968b), that the subject in a verbal learning experiment is actively calling upon his repertoire of past habits and skills in approaching the task. The new learning is superimposed upon this previous network of established habits. Underwood does, however, also recognize the complexity of the serial-learning task and suggests that it might eventually be replaced by a simpler task that will permit a surer understanding of the functional stimulus-response components.

Horton and Dixon (1968) in their summary overview of the summer workshop in 1966 at the University of Kentucky reported that "the dominant theme of the informal discussion centered around the adequacy of general S-R theory as a model of human behavior" (p. 576). That is, the main point was that general stimulus-response theory was not powerful enough to handle all of the complex skills that are characteristic of human verbal learning and linguistic behavior. Battig (1968), for example, argued for a broader theoretical attack on the problems of paired-associate (PA) learning than can be provided by general stimulus-response (S-R) behavior theory. He argued that presently available S-R principles cannot account for all of PA learning, as follows:

> The latter (namely, S-R principles) offer little that is relevant to the specification of how or why these various PA processes combine or interact with one another to determine the complicated multiprocess nature of what ultimately gets learned within the PA task. And since such a complete account must be provided even by a minimally satisfactory theory of PA learning, it also follows that this cannot be accomplished by any theory limited to S-R principles that are derived from simpler behavioral situations (1968, p. 164). (Material in parentheses added.)

The same argument that is applied to paired-associate learning in the above quotation can be applied here with perhaps even greater force to the serial-learning situation. The more complex serial-learning task provides a unique opportunity for the researcher to study the development of selective attention to cues and organizational strategies for storing materials in memory. If one is interested in the control processes, one needs a task rich in opportunities for the subject to display effects of such processes.

Thus, students of human learning have championed both sides of the argument about whether or not the most basic principles are to be discovered through concentration on one type of learning task. Serial learning is complicated, as we can quickly agree. But this is no valid objection to studying it. The very complexity of the task is what we should study. Surely paralearning factors are worthy of investigation. If we are interested in understanding the task because of its relevance, we must study the task itself, with its complexity intact. On this point the Gestaltists (e.g., Köhler, 1947) are correct. We cannot see how the pieces fit and interact together until we put them together in the relevant task. An even stronger argument is that subjects' acquisition strategy is influenced by the details of the task with, for example, different strategies likely for free-recall and serial-anticipation tasks.

ANALYSIS OF INDIVIDUAL PERFORMANCE

Some researchers have previously argued for the analysis of performance by individual subjects. Bolles (1959) concluded many years ago:

> The time has come when it no longer suffices to look only at the over-all achievement. If we are to understand human learning, we must determine what our Ss are really doing (p. 580).

More recently, Montague (1972) has emphasized the new trend toward consideration of what the subject is doing. He points out the new awareness that the subject is acting dynamically upon the task and materials given him:

> In memorizing, Ss elaborate tasks and materials; they transform, recode, encode, reorganize, give meaning to, or make sense out of seeming nonsense. In remembering they search and hopefully retrieve the product of that earlier labor, decode it into some communicable form, decide upon its accuracy, and about whether or not to say it (1972, p. 225).

This point of view receives enthusiastic support here. The pooled results of many subjects may not reflect truly what the individual subject is doing. An illustration of this comes from the classic study of Hayes (1953), in which the learning curve was adjusted on the basis of individual performance, as shown in Figure 1-2. In this plot the trial-by-trial results of rats learning a brightness discrimination were replotted relative to the critical trial in which each rat achieved the learning criterion. The trial at which each rat reached criterion of learning was determined, and performance for each trial was plotted backward from the criterial trial. Instead of the smooth progress of acquisition, displayed by the untransformed results for all subjects, the curve of performance relative to each rat revealed a rather precipitous jump just as the criterion was reached.

Kayson (1970) suggested that the subject comes to the experimental session with a hierarchy of plans or strategies to use in order to solve the experimental task—which is, of course, to learn the list in a serial-learning experiment. The subject will begin with the use of one strategy and stick with it if he makes satisfactory progress. If not, he will move

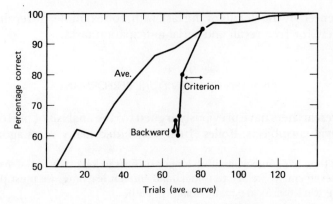

Figure 1-2   Comparison of traditional average learning curve with the backward curve, from Hayes (1953). Copyright © (1953) by the American Psychological Association. Reprinted by permission.

to another strategy, and so forth, until he finds one that will work. Each strategy might be said to require the use of a different functional stimulus for learning.

These control processes are now coming in for increased attention by students of learning. For example, Brewer (1967), finding differential effects of pacing rate for low and high meaningful material, observed:

> Judging from Ss varied comments about their learning strategies, there seems to be a need to control more precisely what Ss do during a verbal learning trial (p. 160).

He was skeptical about the possibility of knowing what the subject was doing even in a paired-associate task because of the possibility of many covert rehearsals during a single overt trial. Also consistent with this argument, Rehula (1960) concludes:

> Perhaps the line of attack in most studies is misplaced in that emphasis has been on the lists rather than the learner. Lists do not produce the curve; the curve represents the way the people learn the lists. The only thing that remains relatively constant over the various experiments is that people are used as subjects. Perhaps the consistency of the curve represents some kind of a perceptual organization, or rather a perceptual limitation on the part of Ss (p. 16).

Reitman (1970) echoes this sentiment, in the context of research in short-term memory, as follows:

> Many of us subscribe to a view that regards human behavior as the pro-
> duct of a complex information-processing system. We recognize that var-
> iations in strategies over time and from one subject to another occur
> and affect our data. Yet we continue to run our experiments with little
> or no reference to the effects of these strategy variations; it is hard to
> see why (p. 501).

Thus, there have been many calls from researchers for analyses of
results for individual subjects. In my opinion, the response to the call
has been inadequate.

An increased attention to what the subject is doing is paralleled by
increased use of notions about hypotheses and strategies in human learning (Cofer, 1968). Cofer (1968) expresses confidence that such processes
exist, but cites the difficulties in identifying and studying these problems
experimentally, as follows:

> One of the difficulties in identifying and studying hypotheses and strate-
> gies in verbal learning has arisen from the tasks we use. In PA and
> serial learning, for example, the only data typically available are the re-
> sponses made to the stimuli presented, and these responses convey remar-
> kably little direct information indicative of other processes that go on.
> This leads the investigator to have to rely heavily on inference if he
> is to speculate about hypotheses and strategies. Even if there were strong
> correlations between predictors like ability tests or measures of personali-
> ty traits and learning scores, the identification of hypotheses and strate-
> gies would be an indirect process with presently available predictors, so
> far as I can see.
>
> We need methods for externalizing what the subject does as he learns
> (1968, p. 530).

Different Terminologies

Perhaps a major detriment to the analysis of individual performance
are the terminologies used by the students of individual behavior. Some
researchers prefer a different set of terms, if not a different philosophy.
For example, Postman and Schwartz (1964) concluded from their study
of interlist transfer between serial-learning and paired-associate tasks
that:

> The results support the conclusion that interlist practice effects are based
> in part on *specific instrumental habits* which are carried over from one
> task to the next (p. 48) (emphasis added).

Later Postman (1969) did use the concept of learning strategy, and showed how it could be controlled experimentally by manipulation of the subject's experience. Restle (1962) makes a case for the use of the term "strategy" as follows:

> The term "strategy" is employed in a sense related to the more common terms, "habit" and "hypothesis," to designate a particular pattern of responses to stimuli. Consider, for example, a rat being trained to jump to the larger of two white circles in a Lashley Jumping Stand. Some possible strategies include; jumping to the left side, jumping to the right side, jumping alternately left and right, jumping always to the side last reinforced. . . . Each such pattern of behavior, if it occurs in isolation for a sufficiently long sequence of trials, can be identified by the experimenter. (p. 329).

Therefore, terms like strategy can be operationalized to make them respectable to the positivist. And any argument should be in terms of the operations, not the words. I do not consider it critical what specific words are used to convey this idea of a mode of attack that may be carried over from previous experience and that directs the distribution of effort among items of the serial task. In some cases the subject can certainly verbalize his plan, but in others he probably cannot. More and more researchers are coming to use cognitive terms and approaches. For example, the recent book by Kausler (1974) reflects this increased emergence of cognitive psychology into the field of verbal learning.

SERIAL-POSITION EFFECT

When Hermann Ebbinghaus (1902) counted the number of promptings required for him to learn each item in a list of ten nonsense syllables, he discovered that most repetitions were required for those syllables appearing near the middle. Fewer promptings were necessary for the final items, and fewest for the first items. He concluded that the "stamping in" of the responses begins at the beginning and end of a series, proceeding faster from the beginning than from the end. Thus, the last syllables to be acquired are just past the middle of the series.

Generality of the Effect

If no special circumstances are employed, the general phenomenon is probably found in all tasks that involve acquisition of multiple-element stimuli. The writers of summaries of learning (e.g., Mednick, 1964) emphasize the generality of the serial-position phenomenon in serial learning, both in terms of the wide range of experimental conditions under which it is obtained and the kinds of subjects that have revealed the effect. The study of Thomas (1971), showing a serial-position curve relating a score reflecting the psychiatric rating of a patient's mental condition and the uncertainty of that rating, indicates the potential significance and great generality of the phenomenon. But, obviously, it is not tied to strictly learning processes.

The serial-position curve of rote learning has been one of the most studied outcomes in psychological research. This result is illustrated in Figure 1-1. Because of the generality of the finding, it would seem to provide the starting point for basic insights into the processes of acquisition and memory for series of items.

Fischer and Norton (1961), considering the question of the relative strengths of proactive and retroactive inhibition, presented series of nine nonsense syllables once and then tested retention by a serial-anticipation trial and by a recognition task. Both retention tasks showed the typical bowed and skewed serial-position curve, although the recognition task produced a flatter function that did not depart significantly from a linear trend. Nevertheless the curves were quite similar, as shown in Figure 1-3, in which different scales are used to plot the results of the different conditions. Also, the rank-order of the performances at different serial-positions were significantly correlated ($p = .883, p < .01$). Although the method of measurement obviously influenced the relative efficiency at the various serial positions (Jensen, 1962c), it did not materially change the shape of the curve. Therefore, the shape of the curve appears also not to be an artifact of the particular method of measurement.

Theoretical Approaches

The general types of theory to describe the serial learning process, and the specific notions given special emphasis in each, may be described under three rather loose categories: associative chaining, position learning, and field organization. These categories are based on the different notions about the effective stimulus for serial learning. Such arbitrary categorizing must admittedly be only a general approximation. Frequently references across these artificial boundaries must be made. Some theoretical positions include proposals for dual mechanisms, while others transcend these categories.

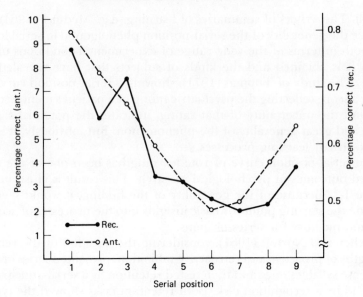

Figure 1-3 Comparison of serial-position curves for anticipation and recognition, after Fischer and Norton (1961). Reprinted by permission from the Journal Press.

ASSOCIATIVE CHAINING

The associative-chaining position holds that the explanation for serial phenomena is in terms of the connection between pairs or groups of items. Thus, presentation of any item, or group of items, as a stimulus has a tendency to call forth a response of the other items.

POSITION LEARNING

The position-learning hypothesis argues that the learning establishes a connection between an item and its position within a series. Therefore, the stimulus for an item is its ordinal position, not the item preceding it in the series.

FIELD ORGANIZATION

The third hypothesis—field organization—is not included as a separate possibility in most discussions. It proposes that some items are learned first because of their superior vividness within the total framework of the stimulus configuration. These are usually the first and last items in the series. Thus, learning consists of establishing an organization or structure for the series.

The Functional Stimulus

This question of the functional stimulus implies that a simple answer can be given to it. Since the various hypotheses do not propose mutually exclusive mechanisms, perhaps the answer can best be summarized as follows: it all depends on what the subject chooses to use. This position is supported by Bewley (1972) in his recent review of the major hypotheses about the functional stimulus in serial learning. After describing the evidence for each hypothesis, he concludes that the subjects can learn by using

> . . . any one of several alternate strategies, the choice of strategies being determined by the set of S and the characteristics of the task. This conception of serial learning suggests that there is no single functional stimulus used by all Ss in all situations. In fact, with some tasks there is no functional stimulus at all, the use of rules allowing the generation of list items with no specific cues or stimuli. The research which has been reviewed here seems to indicate that naive (uninstructed) Ss may choose strategies in a particular order (pp. 210–211).

The Present Approach

The present point of view is that Ebbinghaus' (1902) conception was correct in describing the order of acquisition of items. This progression of "stamping in" is the key to the total process. The unanswered question is what mechanisms control this order of acquisition. The present theoretical orientation is therefore fundamentally similar to that proposed by Jensen (1962a) and by Feigenbaum and Simon (1961, 1962, 1963), who also base their interpretation of the serial-position curve on subject strategies.

The thesis of this book is different, however, in that it concentrates more on the actual acquisition process and on individual subjects. It maintains that a satisfactory explanation of the serial-learning process must look behind the compelling outcome of the serial-position distribution of performance measures. The present approach is to examine the constituent processes in the development of the serial-position effect, as these processes are revealed during the course of learning. In short, the true serial-learning curve must be described in terms of trials, time, or some derived or modified form of these variables, rather than in terms of the relative performance across items at the various serial positions.

PLAN OF THE BOOK

The book is organized into three sections. The first part sets the problem investigated in the book and describes the general orientation and approach adopted in attempting to research a solution. Part 2 is concerned with a description of the paralearning processes themselves, which can account for the distribution of errors among the items in serial learning. The final section proposes a new way of looking at the serial acquisition process, and presents evidence for the validity of that proposition.

PART 1

Part 1 provides, in Chapter 1, the introduction and general orientation to the problem. Chapters 2 and 3 describe the traditional S-R approaches to the understanding of serial learning, oriented generally to the problem of discovering the cause of the serial-position curve in terms of the functional stimulus. In Chapter 2 the effort is generally directed at discovering whether or not the stimulus for serial learning is a specific item or a cluster of items. Chapter 3 asks whether or not the functional stimulus is a particular serial position, or relationship among items. Chapter 4 discusses an orientation to serial learning in terms of mnemonic organizational processes. In this view, the associative stimulus for learning is conceived in configurational terms, with the particular stimulus-component determined by its position in a hierarchy of potential stimuli for association, and by the stage of learning. Chapter 5 presents the information-translation orientation, which is the offering of the present book to explain the serial-learning process. It is an extension of the information-translation hypothesis previously proposed to account for both serial learning and the tachistoscopic perception of spatial patterns (Harcum, 1967b). This hypothesis emphasizes the role in learning played by control processes that reflect the active organizing strategy of the subjects in converting the information in the stimulus array into their mnemonic systems. The approach is set in terms of information-processing models, but without "rigid boxes." The central thesis is that serial learning is characterized by a strategy of selective attention to the items in some order for processing, and for some order of reproduction.

PART 2

Part 2 examines the principal components of the selection mechanism controlling the order of acquisition. Chapter 6 discusses the mechanisms of item differentiation and intrinsic organization according to stimulus characteristics. The basic mechanism reflects the increasing lack of distinctiveness of the items progressively farther from the ends of an array. Chapter 7 deals with the basis for the selection of some item or items to become the mnemonic anchor for the subsequent learning. The mechanism for this is called primattensity, referring to the increased perceptual and mnemonic saliency of an item that is perceived as being the first item, or the starting point in a mnemonic organization of the series. Chapter 8 discusses individual differences in relation to the learnability of items. For different subjects, some items are more familiar, meaningful, or otherwise attention-getting than others.

PART 3

Part 3 of the book presents proposed analyses, evidence, and conclusions. Chapter 9 proposes a different way of looking at the progression of serial learning, following the lead suggested by Jensen (1962a). This method examines the actual acquisition process, using different criteria for learning. It proposes that the serial-learning task is best understood in terms of the learning curve instead of the serial-position outcome. The penultimate chapter (Chapter 10) presents some evidence for the validity of the proposed analysis. Finally, Chapter 11 attempts to show how the proposed macroprocess mechanisms fit into a general schema for microprocesses of information storage and retrieval

SUMMARY

This first chapter described the task of serial learning and pointed out commonalities among this task and other so-called perceptual and memory tasks. The concept of paralearning was introduced and defined to include factors such as performance variables, retrieval plans, and selective strategies of acquisition. These factors were considered to be something different from the actual learning process of association formation.

The learnability of an item was explained in terms of variables in addition to certain intrinsic characteristic of the item. Examples of these were subject effects and context effects. Therefore, conceptions of serial acquisition as an accumulation of simple S-R dyadic associations were considered inadequate.

Examination of individual results was promoted, as was a consideration of what strategies or plans a given subject was using. Therefore, the conclusion was reached that the proper approach for understanding serial-learning phenomena was to evaluate the acquisition curve, rather than the serial-position distribution of outcomes.

The final section gave the plan of the book.

CHAPTER

2

THE STIMULUS: A CHAIN

As is well known in the case of paired-associate learning, subjects often select some component of the nominal stimulus item to become the functional stimulus (e.g., Underwood, Ham, & Ekstrand, 1962). Although these components usually are the ones that facilitate learning, this is not always the case. Subjects probably make a similar selection of a functional stimulus in serial learning. Certainly a large number of studies have investigated the possibility that the subject may, for example, be learning associations between items, or associations of items to their ordinal positions, or some more complicated basis of serial learning (e.g., Ebenholtz, 1963b). This chapter examines the first of these possibilities.

Underwood (1963) emphasized the difficulty in identifying even the nominal, much less the functional, stimulus for serial learning. He pointed to the great difficulty of the double-function paired-associate list, in which each item serves ostensibly as both stimulus and response. Since that task is more difficult to learn than a serial list of nominally the same associations, Underwood suggested that perhaps the functional stimulus in serial learning is not necessarily the prior item in the series. Many other researchers have agreed with this assessment.

Some researchers argue quite strongly (e.g., Tulving & Madigan, 1970) that a search for the functional stimulus is unnecessary, since the subject will use any stimulus that proves to be effective in accomplishing the task. Many researchers and editors disagree with this, however, as a quick glance at the psychological literature of serial learning will verify.

I agree that research is not productive when it is oriented merely toward the question of whether or not the subject has learned position, sequence, or some other particular cue. Nevertheless, the specification of conditions under which a given stimulus attribute is prepotent is informative. It is, of course, probable that the subject can use many cues simultaneously.

The associative-chaining hypothesis, with which this chapter is primarily concerned, is also called the sequence or specificity hypothesis. It assumes that what actually happens when a subject learns a serial list is essentially what the experimenter has instructed him to learn. That is, the subject associates each (response) item with the one specific stimulus item or several other items in sequence preceding it, to which he must give this appropriate response at the correct time.

Since the possible functional stimulus categories are not mutually exclusive, and there may be competition among them on any task, it is difficult to distinguish among them in empirical analysis. Obviously, therefore, the organization of the evidence on stimulus selection does not permit an easy division into the particular categories of possible stimuli. Evidence for or against the specificity hypothesis will necessarily have implications for the hypotheses about other potential bases of learning. Moreover, conditions testing for the functional stimulus have frequently been combined in the same factorial experiment.

TYPES OF ASSOCIATIONS

The specificity hypothesis is complicated by the fact that more than one type of association is possible. Three general types of associations are distinguished: direct forward, remote, and direct backward. These categories, which are themselves not mutually exclusive, will be discussed briefly now, and then in detail in Chapter 6.

Direct Forward Associations

The sequence or chaining theory proposes, in its simplest form, that the subject merely connects each item with the preceding ones in the correct order. For example, McGeoch and Irion (1952, p. 90) see serial learning as direct associations among adjacent items, with each item serving as both stimulus and response. Thus, the association is the connective bond established between two contiguous elements or processes, inferred because presentation of one item comes to elicit the other. This tendency for the presentation of one item to evoke the other is assumed to be directly proportional to the strength of the connecting bond between them.

Remote Associations

Associations need not be restricted to temporally contiguous items. Ebbinghaus (1902, 1913) first formulated the additional concept of remote associations. Using lists derived by selecting items of varying relative positions to one another on a list already learned, he found that such derived lists were learned more quickly than the original lists, although the immediate associations between adjacent items on the new list were totally new. Evidently, items remote in the series were associated to some extent in the learning of the original list. Furthermore, Ebbinghaus (1913) concluded that the more remote the association, the weaker it was. The presence of apparent remote forward, as well as backward, associations in serial learning cannot be interpreted on the basis of a simple chaining theory of serial learning (McGeoch, 1936).

Direct Backward Associations

Ebbinghaus (1913) also found that when he reversed the serial order of the items within his derived lists, he still obtained a savings over the original learning. This indicates that the formation of associations proceeds also in the backward direction, complicating the association process. Such apparent backward association is not doubted, although it may not be due to the association of an item with the items preceding it, but to backward rehearsal (Cason, 1926a) or to artifacts in the experimental situation (Slamecka, 1964).

INDIRECT EVIDENCE FOR SPECIFICITY

Researchers have used both indirect and direct approaches in attempts to answer the problem of the effective stimulus for serial learning. Indirect attempts have been made to show faster learning for items that are easier to associate, or to predict transfer effects on the basis of presumed prior associations between items. Direct approaches have used probes in the form of various different cues in order to determine which ones are more likely to elicit the correct responses.

Associability of Items

Inferential evidence for an associative-chain interpretation is provided whenever high-associative, easy-to-learn items are included in a serial list, with earlier acquisition for these items (e.g., Wright & Bernstein, 1965; Diethorn & Voss, 1967). For example, Diethorn and Voss (1967) varied the location of a four-unit block of words of high forward-adjacent associability within a list of 12 words. The degree of facilitation for serial learning of the block of items was equal regardless of whether the block was located at beginning, middle, or end of the series.

In a study by Rehula (1960), a list of bigrams was constructed to have stronger intraitem associations (i.e., between the two letters of a bigram) or interitem associations (i.e., between the second member of a pair and the first member of the following pair). These manipulations should, and did, facilitate the response learning and the associative hook-up phases of acquisition, respectively. The subjects learning the intraitem-associated list gave more intralist intruding errors, as expected, and those learning the interitem list gave more invented and partial responses. There was also a small tendency for the inventions and partial responses in the interitem-associated list to represent the letter that would have been correct, but coupled with an incorrect second letter. Rehula suggests that the functional stimulus for serial learning may be an extended chain of prior items. If a functional chain is broken, the subject may have to start his recitation again from the beginning of the series.

A different method was used by Voss (1968) who built in associations between items by an experimental manipulation. Voss attempted a test of the sequential hypothesis by varying the number of items in a 16-item list that would actually appear in succession on each of 40 trials. This was done by replacing some of the words in the list at times with an X. To produce a list in which two adjacent items never appeared— namely, a group of one, with zero conditional probability between items—he alternated words and Xs on each trial, with odd words re-placed with Xs on one trial and even words replaced with Xs on alternate trials. He similarly employed groups of 2, 4, and 8 units, with 16-unit sequences achieved by replacing the entire series with Xs on alternate trials, producing a conditional probability between items of 1.00. In this way, the size of groups of adjacent items could be varied, but each word would appear at its proper serial position an equal number of times. Voss found that the number of correct responses progressively increased for the longer groups of items. In addition a serial-position effect appeared, which interacted significantly with the experimental conditions. The extreme conditions of conditional probabilities, with alternation of Xs and words on successive presentations or on successive trials, produced rather smooth typical serial-position curves, presumably because of greater reliance on position cues by the subjects. The other curves were more irregular, with tendencies toward dips in the number of correct responses at boundaries of word and X sequences.

An analysis of intruding errors in the Voss (1968) study showed progressive decreases in frequency with increasing distance between true locus and intruding locus of items for the trials of complete exposure alternating with trials of Xs. The other conditions showed peaks of intrusions corresponding to the size of the clusters of successive items. The subject was apparently confusing the particular item with another item at the same position within another subchain. Although Voss concludes that his results can be interpreted to support the chaining hypothesis, he favors another interpretation. Since the intrusion data for the intermediate-sized groupings did not show progressively decreasing functions with greater remoteness between items, their appearance is not due to simple remote associations. The effect is due to the cue function of the item, which was upset by the confusion in relative position.

This evidence for interitem associability overlaps in an unclear way the evidence for mnemonic organization, to be discussed in Chapter 4. Specifically, the associability of any two items to one another within a series will necessarily be reflected in the overall structure and learnability of the entire series. For example, in a series of items A, B, and C, a high degree of associability between items A and B would probably influence the rate of the acquisition of an association between B and C.

Instructions to Subjects

The relative use of specificity cues can be changed by instructions. Winnick and Dornbush (1963) used continuous presentation of 14 nonsense syllables, but for one of the three groups of subjects, the starting syllable remained the same, while for a second group the starting item shifted progressively ahead one syllable (i.e., second item on trial two, and so on), and for the third group the starting point was determined randomly. One-half of the subjects in each group was given "standard" serial-learning instructions, which merely described the task, and the other was informed that the starting syllable would be varied, and therefore "to learn to associate one syllable with the next." With standard instructions the list with constant starting-point was learned faster, and the one with random starting-point more slowly, as would be expected. The instructions for sequential associations did not affect performance for the list with progressive change of starting syllable, but they did hinder performance for the list with the constant position, and facilitate performance for the list with the randomized starting point. This decrement for the subjects presented with a constant starting point could be caused by the misleading instructions about a shifting starting point or by the instructions to use sequential associations. In view of the improvement for the group with varied starting point after the instruction to make sequential associations, apparently the subjects with constant starting point lost the advantage of this consistency when they were instructed to learn interitem associations.

In order to investigate the effects of differential learning strategies on serial learning, Kayson (1970) varied instructions to his subjects. In one experiment he instructed some subjects to form sequential associations between trigrams in a serial list, and other subjects he told to associate each trigram to its ordinal position. Control subjects received only standard instructions for serial learning, which told them to learn to anticipate succeeding items, but did not suggest a specific method or strategy to accomplish this. Presentation series were followed by recall series. Kayson predicted that position-learning instructions would facilitate learning of low-association trigrams, whereas the sequential instructions would facilitate learning of high-associative items. He used a very nice independent check on his independent variable to determine whether or not his subjects followed the instructions to learn by interitem associations or by associations between items and positions. After a subject had completed the learning task, his reaction time was recorded to probe questions about which trigram followed a given one, or which item appeared at a given position. Subjects were faster in giving the response that was emphasized in the instructions, suggesting that the instructions had indeed been followed.

The group that Kayson (1970) had instructed to learn position revealed some tendency to learn faster, and the control group, having been given no strategy, had the slowest rate of acquisition. Therefore, some time and efficiency in learning were lost while a subject was settling upon which strategy to use. This implies that even a generally less effective strategy may facilitate learning if it is provided early enough to permit progress in actual learning, while some uninstructed subject is using learning time in deciding upon a strategy. As predicted, the position instructions were more efficient for the low-association trigrams but, contrary to predictions, the different types of association had no effect upon the acquisition of the high-association trigrams. As Kayson concludes, the advantage of associating trigrams to positions may be offset by the presumed greater ease of forming interitem associations between high-association items.

Other evidence for a change in the relative importance of cues due to instructions was obtained from instructing the subjects to use mnemonic cues (Delin, 1969a,b). When a subject organizes a list through some mnemonic system, he should show smaller proportions of commission errors relative to omission errors, because errors that do not fit the mnemonic construction can be edited out. Delin (1969a) found some support for this effect for subjects instructed to join adjacent items by organizing them into a bizarre or fantastic image. He also found flatter serial-position curves for those subjects instructed to use the mnemonic system. The flattening was interpreted in terms of increased importance of dyadic associations, with position cues consequently serving a lesser role.

Thus, the particular instructions given to the subject can affect the degree to which he uses interitem associations as a basis for learning. Apparently the researcher tends to gain evidence for sequential associations by appropriate instructions to the subject or to gain evidence also against such associations by the appropriate instructions.

THE TRANSFER APPROACH

A frequent technique for discovering which stimulus is functional for serial learning is to test for transfer to a new task that retains only one of the possible stimuli. Appropriate transfer effects for a given stimulus imply that it was involved in the original learning. On the other hand, a result of zero transfer proves nothing (Postman, 1968a), since the experimental situation may be sufficiently changed to prevent any transfer.

Several paradigms have been used. The transfer may be between two serial lists, from a paired-associate list to a serial list or, most commonly, from serial to paired-associate learning. A retroactive interference design has also been used to determine what kind of associations are unlearned.

Transfer Between Serial Lists

The serial-to-serial transfer paradigm typically compares the acquisition of items that retain their relations to one another on the second list but whose ordinal position has been changed to the acquisition of items that do not maintain this internal relation and whose ordinal position may not be changed. Faster learning of the items with constant internal relations, independent of position, would provide positive evidence for sequential associations from the prior serial learning.

VARIABLE STARTING POSITION

One procedure to differentiate between chaining and position learning is to vary ordinal position in a transfer list while maintaining the internal relations among items. Saufley (1967) contrasted presentation of lists for serial learning by what he called the set and the spin techniques. In the former, namely the set method, the usual procedure of starting each trial with the same item is used. In the latter, the spin technique, the first item for each trial is determined randomly, much as would occur if the experimenter would merely spin the memory drum and let it start where it may for each trial. In either technique the sequence of items with respect to one another never changes. The spin technique yields ordinarily more difficult learning (e.g., Bowman & Thurlow, 1963), presumably because the subjects are not able to learn serial positions.

In Saufley's (1967) study, transfer was computed from a list learned at first by either one of these techniques to later learning by the second technique. Saufley argued that transfer from the set technique to the spin technique should result in a decrement, since subjects had been learning positions, which would not now be an effective cue. On the other hand, changing from the spin to the set technique should facilitate acquisition, since the sequence cues would still be present and the position cues would now be added. The difference in learning between lists of items with high and low interitem associations should be greater using the spin technique since interitem associations were more critical for learning under this technique. Learning of both original and transfer list was carried to one perfect trial. The list of high interitem associations was learned faster under both spin and set conditions and, as predicted, the difference was greater for the spin technique. After allowance was made for the usual postcriterial drop and for the change in method, there was still evidence for the loss of position information in the change from set to spin techniques. This drop was less for items of high associability, however, presumably because for these items the sequential associations had been more important in the set condition of learning than they were for items of low interitem association. Saufley concludes that position provides a "potent source of cues," but that the appearance of even some learning under the spin technique indicates that other cues could be used when position cues were minimal.

Rehula (1960) had subjects first learn lists of 13 bigrams by serial anticipation and then similarly learn transfer lists composed of the original series, a randomization of the same items, or the same series starting with the seventh item but in the same serial order. Since the intact, but shifted, series was retained about as well as the original list, Rehula concluded that the evidence for sequential learning was strong. Nevertheless, there was some evidence for position learning, since the new starting point did, in fact, produce a significant difference in total correct responses. Rehula does point out that this disruption from changed starting point may not be due to prior position learning, but to an alteration in the stimulus situation occasioned by the change in the position of the intertrial intervals. For example, the effective sequential stimulus could be a group of several items, rather than a single item. Moreover, the new eighth item—originally the first item—must now be given in response to a new stimulus item in the shifted transfer list.

DERIVED LISTS

The method of derived lists uses the same items in original and transfer tasks, but varies the internal relations among the items. If the subject originally learned associations between items, negative transfer would ordinarily be expected on the transfer list (Bruce, 1933; Osgood, 1949).

In an important experiment using this technique, Young (1962, Experiment 3) studied transfer from one serial list of adjectives to another. In the experimental conditions, alternate items on the original list retained their relative positions on the transfer list, while the remaining items were randomly rearranged. For the control subjects no items were the same on the two lists. All lists were 12 items long, exclusive of a thirteenth item, which served as the starting cue. The experimental list exhibited negative transfer with respect to the control list, as would be predicted on the basis of interference of old associations with the formation of new associations. However, within the experimental lists the items that had retained their original positions in the transfer task were learned significantly faster than the items with changed positions. The differences between conditions according to a serial-position analysis were significant for all but the first and last serial positions. These results are reproduced in Figure 2-1. Young concluded that the learning was specific to the preceding stimulus item at the ends of the series, but determined more by position learning about the middle. He was, however, concerned about the inconsistency of this conclusion with other findings (e.g., Schulz, 1955), which indicated greater importance of position cues at the ends of the series. There are two problems with Young's argument. First, he concludes that the results for first and last stimulus positions are *not different* because the empirical differences are *not* statistically *significant*. This is the notorious error of accepting the null hypothesis. The second problem with Young's (1962) conclusion is that he performed his serial-position analysis on the raw data instead of making a correction for the overall difference in performance between conditions. A number of authors (e.g., McCrary & Hunter, 1953; Jensen, 1962c; Harcum, 1970a) have pointed out that the shape of the serial-position curve should be evaluated relative to the overall performance level instead of in terms of absolute differences. The method popularized by McCrary and Hunter (1953) converts the performance scores at each serial position into percentages of performance across all serial positions. When this is done for the six relevant positions of Young's data (1962, p. 311), reading approximately from his figure reproduced in Figure 2-1, the percentage values in terms of correct responses for Serial Positions One to Six of the constant-position items are, respectively, 21, 15, 15, 16, 15, and 18. The corresponding percentages for the items of changed location are, respectively, 23, 15, 14, 14, 14, and 19. Therefore, the differential performance across serial positions is generally equivalent for the two classes of stimuli.

Keppel and Saufley (1964) attempted to replicate Young's (1962, Experiment 3) experiment on transfer of serial learning on one list to serial learning of another in which some items were retained in their

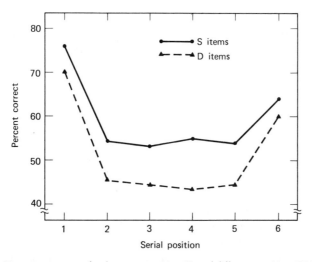

Figure 2-1   Percentage correct for the same-position (S) and different-position (D) item sublists, from Young (1962). Copyright © (1962) by the American Psychological Association. Reprinted by permission.

original positions. Other conditions included a test of Young's proposal for mediation by remote associations. This mediation condition consisted of removing alternate items, shifting the remaining items ahead one position, and returning the removed items in scrambled order to the remaining positions. Therefore, all absolute position cues would be removed, but the internal consistency of one-half of the items would remain. Another condition retained four items in their original locations, but in no obvious pattern. All experimental groups revealed negative transfer. Although the mediation condition and the replication of Young's condition produced equal performance on the transfer test, the difference between randomized and "constant" items was greater in the condition used by Young (1962, Experiment 3). Therefore, the consistency of position seemed to be much more effective than the consistency of one-degree remote associations. Thus, the mediation of associations does not account for Young's (1962) earlier result.

Further evidence for the above conclusion was derived from Keppel and Saufley's (1964) analysis of individual performance within trials on the transfer test for the condition with alternately correct positions of items. Correct performance at a given position was not contingent upon accurate performance for the item two positions ahead, which was the immediately preceding of the fixed-position items. Thus, correct reproduction of an item at an unchanged position was not a necessary prerequisite for accurate reproduction of the next item in the fixed-position chain.

The experimental condition of Keppel and Saufley (1964), which was formed by taking four items from an original list that were retained in the same position in the transfer list, provided further evidence against the mediation interpretation. Although these items did not maintain constant internal relationships with one another, there was a significant difference in the rate of learning for the items in the same position on both lists and those items of scrambled position. Therefore, the subjects under this condition were apparently using position as a cue, rather than some mediational system. Thus, Keppel and Saufley (1964), in their replication of Young's (1962) Experiment 3, failed to find evidence for greater use of the end items for specific associations. There was some evidence, in fact, for the opposite result, which is more in keeping with other evidence (Battig, Brown, & Schild, 1964).

Hakes, James, and Young (1964) found, using derived experimental lists of one, two, and three degrees of remoteness, negative transfer with respect to a control group who learned unrelated lists. The derived list which employed one degree of remoteness actually produced the greatest negative transfer. Later Young, Hakes, and Hicks (1965) used derived lists of 8, 12, or 16 adjectives, all with one degree of remoteness. Negative transfer appeared for the longer lists, but not for the lists of eight items, for which there was slight positive transfer.

The assumption that early interitem associations from first learning would produce positive transfer to the second list may be based on too simple a conception of the serial-learning task. That is, any reorganization of the items from first learning could produce negative transfer tendencies on second learning even if the internal relationships had been maintained. For example, Young (1968) points out that Ebbinghaus' conclusion, that the derived-list paradigm produces positive transfer, differs from expectations about the direction of transfer from more recent data. The positive transfer obtained by Ebbinghaus for learning derived lists may be an artifact of Ebbinghaus' use of random reordering of the original list as his control condition. Such a random derived list would be expected to yield negative transfer, because the early strong correct associations would now conflict with the new response to be learned. The calculated positive transfer of the derived lists of short degrees of remoteness could be only less negative than this control condition and not positive at all. Irion (1946) concluded that the random condition actually produced negative transfer, although Ebenholtz (1972) points out that Irion did not use an unrelated transfer list as a control condition. Young (1968) also notes that Ebbinghaus used a serial-recall procedure and used himself as the well-practiced subject in a series of many experiments.

Later analyses by Hakes and Young (1966) and Ebenholtz (1972) indicate that negative transfer is ordinarily obtained in the derived list experiment, in spite of the conclusion of Ebbinghaus (1964) in favor of positive transfer. The difference is in the use of the proper control group, as mentioned above; a randomized transfer list should produce maximum negative transfer, on the basis of interfering interitem associations, and thus other conditions would tend to produce positive transfer relative to that control condition. Only consistent zero transfer would provide negative evidence, because either positive or negative transfer would indicate an effect of the prior associations. In fact, negative transfer is stronger evidence because of the possible positive effect of item familiarization, which could account for overall positive transfer.

REVERSED SEQUENCE

Young, Patterson, and Benson (1963) had subjects relearn a serial list in reverse order. They argued that general greater positive transfer for the experimental group would favor the specificity hypothesis, whereas such transfer restricted only to the middle items would favor the position hypothesis. There was zero transfer to the second list with respect to subjects who initially had learned an unrelated list. Young et al. found that the reversal of serial order produces positive transfer for only the items in the middle, where the serial position is least changed. The Young et al. result indicates the problems of making conclusions about results that are not significant statistically, but that do suggest some empirical difference, since these researchers did obtain a small difference in trials to criterion favoring the experimental group of subjects (namely, 8.1 to 9.7). The unreliability of the trials measure has been pointed out several times previously in this book; thus, the lack of statistical significance is not too damaging to the specificity hypothesis in view of an almost 20% difference in the dependent variable.

Young et al. (1963) also showed that the errors per trial were not significantly different for the experimental and control groups. Nevertheless, the number of correct responses was greater for the experimental group at 7 of the 11 serial positions, and the largest differences favored the experimental group. Since the number of trials was smaller for the experimental group, and the number of correct responses per trial was larger, one can only speculate what the results would have been if the total number of errors per group had been compared, without correction for the difference in trials.

Contrary to the conclusions of Young et al. (1963), Delin (1969a) did find that subjects had little difficulty in relearning a list of 16 nouns in reverse order, after original learning to a criterion of one errorless trial. He concluded that his results supported an "item-based" functional stimulus.

The basic research design of Young et al. (1963) was used by Bredenkamp and Bredenkamp (1970). Pointing out the problem of proving an experimental hypothesis from statistically negative results, they took into account magnitude-of-effect considerations in deriving conclusions about the experimental hypothesis. Analyses of variance were performed on several measures of learning: number of relative errors per item to the criterion of one correct list recitation; number of relative errors per item to the criterion of two correct list recitations; number of trials to the first correct response per item; and number of trials to two correct responses per item. All of these analyses revealed significant main effects of experimental condition and item position, as well as a significant condition-by-item interaction.

Since different assumptions about the error term in a simple analysis of variance between experimental and control groups produced different estimates of magnitudes of effect, Bredenkamp and Bredenkamp concluded that the results did not clearly support or deny the specificity hypothesis. The significant condition-by-item interaction in the two-way analysis supported the position hypothesis. Examination of individual items revealed no significant difference in positive transfer for Items 1 and 2, but significant differences in transfer for the remaining Items 3 through 10. The serial position curves of transfer per item were not significantly different in terms of rank, however. This argues against the position hypothesis. The correlation between experimental and control serial-position curves was attributed to differences in interitem difficulty, caused by differences in learnability of items because of the position effects. When the results per item were corrected for differences due to this serial-position influence on item difficulty, this correlation was virtually zero. The overall positive transfer was attributed to response learning from the prior task for experimental subjects. Therefore, the authors conclude that their results are contrary to the position hypothesis, and inconclusive with respect to the specificity hypothesis.

SOME CONSTANT POSITIONS

A complementary method to the derived-list technique is to retain some items in their original positions but changing relationships to the other items. This method was used by Eisdorfer (1968) in his study of pacing effects in serial learning for aged subjects. His purpose was to distinguish between what he called cognitive (i.e., position) and S-R (i.e., sequential) strategies of learning. Four groups of subjects learned two lists of eight words on successive days. For the control group the two lists were identical. One experimental group of subjects was given a transfer list in which the second, fourth, sixth, and eighth words were replaced with four similar words, and the order of words in the new list was scrambled. For another experimental group the order of the substituted list was not scrambled, so that the four old words retained their serial position. A fourth group of subjects received the same series of words, but each trial began on a progressively later word (namely, a word from the first position on trial one, second word on trial two, third word on trial three, and so on). Each group was subdivided for assignment to the two pacing rates. The control group showed the greatest transfer, of course, while the scrambled list showed no transfer. The list with four items at constant positions showed significant positive transfer. All of these results were the same for both pacing conditions. The condition of progressive change in starting point, however, did not show any transfer for the fast pace, but a significant degree of transfer for the slower pacing.

Since Eisdorfer (1968) equated position learning with a cognitive approach, and sequential learning to an S-R approach, he therefore concluded that there were more implicit S-R reinforcements for the slower pacing. Also, however, the greater time for responding could have permitted the subjects to make use of positional cues by a proper recoding of the items, which might be possible with the progressive and orderly change of the starting word. With the 10-second pacing, the percentage of transfer was about 32% for the constant position of four items and 45% for the constant sequence with staggered starting point. Thus, the position cues seemed to be more important for the faster pace with this population of aged subjects, whereas for these subjects the slower pace seemed to favor the sequential approach. It should be remembered that the faster pacing presumably increases the arousal level of the subjects, so that the increase in time is confounded with a presumed increase in experimental stress.

McKeever (1968) compared the transfer of adjacent and non-adjacent items from one serial-learning task to another. The derived test list of eight words retained items from each of four previously learned eight-item lists, always at the same serial position as in the earlier lists. The experimental list contained pairs of items that had been previously adjacent, whereas the control list contained no pairs that had previously been closer than three positions from one another. Although the performance of the two groups on the derived list was not significantly different, it did differ when only the even-numbered items were considered—the second member of the adjacent pairs on the experimental list. Performance was not significantly different for the odd-numbered items—which on either list did not involve previously adjacent items. These results show that the subjects benefited from prior adjacent dyadic associations when these were added to possible position cues.

The serial-learning to serial-learning transfer design of Zaffiro (1969) employed two items of the first list that retained the same sequential relation, the same position, both sequential and position cues, or neither of them. These items appeared either at the beginning or middle of a list of ten nonsense syllables. The transfer effect of constant serial position in the two lists was significant, supporting the hypothesis of position learning as the effective cue. The effect of constant position was greater at the beginning of the list than at the middle. No evidence was found supporting an effect of constant sequence, and thus the study failed to support the specificity hypothesis.

SUMMARY

The results of serial-to-serial transfer thus provide some support for the specificity hypothesis, but also for the position-learning hypothesis as well. The start-shift technique, which retains item-sequence constancy to the maximal degree, seems to provide the most consistent evidence for chaining. Even here, however, there is some change in conditions between first and second series because the last and first items were not contiguous before, and now they must be associated. Positive effects are typically greatest when both sequence and position cues can be used by the subjects.

Paired Associate to Serial Learning

The paired-associates to serial-learning design determines whether or not the associations between pairs of items learned in the first task facilitate acquisition of the second task. Pairs of items on the first task are placed in adjacent positions on the second, so that transfer of the early association should facilitate the serial learning if interitem associations are involved.

The classic study using this method was done by Primoff (1938). He found, by comparing serial learning with the learning of a chain of its components, that a serial response is different from and easier to establish than its component associations. The serial learning was easier to establish. Since his experiment has gained importance recently, it will be described in some detail. Primoff's experiment was rather complicated because he used each subject as his own control, with the entire procedure requiring testing of 16 paid subjects for over 2 hours on each of 3 days. The first day a subject apparently learned six practice tasks, composed of two serial and one paired-associate list of words and three similar lists of nonsense syllables. These practice items were unrelated to the experimental tasks. On the second day each subject learned either nonsense or word stimuli; the type of material was reversed on the third day. The subject began with a set of experimental paired associates and a set of control pairs. Then he learned three "preliminary serial lists," followed by experimental and control serial lists with the order counterbalanced across subjects. The experimental list was composed of items derived from the previously learned experimental pairs, with each item serving both as stimulus and response member—what is now known as a double-function list. The control list, however, used unrelated stimulus items, so that the subject had merely become familiarized with the items to be learned serially and had learned no consistent associations between items. On the third day, the subject repeated the procedures of the second day, with word or nonsense-syllable material reversed. In addition, the subject was given a test of backward and forward associations for the material learned that day on the serial test list. In this test, the items were rearranged in temporal order, with each item appearing twice. The item appeared once with a dash to its left, which indicated that the item on the test list that had preceded it should be supplied (namely, a backward association); the other time a dash appeared to its right, indicating that the following item of the serial list should be given (namely, a forward association). At the end of the experiment, the subjects were asked for an introspective report of their feelings and cognitions during the learning, since they had not been instructed about the relations between the tasks. Some subjects had seen the connection and others had not.

The results in the Primoff study were about the same for nonsense and word materials, except for the overall greater difficulty of the nonsense items. For the test serial lists, the experimental conditions, entailing familiarity with the necessary associations, produced faster learning than the control conditions, entailing familiarity only with the items themselves. Moreover, the experimental serial test lists were learned faster than the "preliminary serial lists," which also provided a kind of control condition. The double-function paired-associate (experimental) lists were twice as difficult as the single-function paired-associate (control) items. The fact that the double-function paired-associate list required more trials to learn than did a preliminary serial list of the same associations indicates that a serial task is something other than the formation of the "same" S-R bonds; it is, in fact, more difficult to form the individual bonds. On the other hand, the positive transfer to the final serial task of these interitem associations does indicate that the subject can make later use of the learned associations. The force of this evidence for positive transfer is reduced when it is considered that the double-function list required twice as many trials as the control conditions, and thus the subject should have been more than twice as experienced with those items. Also, of course, the control items had been learned responses to other unrelated items on the prior paired-associate task. Therefore, the typical associative result for backward associations— namely, new response to an old stimulus (Osgood, 1949)—would predict a negative influence on the transfer serial task. Primoff's results thus show that serial learning cannot be equated to formation of a simple direct forward associative bond. His general study has been repeated many times, with supporting results.

Young (1959) studied transfer from a double-function paired-associate list to serial learning of the same associations and also, for different subjects, the reverse transfer from serial learning to a double-function paired-associate list. He confirmed Primoff's (1938) results that more trials in paired-associate learning were required to learn essentially the same associations as in the serial-learning task. Also, more errors per trial and more backward errors per trial occurred for the paired-associate task. The prior paired-associate learning produced significant positive transfer to the serial-learning task, but the reverse was not true. The serial-learning to paired-associate transfer was significantly positive for the first six transfer trials. Thereafter, it was negative, requiring almost as many trials to a criterion of one perfect recitation as the paired-associate list that had been learned before the serial list. Therefore, the shape of this curve was different, showing very rapid progress at first, and then quickly changing to a slow rate of progress. These results indicate that there is tremendous interference between backward and forward associations in the double-function paired-associate list. The tendency to make backward associations is somehow inhibited in the serial-learning task.

The work of Primoff (1938) was further extended by Young, Milauckas, and Bryan (1963) for transfer from a double-function paired-associate list of words to a serial list. The words were arranged so that positive, negative, and zero transfer to the serial list was predicted on the basis of the earlier associations from the paired-associate list— respectively, compatible (i.e., identical), incompatible (i.e., new associations), and unrelated (i.e., dissimilar items). Both the positive and negative results were obtained, as predicted, supporting the argument for the learning of sequential associations in both tasks. The change in contextual stimuli of the two tasks probably contributed to the failure to find perfect transfer in the case of identical associations. There were fewer overt errors per trial for the compatible transfer group relative to the other two groups. As Underwood (1963) points out, this small amount of positive transfer indicates that such prior learning of the correct associations is not the "natural" way to learn them from the standpoint of a serial list. The obvious difference is in the context of the task. When the original pairings in the paired-associate tasks were not the same as those to be learned on the serial task, there was a large negative transfer effect.

Horton and Grover (1968) found positive transfer from a double-function paired-associate list to a derived serial list composed of the prior associations in the forward direction, but not for another list in which associations in the backward direction had been used. Since the nonsignificant difference favored the control group relative to the backward association group, there had to be some negative transfer effects for the backward group.

Apparently two mechanisms can account for the less interference in the serial-learning task. Both are related to the variation in the order of pairs in paired-associate learning, whereas in serial learning items must, of course, be in constant order. The constant order of serial learning means that an item of one-degree backward association has just been seen when the subject would otherwise be tempted to produce it as an intrusion. The second is that an item in paired-associate learning of a double-function list appears twice in one trial, very likely at different positions. To the extent that the subject is learning positions of items, intrusion errors may be mediated by confusion about position.

Serial to Paired-Associate Learning

Both positive and negative evidence for transfer from serial to paired-associate lists have been obtained. Much of the negative evidence has been obtained by Young (1959, 1961, 1962). In one study (Young, 1961), he failed to find evidence for either positive or negative transfer from serial to paired-associate learning, using the same pairing of originally adjacent items and re-pairings of the previously adjacent items, respectively. Later he actually obtained negative transfer when he used two preceding items from the serial list as a compound stimulus for serial learning (Young, 1962).

Martin and Green (1966) also failed to find transfer from serial learning to paired-associate learning, using CVC trigrams matched for meaningfulness. The ten-item serial list was learned to a criterion of one errorless trial. In paired-associate learning at a 2-second presentation rate, items were paired that had been adjacent on the serial learning list or that had not appeared on the previously learned list. The paired-associate performance, assessed by trials to criterion, failed to show a significant difference between the old and the new pairings, although the difference did favor the previously adjacent pairs. There was no serial-position effect in paired-associate learning in terms of the previous position of the familiar parts.

Positive transfer from serial to paired-associate learning was obtained by Jensen (1962f). It was probably important that he used self-paced presentation and explicit instructions about the connection between lists. This presumably would give the subject greater opportunity to make use of any prior learned associations.

In three experiments, Breckenridge and Dixon (1970) studied serial to paired-associate transfer using adjacent pairs, for which positive transfer was predicted on the basis of associative chaining, and previously nonadjacent pairs, for which negative transfer was predicted. A control condition employed unrelated items. In Experiment 1, in which the learning criterion was one correct recitation, results conforming to both predictions for direction of transfer were obtained. In the two subsequent experiments, only adjacent or nonadjacent pairs were used, and the serial list was either partially learned or overlearned. In each case the previously adjacent items were again learned faster as paired associates. A serial position effect in the paired-associate task was obtained in each experiment, with the items at either end in the serial-learning task learned earlier. These results indicate associations between items in serial learning.

In Rosner's (1970) experiment the subjects learned serial lists fastest when there was high associability between successive items. Learning was progressively slower when there was, respectively: low associability but implicit mediational links between successive terms; no interitem associative strength; and high associations between remote items but not adjacent items. The superiority of the list with implicit mediators over the no-association list reflects the facilitation by mediators in serial learning. When these subjects then learned double-function paired-associate lists composed of the previous learned associations, there was no significant effect of the particular serial-learning condition, although all groups were superior to a control group for whom the paired-associate connections were new. The positive transfer from serial learning to paired-associate learning supports a specificity hypothesis about the effective stimulus in serial learning. Since the subsequent paired-associate learning required more trials than the prior serial-learning task, although the associations were the same, other evidence contradicts that hypothesis. The absence of a difference in paired-associate transfer for the various list conditions in the prior serial learning also argues against the specificity hypothesis.

G.J. Johnson (1972) extended the Jensen and Rohwer (1965) study of serial to paired-associate transfer by using a 4:4-second rate of presentation for the transfer list. He used, in addition, conditions for positive and negative transfer and a condition in which both sequential and positional cues were transfered simultaneously. The subjects were instructed about the relations between tasks. Johnson found that positional cues were by far the most effective, although there was also evidence for transfer mediated by sequence. The sequence cue given in addition to the position cue produced only slightly better performance than the position cue alone. Adding sequence cues to position cues did not enhance performance for end items, but it did for middle items. Therefore, there was some evidence for the superiority of the double cues at some (namely, middle) positions.

The compound-stimulus, or cluster, hypothesis was tested by Young and Clark (1964). Their subjects first learned a 15-item serial list, and then a transfer list of 30 items, composed of five 3-item clusters from rearrangement of the first list and five new "clusters." Although the sublists of previously learned and new items did not require significantly different numbers of trials to criterion, an analysis of the trials to learn the second and third members of the clusters did show a significant superiority for the familiar items. A comparison according to serial position in the original list for the second and third items in the clusters showed that the familiar items were learned significantly faster when they had occupied the second, third, and fifteenth positions. Since positive transfer was observed for the second as well as the third item in the cluster, a simple dyadic association could have produced this result. The serial-position data indicates that the formation of the interitem associations is more likely to occur at the ends of a series, than at the middle. Perhaps as Battig, Brown, and Nelson (1963) argue, in what they call the complex-stimulus hypothesis, the end items are quickly associated to position, making them more differentiated earlier, so that interitem associations are facilitated.

Crowder, Chisolm, and Fell (1966) tested transfer from a serial-learning task to a continuous paired-associate task, involving interleaved presentations and test trials. The pairs of paired-associate words had been adjacent, nonadjacent, or not present on the prior serial-learning list. Recall of the adjacent pairs was almost double that of the other two conditions, supporting the sequential associations hypothesis of serial learning.

The differences among results of different researchers naturally have led to a search for the critical variables that determined whether or not positive transfer would be found with this method. Some variables that have been investigated are availability of position information, type of material, presentation rate, degree of prior learning, instructions, and transfer measure used.

POSITION INFORMATION

Ebenholtz (1966a) studied transfer from a serial list of 14 nonsense syllables by using these prior serial items as stimuli for paired-associate learning. The paired-associate learning was significantly correlated with relative position in the original serial learning task. Although the errors of paired-associate learning generally described the typical bowed shape, in terms of the position of items from the serial learning, there was a relative depression for the middle items. Ebenholtz suggests that the general bowed shape of this curve was attributable to the greater association with position for items at the ends of the series, whereas the relative depression for the middle positions was caused by the tendency for the subjects to learn sequential associations at the middle positions. This argument supports a transfer of positional information, because the paired associates were presented in three different presentation sequences. Position information should produce a U-shaped function with maxima at extreme serial positions and minima about the middle, where presumably interitem associations tend to predominate. Superiority for first and last positions probably merely reflected the usual overlearning of these syllables in the original learning task.

Shuell and Keppel (1967a) required subjects to learn 12-adjective lists, to a criterion of one perfect trial, followed by ten trials on a double-function paired-associate list. For an experimental group the paired-associate lists maintained the pairings of the serial list, whereas for a control group the words on the two lists were unrelated. The location of the starting point of the serial list was varied for one-half of the subjects in each group. While substantial positive transfer was obtained from both experimental conditions, transfer was greater for those subjects with the varied starting point of the serial list. Presumably these subjects were less likely to have associated items in the serial learning to a specific position and were thus more likely to have formed sequential associations among items. The subjects with constant starting position did, in fact, show a serial-position effect on the transfer (paired-associate) task in terms of location of the items on the prior serial task.

Muir and Youssef (1971) found positive transfer from serial to paired-associate lists when the starting item for serial learning was varied from trial to trial. Presumably the subject was thereby forced to learn interitem sequential associations, since the possibilities for multiple-element chaining and position learning were thus drastically reduced.

TYPE OF MATERIAL

The nature of the stimulus material can influence the direction of evidence for various functional stimuli. Therefore, Horowitz and Izawa (1963) suggested that the chaining hypothesis is oversimplified. They concluded from a study of transfer from serial learning to paired-associate, and paired-associate to serial learning, that subjects tend to learn sequential associations with material of low similarity, but to learn position with material of high internal similarity. Moreover, for lists of low internal interference they concluded that the effective stimulus tends to be a cluster of preceding items. This interpretation accounts for three major results of their study: the greater speed of serial relative to paired-associate learning, the absence of backward errors in serial learning, and the differences in the direction of transfer as a function of strengths of interitem associations.

Using the same list of adjectives that had been employed with positive results by Horowitz and Izawa (1963), Young and Casey (1964) failed to find a transfer effect from a serial-learning task to a paired-associate task, even though nominally the same associations were required for successful performance of each task. This suggests that the previous positive results of Horowitz and Izawa may have occurred because a control for practice and warm-up effect had not been included. Thus, the argument for associative chaining was not supported.

Serial to paired-associate transfer of a 13-item list was investigated by Horton and Turnage (1970), using a mixed serial list and a single-function paired-associate list. Varied were item meaningfulness and the degree of training on the serial list. Positive transfer was discovered over the first five trials of paired-associate learning and for the criterion of any four correct of the 6-item subset of control or experimental items. However, trials to the criterion of one correct presentation of the total subset of six control or experimental items revealed superior performance for the control items. Thus, consistent with previous results, the positive transfer effect occurs early and then is lost. There was, moreover, a significant interaction of item meaningfulness and performance on the early paired-associate trials; for the meaningless and low meaningful items the paired-associate performance was superior for previously learned items, but it was inferior for the high-meaningful items (two-syllable nouns). However, the trials to complete learning showed universally negative transfer for all conditions of meaningfulness.

Horton and Turnage (1970) found the usual serial-position effect in the paired-associate task for experimental items ordered according to their position in the previously learned serial task, but not for control items. Bowing was progressively greater the less meaningful the items, indicating greater reliance on position cues for the less meaningful material. The degree of original serial learning was not a significant variable, suggesting that differential familiarity with items from the prior serial learning was not the cause of the superior transfer for end items.

PRESENTATION RATE

Erickson, Ingram, and Young (1963) tested the hypothesis that the failure of transfer from serial learning to paired-associate learning occurred because the paired-associate task typically did not allow enough time for the subject to scan the memorized serial list in order to recover the dyadic associations. For this purpose, they speeded up the serial-learning task, in order to increase the availability of the serial associations, while at the same time allowing more time for the paired-associate response, thus giving the subject more time to search his memory for the correct association. The overall results were negative with respect to the hypothesis, however. But a serial-position analysis revealed significant negative transfer for the pairs from the middle positions on the serial list, but significant positive transfer from the terminal position. Specifically, with regard to position on the prior serial list, the transfer was zero at the first position, significantly negative about the middle, and significantly positive for syllables from the end. This result was generally the reverse of expectations from the assumption of a scanning of memory from beginning to end of the original series.

The subjects of Heaps, Green, and Cheney (1968) learned a serial list of ten items and then a paired-associate list of adjacent couplets at either a 2:2 or 6:6 rate. Control subjects learned pairs that had not appeared on their prior serial list. Positive transfer was found only for the 6:6-second paired-associate learning. The authors suggest that a slower rate allows the subject to scan his memory of the learned series to recover the appropriate dyadic associations. Since the transfer was not obtained for the 2:2-second rate, the sheer familiarity of previously learned items is probably not the cause of the positive transfer.

PRIOR LEARNING

Crowder (1968) extended the work of Crowder et al., (1966) by varying the degree of the prior serial learning. He argued that the negative transfer consistently obtained in tests of effects of prior serial learning on subsequent paired-associate learning is due to weaknesses in the transfer measure. Using a continuous paired-associate learning task, in which retention for a once-presented pair is tested after a period of tests and presentation of other items, he discovered as appropriate both positive and negative transfer effects from the prior serial learning. The paired-associate performance on previous adjacent items showed positive transfer, increasing with the degree of prior training, whereas the paired-associate performance for previously remote items decreased as a function of degree of prior training. The paired-associate learning of previously remote items showed intrusions of the items that had been adjacent in the original serial learning. Crowder concludes that his results support the chaining hypothesis and adds a methodological comment which strikes a sympathetic note here:

> Implied by these results is the possibility that failures to find transfer
> in the complete mastery of a paired-associate list, as frequently reported

in this literature, have more to say about the complexity of paired-associate learning than about the mechanism of serial learning (1968, p. 500).

INSTRUCTIONS

Postman and Stark (1967) point out that Young (1961) and Young and Casey (1964) found a transient positive-transfer effect early that might be dismissed as merely response familiarization, but might even mean something more. Postman and Stark therefore tested serial to paired-associate transfer on a double-function list for one group of subjects learning the same associations and for another group learning the same items, but all new associations. The control group learned all new items on the paired-associate test. Some subjects were instructed about the relationships among associations between the two tasks, while other subjects were not told about the relations between the items. Each subject was tested under one of the transfer conditions with one set of instructions, but three times in three cycles of the experiment. The mean number of correct responses on the first transfer test of the first cycle revealed significant effects of transfer condition and a significant interaction of condition with instructions. Greatest positive transfer appeared for the subjects learning the same associations, with the instructed group surpassing the uninstructed group. The re-paired associations showed a relatively small, but significant, negative transfer. Since this experimental group had enjoyed familiarization with the stimuli, this result cannot be attributed to familiarization, but to interfering prior associations. The results were equivalent when evaluated over all of the ten transfer trials that were used in the first cycle. Over cycles, the practice tended to increase the amount of positive transfer and to reduce the negative transfer.

Postman and Stark (1967) found that the instructions were ineffective for the performance of the subjects learning re-paired associations. They conclude that the positive transfer from serial-learning to paired-associate learning indicates the effectiveness of prior items as cues in serial learning. Since such transfer was far from perfect, other bases of learning are indicated—including position cues. Therefore, the study of Postman and Stark indicates that subjects can under some conditions learn direct associations between items.

Stark (1968) also obtained evidence for positive transfer from serial learning to a double-function paired-associate list. This positive transfer occurred at all serial positions and at all stages of practice, presumably because the transfer task was made easier by instructing the subject about the relation between items in the two tasks and by decreasing the presentation rate in the paired-associate transfer task. This study provides further evidence for the effectiveness of the specific prior item as a stimulus in serial learning.

Further evidence for the effects of instructions on serial to paired-associate learning was obtained by Lesgold and Bower (1970), who instructed the subjects about the relationships between the tasks. Findings of effects of instructions would indicate a strategy-selection interpretation of learning, whereas no effect of a variable such as instructions would imply a unitary associational serial-learning process. Three groups were used in each of two experiments: two experimental groups first learned the serial task, and then a paired-associate task employed adjacent pairs from the earlier series. One of the groups was instructed about the relation between groups, and the other was not. Control groups learned only the paired-associate list in Experiment 1; they learned an unrelated serial list in Experiment 2. Stimuli were letters in Experiment 1 and were words in Experiment 2. In the serial task, 15 items were presented in temporal groupings of three. For the serial-learning task, transition-shift probabilities computed from the recall protocols indicated that subjects tended to recall in triplet chunks. They often missed the first item of a triad even though they had got the last item of the previous triad correctly. On the other hand, they tended to get the remaining two members correct if they had got the first item correct and vice versa. On the paired-associate transfer task, only the instructed group showed positive transfer on the first transfer trial, although the uninstructed group eventually surpassed it because of a faster learning rate. The transition shift probabilities fit the triplet-organized result described above only for the instructed group. The instructed subjects were using the information from the prior serial task, but they were not learning the paired-associate task as well. The results were interpreted in terms of "cognitive control of transfer." The instructed subjects tended to establish a strategy of approaching the paired-associate task that was apparently less efficient than that of the uninstructed group. Moreover, the presence of some strategy tended to retard the adoption of the better approach. Lesgold and Bower suggest that the serial task was more integrational in character, whereas the paired-associate task had more of an S-R character, involving simple dyadic association between the nominal stimulus items and response items.

TRANSFER MEASURE

Postman and Stark (1967) and Stark (1968) argued also that the generally negative evidence for positive transfer from serial learning to paired-associate learning may have been the result of rather insensitive measures of transfer. Specifically, the measure of trials to criterion of complete learning is insensitive because it is heavily controlled by just the most difficult items alone. The degree of variation in trials to criterion as a measure is indeed gigantic. For example, Smith and Stearns (1949) report that the variation among subjects in number of trials to learn 13 two-syllable adjectives was from 2 to 57.

SUMMARY

Although the results of serial to paired-associate transfer are not unanimous, there is still substantial evidence for the specificity hypothesis. Since negative evidence in the form of zero transfer cannot disprove the hypothesis, the positive evidence carries more weight.

Unlearning

Noting the inconsistency in the literature with respect to transfer studies of the effective stimulus in serial learning, Giurintano (1973) tested position-learning, chaining, and dual-stimulus hypotheses within the same complex experimental design. He had subjects first learn a serial list, followed by a paired-associate list, and then recall, re-order, and relearn the original serial list. Specific predictions were made for the relative performance of multiple different transfer paradigms. Giurintano interpreted his results as tending to support the chaining hypothesis, but he cautioned that other conditions and procedures might produce a different result.

His comprehensive research design and cautious attitude about conclusions on the functional-stimulus question represent a growing awareness of researchers about the general tenor of the final solution. Probably, therefore, the subject can learn sequential associations, which must be unlearned if they conflict with requirements of the new task.

CUE PROBES

Another, more direct, technique of discovering the functional stimulus in serial learning is to present a series for one or more trials and then to record the subject's accuracy of response to probe stimuli representing different cues. This technique was employed by Woodward and Murdock (1968), who used three types of probe cue in a short-term memory task for words. The probe was a number indicating the position of the item to be recalled, or a word that had preceded the item to be recalled, or both. When a single probe was used to test recall for a single item after a single exposure, the position probe was more effective than the sequential (word) probe, particularly at the ends of the series. The typical bowed serial-position curve was found, showing a greater recency than primacy effect. A second experiment, designed to increase the overall performance level, presented the stimulus strings five times before the cued recall. The characteristic serial-position curve was again obtained, with no differences among types of cues. The authors concluded that the sequence and the position cues were about equally effective, and that a combination of the two did not improve recall. Prior instructions about type of probe did not produce much of a differential effect.

Woodward (1968) used short-term memory for a serial list to investigate the effective cue for serial learning. In one experiment, lists of high and low acoustic item similarity were shown once, twice, or four times, at different rates of presentation. Retention was tested by a probe for serial position, for sequential dyadic association, or by both cues. The main effect of probe type was not significant, but probe type did enter a triple interaction with list similarity and serial position. Although each type of probe produced a typical serial-position curve, with greater recency than primacy effects, the outcome did not permit an easy description; the position probe produced a somewhat flatter curve over the middle positions, particularly for highly similar words. Signal detection analyses of performance (Swets, Tanner, & Birdsall, 1961) at the various serial positions in the first experiment indicated differences in beta, which is a measure of the criterion established by the subject for giving a positive response. A value of 1.0 indicates an optimum rational strategy, whereas values greater than 1.0 indicate too lax a criterion, and those below indicate excessive stringency. Woodward's results revealed a rise in beta from about .8 at the first two positions, to a maximum of about 1.0 for Positions Three and Four, and then a progressive drop to about .2 for the ninth and tenth positions. However, the d' value, which is a signal-detection measure of the subject's sensitivity (storage capacity of memory), showed a stronger effect of primacy, except that the tenth (last) position was greatest of all positions.

In a second experiment Woodward (1968) used only the sequential and position probes. The serial-position curves again were bowed, with greater recency effects. The interactive effect of probe and position was significant; the position probe was superior at Positions Eight, Nine, and Ten, but not at the remaining positions. The low-similarity words showed a more skewed curve than high-similar items, showing poorer recall at Positions One through Five, and superior recall at the remaining positions. The d' measure showed the typical bowed curve, but with greater primacy effects. For the position probe, d' was greater than for the sequential probe at the end positions and not the middle positions. The values of beta tended to drop from first to last items, with larger values for the position probe at the first six positions, and then larger values for the sequential probe for Positions Seven through Ten. Presentation rate did not affect rate of recall of items at the beginning of the list (i.e., primary memory). Woodward suggests that his results and those of Woodward and Murdock (1968) support Youssef's (1967) two-factor theory. That is, probe data collected from a single trial tend to show differential effects of probe type, because the process is primarily associational, whereas probes after multiple trials fail to find differences between probe types, because the process has become integrational.

Voss (1969) had subjects learn a serial list of 12 high-frequency words to different criteria and tested retention by asking the subject to: (1) recall as many words as possible in any order; (2) report the word following a probe word; or (3) report the word appearing at a given serial position. Learning was continued to mastery of the list, after the interruption. As would be expected, the subjects could recall more items than they could correctly reproduce by either method. The sequential probe produced more accurate responses than the position probe. Serial-position analyses for the recall condition indicated a serial-position effect for each stage of learning, except for the absence of a clear recency effect for the conditions of minimal original learning. The subjects also could recall more items than they could anticipate, on the trial either immediately before or after the interruption for the test. For the sequential probe, the items near the beginning were most accurately reproduced, again with the recency effect appearing only later in learning. Of great interest, however, was the fact that anticipations before and after the probe test exceeded the number of correct responses to the sequential probe, even for both the cases of learning to a criterion of one perfect trial and for a list overlearned by ten trials. This result shows that all the cues for learning and retention are not present in a probe test. In particular, the configuration of the total situation is not reproduced with fidelity.

The results of the recall test in the Voss (1969) experiment indicate that there is a difference between item learning and item placement (Slamecka, 1964; Voss, 1966). The serial-position effects of item recall support the conception of serial learning as a strategy of item acquisition, with the initial items learned first, and then the final items. The results of both sequential and positional probes do not provide strong support for either the sequence or position-learning hypothesis, since subjects could anticipate more items than they could reproduce from the probe. Of course, the problem of change of set is important here since the probes, for example, were given verbally and the anticipation trials were presented visually.

Schwartz (1970a) investigated the effective stimulus for one-trial serial learning of ten-word lists. He used a position probe and also probes for forward and backward sequential associations. The shapes of serial-position curves were about the same, showing the typical bow and a greater recency than primacy effect. Overall performance for the different probes was not different. There was a slight tendency for the position probe to produce a greater recency effect, and to be slightly less effective for the middle items. These curves, corrected for guessing, showed a similar shape, but with greater primacy than recency effects, because guessing was greater for the terminal items. Again, there was a slightly greater bow in the position-probe data. The curve of d' as a function of serial position also showed slightly greater primacy than recency effects, again with greater bowing for the position probe. Schwartz (1970b) later provided further evidence for a dual process of serial learning, with positive evidence for items at each serial position.

Posnansky, Battig, and Voss (1972) argued that transfer tasks suffer from the problem of ambiguity with respect to what was learned originally and how it was used in the second task. Also, Voss' (1969) evidence for changes of process at different stages of serial learning also indicates added ambiguity depending upon the stage of original learning. The Posnansky et al. technique was new. It employed serial recall after each trial, with items scored as correct only if their correct position was indicated. Subsequent retention of items at specific positions was probed by a diagrammatic representation of position, by a prior item, or by a cluster of three prior items. For experimental subjects an item correct on the serial recall was probed, whereas for control subjects the probe was not contingent upon a prior correct response. The different probe-types were given in selected sequences, starting with either the position or prior-item probes. Although both position and prior-item probes showed serial-position effects, the effect was stronger for the position probe. Again, the position probe was especially ineffective for the middle positions. The addition of the three-item probe added little to the effectiveness of position probe or single prior-item.

The ultimate in probing for the functional stimulus in serial-learning was accomplished by Posnansky (1972). In an elaborate study using both serial-recall and serial-anticipation learning with 15-word lists, and probes for position, prior item, and three prior items, she discovered that subjects used all three of these potential cues for learning. Even though a subject established a preferred cue, nevertheless he gave evidence for using each of them on occasion. No serial-position effects were found for the prior-item probe or for the three-item probe. The position probe did show that this cue was used most for items at the ends of the series. Thus, Posnansky concludes that the prior searches for the functional stimulus in serial position had to produce contradictory results, because subjects can, and do, use all cues.

The evidence from probe stimuli therefore provides evidence for use of both position and sequential cues. The results support the general conclusion that the probe stimuli are relatively effective for end items and the sequential associations for middle items.

COMPOUND-STIMULUS HYPOTHESIS

A compromise approach to the question of the effective stimulus in serial learning incorporates the preceding two arguments; it can be considered a compound-stimulus explanation. The compound-stimulus hypothesis (Young, 1962; Horowitz & Izawa, 1963) considers the stimulus to be some combination of prior items. Closely allied to this is the notion of no stimulus, but merely response integration (Jensen, 1962b). An earlier statement of this general view was offered by Newman (1936). He hypothesized, as a process by which configuration mediates learning, a "non-sensory" Gestalt of the whole series as a part of the stimulus for each successive response. This concept implies that in learning each item is associated with its position in relation to the whole series.

EVIDENCE FROM TRANSFER BETWEEN SERIAL LISTS

By studying transfer between two serial lists of 12 bigrams, Battig, Brown, and Schild (1964) attempted to evaluate the relative importance of associations between adjacent items, learning of serial positions, and learning of more complex relationships. Groups of three items were repeated on the transfer list in the same positions adjacent to one another, in different positions but still adjacent to one another, or in the same serial positions but not adjacent to one another. When adjacent to one another, the cluster of three items appeared near the beginning or middle of the series, respectively. Two degrees of initial learning were employed. The totals of errors on the second list were smaller for the two conditions of the clustered transferred items, whether or not the position of the cluster was changed. Battig et al. concluded that the beginning of a serial list can be learned by simple chaining or position learning, while the middle of the series can be learned by more complex associative clusters.

EVIDENCE FROM PAIRED ASSOCIATES

A more eclectic view was offered by Battig, Brown, and Nelson (1963). They argued that the subject develops a unique approach, which may involve some combination of position learning and multiple associations. They found that a paired-associate list was equally difficult to learn if the constant ordinal positions were maintained only until each pair had been correctly reproduced once, as when the relative position of pairs was constant throughout learning.

EVIDENCE FROM PROBES

Heslip (1969a) tested the cluster hypothesis of the functional stimulus in serial learning (Horowitz & Izawa, 1963) by giving two-item prompts on test trials for selected items after every third trial of learning by the anticipation method. For the test trial, two adjacent items from the series were presented as in the acquisition procedure, followed by an X. The subject was to report the item that was represented by the X in the sequence. Since the subject had only the preceding cluster of two items to cue his response, with no indication of position, his performance on the test could be compared to his level of accuracy on the acquisition test that did produce the position cue also. In this way Heslip proposed to determine whether or not the subject was performing better with the additional cue of position.

The serial-position results by serial anticipation were, in fact, closely approximated by the cluster-prompting technique. There are two problems in interpreting this result, however. The first is that a correct response of serial anticipation was counted if the subject had got that item correct on either one or the other of the last two trials before the cluster test. This would, of course, tend to inflate the number of items that were apparently learned. The second problem is that the cluster test also inflated the number of correct responses by giving the subject longer to think of his response and to make it. This occurred because the subject was to make his response during the 2-second interval that the X was visible. This is precisely the interval that is customarily not counted as correct during serial-anticipation learning. Although the response interval in Heslip's technique is equated, for the cluster probe it is delayed so that the subject had the 2 seconds in which the prior item was visible to think of his answer. It is not possible to know whether these two sources of distortion in the number correct were the same for both conditions of testing.

The most convincing evidence from the Heslip (1969a) study, nevertheless, was the fact that the subjects did not know the length of the 13-item list during postexperimental interviews. Of 156 subjects, 71 guessed that it was 10 items long, 57 judged it to be 8 or 9 items long, and only one reported the number correctly at 13! I interpret these results to mean that the subjects were led to use a sequential-association approach to the serial-anticipation task in this study because the interpolated tests called for that kind of learning. Assuming that subjects can use both position and sequence cues, it would be most inefficient for the learner to adopt one set of cues for the serial-learning tests, which would then be essentially worthless for the interpolated cluster-probe tests.

Heslip (1969c) attempted another direct test of a two-item cluster hypothesis—that only two items given in proper sequence should elicit the correct response as often as a normal situation of anticipation learning, which provides all cues to responding. He used high-familiar and high-association items in one experiment and high-familiar and low-association items in a second experiment. The cluster-probe test was accomplished at various stages of the acquisition process by using, in addition to the memory drum used for the learning task, a second memory drum in which two cue syllables could be given in sequence, followed by a red X to indicate when the third syllable to complete the triad sequence should be reproduced. Results of this test could be compared to the results when the complete series was presented in the same memory drum used for the learning trials. For both lists of items the results for the two-item-cluster cue approximated those for the complete series, although there was some remaining advantage when the total series was presented for a cue. Again, the use of the cluster test, because it was essentially a sequential test, could be equivalent to telling the subjects to learn interitem associations.

SUMMARY

This chapter began the search for the functional stimulus in serial learning. The first and obvious basis to be considered was the formation of direct forward associations between the immediately prior item or items in the series and the subsequent item. Evidence both for and against this hypothesis was presented. The evidence thus indicates that under some conditions the subjects do learn associations between succeeding items, or between several prior items and a response item. Such associations do not appear to be necessary prerequisites for serial learning to take place, however.

It seems clear that serial learning is not simply the formation of dyadic associations between pairs of items. Although the cluster hypothesis has typically been considered mainly an extension of the chaining hypothesis, it nevertheless is essentially a compromise interpretation, between the simple-chaining and position-learning hypotheses. As such, it is probably closer to the truth. If the concept of cluster is extended to include all of the prior items in the series, instead of three prior items, for example, then the difference between position learning and item association is virtually reduced to a semantic argument.

CHAPTER

3

THE STIMULUS: A POSITION

If the serial-learning task does not require merely the formation of associations between items, it may then be facilitated by the association of each item to its ordinal position within the series. The subject may learn that an item is the fifth in the series, for example, without learning what particular item it follows. This interpretation of serial learning has also received extensive support in the psychological literature.

Not all of the support has been recent. Ladd and Woodworth (1911) asserted long ago that subjects form associations between individual items and their positions within the list. They conclude that this accounts in part for the disadvantage of learning a series in parts, because for many of the items absolute position within the entire series is not a strong cue, and relative position within each part provides ambiguous or conflicting cues. McGeoch (1936) also suggested that items were associated to serial position.

Workman (1951) emphasized this possibility of position association. He quoted Woodworth and Poffenberger's (1920) conclusion that association to position within the list is an important factor in serial learning. Woodworth and Poffenberger argued that particularly the first and last members are strongly associated to positions; the effort to begin the list elicits the first item, and the last item is often reproduced correctly even though the item before it is not given correctly. The items about the middle of the series, they maintained, are not strongly associated to their positions, because the positions themselves are not well differentiated. Their proposition anticipates the following discussion very well.

In a very interesting study on several counts, Mellgren (1967) obtained evidence that subjects can use sheer spatial position as a learning cue. He also found that the learning was facilitated when the position cue was part of a "better organized" spatial dimension.

The evidence for position cues in learning has also come from widely differing types of research designs, again varying in the degrees of directness in the approach. These investigations include studies of the effects of consistent item ordering in paired-associate learning, as well as in serial learning, of addition or enhancement of position cues, and from studying position-related intruding errors and probed recall for knowledge of item position.

PAIRED-ASSOCIATE LEARNING

There is evidence from paired-associate learning that the position of the pairs affects the rate at which they are learned. The cue provided by consistency of relative position is not necessary, of course, just as it is not necessary for serial learning. If, nevertheless, the subject uses the cue in paired-associate learning, it is reasonable to assume that he also may use it in serial learning.

Newman and Saltz (1962) and Ebenholtz (1965) reported that a constant order of pairs in paired-associate learning facilitated the learning, even when the order of stimulus terms was randomized on the test trial. This indicates the use of a positional cue as part of a compound stimulus in paired-associate learning. Later, Newman (1966) presented evidence that the effect of constant order improved performance in the acquisition of the pairings, but it did not facilitate learning of the pairs themselves.

An attempt was made by Martin and Saltz (1963) to discover whether or not a facilitating effect of constant order of pairs in paired-associate learning could be attributed to the learning of position cues. The subjects learned ten-item paired-associate lists for ten trials, with retention tests after the fifth and tenth trials. Different groups of subjects saw the same order of pairs on all learning and test trials, a different order on all trials, the constant serial order for all presentations except the second test trial, and a constant order only on the first five learning trials. There was no significant facilitative effect of the constant order of presentation. A subsequent serial-learning test of response terms, in the same or varied order from the earlier constant position, produced positive evidence for facilitation resulting from constant order in paired-associate learning. It is not possible to conclude whether this result was due to position learning of the response terms or to sequential associations among response terms, however.

When the pairs were presented in a constant sequence, Rubin and Brown (1967) found facilitation of paired-associate learning. Moreover, the pairs at the ends were consistently learned first. When the response items were subsequently placed in a serial-learning task, to be learned by the anticipation method, the serial learning was faster for those items appearing in the same serial position on later tasks, relative to the groups for whom the order was changed from the constant order of the paired-associate task and also relative to the group for whom the original paired-associate learning did not manifest a constant order.

Battig, Brown, and Nelson (1963) presented evidence for a facilitative effect of a constant sequence in paired-associate learning, and pointed out possible methodological reasons for earlier failures to find such evidence. However, Battig et al. concluded that this positive effect is not caused by serial learning of items for three reasons: there were no serial-position effects in the paired-associate data; the subsequent serial learning of either stimulus or response terms in constant order was not facilitated; and the serial learning of changed-order items was superior for those items that had retained the same serial position as in the paired-associate series. This latter finding supports the idea of a learning of serial position in paired-associate learning. Battig et al. conclude that the positive effect of position learning shows up only later in the learning. Perhaps initially the position cue is both helpful, because it aids differentiation, and also harmful because it offers a cue for a different, less effective strategy. Apparently, subjects later abandon the position cue in favor of the stimulus cue alone; nevertheless, the initial differentiation effect is carried over even though the strategy is abandoned. This conclusion is supported by an experiment in which Battig et al. maintained the constant serial position of each pair until it had been reproduced correctly once and then varied it. The learning was not different from a list in which the order was forever constant. Further support for this "complex-cue" hypothesis was the fact that the relative number of commission errors was smaller for the constant order of paired-associate presentation.

The evidence thus rather consistently favors the conclusion that a constant serial order in paired-associate learning favors acquisition of the pairs. Since in paired-associate learning the subject is instructed to learn specific associations between items, as he also is instructed in serial learning, it is a reasonable inference that he also uses position information as a cue when that information becomes an aid because of constant serial position of items.

ORDER CONSISTENCY IN SERIAL LEARNING

Another way to assess effectiveness of position learning is to assess the effect of maintaining a constant position of an item in serial learning from trial to trial. Obviously if subjects are learning serial position, invariance of this cue will facilitate acquisition of the material.

Derived Serial Lists

Evidence of a position-learning view of serial learning was presented by Nagel (1912), who had subjects learn original 12-syllable lists to one correct presentation, or overlearn them. Nagel changed lists by replacing alternate items with extra syllables. Where the syllables corresponded to the same position that they had before, there were fewer trials for relearning. The results for one subject showed savings of 16.39% for a criterion of one presentation, and 10.28% with overlearning. Nagel concluded that lists learned with only one correct presentation need fewer repetitions to relearn in a different order. He also found that when the subject knew the whole series, he could reproduce only one-third of the individual interitem connections.

Ebenholtz (1963b) found faster learning for alternate items in a transfer series if their location was the same as on the original list. This was true relative to control data on rearranged lists as well as for control data obtained on unrelated items.

Maisto and Ward (1973) examined serial-to-serial transfer with experimental items retained in their same ordinal position and control items switched to new positions. Some of the subjects were instructed about the relationships between the original and transfer lists. On the basis of the contention of Battig and Lawrence (1967) that serial recall provided more sensitive tests of differences, the authors used both serial recall and anticipation procedures. On the eight trials of the transfer list, there were fewer errors for the experimental items, for which the position had not been changed. Significant interactions indicated that the positive effect of position learning appeared only for subjects instructed about the relations between items on the first and second lists. Also, the transfer of position information was greater when subjects learned by serial anticipation on either the first or second list. Therefore, position seems more likely to be a functional stimulus if the anticipation procedure is used than if serial recall is used, even when subjects are informed of the relation between original and transfer series.

The study by Bredenkamp and Bredenkamp (1970) was mentioned in the previous chapter. They obtained mixed evidence with respect to the position-learning hypothesis from the learning of a reversed order of a serial list. Positive transfer was attributed to item familiarity. Since generally the transfer was independent of serial position, although the locations of middle items were less changed that those for the end items, the authors concluded that the evidence was against the position-learning interpretation.

Constant Position, Varied Associations

An unpublished study by Cogan and Ericksen, cited by Young (1968), investigated the serial learning of adjectives when different items were replaced by neutral symbols on selected proportions of the learning trials. They appeared, therefore, on 33, 66, or 100% of the trials. The performance at each serial position was reported in terms of "mean correct per trial." Since this measure was not further described, it is not clear whether these figures are based on total trials to criterion without regard to the number of appearances of an item, or with respect to the number of trials on which the item actually appeared. The reported data indicated about half as many correct responses for the 33% group as for the 100% group, with the 66% group falling in between. Assuming that the performance is adjusted to the number of appearances of an item, the poorer performance for the partial-presentation conditions may reflect the interfering effect on interitem associations of the substitution of items and symbols. It may also reflect the fact that the subjects were forced to rely more on position learning for the experimental conditions. Both factors could have been operating, of course. Thus, either a sequential association or position-learning view could account for these results.

Assuming that the Cogan and Ericksen results were reported in terms of total trials, the performance of the 33% group is too good; with only one-third the number of exposures, they produced about one-half as many correct responses. The 66% group produced about 70% as many correct responses as the control group. The occurrence of better performance than a reasonable expectation on the basis of the percentage of appearance could indicate a greater efficiency of position learning over sequential learning, since the subjects reported using a position-learning strategy more often as frequency of occurrence decreased. On the other hand, the subjects could be emitting and rehearsing the missing items on the substitution trials and thus increasing the number of effective appearances. Thus it appears that little evidence can be gained from the overall performance levels.

Young (1968) also notes, however, that the shapes of the serial-position curves become consistently more asymmetrical as the frequency of substitution increases. The data are replotted in Figure 3-1 in terms of the percentage of the total errors that appeared at each serial position, in order to correct for apparent changes of shape due to differences in totals of errors (McCrary & Hunter, 1953; Harcum, 1970a). The three curves represent the percentage of occurrence of the response member (ORM). Clearly, the point of poorest performance shifts toward the end of the list as the proportion of substitutions is greater. Young (1968) does not offer an explanation for this effect. The most obvious factor to account for this difference is the increasing frequency with which the subjects use a position-based learning strategy. This conclusion follows from the argument of Harcum and Coppage (1965b); its implications will be discussed fully in Chapter 5.

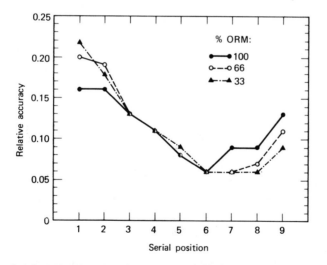

Figure 3-1 Serial-position accuracy for various percentages of response occurrence, after Young (1968). Reprinted with permission from R. K. Young, in T. R. Dixon & D. L. Horton (Eds.) *Verbal Behavior and General Behavior Theory*. Prentice-Hall, 1968.

Shifted Beginning

One technique for keeping the between-item associations constant, but at the same time removing the constant-position cue, is called the "spin technique." The procedure is to vary the starting item for each trial, for example, as would occur if the experimenter merely spins the memory drum between trials, starting a new trial wherever the drum happens to stop. Thus, the internal relationships of the series are maintained as cues for learning, but item position is not a directly usable cue.

In order to test the position-learning hypothesis of serial learning, Ebenholtz (1963b) predicted faster learning of a serial list presented in the usual way, relative to a condition in which the same sequence of items started randomly with different items on each trial. This prediction was supported by the data. Also, the intralist intruding errors were closer to the correct location on the conventional list—that is, the errors were less remote—indicating more accurate position-localization for that group.

McManis (1965) also contrasted the normal technique of a constant starting item for serial learning with the spin technique in which the starting item was randomly determined. Stimuli were lists of trigrams or lists of words having intrinsic between-item associations (e.g., thirsty-hungry). For both classes of stimuli the errors in acquisition over ten trials were fewer with the constant starting position. The strength of the tendency to learn by association to serial position is indicated by the fact that the subjects did not rely on forming sequential associations even when the associations between adjacent items already had some strength prior to the experiment. Two characteristics of this experiment should be noted, however: (1) the subjects were not told of the existing structure within the word list, and only ten trials might not have permitted time for them to discover it; and (2) the subjects were given the identical three items at the beginning and end of the list to "allow them to get into the sequence." These items could have helped to mask the starting and end points of the list (Lippman & Denny, 1964).

Keppel (1964) investigated retroactive inhibition for serial recall of series when the first item was varied or kept constant on succeeding trials. Experimental subjects studied an interpolated list while control subjects worked a neutral puzzle. The original learning was faster in terms of trials to criterion for the subjects with constant starting position, as usual. Only when the series started constantly on the same item was there a typical serial-position curve; variation of the starting item failed to produce a significant effect of serial position. After the interpolated task, the subjects who saw a constant first item were asked for unpaced serial recall of the items on the original lists, and the subjects with varied first item were asked to recall the items in the correct relative order starting with any item. Retroactive inhibition exerted a significant effect only for the condition of constant starting position. Thus, subjects were learning positions in the serial tasks with constant starting positions.

Zavortink and Keppel (1968) contrasted the amounts of retroactive inhibition on re-ordering of an original serial list produced by learning interpolated paired association when the original serial list was learned with constant or varied starting points (namely, the spin technique). With the spin technique, subjects are less able to use position cues for acquisition and are more dependent upon interitem associations. Since the interitem associations would be inhibited more by the paired-associate learning, which employed a double-function list of pairs from the original serial learning, the retroactive inhibition should be greater for the group learning the serial task with varied starting position. The results generally supported the predictions. In addition to a greater retroactive-interference effect for the series with varied starting positions, there were more intruding (previously correct) associations from the original serial-learning task in the interpolated paired-association task. Therefore this study provides evidence for learning of both sequential chains between items and item position. The former is indicated by the presence of a retroactive effect for the group with constant starting position, and the latter is shown by the greater effect of interitem interference for the group with varied starting positions.

Instead of a random change in the starting point, Winnick and Dornbush (1963) changed the starting item systematically. They found that with standard serial-learning instructions and constant serial position a series was learned faster than when serial positions were progressively changed. Although the relative position (interitem associations) were constant from trial to trial, the absolute positions varied for the experiment groups.

Consistent with the results for paired-associate learning, the acquisition of serial lists is facilitated if the items are presented in constant positions. Presumably, subjects are using the position cues in addition to, or in place of, the item-specific cues.

CONFLICTING SPATIAL CUES

Mandler and Anderson (1971) presented 12-word series in both horizontal spatial array and temporal sequence with independent variation of the relative spatial order and temporal sequence. Over several trials the order of each mode could be constant or varied. In one experiment, after the last presentation of a series the subject was told to reproduce either the spatial or temporal order of that last presentation. In a second experiment he was informed about the relevant response dimension before presentation of the stimuli. In both experiments the subjects reproduced the temporal dimension more accurately than the spatial, but gave evidence for processing both types of information. Both prior knowledge of recall mode and constant ordering across trials improved performance, of course.

In a third experiment of Mandler and Anderson (1971) only eight words were presented for just a single trial, and the subject was asked to reproduce the word falling between two other probe words, either in the original temporal or spatial order, as instructed. The correlation between spatial and temporal orders was varied from 1.0 (i.e., left-to-right order), to about .5, and 0. One-half of the subjects had to pronounce the words as they were presented. Again the temporal dimension for recall was most effective, as was prior instruction about the relevant dimension. Correlation of temporal and spatial position again produced best performance. Probe position was not significant, although it should be noted that the probing method precluded the testing of either the beginning or end positions. The interaction of probe position and pronunciation group was significant, however, reflecting the absence of a position effect for the nonpronouncing group and a strong recency effect for the pronouncing group. The performance for perfect correlation of temporal and spatial cues was fairly well predicted from the contingent results of each basis of recall with zero correlation, indicating independent use of the two ordering dimensions.

POSITION CUE ADDED

If a facilitation effect of adding position cues to a serial list is found, then inferential evidence is provided for position learning in the serial task. This result has been obtained; Voss (1956) did find that his subjects used spatial cues added to other cues during the learning of temporal sequences.

Ebenholtz (1963a) studied transfer between a serial-learning task and a so-called position-learning task in which the subject had to learn to associate nonsense syllables with vertically oriented arrays of spatial positions. When relative temporal and spatial position in the two tasks was the same, transfer was greater, but not perfect. Therefore, in addition to the evidence for position learning, there was also evidence for specific associations among items. Ebenholtz argued, on the basis of presumed easier learning of positions than specific associations, that position is the first cue to be used—while the ends are being learned—and then specific associations are formed about the middle where position discrimination is poorer.

Jensen and Blank (1962) failed to find an advantage in serial learning of presenting to the subject constant information with each item about its ordinal position. Using the same technique, Leonard and Tangeman (1973) also consistently failed to find a positive effect of numbering. The items were CVC trigrams of intermediate meaningfulness. The authors offered four hypotheses to account for the negative results, including the possibility that the subjects ignored the numbers.

POSITION-BASED INTRUSIONS

Melton and von Lackum (1941) tested recall and relearning of ten three-consonant syllables, using proactive and retroactive inhibition paradigms. Although they found that subjects made relatively few intruding errors in a subsequent series because of substitutions of an item from a previous list, nevertheless the intrusions that did occur tended to appear close to their original position on the prior list. This effect was greater for formally similar lists than for dissimilar ones. Therefore, subjects were learning the serial position of items, and the interference reflected a confusion of list membership. As Melton and von Lackum conclude:

> Apparently the factor of serial position similarity is an important determiner of inter-list intrusions even when the similarity of the lists is very great. In fact, it is suggested that the serial position factor is not sufficient to produce a significant number of intrusions unless there is also a formal similarity of the materials learned (1941, p. 170).

Also, Melton and von Lackum point out that intrusions attributable to serial-position similarity tend to drop out earlier in the relearning process than those intrusions not related to serial position.

When Voss (1968) introduced clustering of items in lists for serial learning, he found that subjects made intruding errors from the same relative positions within clusters. Apparently the subject learned the relative position within a cluster, producing an intruding error when he made a mistake in identifying the correct cluster.

The evidence for position learning in a serial-learning task was summarized by Dey (1970), who added empirical evidence for it. He used continuous presentation of six-item lists, with the first syllable printed in red; actually the subject learned two six-item lists substituted for one another haphazardly. Position learning was inferred when the subject gave an intruding association from the wrong list at or near the proper serial position. Over one-half of the interlist intrusions were from the proper serial position, in spite of the fact that there were more possible incorrect positions than correct ones. Therefore, the subject was associating an item to a serial position, at least to some extent.

TRANSFER STUDIES

As mentioned in the previous chapter, a number of studies (e.g., Mueller, 1970; Horton & Turnage, 1970; G. J. Johnson, 1972) obtained evidence for position learning in transfer studies. Two examples of transfer designs are transfer from serial to paired-associate learning, and unlearning in a retroactive design.

Serial to Paired Associate

After serial learning, the subjects of Mueller (1970) learned a list of paired associates composed of positional indicants and the preceeding item from the serial list. Whether the paired-associate list was single function or double function, there was a positive effect from the previous learning. The typical bowed serial-position curve was found for pairs taken from the various ordinal positions from the serial list.

Mueller and Jablonski (1973) obtained positive transfer from serial to paired-associate learning, using items from a prior free-recall task in the control condition. Items related to each other from position in the prior serial learning revealed positive transfer on the paired-associate task. For example, the number "one" was the stimulus on the paired-associate task for the item from the first serial position on the serial learning task. Also, items randomly arranged from the position cues on the prior serial-learning task exhibited negative transfer. For example, the number "five" was the stimulus in the paired-associate task for the item that had been first in the serial learning. Both of these effects indicate transfer due to the learning of position on the prior serial-learning task.

G. J. Johnson (1972) found evidence for stronger transfer effects of position cues than for sequence cues in serial to paired-associate transfer. The position cues were less effective for middle than for end items, and the addition of sequence cues to position cues was of greater benefit for the middle items. Therefore, position cues appeared to be of greater value in fostering learning of the end items.

The differential importance of different cues at different item positions within a series has not been unambiguously established. Although Ebenholtz (1963b) found that position learning was more important for items at the ends of the series, for example, Young (1962) concluded, on the other hand, that position was more important at the middle of the series.

Young, Hakes, and Hicks (1967) investigated the extent to which position learning in a serial-learning task would transfer to a paired-associate task in which position numbers were the stimuli. The transfer was positive for positions near the ends of the serial list, but negative for items about the middle. These effects were increased when subjects were instructed about the relations between tasks.

The experiment by Young, Hakes, and Hicks (1967) was followed by Winnick and Dornbush (1968), again using a design that assessed effects of prior knowledge of future serial position. Subjects were given absolute or relative knowledge of the later serial position through paired-associate learning in which the stimuli were numbers for absolute position or numbers that indicated only the proper relative order. For control groups the stimuli were either numbers giving no information about either absolute or relative position, or words which of course did not convey position information. Response items for the paired-association learning, which also served as the stimulus materials for the serial learning, were nonsense syllables. The two experimental groups learned the serial list fastest, with the groups previously learning absolute position performing the best, by far. The groups given inconsistent, unrelated numbering actually performed slightly worse than the control group learning with word stimuli, presumably due to negative transfer, because the prior numerical associations were incorrect. Therefore, relative, as well as absolute, prior information about the position to be occupied by items in serial learning facilitates the subsequent serial learning. The clear implication of this result is that serial position can be an effective cue in fostering serial learning.

Unlearning

Keppel (1966) used a retroactive-inhibition transfer paradigm to investigate what is unlearned in serial learning. Since responses from original learning remained, as shown by a free recall test, whereas some information about serial order was lost, as shown by a re-ordering test, he concluded that subjects were unlearning serial positions, at least to some extent.

PROBE CUES

Results of three techniques for the use of probe cues will be described. The first one (Gamble & Wilson, 1916) uses item probes, but examines the data for evidence that the subject was also making use of positional information. The second technique probes directly with the position cue (e.g., Voss, 1969). In the third method, the subject is given an item and asked to recall the spatial position occupied by that item (e.g., Schulz, 1955).

Supplemental Spatial Cues

An experiment by Gamble and Wilson (1916) indicated that in learning a list the location of items had been better learned than the associations. Gamble and Wilson exposed 18 nonsense syllables in a matrix of three horizontal rows. The subject was to learn the syllables in pairs, so that later when given an odd item he would be able to reproduce an adjacent one, either preceding or following, depending upon instructions. After several readings of the series and a 3-minute rest in which rehearsal was prevented, the subject attempted to perform the instructed task. On the test the individual (probe) items were sometimes given at changed locations, and the subject was also asked what the proper location had been. The subjects were able to give the correct item associations about 49% of the time, but were correct about location about 75% of the time. Moreover, the associations to the correct syllable were consistently more correct when they were presented in the same spatial position for learning and testing. When an item was correctly localized, the associated syllable was correct 80% of the time, but when that item was incorrectly localized, the associations to the paired syllable were only 15% correct.

Four of the seven subjects in the Gamble and Wilson (1916) study reported making conscious use of associations to spatial position. However, disturbance by the change in test position was not limited to these particular subjects.

In a second experiment Gamble and Wilson (1916) compared sequential probed recall after whole presentation, on a tablet as before, or after sequential presentation on a memory drum, attempting to keep the presentation time constant. Although the data were not totally convincing, the whole presentation revealed superior recall of correct associates. Gamble and Wilson conclude:

> These experiments, as far as they go, tend to show what was indicated by the numerical, and proved by the introspective, results of the earlier experiments, namely, that *associations of spatial position may be not merely a concomitant but also a really mediating factor in the recall of one nonsense syllable by another.* The argument based upon the later experiments runs as follows: *Syllable sequences are better recalled if the series are presented for memorizing in such a fashion as to foster formation of place associations* (1916, p. 97).

Position Probes

Much of the positive evidence from positional probes was summarized in the preceding chapter, since experimenters often employed sequential and positional probes in the same study (e.g., Posnansky, 1972; Schwartz, 1970a; Voss, 1969; Woodward, 1968; Woodward & Murdock, 1968). Only three studies will be mentioned here.

In Voss' (1969) study, the subjects showed high accuracy for the initial serial positions early in acquisition when tested by a position probe. This level was maintained. The serial-position curve was present early; there was little change with practice. As with a sequential probe, the number of correct anticipations on preceding and following trials exceeded the number of correct responses to the position probe. Intrusion errors in the positional-probe conditions showed a decrease in both frequency and degree. The backward and forward intrusions began with about equal frequencies, but then revealed a greater frequency of forward than backward intrusions, without a change in the overall number of intrusions or in the absolute size of error. For a sequential probe, on the other hand, the intrusion frequency decreased, along with the absolute size of the errors.

Using a somewhat different method, Hicks, Hakes, and Young (1966) had one group of subjects recall serial position of each item after serial learning, while another group of subjects was cued by a given serial position and asked to recall the item at that serial position. For both of these conditions serial-position curves of accuracy were obtained, with primacy effects greater than recency. Thus, the subjects were learning position—better at the ends and best for the beginning portion of the series.

The effect of instructions was assessed by Kayson and Winnick (1974). Subjects instructed to use position cues indicated by latency of responses to position probes that they had in fact used position cues more often than control subjects or subjects instructed to use sequential associations. Moreover, the position instructions were more effective for material of low interitem associations.

Probes for Position

The classic experiment on item probe for the learning of position information was done by Schulz (1955). Schulz investigated the generalization of knowledge of position during serial learning to various degrees of mastery of ten syllables varying in intralist similarity. After a given criterion of mastery was reached, the experimenter called out a syllable, and the subject was instructed to give quickly its ordinal position. The number of subjects incorrectly naming a position described a typical serial-position curve. This curve corresponded closely to the serial-position curve of failures of correct anticipation during learning. These results applied generally to all experimental conditions. High intralist similarity of items reduced the size of subjects' errors in naming the position of an item, although it exerted minimal effects on the frequency with which subjects reported the position with perfect accuracy. The effect of level of list mastery was not large, particularly for the low-similarity lists. Schulz suggested that one possibility for this is that position is learned very early. This possibility is supported by the results and conclusion of Battig, Brown, and Nelson (1963) that position cues are learned early, but are then abandoned in favor of other cues. Schulz favored another interpretation, however—that the subject actually does not learn serial position in terms of an ordinal number. Since the results are so closely related to the serial-position curve of learning, it may be that the subject was merely reconstructing position for the test on the basis of whatever cues he used to learn the list, although the subjects had been given the instructions to respond rapidly in order to prevent such a "rerecitation" of the series.

Heslip (1968) investigated whether or not evidence for a position-learning interpretation of serial learning was an artifact of the subjects covertly rehearsing and counting the items to the probed item. His task for the subject was to learn a serial list to a selected criterion and then to indicate recall of items by placing a test word from the list in its proper relative position within a spatial array as quickly as possible. Two groups of subjects learned the list to a criterion of one perfect trial.

One of these groups was instructed to recite the sequence of items from a known location to the test item before responding, in order to stimulate prompting of position recall though sequence recitation. The second group was told to respond immediately on the basis of the judged relative position of the item. Only the time to make the response was recorded; the accuracy of the response was not considered. The recitation group took longer to respond, of course, revealing the typical asymmetrical curve except for the items at either end. These items were placed about as rapidly as the position-only group, indicating the strong tendency to attach these items to position. Although the bowing of response distributions for the position-only group was slight, this must have resulted from the absence of a requirement for accuracy of placement, although this factor was not considered by the author. The results for this group were useful primarily as a measure of time required for making the overt response. The reason for this conclusion is the absence of an overall difference in performance between this group and another group tested in the same way, but having received only five training trials. This group with less training performed equally well for each position, probably indicating minimal effects of learning, since serial-position effects appear on even the first trial of the acquisition of a serial list under the usual conditions of presentation (Robinson & Brown, 1926).

Hintzman and Block (1971) and Hintzman, Block, and Summers (1973) provided evidence that subjects instructed to learn series of items did incidentally learn time tags for items within the series. The subjects could later, under some conditions, provide information about the relative location of the items within the series. According to Hintzman et al. (1973) these time tags are not associated only with a pure temporal dimension, however, but with other contextual cues, such as list membership.

Heslip and Epstein (1969) gave five groups of subjects respectively five levels of practice (namely, 4, 8, 12, 16, and 20 trials) on a serial list of 13 words, and tested accuracy of placement of each word on a spatial array immediately after the learning trials. A correct-anticipation score was derived by counting the number of times that a word was correct on the acquisition trials on either of the last two trials before learning trials had been terminated. The results indicated that after four trials of acquisition, the correct anticipation and correct placement measures were not different, but thereafter the correct anticipations exceeded the correct placements at each serial position except those near the ends of the array. This comparison of acquisition and position placement is not altogether fair because, as mentioned with respect to the Heslip (1968) study, allowance was made for failures to respond correctly on one of the acquisition trials, but perfect accuracy was required for the placement responses. For example, subjects in serial learning often learn the general location of an item before the exact location of that item is learned. During the acquisition phase a subject can, for example, give an item at the seventh position that would be correct at the eighth position. When he sees that the item is incorrect at the seventh position, he may give it again at the eighth position and be credited with a correct response. It would be entirely possible, therefore, for a subject in the Heslip and Epstein procedure to anticipate an item correctly in this way and still mislocalize it by one position on the placement test.

In the Heslip and Epstein (1969) study, the fact that the subjects were learning the general location of items was supported by an analysis of the average deviation of the placement responses. In spite of the fact that control subjects, who made the placing responses without having seen the list, revealed symmetrically bowed curves, with greater accuracy about the middle, the experimental subjects performed the placing responses most accurately for items near the ends. The bowing of the curves for the control group obviously represents the differential possibility for errors of different magnitudes at middle and end positions. For example, an item at Position Seven can only be misplaced as far as six positions away from the true location, whereas an item at Position One can be mislocalized 12 positions away. This concept underlies the measure of distinctiveness proposed by Murdock (1957).

Heslip and Epstein (1969) asked the subjects at the end of their experiment to guess how many items had appeared in the original list. In fact, only one of the 130 subjects correctly guessed the number, indicating, as had the earlier result of Heslip (1968), that subjects had not been associating items to ordinal position. This is an incredible result on two grounds. First, the number of correct guesses is probably too small if the subjects were merely guessing. Assuming that no subject would guess fewer than 6 items, or more than 20, even with a rectangular distribution of guesses within that range, there should have been over 8 correct guesses. Second, the subjects had just been tested on correct placement on items using a 13-position array. Surely the subjects must therefore have inferred the correct number of items in the list unless something in the instructions of the placement test implied that 13 was *not* the correct number! But if this were true, the coherence of the serial-position data adds to the puzzle.

In a second experiment, Heslip and Epstein (1969) employed the same procedure as the first experiment except that the experimental subjects were tested with a sequential probe. They were given, singly in random order, the starting cue and each one of the first 12 items, and asked to report the item following that stimulus. The performance was again superior for the control group after 12 and 20 trials, but not after only 4 trials. The number of correct responses was greater for the subjects given the sequential probes than for those given the position probes.

Ahmed and Voss (1969) supplemented the previous study of Voss (1969) by using a different retention task. After one of five degrees of serial learning, the subjects were asked first to recall the items and then, given each item, to indicate its position along a line representing the serial list. The dependent variable was the deviation of each such placement from the true location of the item. As predicted, deviations decreased with increasing trials, with reductions of about 50% after only one trial. Also as predicted, the placement after a single trial was more accurate for the recalled than for the unrecalled items, although thereafter the difference disappeared. When the interruption of learning occurred about midway through the learning of the list, most accurate placement occurred when the item had been correct on the preceding criterion trial and had been correctly recalled. Ahmed and Voss note that at this stage of learning the subjects tend to place an item about the middle of the series if they do not know where it belongs, because they know that the middle positions represent the unknown items and positions—a point made previously by Slamecka (1964). These incompletely learned lists show the typically bowed serial-position curve with greater "primacy" than "recency" effects. Thus, it appears that a learned serial list is one in which the subject has knowledge of the serial positions of the items.

CONCLUSIONS

The methodological problems in trying to answer the question of the effective stimulus for a specific serial-learning task have been shown to be formidable. For example, in Chapter 2 it was pointed out that failure to find positive transfer between paired-associate and serial learning may sometimes result from the use of trials-to-criterion as the measure of learning, which is a highly insensitive measure (Bahrick, 1967; Postman & Stark, 1967). Postman (1968a) goes on to say:

> The methodological point which deserves emphasis at this juncture is that while tests of transfer normally yield information about what has been learned, they will often provide only ambiguous evidence about

how a task was acquired. Failure to find transfer may rule out certain classes of functional stimuli; the uncertainty of interpretations based on positive transfer increases with the number of different assumptions about the functional stimulus which are consistent with the observed transfer results (Postman, 1968a, p. 565).

Voss (1968) places little value on studies of transfer from serial to paired-associate learning. He emphasizes the difference between studying the processes of serial learning and studying the results of prior serial learning. Therefore, a result of positive transfer could occur because subjects could use in the paired-associate task what they had learned in the serial task in a number of different mediating ways. In order to conclude that a particular stimulus had been used in the prior task obviously the other possibilities must first be eliminated, and this is certainly not easy.

Other authors (e.g., Battig & Lawrence, 1967; Young, 1968) are disenchanted with the typical serial-learning task itself. Battig and Lawrence (1967) suggest that much of the confusion about what is learned in serial learning is caused by the use of the insensitive traditional anticipation technique. They conclude that the superiority of a serial-recall procedure is probably due to the separation of the learning from the measurement of performance. Both functions must occur simultaneously under the anticipation procedure, of course.

Underwood (1963) suggests that the functional stimulus for serial learning might not have been found unambiguously because there are many possible bases for learning. Also subjects may be using different cues at different times depending upon such characteristics of the experimental method as the instructions to him. Postman, Adams, and Bohm (1956) found that subjects instructed to learn the serial order of a list do, in fact, retain more information about order. They do this at the expense of the total number of words recalled. Thus, the instructions determine what attributes of the learning situation the subject spends his effort on—a paralearning effect. The same conclusion is reached by the results of Mandler and Anderson (1971) from prior instructions about recall modality for sequences with different input sequences of temporal and spatial modalities.

Coppage and Harcum (1967) and Harcum, Pschirrer, and Coppage (1968) pointed out that the subject in serial learning always has to make a choice between different bases of organizing a serial list for learning. Saufley (1967) is careful to point out that his paper was aimed at discovering what cues tend to be used in serial learning, rather than to insist that there is only one stimulus.

Young (1968), as a result of his survey of the literature on chaining versus position learning, concludes:

> All of this suggests that serial learning involves a relatively idiosyncratic situation in which the subject may learn by chaining, by position, or both, in which case the results could be explained by the position hypothesis when the design of the experiment is such as to expect learning through the use of position cues and, conversely, by the chaining hypothesis when the design of the experiment is such as to expect serial learning to occur through the use of sequential associations (p. 142).

Keppel (1965) and Breckenridge, Hakes, and Young (1965a) also support his possibility of simultaneous use of chaining and position cues.

The present position is therefore that the question of the stimulus for serial learning has, unfortunately, often been asked in the wrong way. Frequently it has been asked in the context of a general simplistic solution that would apply to the learning of each list to be acquired. The tacit assumption is that there is, in fact, an answer to this question. However, the research has thus far been geared to answering the question of what factors *can* be effective stimuli in serial learning. The studies have attempted to isolate the variables in serial learning, as is appropriate for the first stage in a science. But the long history of research in serial learning would seem to provide the opportunity for even more analytic study.

To ask "What is the stimulus in serial learning?" is like asking "What is the stimulus for learning to bar press in the Skinner box?"; "What stimulus does the rat use to learn the maze?"; "What is the stimulus for elicitation of the sexual response in the male rat?" In the case of the stimulus for a learned instrumental response, Hilgard and Marquis (1940) conclude:

> In many experiments there is no specific conditioned stimulus which is turned on and off under the control of the experimenter. In these instances, the total situation confronting the subject may be considered as the analogue of the conditioned stimulus. The particular aspects of the situation to which the subject is responding can be discovered only by experimental variation of the situation (p. 68).

The generality of this kind of result and conclusion is illustrated by Maier and Schneirla's (1964) statement with respect to the functional stimulus for serial learning of a maze by a rat. They point out that by constructing different mazes and by introducing various sensory differences, one at a time, it is possible to determine experimentally just what sensory modality the rat can use in learning a given maze. They conclude that probably *any sensory differences that the rat can discriminate can be used for this*. It is an empirical question to determine which sensory differences can be most effective and which are preferred for use. Furthermore, Maier and Schneirla add, there may be individual differences among rats, depending upon such factors as idiosyncratic differences in sensory acuity and intelligence. Finally, they suggest that, even in the rat, the responses are often determined by complex stimulus patterns and thus are not necessarily simple responses to a preceding stimulus. This is a clear argument against a simple chaining explanation of serial learning, even in a lower animal.

Even greater breadth of the argument for the use of multiple cues in the control of behavior can be extracted from Beach's research (1942) on sexual behavior of the male rat. Beach found that the experienced male rat can, and will, use any stimulus modality that is available to him in locating the female rat in estrus. Each one, or combinations of two bases of discrimination, could be eliminated without degrading performance. Therefore, *no specific stimulus was essential for successful performance*, although obviously the male required at least one channel of sensory input to make him aware of the cooperative partner.

To complete the analogy, we can say that the subject in a serial-learning experiment can select any of several bases for learning the correct responses, and he can also use such bases in combination. As will be argued in the next chapter, the effective stimulus is actually a dynamic configuration of stimuli. The learning involves the construction of a mnemonic organization of the multiple elements within the task. This interpretation is similar to the "multiple-cue hypothesis" proposed by Young, Hakes, and Hicks (1967).

The present chapter thus illustrates the futility of looking for a simple answer to the question of what stimulus initiates and fosters serial learning. The subject can learn both associations to a previous item or items and associations to relative positions. Such bases of learning are, moreover, not mutually exclusive. The subject can, in fact, learn a given list by using some combination of both bases for learning, with emphasis on position for end items and sequence for middle items. The base that is more important apparently depends upon the conditions of the experiment, and also presumably upon the predilections of individual subjects.

If a given subject does not use a particular basis or cue for learning a list, this does not prove that he cannot, will not, or does not ordinarily use that basis for learning. The false dichotomy between chaining and position learning, popularized by some researchers, has provided a false trail for research on the problem of serial learning. The evidence against a simple associationistic point of view was ample prior to 1950.

SUMMARY

This chapter has presented evidence concerning the stimulus attribute of position as the basis for learning serial lists. Association to serial position often does contribute directly to serial learning. Since such association is not a necessary condition for serial learning to occur, it therefore is merely another of the multiple cues that subjects may use to master a serial task. It was concluded further that position learning also was not exclusively responsible for serial learning. Subjects typically learn each list through some combination of stimuli, with the relative importance of each dependent upon the conditions of the experiment, the relative position within the series, and the stage of learning.

The investigations of the effective stimulus for serial learning have now matured to the point that even though evidence for only one stimulus type is obtained, the possibility for another basis under different conditions is conceded (Giurintano, 1970). Therefore, the search for the functional stimulus must continue.

CHAPTER

$$\boxed{4}$$

THE STIMULUS:
A CONFIGURATION

The thesis and evidence of this chapter argue that serial learning involves the selective use of multiple cues. Furthermore, the selection of a cue for learning a specific item is the result of a dynamic approach to the task by the subject. For example, the relative importance of each stimulus dimension will depend upon the stage of learning and the subject's organizational strategy at that stage. Anderson and Bower (1973) have taken a similar open attitude about the possible "solution" to the problem of functional stimulus in serial learning. Their model of human associative memory (HAM) also does not require a particular basis of serial learning; the encoding of a series, in their view, could vary with the conditions of the learning situation and the characteristics of the subjects.

Long ago, Ladd and Woodworth (1911) emphasized the importance of hierarchical organization of units. They argued that: "The process embodies great multiplicity, and at the same time much unity" (p. 570). This paradox about the effective stimulus—the multiplicity and the unity—presents the challenge to further analysis. The question becomes: What part or property of a total changing configuration becomes for this subject the effective cue at this particular stage in the acquisition process?

The present proposition about the functional stimulus is that it is a configuration of several stimuli, which changes as the subject makes progress in acquiring the series. This hypothesis is therefore called the *hierarchical configuration hypothesis,* in order to imply that the best-cued, most discriminable, easiest item within the configuration is learned first; then another item becomes the most discriminable item to be learned. Attention is focused on the most discriminable unlearned item in the particular configuration, and it becomes the one to be learned next. Therefore, the items in a series are learned in an order that is determined by the existing configuration at the various successive stages of learning. The existing configuration is determined by the intrinsic associability of an item, by salience of position, by direction of attention, or by any number of additional factors. It is, therefore, the result of a dynamic organization of the learning task by the subject. Bugelski (1965) referred to a "confluence" of remote-association effects, as opposed to individual S-R associations. This conception appears to be quite similar to the organizational hypothesis promoted here.

The stimulus configuration includes intralist and intratask stimuli, as well as contextual, extra-experimental stimuli. The contextual stimuli, which include cues from the apparatus, experimental room, and other situational stimuli, are presumed to be generally more important early in the task, and therefore for acquisition of the first item. The interitem associations gain importance as learning progresses. The task stimuli influence the relative importance or relevance of the different stimulus dimensions.

Any student of learning will concede that mnemonic organization of stimuli generally improves the retention of that material. The Gestalt theorists have argued, in fact, that learning is an organizing process. For example, Köhler (1947) states that learning usually proceeds by rhythmical subgroupings, and that intentional memorizing is synonomous with intentional organizing. His position is that "strong association occurs only among such items of the series as become parts of well-defined groups" (p. 267). Köhler goes on to quote G. E. Müller as saying that a series of items is learned essentially by synthesis in which the members of the series are combined into groups. Thus, paralearning mechanisms, in the form of factors that aid discrimination of the parts that are to be associated, become very important in the overall process of learning.

Other early writers supported the importance of organization in learning. Woodworth (1938) concludes that learning does not start with elements and unite these, but it starts with groups, or even with the whole series, and proceeds largely by analysis and the finding of parts and relations (p. 35).

He pointed out the similarity of this point of view to the Gestalt position. Other theorists have also argued for a dynamic process of associations among items and positions in serial learning. For example, McGeoch (1942) concluded:

By means of remote associations a series is interconnected, woven into a whole which is more complexly organized than serial succession alone would indicate. This positive fact is of high importance to an understanding of mental organization (p. 89).

Thus, associationists have also argued for the importance of grouping in learning, either in terms of the analysis of groups or in terms of organization into groups.

Others have proposed, however, that the associationistic view does not go far enough. Asch (1968), for example, has been an eloquent spokesman for the antiassociationistic view. He takes the traditional associationistic theorists to task for what he judges to be their overly narrow conception of what can be a stimulus for association, and deplored the domination of learning theory by the "elementaristic" approach. Asch further argues that the same types of mechanisms underlying object perception, language acquisition, and the learning of logical connections should be considered by theorists in attempting to understand learning and memory. He denies, furthermore, that the use of language can be understood in terms of the assumption that sentences are generated from sequential dependencies upon words. Asch proposed a greater concern for the relations among events, since association by contiguity ignores the structure added by the learner as he operates on the material given him. The learner is actively constructing organized structures as he learns. Asch concludes:

The associationistic emphasis on arbitrary connections is not equipped to treat these phenomena. It slights precisely those effects of experience that produce changed ways of perceiving and understanding.

At the same time recent investigations make it increasingly clear that the paradigms of rote learning are by no means free of relational operations. These advances promise to bridge the gap between rote and other phenomena of learning. They also provide support for a cognitive interpretation of associations. These developments should open the way to a freer examination of the presuppositions that have dominated the rote learning area and of the limited conception of science that it fostered. In general, the erosion of thinking about cognitive processes under the influence of behaviorism is receding. It is becoming easier to reconsider the positivistic equation of a law of nature with an empirical regularity. It is becoming more difficult to rule out the thought that associative phenomena refer to central processes, not themselves behavior, which control behavior. It may even be in order to entertain the possibility that it is not necessary, nor perhaps fruitful, to be an associationist in the study of associations (1968, p. 227).

The current trend of research and theorizing pursues the direction proposed by Asch. In his discussion of the EPAM model of learning, Gregg (1972) argues similarly that

the nominal stimuli provide a variety of cueing possibilities, and that these are organized into a complex structure capable of generating the desired verbal response sequence (1972, p. 4).

Recent books by Tulving and Donaldson (1972) and Melton and Marin (1972) indicate the new concern for organizational or encoding principles in human memory. Melton and Martin point out the recent revival of the controversy between the positions which holds that association is the basis of organization, in opposition to the argument that organization is the basis of association. They go on to suggest that the current interest in coding may provide the rapprochement between association-istic and organization theories, as well as foster the destruction of the topical boundaries between concepts such as perception, memory, and learning. N. F. Johnson (1972), for example, discussed how a coding model can account for serial ordering of behavior in terms of associations of items to a code, but not to one another. Also, Estes' (1972) concept of a reverberatory loop between a "control element" and a feature to be remembered provides a basis for understanding how meaningful organization can facilitate learning. The more permanent the control element, the more persistent the recall of the feature.

Anderson and Bower (1973) also are able to accommodate the principles of grouping and organization in serial learning in their neoassociationistic model of human memory. Thus, the trend is now toward the use of models that incorporate cognitive codes and controls, rather than simple associations between items. Hopefully, this book will augment this trend.

Since the stated goal of this book is to account for both the acquisition of entire series, and also the acquisition of individual items, the levels of analysis and focus of attention change as appropriate. Therefore, from time to time I invoke seemingly incompatible mechanisms, such as organizational strategy and forward association, in the same general context. I do not see these as truly incompatible, but merely lying at different points on a scale of organizational complexity, with the simple associations representing the lowest order of organization—a group consisting of just two members. Certainly it should be possible for two items to be so highly associable that contextual cues are irrelevant.

Obviously, the topic of this chapter, which considers evidence for mnemonic organization in serial learning, is quite similar to and overlapping with the material in Chapters 6, 7, and 8, which take up later the questions of item differentiation and intrinsic organization of a series, the structural attentional bases of ordering, and idiosyncratic attentional bases of ordering, respectively. The difference is that Chapter 4 will make a general case for the relevance of organizational strategy by the subject for serial-learning tasks. Chapters 6, 7, and 8 will consider the evidence in more detail under the particular rubrics as described above.

ORGANIZATION IN OTHER LEARNING

A case will first be made briefly for the general relevance of organizational principles to other learning tasks. The conclusion that organization facilitates learning is amply supported by the classic as well as the recent literature. Katona (1940) argues, for example, that grouping is a fact of learning.

Dashiell (1942) had subjects memorize lists of 14 monosyllabic words under instructions to recall a certain number of syllables, but not their order of presentation. Results showed that eight out of nine subjects showed measurable tendencies to regroup words into what he called sequences that represent certain separate thought contexts. Dashiell concludes that his results support organizational emphasis in interpreting memory, but cautions that association emphasis must be recognized as supplementary.

Later well-known evidence of Bousfield (1953) and Tulving (1962) for free recall of "unrelated" and randomly arranged items supports Dashiell's thesis. The subjects tended to organize the items into coherent clusters or subjective categories for the subsequent recall. Tulving (1964) showed that free recall performance increased along with the subjective organization of the material from trial to trial. Chunking is the term used by Miller (1956) to refer to this organization or recoding of items into memory in terms of larger units than bits. This process can greatly increase the number of items in a stimulus array that can be correctly reproduced.

The use of possible ways for organizing stimuli appears to improve as learning skill improves. Wapner and Rand (1968) presented colored lights at six spatial positions in various temporal orders to subjects of ages 8 to 18. The older subjects were more accurate in learning the series and were more likely to use organizational relations in reporting their responses.

Postman (1954) has shown that training in organizing (coding) outline-form stimuli into categories improved memory for the forms. Moreover, the relative efficacy of this training improved as the retention interval was increased up to two weeks. An apparent reason for this is that errors in violation of the coding rules tended to drop out. Also, Postman found that training in the use of a code reduced the amount of retroactive interference. This paralearning effect is consistent with the conclusion of McGeoch (1942) that functional isolation of original and interpolated material by cognitive means reduced the amount of interference. McGeoch summarized the evidence as follows:

> These results and others imply that retroactive inhibition decreases with an isolation of the interpolated activity from the original, an isolation which may be brought about in a number of different ways, among which instruction and set are very influential (1942, p. 479).

Thus cognitive boundaries of organizational groups can somehow insulate members of the group from interference between members of different groups. This appears to be a general principle, applicable to other tasks in addition to serial learning. It will be discussed in greater detail in Chapter 6.

ORGANIZATION IN SERIAL LEARNING

In serial learning, organization is important in each segment of the total process. The stimulus factors first foster certain groupings of items. These are supplemented by central mnemonic encoding mechanisms and also by retrieval and output factors that may require their own codes.

Temporal Factors

RHYTHM

Temporal grouping or intrinsic organization of items seems to be a natural process in the intake of information. For example, Ebbinghaus (1913) found it impossible in his studies to avoid some grouping and accenting in reading the syllables. He therefore established a regular arrangement (trochaic rhythm) for grouping, which he followed under all learning conditions.

Neisser (1969) showed that rhythmic grouping of digit strings influenced intruding errors in short-term memory. Only when successive strings had similar grouping patterns (rhythms) were serial intrusions greater than chance.

Recall.   Using both serial-recall and free-recall measures of retention, Kaufman (1967) inserted differential temporal spacing into sequences of 24 words presented aurally. Clustering of responses was shown by greater probabilities for responses within groupings, as well as a carrying over under some conditions of such clustering tendencies from one task to another. Kaufman concluded that subjects showed organization among the experimenter-provided groups of items, and also within these groups. The within-group organization was obviously determined by the individual subject.

That temporal chunking would aid learning, particularly for longer series, was predicted by Kayson (1970). He presented 12-item and 20-item lists of trigrams in temporal chunks of 1, 2, or 4 items, using a serial presentation and recall method. There was some suggestive evidence that the 2-item chunks were learned fastest and the 4-item chunks the slowest for the longer list. Kayson suggested that the deleterious effect for 4-item chunks was produced by the difficulty for subjects to keep in mind what they had to do in that condition.

A number of studies by Bower and his co-workers (e.g., Bower & Springston, 1970; Lesgold & Bower, 1970; Winzenz, 1972) have shown grouping effects on serial learning and recall. Lists of 15 items in triplet temporal groupings were used by Lesgold and Bower (1970). They found serial recall organized about the breaks between the triplets, measured by both transitional probabilities of correct response—namely, contingent relations between adjacent items—and by number of correct pairs within the same triplet as compared to correct pairs across different triplets.

Bower and Springston (1970) tested the hypothesis that temporal pauses within a letter series determined the coding boundaries. If this hypothesis is correct, the pauses that facilitate coding, in terms of either pronounceability or meaning, should produce superior recall of the series relative to instances in which the pauses did not support an easy encodability of items. In fact, a series of letters in which the pauses bounded meaningful units, as in the sequence FBI PHD TWA IBM was much easier to recall than the same series of letters with pauses breaking up the meaningful units. The latter were formed by moving the last letter to the front, and maintaining the three-letter units, as follows: MFB IPH DTW AIB. In one experiment, recall of the nonoptimal series was only about 25% of that of the optimally spaced series. Serial-position curves were modified by changes at the boundaries produced by the chunks of letter units. In addition to these fluctuations in recall of items, transition error probabilities showed large increases in recall of items following a pause, indicating a boundary of a chunk. This value progressively decreased for the remaining two items within each triplet. Therefore, the pauses were more potent bases of encoding than were the meaningful units. When there were no pauses between meaningful triplets, the transition error probabilities showed boundaries at the limits of meaningful or pronounceable triplets.

Using a series composed of meaningful units of one quadrigram, two trigrams, and one digram, Bower and Springston again found that recall was greatly facilitated when the pauses and the meaningful units fostered the same chunks for encoding. Their results are illustrated in Figure 4-1 for the case of sequences beginning with a digram. The pause boundaries forming units of 4-3-3-2 or 2-3-3-4 are indicated by the dashed and solid curves, with pauses further indicated by the omission of lines between points. Clearly the pauses which correspond to the meaningful units produce fewer shifts from correct to incorrect, or incorrect to correct, reproductions of successive letters. These transitional shift proportions show large jumps across the pause boundaries, with decreasing values for the succeeding letters within a pause-defined group. Thus, the pauses determined the mnemonic organization of the series.

The subjects of Winzenz (1972) learned repeated strings of items, with test items reappearing in the series; noise (filler) items were not repeated. These subjects attempted to recall each string immediately after it was presented. The spacing of test items was either constant or varied. For example, the string of letters TONESTATENOTEATALL could be grouped this way: TO NEST ATE NOT EAT ALL; TONE STATE NO TEA TALL, or TON ESTATE NOTE AT ALL. The constant groupings showed a marked improvement on successive repetitions, but the changed groupings failed to improve with repetition. For a constant spacing of letter series, the individual words were recalled as a unit, or not at all, indicating the cohesive integrity of an organizational group or chunk in recall.

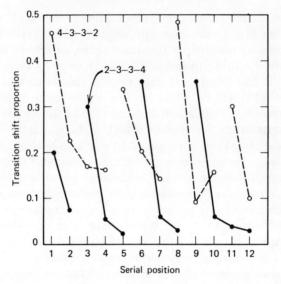

Figure 4-1   Transition shift proportions for recall of sequences beginning with a digram and employing two different pause structures, from Bower and Springston (1970). Copyright © (1970) by the American Psychological Association. Reprinted by permission.

Anticipation.   Restle (1972) studied effects of differential rest pauses (i.e., phrasing) in serial anticipation, using a series or pattern of lights. The subject's task was to learn by serial anticipation which of 6 lights was to come on within a series of 16 lights, after previewing the series one, three, or five times. The preview sequences employed differential spacing between presentations of succeeding lights, varying around an average of 0.3 seconds for a fast sequence and around 0.8 seconds for a slow sequence. The different pauses could be "well placed" or poorly placed to facilitate mnemonic organization. A control condition employed uniform 0.3-second pauses between all lights. Whereas the good phrasing in the previews facilitated accurate serial-learning performance, and the poor phrasing inhibited serial learning, there was no difference between the differential speeds of presentation. Thus, the phrasing effect is due to the structuring of the series, rather than to the increase of time at important points in the series with the good phrasing.

In a second experiment Restle (1972) showed that very fast presentation can be harmful to learning and that periodic or inappropriate phrasing can also be harmful. Restle concludes that grouping into phrases is helpful if it follows the natural internal organization of the sequence and harmful if it facilitates an organization that conflicts with the natural one.

Lippman (1971a) presented series of 16 nonsense syllables either in the conventional way for anticipation learning, or in temporal-spatial clusters of four, keeping the total presentation time constant. There was no difference in total number of correct anticipations, although "isolation" effects favored the first items of clusters, and each cluster produced an approximation of the serial-position curve. The cluster condition revealed more intralist intrusions from other clusters relative to the control data treated in the same manner. Presumably there was confusion in terms of relative position within clusters.

In a second experiment, Lippman (1971a) tested the hypothesis that the lack of difference between conditions in the first study was due to complete canceling of facilitative clustering caused by isolation-differentiation of items and inhibition caused by the greater intraseries interference of different items having the same position within different clusters. Accordingly he predicted that a task that retained the advantage of isolation effects while reducing the interference effects of the clustering would show overall superior performance for the clustered condition. In a reconstruction task the subject was given the items on 16 cards and was asked to place them in order. This procedure should have reduced overt intruding errors. The number of correct placements was significantly greater for the clustered list, as predicted. Again the subunits of the total series revealed serial-position effects. These results support the idea of stimulus distinctiveness as a basis for item selection for serial learning.

Thus, placement of differentially-sized temporal intervals between items provides tempting boundaries or reference points for the chunking of information. When these reference points appear at locations which support meaningful units of material, encoding of the information is facilitated, along with subsequent retrieval and recall. But several studies (e.g., Bower & Springston, 1970; Restle, 1972) show that mere provision of reference points does not insure an aid to retention. If the reference points conflict with natural internal boundaries of the material, the overall result will be detrimental.

Spatial Factors

Differential spatial arrangements can also be the basis for mnemonic groupings and encoding. For example, the difficulty of reading English prose with mislocated spacing is a well-known example of Gestalt principles. The following is a simple example of something written to make it appear to be an unfamiliar language:

REA DINGTH ISI SNO TVER YEA SY

McLean and Gregg (1967) presented strings of 24 letters distributed on separate cards in groups or chunks of 1, 3, 4, 6, or 8 items. When the subjects recalled the string of letters, either in forward or backward sequence, they indicated by temporal pauses in their verbal reports that they had maintained the temporal and spatial chunking in their mnemonic organization of the task.

Wilkes (1972) presented strings of 15 consonant letters typed on a card with spaces between letters to produce five groupings. For one group of control subjects the grouping was constant, with five groups of three, while for an experimental group the size of the groups varied randomly. The subjects read the letter string aloud and then attempted to recall the letters. Control subjects tended to pause in the reading at positions corresponding to the spatial breaks, whereas the experimental subjects were far less consistent in pausing at breaks. The subjects with constant groupings (consistent spacing) learned faster. In addition, those of the subjects who paused longer at the breaks learned faster. The control subjects constantly used a triplet grouping. Of the six experimental subjects who eventually reached the criterion of three successive correct recalls, three of them settled on a triplet grouping, and three consistently used some other idiosyncratic grouping. But, importantly, they all did establish a mnemonic organization for recall.

Other Structural Discontinuities

Other physical discontinuities can also serve as a basis of organization. Any time a subject can discriminate a difference, he can potentially use that difference as a basis of coding, categorization, or organization. Many examples of this can be cited; some are given below.

MODALITY SHIFT

Chan and Travers (1965) found an isolation effect in free recall of seven-syllable lists when the sensory modality of presentation was switched from auditory to visual, or from visual to auditory, on the second or fifth syllable. Effects were greater for presentation at a rate of 0.5 seconds per syllable than at 0.37 seconds per syllable. At the slower rates, the recency effect was greater than the primacy effect, but the reverse was true for the faster rate. At the fifth syllable the isolation effect was greater than at the second, presumably because the contrast (surprise) effect was greater at that position.

In a later similar investigation Chan and Travers (1970) studied free call of series of four auditory or visual "blip" patterns, switching modality at various serial locations. In contrast to the earlier results, the "switched" item, as well as the "switched-back" item, showed a decrement, particularly when it occured later in the series. These results were attributed to the disruption of expectancies. Presumably the surprise of the switch interfered with performance on this different task, which involved shorter-term memory of less-meaningful items. Therefore, a factor that can aid mnemonic organization can also disrupt it—a conclusion that has been reached earlier.

DIFFERENT VOICE

The so-called prefix effect in short-term memory was investigated by Neisser, Hoenig, and Goldstein (1969) in order to test the hypothesis that short-term memory for verbal storing is best understood in terms of a constructive process similar to the production of speech. The prefix effect, discovered by Conrad (1958), was a decrease in recall of a digit string when the subject had to reproduce a redundant (irrelevant) digit before recalling the experimental items. According to Neisser et al., the deficit was produced because the subject unnecessarily actively organized the irrelevant item along with the relevant items, thus increasing the informational load. Therefore, any experimental manipulation that would reduce this tendency would reduce the prefix effect. Positive results were obtained by using a prefix "zero" spoken by a different speaker, and using a prefix of three zeros, which formed a separate organizational chunk and thus was insulated from the experimental items. The break in cognitive structure eliminated the prefix effect by placing prefix information in a different chunk.

DIFFERENT COLORS

Wishner, Shipley, and Hurvich (1957) found that differentiating lists of nonsense syllables by different colors of ink for different segments of the list and instructing the subject that more than one list was involved facilitated the serial acquisition. Also the shapes of the distribution of errors over serial position were changed, with dips in errors where the lists were thus demarcated.

Wing (1964) also provided some evidence for faster learning of a 12-item list of nonsense syllables when the first and second 6 items were printed in different colors of ink. There was also a slight dip in errors about the middle of the series where the color changed. Since these effects were greatly increased when the subjects were instructed to learn the differentiated list as two smaller lists, organizational strategy can affect rate of learning.

WHOLE-PART

In several studies Fingeret and Brogden (1970, 1972, 1973) studied part-whole serial learning of various arrangements of items of two types. For example, lists of two-digit numbers and nouns could be interleaved in various combinations. The transition between clusters of similar items could produce fewer errors—an isolation effect (Fingeret & Brogden, 1970), or it could produce more errors—a transition effect (Fingeret & Brogden, 1972). Either result indicated effects of organizational strategy in serial learning.

In their 1973 study, Fingeret and Brogden had subjects learn series of 16 two-digit numbers presented one-half of the time as words or digits, respectively, in different patterns. The experimental groups saw words and digits on alternate items, or in double, quadruple, and octuple groups. Different control groups saw only words, only digits, or random arrangements of words and digits; these individual control groups were combined, because their results were not different. The shapes of the serial-position curves were generally similar because of the usual powerful primacy and recency effects, but the quadruple alternation produced a somewhat depressed curve of errors about the middle, and the octuple alternation produced a marked dip in errors about the ninth item. The results were interpreted in terms of organizational principles transferred from prior experience with similar serial tasks. The larger clusters of similar items provided an organizational basis for learning.

ORGANIZATIONAL RULES

Restle and Brown (1970b) showed that subjects tended not to learn a patterned sequence of six lights in terms of simple chains or simple positions. The performance was too accurate to be explained by simple dyadic associations, considering the number of repeating stimuli followed by different responses (i.e., branches). Also, the subjects were not consistently using clusters of items, since performance was not strongly related to the length of memory span required for accurate performance. The distributions of errors were not tied to relative position, eliminating this, too, as a basis of learning. The errors were determined by rules discovered within the sequence, which generated the specific patterns. This supports an interpretation in terms of learning and applying the rules by which the patterns were generated when the serial-learning task employs such patterns. The distributions of errors follow discontinuities of structure, such as continuations of runs. Restle and Brown (1970b) argue that the "conventional" theories of learning are inadequate because they do not consider the subject's ability to generate rules to guide his performance.

Restle (1970) has since elaborated his proposition for learning patterned series. He cautions that his approach is relevant to serial patterns, which lend themselves to organization, and is not useful in connection with arbitrary sequences, which have no built-in organizational basis. Nevertheless, there is similarity to the present theoretical argument in that the subject learns certain parts or levels of the organizational trees (hierarchies) before others.

Discontinuity of Meaning

Learning and memory are facilitated if the material to be learned can be easily organized into a meaningful whole, because it contains some unifying internal structure. Such structure can be produced in many ways.

SENTENCE ORDER

Ebbinghaus (1902, p. 626) concluded that the formation of associations between various elements is extraordinarily facilitated by the belongingness to a whole. He pointed out how meaningful sentences of poetry can be learned faster than comparable lists of nonsense syllables.

The internal linguistic structure of meaningful prose typically provides bases for organization into mnemonic units. For example, Miller and Selfridge (1950) did, in fact, show that subjects learned word arrays faster when the arrays exhibited a closer approximation to the English language.

O'Connell, Stubbs, and Theby (1968) had subjects learn strings of words with varying degrees of internal structure (morphology and syntax), using serial presentation trials at 1- and 3-second rates, followed by unpaced serial recall. They predicted that the faster rate, being closer to a reading rate, would produce a greater facilitative effect of the structure within the series. Although a facilitation of structure was obtained, this organization variable did not however interact significantly with presentation rate.

Simpson (1965) showed that greater approximations to English improved serial anticipation learning of 30-word lists; also the serial-position curve was affected by the grouping "boundaries." A list with words ordered to form meaningful prose did show the typical serial-position effect, but with a highly irregular curve because of different effects of phrasing and meaningful context. The series with words in random order, and therefore without obvious internal boundaries for organization, showed a very smooth, typical serial-position function. The list with intermediate structure, having meaningful five-word segments, but with these segments in scrambled order, showed the typical serial-position curve. Nevertheless, this curve also showed a consistent local effect about the partitions that corresponded to changes from one meaningful segment to another. Specifically, the first item of the subsequent segment showed a peak of errors, and the one following it showed a dip.

In a later study, Simpson (1967) again studied serial learning by the anticipation method, using lists of words arranged to produce English sentences or rearranged in sequences having a low approximation to English. The serial-position curves for 15 words were plotted in terms of percentage of total performance for that condition, in the manner of McCrary and Hunter (1953). The overall shapes of these curves in terms of errors were not significantly different, although the curve for the meaningful sentences was somewhat flatter. The serial-position curve based on percentage of correct responses was considerably flatter for the low-approximation condition, however. This latter result was predicted from Jensen's (1962c) analysis, because the low-approximation condition was less accurate overall. These data actually showed a decrease in errors from beginning to end, and relatively little bowing. Therefore, the organized material produced the atypical serial-position curve; the unorganized material, having only the temporal basis of organization, revealed the typical temporal-position basis of organization as shown by greater bowing of the curve.

Brent (1969) studied the effects of four levels of linguistic structure on serial-anticipation learning. Lists of varying length were presented in meaningful paragraphs, in meaningful sentences, in sentences with nouns interchanged, and in groups of words composed of rearrangements within the sentences. Brent predicted that difficulty of learning would increase with the number of linguistic units, independent of the number of words, and that errors would "scallop" about the borders of linguistic units because errors within a unit would be rare. Furthermore, he predicted that the subject would use the highest level of linguistic structure that was available to him. Specifically, the scallop of errors would bound the highest level of linguistic unity available, rather than some subordinate level. Length was varied by deleting adverbial and adjective modifiers, without interfering with the overall coherence of the narrative. The number of items in that task did have a small effect on errors of anticipation, although the strong effect of the number of linguistic units was larger. The serial-position results were exactly as predicted. The paragraph organization showed minor scallops at the beginning of the sentences and little evidence for a serial-position effect. For the sentence structure there were both larger scallops at the beginning of sentences, with larger overall serial-position effects, particularly for the rearranged sentences. For isolated words the serial-position effect was large, with minimal scalloping.

Brent (1969) also found that, as the meaningful organization increased, the proportion of omission errors decreased, and the proportion of semantically or syntactically equivalent errors increased. This suggests that the subjects were using the linguistic structure to aid learning. For disconnected sentences there was, of course, a marked difference according to the number of sentences. The fact that there was little effect of the number of sentences in a paragraph supports the idea that the subject tends to use the larger (paragraph) organization when this level is present, as opposed to the level of sentence organization.

In a second experiment, Brent (1969) presented a paragraph series at either 0.5-, 1-, or 3-second unit rates. He predicted that the subject would be more effective in using the linguistic structure when he had more time, thus showing more scalloping at the intermediate rate, and little scalloping at the fastest rate. These results were partially supported, since scalloping increased with the increase in rate from 3 seconds to 1 second, but much scalloping, and little serial-position effect, was present even at the 0.5-second rate.

The results from material with meaningful internal structure thus show faster learning and "poorer" serial-position curves. This means that subjects prefer to base their learning strategy on meaningful relationships, and rely on position cues more or less by default when the other cues are not available or not particularly useful. Although it seems trite to say it, the serial-position effect depends upon the subject using position clues in his strategy of learning.

HIGH INTERITEM ASSOCIABILITY

Guilford (1927) hid coherent schemes within serial lists that could be the basis for an organization of the items. The schemes could, for example, be regular number progressions or words forming approximations to familiar English sentences. If the subjects discovered the constructional scheme, learning was facilitated.

Freeman (1930) argued that subjects actively select stimuli to associate on the basis of formal instructions, self-instructions, and "occasional instructions"—those given by the configuration of the stimuli. Thus, items are always associated in some context. Using paired-associate learning and varying such contextual stimuli as extrinsic aids (rhythm and spatial localization), intrinsic relations (rhyme and identity), formal generative rules, and symbolic relations (suggested meaningful word sequences), he found facilitation of learning. He proposed that the contextual aids were helpful to learning because subjects assimilated or integrated them through "secondary operations" into a contextual organization. He argues that the organism adopts some certain strategy for assimilating a particular series of items, and concludes:

> Sooner or later it becomes aware of its procedure; or the significance may be identified in the items themselves. This exposition is, of course, only a hypothesis. But it offers the possibility of leading us out a bit from that blind alley into which most considerations of context (or meaning) usually take us. Certainly the time has passed when we can treat *context* as a mystical factor in associative formation—a thing to be brought quietly into the realm of psychological thought only where logical distinction fails to provide adequately for its absence (1930, p. 211).

Ellis and Manning (1967) employed dot patterns of scaled similarity as stimuli in a paired-association task. Both a fixed sequential order of the pairs and a high similarity between adjacent pairs in progressive order facilitated the learning of an association between them. The consistent structure of the task by sequential ordering and by similarity ordering facilitated the learning equally and produced fastest learning when both structural bases of ordering were present. These results occurred even though the subjects were not aware of the structural cues which they were using. Although it is not clear from the original report, it is apparent from a later report (Ellis, 1970) that the ordinal position of the items was changed progressively from trial to trial, while the sequence of pairs was maintained. This would account for the fact that the subjects were not aware of the structure provided by the serial ordering.

Weingartner (1963) employed lists of 16 words for serial anticipation learning in which all words were free-recall associates of one word. These words could be grouped into four groups of four in which the words in a subcategory were more closely associated to one another, as determined by a previous factor analysis. Learning was fastest when the list retained the greatest degree of internal associative structure, and slowest when the serial order was scrambled among all four categories. When only the first and last groups of four items, or only the middle eight items were so shuffled, the difficulty of learning was intermediate. About 71% of the errors were made at the middle eight positions with the maximally organized list and about 61% with the least-organized list and the list with only the end groups of items in shuffled categories. The condition with the middle two categories (eight items) in scrambled array resulted in about 76% of the errors. Battig (1966) also found that blocking of formally similar trigrams in free and serial recall improved performance. Presumably the list of blocked items was easier to organize.

Tulving (1965) found that serial learning and free recall were superior for a group of words ordered in such a way as to maintain the adjacency of items that had been frequently reproduced in adjacent positions in a previous free recall study. The subjective organization that had presumably facilitated free recall for one group of subjects also facilitated free recall and serial learning for a different group of subjects.

Underwood and Zimmerman (1973) found that internal organization within a serial list facilitated both learning and recall. The structure was produced by hierarchical categories for common nouns—for example, living things, animals, and domestic animals. The authors emphasize that the structure was the result of preexperimental factors that the subject brought to the laboratory with him.

Internal organization of the items in a series can, on the other hand, hinder serial learning if the previous organization is inconsistent with the associations to be formed in the serial task. For example, Wood (1969) showed clearly that subjective organization within a group of words as part of the process of free recall learning interfered with subsequent serial learning of those items. Presumably the temporal organization required in the serial task was in conflict with the previous interitem organizations.

ASSOCIATIVE ORDERING

Harcum (1975) investigated serial learning of ten items having different associative values when the items were ordered in sequence from low-to-high values or high-to-low values. A control list consisted of items each having about the same association value as the average of the experimental items. Arguing that the items at the beginning would be learned first, as an anchor for the subsequent learning, and that organized lists would be favored in learning, he predicted that the ascending order of difficulty would be learned fastest, followed by the condition in which the list was organized in terms of descending order of difficulty. The results in terms of mean errors per serial position under each condition yielded, as predicted, fewest errors for the ascending condition and the greatest number of errors for the control, unorganized series. The shapes of the serial-position curves generally reflected the differences in association value for the items at the various positions. A comparison of the descending and control curves, however, showed virtually no effect of conditions for the items at the beginning of the list. Since association values of the items in descending order were substantially higher for these positions, apparently the variable of position was of greater importance than the association value for these items.

The particular control condition in the first experiment of the Harcum (1975) study was selected on the assumption that a homogeneous group of items would be equally difficult to learn relative to an ordered heterogeneous group of items having an equal arithmetic average of association values. This assumption was checked, and found invalid, in a second experiment, for which the results were summarized in Figure 4-2. The means of errors for items of various association values are shown for both the heterogeneous and the homogeneous series. The heterogeneous items are labeled as "mixed" association values, and homogeneous items are labeled as having "same" association values. Clearly the homogeneous items produce fewer errors, at least for those items of the mixed list at about the same associational level. Harcum inter-

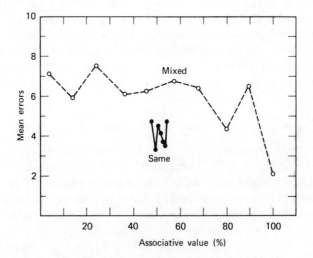

Figure 4-2   Errors in learning series of items having mixed or homogeneous (same) association values, after Harcum (1975). Reprinted with permission of publisher.

preted this to mean that item position basically determined the organizational strategy of the subjects with the homogeneous items, whereas the heterogeneous nature of the mixed list produced a different, competing basis for organization. The conflict between the two possible organizational tendencies yielded a more difficult task overall. Harcum argued that the unorganized array of heterogeneous items produced interference in terms of competing strategies, even though the formal intralist similarity was low—a condition that ordinarily produces reduced interference.

Harcum's (1975) conclusion was further supported by inspection of the serial-position curves. The curves for percentages of total errors at each item position in Figure 4-3 show a more regular serial-position curve for items of the same association value. The items at both extremes of the mixed series were favored presumably because of their positions, but the remaining items did not show a large effect of position. This indicates that these final seven or eight items were acquired through a strategy that was based primarily on interitem associations.

Harcum's (1975) comparison of mixed and homogeneous serial lists showed that the difference was primarily in terms of item differentiation. Evidence for this came from a comparison of serial-position curves for omission and commission errors. Omission errors revealed essentially equivalent shapes of curves for the two types of lists; Harcum and Coppage (1969) argued that omission errors reflected the subject's strategy

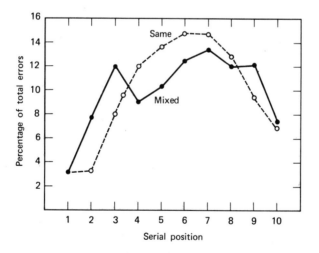

Figure 4-3 Percentage errors per serial position for items of same or mixed association value, after Harcum (1975). Reprinted with permission of publisher.

of learning a series from the temporally first to last items. In the Harcum (1975) study, the commission errors, on the other hand, were responsible for the differences in total errors between the two lists. The items of same association value revealed the symmetrical serial-position curve, which Harcum and Coppage (1969) attributed to confusion among position. The mixed series also showed the positional advantage for the end items, but thereafter they revealed virtually no effect of position. Therefore, the argument for relative importance of position and item cues depends upon the intrinsic bases of organization that are easily available to the subjects.

SUBJECT MEDIATION

Thieman (1973) found that retention of serial lists was superior when the subject used mediators generated for the learning task. The greater the degree of meaningful processing by the subject, the better the retention.

Smith and Noble (1965) showed that a mnemonic "hook" system had essentially no advantage in serial learning of high-meaningful items, but a slight advantage for items of medium meaningfulness. The mnemonic system was most effective for subjects of lower initial ability. Recall and relearning were consistently superior for the material learned with the mnemonic system. From these results it appears that subjects of higher ability are better able to generate meaningful mnemonic aids, and that such aids are less helpful if the material to be learned is itself already meaningful.

The results of Bruce (1974) support the contention that subjects of higher ability are better able to use mnemonic schemes. Bruce tested fourth-, sixth-, and eighth-grade children on a serial-learning task involving as the stimulus items structured (predictable) changes in a permutation of symbols or random (unpredictable) arrangements of the symbols. The structured series yielded fewer errors; this advantage showed a disproportionate increase for the older children. Thus, the more mature child is better able to use the internal structure within a series.

Levin and Rohwer (1968) found that the provision of a unifying structure only on the first of five trials improved the accuracy of serial learning for a group of fourth- and fifth-grade children. Later, Levin (1969) tested the hypothesis that better-organized learning materials produce deviations from the smooth serial-position curve to be anticipated from materials to be learned merely by rote. Lists of 12 high-frequency nouns were presented within various organizational frameworks provided by a single sentence, by 2 through 12 unrelated context sentences, or by no context—the control condition. Different groups of fourth- and fifth-grade children served as subjects under the various conditions of list organization and of testing either by serial recall or anticipation learning. All conditions of anticipation learning, except the one in which there were four context sentences, revealed a significant quadratic trend, indicating a symmetrical bow in the curve. There was virtually no asymmetry of the function. There was, however, an increasing tendency for a linear trend to appear as the number of context sentences increased, and the internal organization was thus decreased. But only for the unorganized condition was the linear trend significant. Thus, for only the disorganized series was the typical serial-position result obtained at a significant level—both linear and quadratic components significant.

Levin and Rohwer (1968) analyzed the serial-recall data in terms of transitional error probabilities—the proportion of times a succeeding item was correct given that the preceding one was also given correctly. For these data the most-organized list was characterized by a significant quadratic component, with the linear trend not significant. On the other hand, the least-organized series showed significant linear trends, but not quadratic trends. These results clearly support the hypothesis that the unorganized material is learned more by rote, and therefore the temporal ordering controls the order of acquisition. The organized material is acquired more in terms of the various linkages between items and thus is less tied to the temporal order of presentation. Therefore, the organized material fails to produce the clear-cut serial-position effect when relative position is defined temporally. Delin (1969a) also found a flatter serial-position function when the subjects had been instructed to use a mnemonic system.

Bower and Clark (1969) demonstrated the advantage of allowing the subject to construct a narrative story to incorporate ten nouns in a series to be learned. For a group of 12 lists, the immediate recall of each list was virtually perfect for both experimental subjects and their yoked controls, who were matched for study time, but were not instructed to invent the stories. The recall for the subjects who constructed the stories was six or seven times that of their controls who had not constructed the stories. The number of intruding errors for the organized lists was low, indicating that the stories promoted discrimination and reduced interference among items and lists.

The paucity of commission errors when a series has been meaningfully organized is supported by results of Delin (1969c). In Delin's study the proportion of omission errors increased as the completeness of the mnemonic instructions increased, although overall performance improved with the additional mnemonics.

A number of studies by Blick and his co-workers obtained positive effects of mnemonic aids in free recall (e.g., Pash & Blick, 1970). Pash and Blick (1970) showed, for example, that although instructing the subjects to use a mnemonic in free recall did not facilitate performance, those subjects who gave evidence of actually using the mnemonic did reveal superior performance. Kibler and Blick (1972) found that an experimenter-supplied first-letter mnemonic produced superior free recall, relative to subject-supplied mnemonics, using retention intervals from immediate recall to four weeks. Apparently the reason for this was simply that the subjects were not able in the time allowed to construct a first-letter mnemonic, for the 19 words in the study, that was as comprehensive or meaningful as the one supplied by the experimenters. Buonassissi, Blick, and Kibler (1972) later compared experimenter- and subject-supplied descriptive story schemes in free recall of words. At various retention intervals up to 12 weeks, the two conditions did not produce differences in recall. Therefore, the results of experimenter- versus subject-supplied mnemonics seem to be tied to the specific type of mnemonic aid and whether or not that aid is supplied by the experimenter or the subject himself.

Blick, Buonassissi, and Boltwood (1972) asked subjects to report what kind of mnemonic they would use in a serial-learning task. Most often subjects reported that they would use some system based on first letters of the items. Other strategems involved imagery, descriptive stories, mediation, and phonetic and semantic clustering. Since these categories corresponded closely to those reported by the subjects of Blick and Waite (1971) as actually used for free recall, Blick et al. (1972) concluded that the free-recall and serial tasks were almost indentical tasks as far as college students were concerned.

Context

One difficulty with transfer studies aimed at discovering the functional stimulus is that the context of the original serial learning cannot be reinstated for the second task. McGeoch (1932) proposed that loss of context, along with retroactive inhibition, formed a major law of forgetting. This general effect of loss of context or failure of retention will be discussed more completely in Chapter 6.

The transfer loss can be attributed to general situational effects or to specific changed associations between items. McGeoch (1936) puts it this way:

> On the positive side, any theory will need to consider the influence of the change in set which accompanies the methodological shift from learn-

ing by the anticipation method to recall by the association-method where the direct sequence is not necessary. It should take account, also, of the fact that by the association method there is a breaking up of sequence and of the antecedent context of each word since the stimulus-word is not now aroused by the preceding word and recalled by the S, but is spoken by E. It becomes, thus, a different stimulus-word (p. 243).

McGovern (1964) provided evidence in the A–B, A–C paired-associate paradigm for the unlearning of both contextual and specific associations. Obviously the differences between the so-called general and specific effects are not discrete or mutually exclusive. This nevertheless is a convenient organizational device.

GENERAL CONTEXT EFFECTS

Asch (1968) points out that contextual stimuli can be any part of the experimental environment, but the context is often treated as though it were a single stimulus. Hintzman and Block (1971) and Hintzman, Block, and Summers (1973) emphasized this multifarious quality of total contextual stimulation, as well as its dynamic quality. Evidence for a general effect of changes in context was discovered early.

Bilodeau and Schlosberg (1951) found that the effects of retroactive inhibition are lessened if the interpolated material is learned under different stimulating environments. A gross change in room conditions, experimental apparatus, and subject posture during interpolated learning produced a large decrease in retroactive inhibition. Greenspoon and Ranyard (1957) also found that learning the interpolated list under different environmental conditions from the original list reduced retroactive inhibition in a serial-learning task. Watts and Royer (1969) have reduced the retroactive effects in a free recall measure by merely printing the interpolated stimuli in a different color of ink.

Irion (1948) showed that paired-associate retention decreased as an increasing function of the length of a rest pause in the acquisition process. This loss was attributed to a change of "set," including factors such as changing attention to environmental and internal cues, and changing postural and other adjustive mechanisms.

Jenson (1962f) proposed also that prior failures to find very large transfer to serial learning of the same associations established in paired-associate learning were due to a change in "set" between the two tasks. Accordingly he predicted that the transfer would be greater from paired associate to serial learning if the serial list began with a stimulus item from the paired-associate task, than if it began with a former response item. Presumably the initiation of the serial list with a former stimulus item would help maintain the set that had been established in the paired-associate learning. The subjects were informed of the relations between the two tasks. Positive transfer was obtained relative to a control group learning the serial task without prior paired-associate learning. Since the stimulus items consisted of highly available responses (i.e., colored forms), it was felt that response-learning factors could be ignored. Analysis of performance for individual items supported the set idea. For the serial list starting with a stimulus item from paired-associate learning, the former response members revealed drops in errors relative to the former stimulus members. Presumably the subjects were accustomed to responding with the response terms, but not with the stimulus terms.

Further evidence in Jensen's (1962f) study came from the learning curves for selected items, which showed gradually decreasing trends of errors for the control group and for the group starting with a former stimulus item, but an increase in errors initially for the group with the changed set (i.e., starting with a response item from paired-associate learning). Thus, the group starting serial learning with a "response" term finds the paired-associate strategy unsuccessful and then shifts to a strategy more in keeping with the serial-learning task. Jensen proposes that the items in serial learning are not serving as stimulus and response, but that they are acquired merely as an integration of responses.

Peterson (1963) attempted to integrate ways of looking at so-called immediate memory and learning experiments by adding the concepts of "cue learning" and "background conditioning" to the concept of stimulus trace. The former refers to the formation of sequential dependencies among individual items to be learned, and the latter refers to the building of relationships between the nonspecific cues in the environment and the responses of the subjects. This process would be of particular importance in establishing the recall of the first items in a sequence. Peterson (1963) presented data that indicated that these two types of association were not perfectly correlated. For example, background conditioning is used to account for changes in the order of reporting items (e.g., Deese & Kaufman, 1957) that are often attributed to changes in subject's strategy. Interference among items could be produced by the association of each item to the context or background stimuli. This concept of background conditioning appears closely related to the concept of list membership.

SPECIFIC CONTEXT EFFECTS

Dulsky (1935) studied recall and relearning of paired-associate learning of nonsense syllables with varied colors of stimulus and response backgrounds. Any change in background colors interfered with the number of items recalled and with the accuracy of recall. Relearning was also more difficult. This was attributed to interference of the incorrect association of a changed background color to the response with the correct association between stimulus syllable and the response.

Underwood, Ham, and Ekstrand (1962) presented trigrams or words on colored patches for paired-associate learning trials and then tested for transfer when either color or verbal cue was removed. They predicted that the more meaningful stimulus would be the functional stimulus—namely, colors over trigrams and words over colors. These predictions were supported; transfer was nearly perfect for color alone with trigrams in the compound stimulus, and words were more effective than color when they had been included in the compound. The complete transfer for color as the cue with the trigram-color compound indicates that the results were due to cue selection rather than to a change in the stimulus configuration.

An effect of associative context on retrieval in recognition memory has been shown by Tulving and Thomson (1971). A word presented as part of a pair of associatively related words was later not recognized as often if the context word was missing or changed. Thus, the subject was making the irrelevant word a part of his mnemonic code, which was not the same code for the word without that same context.

Positional Anchoring

The possibility that the subjects use positional anchors for mnemonic organization of a series depends, of course, on evidence that the subjects use positional cues. This was documented in the previous chapter. In this section of this chapter, the emphasis is on the specific use of end items as reference points for the organization of learning.

PAIRED-ASSOCIATE LEARNING

Ebenholtz (1966b) showed that a serial-position effect could be obtained in paired-associate learning for digit stimuli ordered according to their ordinal values, as well as for nonsense-syllable stimuli ordered according to their ordinal position in a prior serial-learning task. He concluded that subjects had been learning serial position in the prior serial-learning task and that response to positional organizing cues produces the serial-position effect.

CONTINUOUS SERIAL LISTS

Eysenck (1959) compared continuous and discontinuous presentation of 15-item lists of adjectives. The typical bowed serial-position curve appeared for both conditions. The measures of trials (number of errors) to the first correct response and of total errors to a criterion of one perfect recitation revealed similar serial-position curves, with more errors for the continuous series.

Asch, Hay, and Diamond (1960) obtained a serial-learning gradient when pauses between trials were omitted, and they concluded that the

> learner's knowledge of the ends of the series constitutes one condition of the serial gradient. It seems necessary to conclude that the gradient requires, as one condition, a particular cognitive operation, namely, the identification of the beginning and end of the series and the location of items with respect to these boundaries (p. 196).

Asch et al. (1960) also added a spatial dimension to the temporal one in serial learning, finding important effects on the rate of learning and on the patterns of interfering associations. Thus, they concluded that serial learning cannot be accounted for by simple associations:

> Further, when the entire set of positions is perceived as mutually interrelated within a configuration, the associations occuring will be a function of the *Gestalt*-properties of the configuration. This is, indeed, what we find (p. 195).

Bewley, Nelson, and Brogden (1969) found that any experimental treatment that reduced ordinal position effects in serial learning contributed to the difficulty of the task. Thus, bowing of the curve was positively correlated with the speed of learning. The serial-position curve was flattened by using closed-cycle (continuous) presentations and by varying the starting ordinal position over trials.

VARIED STARTING POINT

Keppel (1964), using a retroactive inhibition paradigm with serial learning, found evidence for the use of both positional and chaining cues. When the starting item for the list was varied from trial to trial, the learning was hindered with respect to the usual condition of constant location of the starting point. Obviously the subjects had been thus prevented from using a position cue. However, for the second list learned in this varied manner, the learning was equal to that for constant serial position. Therefore, as Keppel (1964) concludes, the sequential cue alone for learning can become as effective as the position and sequence cues together.

Woods and Epstein (1969) provided further evidence that the intertrial interval contributes substantially to the serial-position effect and that this effect is the result of the cognitive anchor that it provides. In a 15-item series, using a standard anticipation procedure, control subjects were given an intertrial interval filled with asterisks and with the number "1" placed to the left of an item, which was thereby designated as the "first" item in the list. Although it is not clear from the experimental report, presumably the item designated as "first" was always the one following the asterisks. The experimental subjects observed exactly the same stimulus conditions but, after the first trial, the temporally first syllable was determined randomly. For the control group the classical serial-position curve appeared. For the experimental group, again there was the skewed serial-position function, but the bowing was much less and the number of errors was greater. As had been observed by Bowman and Thurlow (1963), the item that had been designated "first" produced more errors than the item following it; actually Woods and Epstein plotted the designated-first item as last and the one succeeding it as first. The appearance of the usual serial-position curve for the experimental condition, plotted around the designated-first item, indicates the importance of the cognitive apprehension of an anchoring item.

Woods and Epstein (1969) also plotted serial-position curves in terms of temporal position within each trial. This does not affect the control curve, of course, since the temporal primacy, the designation of a "first" item, and the first item after the asterisk break were all the same for this group of subjects. For the experimental group, the plot according to temporal serial position did not show significant serial-position effects. Woods and Epstein conclude that these data indicate the effects of recall, rather than learning, and that recall therefore does not show a serial-position effect. Thus, they argue, the serial-position effect is associated with the learning process, and not the recall process. This argument is not convincing, however, since the difference is not between learning and recall, but between two possible competing ways for subjects to organize the material for learning—to direct the ordinal strategy of learning. Given the clear cues for a designated first item on each trial, why should the subject show effects of the transient temporal organization on each trial? The randomization of starting points merely cancels out the serial-position effects caused by the cognition of a first anchor item, which the experimenters virtually instructed subjects to use. Thus, the results support those of Bowman and Thurlow (1963) that the serial-position function will be organized around a natural break in the series even when the temporal primacy effect is varied on each trial. These data support the hypothesis that a cognitive anchor and position relative to that anchor play a major role in the generation of the serial-position curve.

Isolation Effect

The isolation effect (von Restorff, 1933) has frequently been cited as evidence for the Gestalt-organization view of serial learning. An item made perceptually or cognitively different (i.e., isolated) is learned or recalled more quickly or more accurately (e.g., Pillsbury & Raush, 1943; Jenkins & Postman, 1948). In a sense, each effect of a discontinuity in a series is an isolation effect. Presumably the boundary between types of items causes a cognition of a difference at that point, which can be used to organize the series.

There have been literally scores of isolation studies. They are just mentioned here; they will be discussed more completely in Chapter 7, in terms of changed orders of acquisition for isolated items.

Response Factors

A multifactor approach, such as the present one, must identify effects caused by possible responding biases from responding parameters on the coding system that the subject uses. The response requirements can provide also an organizational basis for the learning. This can affect learning performance in two ways: providing a basis for mnemonic organization to be consistent with the response requirement, and affecting the subject's criterion for making an overt response.

POSITION CODING

In free recall of unrelated material the subject supplies, for example, conceptual bases for organization, and this is reflected in the overt ordering of recall (Tulving, 1962). The requirement for serial recall places a constraint on the response ordering, which probably also provides a constraint on the selection of coding cues. For example, Waugh (1961) showed that the requirement for serial recall at first inhibited performance, but later facilitated it. Thus the basis provided by the serial structure of the list was a factor in the organization of learning.

The responding condition may be important because it contains the cues (context) for retrieval. Tulving and Pearlstone (1966) provided evidence that subjects may have available traces of categorized words for free recall, but be unable to gain accession to the trace for the recall test. When the subject was given a cue to aid his recall, the number of items recalled increased, thus indicating that the recall failure was due to a problem of retrieval of material stored in memory rather than to a failure of memory itself.

RESPONDING CRITERION

Murdock (1968) has argued on the basis of short-term memory for word lists, using both sequential and ordinal probes, that the typical greater recency effect is due to a more lax criterion for responding with items from the "recency" end of the series. When allowance is made for the fact that the subject responds more often for items at the end of the series, these items show a lower "hit" rate. A signal-detection analysis supported this interpretation. The measure of responding criterion—beta—showed a progressive decrease from first to last item, with both types of probe. The sensitivity measure—d'–showed the typical serial-position curves with greater recency than primacy effects. Murdock also employed a serial-recall procedure with a ten-digit list, and thereby increased the magnitude of the primacy effect—although the last digit was still reproduced with remarkable accuracy. Thus, he concluded that the probe technique underestimated the magnitude of primacy effects, presumably because of the criterion shifts and the loss of context. He argued that the ubiquitous serial-position curve reflects, therefore, both effects of memory traces and recall processes.

Murdock (1968) also used a short-term memory procedure for recall of ten-word lists, cueing the subject either before or after presentation about whether the recall should begin with items at the ordinal beginning or end of the list. The postcue condition revealed greater recency than primacy effects, with a stronger recency effect for the condition in which the last items were reproduced first. For the precue condition, the order of report strongly controlled the direction of the asymmetry of the curve, with a marked primacy effect for the reports with initial items first and a marked recency effect when the end items were reported first. These results were the same as those of Harcum, Hartman, and Smith (1963) for spatial arrays of ten items tachistoscopically exposed simultaneously.

Murdock (1968) interpreted his results to indicate "output interference." Since the effects of pre- or postcueing on overall performance were minimal, Murdock concludes that this variable did not influence the capacity of the short-term memory system, but merely input-output interactions. Thus, the capacity of short-term memory is not changed, but the items that enter it for storage are affected. The items at either end of the array are likely to enter, but those in the middle become "compressed" in the fixed amount of storage space that remains.

CONCLUSION

The evidence thus indicates that learning a series includes learning the organization, grouping, and relative position of the individual items.

However, these factors could not cause the serial-position curve except as they facilitate or hinder the operation of other processes. For example, positional learning would enhance vividness and ease of differentiation among items. As Waters (1948) concludes from his review of the literature, perceptual organization is not the sufficient cause or condition of learning. In the terms of this book, it is a paralearning factor.

The time has come to look for processes and mechanisms, and not to concentrate on isolating single variables and examining results. The important goal should be to find out how the known variables work together to produce a given constellation of results for a given subject who is learning a given list. The evidence indicates that the subject can use many cues in a complex way. For example, when Anderson and Bower (1972) examined the effectiveness of probe cues on the recall of parts of meaningful sentences, they found under some conditions superior recall when the exact context of multiple cues was retained. Under other conditions the recall was predictable from the independent combination of probabilities from individual cues. Therefore, there was evidence for both Gestalt and associationistic approaches to a theory of memory.

Battig and Young (1969) point out that transfer studies may tell more about what happens afterward, rather than what happens during the actual course of serial learning. They used a serial-recall procedure to test performance after each exposure of a series, using two different sequences of the items on alternate trials. The two sequences varied the degree of constancy of item position and item sequence. Constant position of items seemed to facilitate recall more than constant sequence. The authors concluded, moreover, that the study contained evidence for both learning of sequential connections and positional connections, but that some additional factor was needed to account for all of the results. They refer to this as "a kind of rule-learning process." With this kind of test the subjects are apparently led to search for the rule by which one sequence is converted to the second on the alternate trial.

The organizational strategy approach proposes that the first and last items of a serial list are learned first because of their superior vividness, because such isolation of boundaries facilitates learning. The theory maintains that learning a series involves forming it into a Gestalt, localizing the individual elements with respect to the total configuration. In general, a serial list becomes a Gestalt when the beginning and ending syllables, which separate the figure from the ground, are learned and when the whole list is synthesized into a relatively meaningful whole.

Mandler (1962) argues for overlearning as a cause for the processes to change from associative to "structural"—that is, overlearning of ends of serial-learning series. Youssef (1967) proposed a similar dual process of serial learning. The first is the establishment of associative connections, which is followed by an integrative process. Mandler (1968) denies, however, that "rote-learned" lists for serial recall are learned in the same way that is characteristic of a structured series. He states,

> Rather, serial recall initially involves two components, an organized component for the early items and a primary memory component (cf. Waugh and Norman, 1965) for the items presented just prior to recall. The first three to five items are organized in the sense that some categorical or sequential (e.g., syntactic) organization is applied to them, and they are stored accordingly (1968, p. 117).

Mandler and Mandler (1964) examined serial-position curves for serial-anticipation learning of short meaningful sentences. The curves did not show the typical primacy or recency effects; instead, the core idea of the sentence was favored in the first test trial. They argued therefore that the serial-learning task should be interpreted in terms of "memory" instead of "learning." The present interpretation is that the subjects tended to use meaningful sequence cues instead of positional cues.

Neisser (1967) concludes that the active processes in short-term verbal memory include what has variously been called rehearsal, recoding, or grouping processes. He implies that the advantage of recency in auditory short-term memory is due to "echoic memory"—a temporary auditory storage, whereas active mnemonic reformulation accounts for a so-called primacy effect when recall is in the same order as the presentation order. Neisser proposes for the higher mental processes that cognitive ordering in both temporal and spatial dimensions is important in establishing cognitive structures for memory.

Harcum and Coppage (1965b) have emphasized the two main features of the results in the acquisition of a series of elements; one is the piling up of errors near the middle of the stimulus configuration, and the other is the asymmetry of the distribution. Thomas (1968) supports the argument for two factors in the composition of the serial-position curve, on the basis of a mathematical analysis of the curve. It seems likely that the bowing of the serial curve is due to a buildup of some kind of inhibition or interference about the central items of the series. There is ample evidence that, under some circumstances, the subjects are responding to the stimulus of relative position in addition to, or instead of, the stimulus of the item itself. Thus, this mechanism may alternatively be considered as a confusion among position labels. The second feature of the serial-position effect is the usual asymmetry of the element-position function. Harcum and Coppage (1965b) have argued that the assimilation of items in a series is oriented and directed by organizational factors in memory. This organizational process determines which items are identified cognitively as first. These items tend to be a kind of anchor for the subsequent mnemonic organization.

The relevant stimulus thus seems to be dependent upon organizational factors that emerge from the total experimental experience of the subject. Not only is he able to use many cues, he orders these cues into hierarchies of preference, with the preferred cue depending upon what hierarchy is appropriate to the task, and at what stage of the hierarchy he has reached. The process is dynamic, and thus changes with feedback about the success of a given strategy. Therefore, the answer to the question of the functional stimulus for serial learning must be the classical answer of the psychologist to such simple questions: It all depends!

SUMMARY

This chapter has presented evidence that serial learning is facilitated and directed by organizational strategies of learning and memory. Because of this, cognitive factors are important. The subject can use any basis of differentiation of items in order to use them as stimuli for learning, and he may similarly use any available cues as the basis for selecting the correct responses. It is proposed that the various items represent potentially changing hierarchies of cues, with the choice of a cue dependent upon the existing configuration of stimuli at the stage in which another item is to be acquired.

CHAPTER

$$\boxed{5}$$

THE INFORMATION-TRANSLATION CONCEPTION

A successful theoretical approach to understanding performance in serial learning and memory must be broad enough to include mechanisms on both the input and output edges of the ecphoric processes. Noble (1961) proposed that methodology for future research in verbal learning should include specific phases in the area of individual differences, repeated-measurement designs, and theorizing that is sufficiently broad in scope to incorporate all of the empirical findings. Narrowly conceived ideas about what processes are relevant may bypass important parts of the total process. Asch's (1968) argument for a study of relational properties in rote learning, in terms of cognitive processes, was quoted in the previous chapter. The present effort aims to be sufficiently broad to satisfy the above requirements.

LANGUAGE OF MODEL

An effort must be made to avoid reducing the issues of theoretical approach to arguments about words, since processes are frequently described by some researchers in words that are objectionable to other authors. Apparently some authors are so fearful of being considered unscientific and nonrigorous that they refuse to use in their writings words that they use daily, even in academic discussions. I agree with Hebb (1958) that molar terms are suitable for molar descriptions, and molecular terms should be reserved for their own appropriate level of description. Fortunately, the trend has been toward the acceptance of cognitive concepts and terms. Probably the books of Neisser (1967) and Gibson (1969) have been influential in promoting this trend.

Kendler (1952) stresses the futility of arguing about the choice of a theoretical model. The validity of concepts, he says, is tested by tying them to observables and testing the adequacy of their explanatory capabilities. Many arguments among psychologists settle down to the selection of words, as, for example, the differences between the cognitive theorists and the stimulus-response theorists:

> Firstly, the two appear to possess somewhat different thinking styles. Aside from certain scientific requirements, the selection of the specific terms in a theoretical structure seems to be determined by the personal needs of the theorists. . . . I suspect that if Hull had labelled what he now calls habit strength "dynamic cognitive field expectancies" without modifying its postulated relationships to the independent variables, much opposition of this concept would disappear and probably some new opposition would arise from certain quarters (Kendler, 1952, p. 273).

Kendler (1952) is correct. Nevertheless, it does appear that cognitions are staging a comeback, along with a renewed belief in the helpfulness of verbal reports.

VERBAL REPORTS OF STRATEGIES

Verbal reports are very often unreliable. This is, however, not a good reason to ignore them. Such "unreliable" data can, in fact, support an otherwise circular argument for a particular strategy of learning employed by the subjects (e.g., Harcum, Pschirrer, & Coppage, 1968). When such a correlation is found, support for the validity of the measures can also be inferred. Empirical success is the true criterion.

Miller, Galanter, and Pribram (1960) argue strongly not only for the existence of a learning strategy by the subject, but also for the possibility of discovering what it is. They propose the simple approach—merely to ask the subject what he is doing. Although Miller et al. recognize the problems of assuming that the subject actually knows what he is doing, they doubt that it is useless to believe him. They conclude:

> This skepticism may indeed be justified in many cases, especially those dealing with emotions and motivations. But it seems foolish to refuse to listen to the person under any circumstances. What he says is not always wrong. More often what he says would provide a valuable clue if only we were able to understand what it meant (1960, p. 126).

The verbal report will probably not be helpful in the case of the more peripheral or microprocess mechanisms, such as perception of visual images or the actual process of forming learned associations. For example, it is controversial whether or not the subject can report the visual image with fidelity (Hershenson, 1969; Harcum, 1970b). This problem remains in the possible distinction between "short-term" and "long-term" memory. For the content of molar central processes, however, such as the basis of selecting a style or strategy of solving a problem, the verbal report should be more valid and valuable.

EVIDENCE FOR MULTIPLE PROCESSES

The evidence points to multiple causation of the serial-position phenomenon. Postman (1961a) supported a two-stage interpretation of verbal learning (Underwood, Runquist, & Schulz, 1959). He proposed that the response-integregation stage for learning an item is bounded by the trial on which it is first given correctly, whereas the associative stage is completed when that response is given in its correct position. He found that high-frequency words (Thorndike & Lorge, 1944) were integrated faster than low-frequency words, but that there was no effect of word frequency on the associative stage. In the study by Lindley (1963), the association values of nonsense syllables from 30–80 % (e.g., Archer, 1960) seemed to have more effect on the serial learning than did the measures of pronounceability or familiarity. A stage analysis was performed following Postman's (1961a) definitions of response integration and associative-connection stages. Since the meaningfulness of syllables facilitated response integration, but did not affect association formation, the two-stage hypothesis was again supported.

Further evidence that serial learning does not involve a monolithic process was provided by Voss (1966). Voss varied the probability that certain items at certain positions in four- or eight-item series of adjectives could change from trial to trial and also the probability ratio that one or the other item would appear on each trial. Correct anticipation of either possible item was scored as correct. Performance decreased as the number of varied serial positions increased, either because there were more items to learn, or because the number of adjacent associations changed, or both. In another experiment, all items were varied probabilistically in either four- or eight-item lists. Both the probability of one or another item appearing was varied, along with the conditional probability that one item would follow another. For the four-item series, the conditional probability was not a significant variable, and with 100% conditional probability between items the consistent appearance of only one item produced faster learning than when it was replaced by another item for some proportion of the presentations. The greater the probabilistic variation, the greater the serial-position differences, with a flat function for the unchanged list and with fewest errors at the second position for the remaining conditions. For the eight-item lists, the conditional probability was a significant variable, but only later in learning. Again the constant appearance of one item was superior when the conditional probability between items was 1. The eight-item series showed the typical bowed shape, again with greater bowing for the lists with greater changes.

Analyzing the omission errors before and after first correct anticipation, Voss (1966) found that for the four-item series both conditions of probabilistic variation showed significant effects before the first correct response, but only the item variation was a significant factor thereafter. For the eight-item data, both scores of variation were significant. For the four-unit case the omission errors before first correct anticipation showed a slight linear increase across serial positions, but bowing up about the middle after that response. The eight-item curves were bowed up both before and after the first correct anticipation. For lists of both lengths, the intrusion errors were larger about the middle items, with more perseveratory than anticipatory errors.

To account for his results, Voss (1966) proposes that there are four processes of serial learning. The first, immediate serial memory, shows little variation across serial positions, with slight increases in errors across the four items in his study. For the longer series of eight items, the span of memory breaks down; thus this process affects only the items at the initial serial positions. The second process is item learning (cf. Underwood & Schulz, 1960)—the subject becomes familiar with the items of the study. The third process is called item placement, in which the subject learns to place an item at its correct serial position. From the intrusion data Voss concludes that the subject learns first the location of items about the beginning of the series and a general knowledge of the location of items from middle to end. He also concludes that the item learning occurs earlier, and the fourth process—sequential learning of adjacent associations occurs later. This process is more important in longer series and at later stages of learning. Furthermore, an interaction between item probability and contingent probability indicates that the more frequent items are learned first and also are associated sooner with the adjacent item.

Voss (1969) showed that the subject was able to localize first-learned items about as soon as the item itself was learned, whereas later-learned items were not localized at first. The subject first learned the item and then, only later, learned its position. The learning of the other items occurs according to the shape of the serial-position curve. Voss concludes that the serial-position effects of item learning are important, as follows:

> Specifically, the result implies that the major factor contributing to the shape of the serial position curve probably is the order in which the items are learned per se, and not interference between items (Feigenbaum & Simon, 1962). Furthermore, the order in which the items are learned may be taken as evidence for the position which states that the serial list may be viewed as a perceptual dimension and the items at the beginning are first learned followed by the last items, i.e., those items that may be discriminated more readily (1969, p. 224–225).

Differences in tasks undoubtedly account for changing importance for some factors. For example, the possible differences between short-term and long-term retention are important for immediate recall, where timing differences could differentially affect performance, but they would be less important for serial-anticipation learning. The possibility of encoding or decoding is important in all tasks at all stages of processing.

Short-term versus Long-term Retention

Murdock (1962b), Postman and Phillips (1965), Glanzer and Cunitz (1966), and Atkinson and Shiffrin (1968 a, b) provided evidence for two mechanisms in free recall. Murdock (1962b) found that the recency effect was not affected by rate of presentation or by length of series. Postman and Phillips (1965) and Glanzer and Cunitz (1966) eliminated the recency effect by delaying the recall, but they did not materially affect the recall of the remainder of the items. Results such as these have led some theorists (Waugh & Norman, 1965; Atkinson & Shiffrin, 1968 a, b) to propose two systems of memory: a short-term storage and a long-term memory.

Baddeley and Patterson (1971) and Craik (1971) have reviewed recently the literature on the relations between short-term and long-term memory. Baddeley and Patterson (1971) conclude that two factors determine what is remembered and what is forgotten. The first stage in the selection of information is accomplished by "buffer stores," including such mechanisms as the iconic storage proposed by Neisser (1967). They propose that

> these buffer stores should probably be regarded as an integral part of the information processing system, perhaps as much concerned with perception and pattern recognition as with memory storage (pp. 241–242).

The short-term components of the process would presumably be less accessible to introspective report.

Deese argued, however, that encoding in a verbal learning experiment was an all-or-nothing proposition (Cofer, 1961a, p. 39). Thus, the variations of conditions affecting word recognition that are important in tachistoscopic presentation are not important, since such recognizability is guaranteed if the words are encoded at all. In most verbal learning and memory experiments the sensory buffer can be ignored (Tulving & Madigan, 1970).

Of primary concern here are those long-term mechanisms that are common to the paralearning processes of the various tasks. Deese (1961) assumed that the same verbal processes pertained to free recall and paired-associate or serial learning. The differences in relationships he would attribute to differences in reinforcement contingencies and scoring techniques.

Encoding

Greeno and Bjork (1973) point out that the new interest in the study of cognitive processes, such as attention, encoding, search and rehearsal strategies, constitutes a kind of scientific revolution. The most significant theoretical development, they propose, is the increased structural complexity of the models of information processing and memorization. The increased complexity has included notions of multilevel functioning, such as an executive control of various processes. Thus, information is also selectively stored in what Shiffrin and Atkinson (1969) have called "control processes." These processes include rehearsal, coding, and recoding, and they should be much more accessible to conscious report by the subject.

Restle (1973) and Melton (1973) have disagreed about the concept of "coding." Restle (1973) prefers to restrict the concept to detection of patterns in the external environment and the application of a set of symbols to them. Thus, the code is given to the organism, in the stimulus configuration, rather than being imposed by the organism on nonsensical material. Melton (1973) prefers a broader use of the term, to refer to any system that the subject uses as a representation of the stimulus. The code may be so narrow that it is merely an instance of the nominal stimulus, or it may be as broad as the final stored result of the subject's information processing mechanisms. The present conception follows the one proposed by Melton, which includes also Restle's pattern perception definition. Therefore, the encoding can be based on central factors: of meaningfulness, familiarity, and similarity of items, for example, or on input or output dimensions of the task.

Bower (1970) argued that perceptual groupings are stored as chunks in memory, and serial recall involves primarily the assembly of these units. He summarizes his general conclusions, which he acknowledges are not new, in terms of the subject as an information processor equipped with learning programs:

> The first general idea is that a preferred strategy of the adult human in learning a large body of material is to "divide and conquer": that is, subdivide the material into smaller groups by some means, and then learn these parts as integrated packets of information. The bases for the groupings can be richly varied depending upon the nature of the material and the person's mental set (1970, p. 41).

Bower states that the chunking is influenced by cognitive control factors, such as attention, which are controlled by physical differences in homogeneities in the stimuli, as well as by contextual stimulation and previous organizations of stimuli.

CENTRAL FACTORS

Melton and Martin (1972) point out the emergence of the concept of central coding as a new emphasis in research on human learning and memory. In fact, evidence for a central encoding factor has been available for some time.

Underwood and Keppel (1963) found evidence for both positive and negative effects of encoding in free recall of trigrams. The subjects were or were not instructed that the letters of the nonsense trigrams could be rearranged to produce meaningful words. Whether or not the effect was facilitative depended upon the trial that the subject was first allowed to write the responses in any order and upon the availability of instructions. The inhibitory effects were attributed to the different rules for meaningful rearrangement of each item and the consequent problem of encoding and then later decoding when the nonsense response was required. For example, a direct encoding of a nonsense trigram that maintained the output requirement could be more efficient than coding the trigram into a word and back again for recall. Consider the nonsense trigram DNO, which could be encoded as "Don't Know" for subsequent recall more easily than by the rule of moving the first letter to last, then remembering for recall both the meaningful word and the rule by which it had been encoded.

The information processing theory of Simon and Feigenbaum (1964) employs the concept of central encoding. The first stage of learning required the development of an image or concept of the item. This image is then discriminated through experience from other stimilar images, producing a new composite image of the stimulus-response pair. This theory was tested with positive results against selected data from paired-associate learning.

Subjects' strategies or responding sets have been shown to influence performance in serial-learning tasks. For example, Underwood (1952b) provided evidence for the transfer of a responding set from one task to another. Subjects who performed a color-naming task, which required a response to every stimulus, subsequently made more overt errors on a serial-learning task that subjects previously performing a symbol-cancellation task. The frequency of overt errors was not related to overall rate of learning, as measured by trials to criterion.

INPUT-OUTPUT FACTORS

The details of both input and output ordering can influence the way the subject organizes the elements within an array. The input and output cues can support the same or different bases of organization.

The characteristics of the input can provide a basis for encoding and therefore retrieval of multiple-element stimuli. Tulving (1968) describes one basis as follows:

> Serial position or temporal dating of items in the input phase may constitute another kind of auxiliary information which can serve as a retrieval cue. Such information may be greater for early and late input items than for the middle ones and may be initially more powerful and yet decay more rapidly than other retrieval cues (1968, p. 14).

The results of Taylor and Taub (1972) supported the argument that subjects could code serial lists in terms of differences in spatial position. Stimuli were nine single letters presented serially in a memory drum in either the standard manner (i.e., all at the same location), in spatial sequence from left to right, or in haphazard temporal-spatial sequence. Recall tests after each presentation of the sequence were unconstrained except that the subject had to write no more than nine letters in nine open boxes arranged horizontally on the page of the test booklet. The subjects presented with a coherent spatial array tended to use spatial encoding in addition to a temporal basis of recall.

Deese (1968) argues that the organizational structure of the output—the manifest sequence—is not determined by contiguities between items but by an underlying organization or structure that can generate the manifest sequences of free recall. Thus, he says:

> The left-to-right or readout feature of memory and related phenomena is not one of the essential structural characteristics but is determined by the human limitations in information processing (1968, p. 99).

This argument seems to be the same as the one proposed by Lashley (1951).

Slamecka (1967) provided evidence for the importance of output factors. He had subjects learn lists of ten trigrams or ten consonants, using alternating trials of serial presentation and serial recall. The recall required the subject to write, at his own pace, items in a prescribed serial order, starting with the designated item and without skipping or making later changes. The subject was told that there were ten items in the series and to indicate missing items by a dash at the appropriate place. One group of the subjects learned by the usual procedure for serial learning—namely, items presented in temporal succession at one position in a window of a memory drum. A second group was presented with items at ten respective horizontal locations in a long window of a memory drum, but with the spatial left-to-right ordering not corresponding to the temporal ordering. The subject was instructed to order his response in terms of spatial sequence. A third group saw both irrelevant temporal presentation and varied absolute position of items from trial to trial. The task was first to reproduce a cued starting item, then the consistent spatial arrangement toward the right and then to recycle from the left to complete the sequence. The results revealed that, for both trigram and consonant stimuli, the group with only relative-position cues took about 51% longer to learn to a criterion of one errorless trial than did either of the other two groups. The serial position functions in terms of required responding sequences showed the typical bowed result, with the last-learned items appearing on the average about Positions Six and Seven. Thus, absolute position was as effective as temporal position for a learning cue. Slamecka emphasized the importance of the output order on serial position curves as follows:

> The obtained primacy and recency effects correspond to the prescribed *output* orders, and not to the input orders, which were quite different. Were order of arrival the determining factor, the curves would have different shapes entirely. Such an observation is possible only when input and output orders are experimentally separated as they were here, and it suggests that the characteristic form of serial position curves is given to them solely by the output requirements of the task (1967, p. 65).

Slamecka (1967) goes on to point out that, since absolute position cues alone could promote serial learning, then the fundamental process of serial learning seems to be position learning. He concludes that his results show the inadequacy of a memory model such as that of Conrad (1965), which assumes that items are stored in temporal order and must be retrieved in the same order—at least for the case of repeated trials.

Heslip (1969b) studied the effects of input condition using Slamecka's (1967) general design. One group of subjects was given ten-item consonant series at a constant location in a memory drum in the same temporal sequence to be used in subsequent serial recall. Items were to be recalled left-to-right on a recall slip. For a second group, items were presented at ten horizontal spatial positions, but in a haphazard temporal sequence relative to the required left-to-right spatial ordering of both input and output. The results of the two groups with temporal input paralleling output order were identical both in terms of trials to criterion and shapes of serial position curves. But the remaining group, with inconsistent temporal input and output, took much longer to learn, and the serial-position curve showed much less of a primacy (or left-superiority) effect. The greater symmetry of this curve, Heslip attributed to less consistency in the positional strategies among this group that was forced to learn on the basis of position cues only. The subjects with paralleling temporal input and recall information apparently consistently used the temporal ordering in their strategy of learning.

Heslip and Engelbrecht (1969) attempted to resolve the discrepancy between the Slamecka (1967) and the Heslip (1969b) results by replicating both studies. Their results did replicate Heslip's earlier finding of relative superiority in recall for temporal input cues corresponding to temporal output cues. Contrary to Slamecka's earlier results, they obtained this same result even when using his procedure.

These effects of input and output bases of encoding suggest that the subject's strategies of encoding strongly influence which items of a multiple-element array are learned first or better. Miller (1963) makes this point with respect to the elementary perceiver and memorizer (EPAM) model of Feigenbaum and Simon (1962, 1963). This model describes a strategy of acquisition of the items within a series in terms of the order of their acquisition. Miller argues:

> The implication of EPAM I is that a serial position curve does not reflect any deep or fundamental properties of human memory, but is a simple consequence of the strategy most people will adopt when confronted with this particular problem (p. 326).

In other words—the terminology of this book—the serial-position curve is the result of paralearning factors.

THE PROCESSES

The theoretical implications of the general information-processing approach can be summarized at two levels. These correspond, respectively, to what Feigenbaum and Simon (1962) have called microprocess and macroprocess. First, the suggested mechanisms can be arranged in a machinelike model, giving primarily a molar, or macroprocess, description of them. The machine model follows the lines suggested by, for example, Broadbent (1958), Bryden (1967), Atkinson and Shiffrin (1968a, b), Shiffrin and Atkinson (1969), Sperling (1967), Mandler (1967a), and Masani (1967).

The mechanisms correspond closely to my previous description (Harcum, 1967b), although the earlier paper concentrated more on describing the processes than on speculating about the specific mechanisms. The information-translation conception (Harcum, 1967b) is essentially a modification of the macroprocess postulates of Feingenbaum and Simon (1962).

Molecular Level

Some speculations about what the mechanisms might represent at the molecular level will be discussed briefly in Chapter 11. In that final chapter some effort will be made to point out similarities of the present argument to some of the more detailed quantitative approaches to memory for multiple-element stimuli as represented in Norman (1970). In particular, a memory-search model, such as the one by Shiffrin (1970), exhibits several points of similarity to the present argument.

Macroprocesses

The information-translation approach (Harcum, 1967b) is best illustrated by Lashley's (1951) example of the translation of languages. A sensory input is first translated into the subject's conceptual or coding system. The information is then translated into a language that is appropriate to the required responding system, or into the subject's preferred method of response. This translation process is compatible with the stimulus and response variables; it it best conceived as a strategy of organizing information for reduction into memory. The general outline of the theory is sketched in Figure 5-1. The vertical dimension of the table corresponds roughly to the temporal interval between stimulus input at t_1 and the overt response at t_7. The processes that have been inferred as intervening in the reproduction of multiple elements include element differentiation and organization, selective analysis of persisting traces, and the idiosyncratic strategy for codifying the information for storage in memory. These are not discrete, either in terms of temporal relations or in function.

As Harcum (1967b) points out, this theoretical analysis is most easily applied to the pattern-perception task and to the single trial of serial learning. In a sense, it conceives of the pattern-perception task as a miniature process of serial learning or, alternatively, of the serial-learning task as a perception and reproduction of a temporal and/or spatial pattern of multiple elements. Obviously, both tasks potentially can involve both intake (perceptual) and output (memory) processes, as well as central codification and organizational mechanisms. The immediate memory for a string of words, letters, or digits is influenced by the subject's memory for specific items as well as structural rules derived from preceding strings in the experimental session (e.g., Hebb, 1961; Keppel & Underwood, 1962b; Wilkes, 1972). Similarly, serial learning is strongly influenced by differentiability among items that affects attentional-perceptual factors (e.g., Wishner, Shipley & Hurvich, 1957; Coppage & Harcum, 1967). Finally, both tasks are strongly influenced by the verbal and other habits of organization that the subject brings with him to the experimental situation (e.g., Guilford, 1927; Simpson, 1965, 1967).

Mandler (1967a, p. 23), proposes a model for information processing that is quite similar and compatible with the information conception

TABLE 1

A Theoretical Description of the
Processes in Serial Learning
and Pattern Perception

t_1: STIMULUS

t_2: Differentation

(Configuration, type, location, visual
capacity, context)

t_3: Intrinsic Organization

(Spatial primacy, temporal primacy,
configuration)

t_4: Selection

(Instructions, habits, stimulus characteristics,
response configuration, number of scans)

t_5: Codification

(Meaning, temporal concepts, spatial concepts, central state, personal schemata)

t_6: Response Selection

(Compatibility, knowledge of
responding order, syntax)

t_7: RESPONSE

Figure 5-1   Theoretical mechanisms underlying the serial-position effect, from Harcum
(1967b). Copyright © (1967) by the American Psychological Association. Reprinted by permission.

proposed by Harcum (1967b), as well as the model for sequential behavior proposed by Bryden (1967) and, as Mandler points out, with many
other models. He describes how the processing of language information
requires two sets of elements: (1) a set of rules, transformations, or
programs; and (2) a set of units or building blocks. Mandler's (1967a)
model is illustrated in Figure 5-2. Mandler is careful to point out that

his model is merely a way to conceptualize the information processing system, given as a convenient aid to memory. Mandler's model includes, between input and output, three processing programs: one for stimulus selection, one for coding the material, and one for selecting an output routine. The operating program is similar to Shiffrin's (1970) "executive decision process," to Neisser's (1967) "executive," to Lashley's (1951) concept of analysis at a different level. This similarity of ideas illustrates the futility of arguing about small details about the language or drawings of a model. The present conception does not carry the boxlike conception too far. Craik (1971) favors making a distinction between primary memory and secondary memory, but concludes:

> The present tendency today seems to be away from mechanistic models with rigid boxes or stores and towards a flexible system with a large part played by such optional control processes as attention, rehearsal, and strategies (p. 236).

The output program controls the "accessibility" or "retrieval" of the coded information, but not its "availability." Of these output programs, Mandler lists three types: associative cues, general accessibility rules, and generative rules. The associative rules seem to be more relevant to the response-learning phase of acquisition rather than the hookup phase. The associations are primarily involved in interference and unlearning.

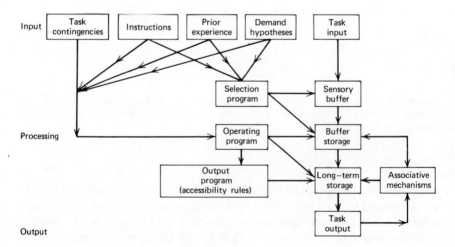

Figure 5-2   General theoretical model proposed by Mandler (1967a). Reprinted by permission of the publisher.

Harcum and Coppage (1969) elaborated the translation hypothesis to account for the distribution of errors in serial learning. The evidence indicates that the acquisition of patterns of multiple elements is a higher-order analysis of the persisting traces. This must be accomplished in some order of elements. Thus, a basic task is to study the serial order of behavior. Since any basis of differentiation within the stimulus array could influence the order of analysis of items, the important problem is to discover what determines which element will be processed first. This element serves as the reference point, or anchor, for the subsequent processes.

The information-translation hypothesis as it applies to the theoretical foundation for the serial-position effect is illustrated in Figure 5-3. The abscissa represents serial position of the items, and the ordinate represents the distinctiveness of individual items in the units suggested by Murdock (1960). One unit of distinctiveness is defined as equivalent to one degree of difference in the ordinal position between any two items. The total positional distinctiveness of an item is determined by the sum of its various degrees of remoteness from each of the other items in the series. The distinctiveness of an item is assumed to be positively correlated with the ease of learning.

The two factors illustrated in Figure 5-3 obviously account for the main features of the serial-position curve. These have been consistently found as components of the overall curve. For example, Voss (1956) obtained both linear (asymmetrical) and quadratic (bowing) trends in

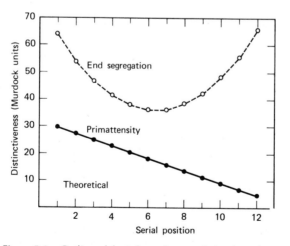

Figure 5-3   Outline of the information-translation hypothesis.

error performance for temporal serial positions for both motor and verbal sequences of 8, 12, 16, 20 and 24 items. He argued that the linear trend was perhaps related to rehearsal from the beginning and the bowing to task difficulty. The interpretation in Figure 5-3 is quite similar. The distinctiveness or "end segregation" function reflects increased difficulty of discriminating the items as they are more distant from the ends of the series. The "primattensity" function represents the subject's tendency to learn the temporally first items first. A third basis for the selection of a strategy for serial learning cannot be illustrated in Figure 5-3, because its effect does not consistently favor some positions over others. It consists of unsystematic biases among items resulting from differences in "learnability" of individual items. This learnability is not totally intrinsic to the item, of course, but depends also upon such characteristics of the learner as verbal experience and cognitive-perceptual style.

END SEGREGATION

The upper curve in Figure 5-3 represents the relative degrees of total distinctiveness of items due to their saliency with respect to the ends of the series. The end items show greater distinctiveness, because they include larger degrees of remoteness from certain items than is possible for those items that are nearer the middle of the list. The hypothesis states that the relative distinctiveness of items provides a basis for the subject to select a cognitively first item more easily, as part of a strategy that determines the sequence for acquisition of items.

Kausler and Trapp (1963), in a supplement to an earlier study (Kausler & Trapp, 1962), added a control group in order to test the hypothesis that the addition of "irrelevant" cues to an eight-item serial list aided learning because of the added distinctiveness to individual items. The addition of the irrelevant cues hindered learning, however. Presumably this was due to the subjects' distraction by attention to the irrelevant cues. Kausler and Trapp reported a significant effect of cue condition on "percent scores" at the various serial positions, but did not state which condition yielded fewest errors in learning. These scores apparently represented the percentage of the total number of correct responses at each position and thus did not describe the absolute performance. Presumably the no-cue condition was best on this measure also. Since the serial position curve was flatter over the middle serial positions, presumably the added distinctiveness was more important for items about the middle of the series. The serial-position curve for the list without irrelevant cues was more asymmetrical, suggesting a greater consistency for beginning-to-end learning when only the intrinsic (position) cues are present. This result would be consistent with the argument for superior learning where there was less ambiguity about the most effective strategy for the order of learning the items.

Kayson and Winnick (1974) found that, for low-association trigrams, instructions to learn position cues were more effective in serial recall than instructions to learn sequence. For high-association trigrams the type of instructions was not important. Moreover, the bowing in the curve was more pronounced for position-learning strategies and for low-association stimuli.

The results of Cogan and Ericksen (Young, 1968), cited in Chapter 3 (Figure 3-1), revealed a greater asymmetry of serial position curves as the frequency of substitution of filler material for selected items on certain trials increased. This was interpreted, on the basis of the argument proposed by Harcum and Coppage (1965b), to mean that the subjects were forced to rely more on position cues for the serial learning. These differences in the asymmetry of these serial-position curves strikes me as being very important theoretically. The reason for this is that the theories of the serial-position effect have experienced little difficulty in accounting for the bow in the curve, but real problems in accounting for its asymmetry. The asymmetry of the serial-position curve has become a useful dependent variable in deriving and testing theoretical predictions (Jensen, 1962c; Harcum & Coppage, 1965b; Glanzer, 1966, 1968; Harcum, 1967a, 1970a).

Since the greater asymmetry in Figure 3-1 is associated with position learning, it follows that the factors that produce asymmetry, as well as the one that determines the bowing, are of greater relative importance when the subject is using a position-learning strategy. It is more important then for him to establish an anchor for the subsequent organization of the series. Each substitute member therefore becomes less useful as an anchor, and the subjects come to use the first-item position more consistently. Thus, the distribution of errors becomes more skewed for the reasons Harcum and Coppage (1965b) suggest; for each subject the order to acquisition is more likely to begin with the temporally first item as an anchor, and the remaining items are more likely to be added in a sequence that corresponds to the temporal order of presentation.

PRIMATTENSITY

This second dimension of distinctiveness, which is related to position, is illustrated by the lower function in Figure 5-3. It refers to the saliency of items resulting from the direction of the subject's effort in selecting the items at one end of the series to be learned before those at the opposite end. Thus, the temporally first item is assumed to be more distinctive because of the subject's greater tendency to select that item as cognitively the first item in the series. This factor is labeled primatten-sity from "prime," meaning first, and "attensity," meaning the subjective intensity or impact of a stimulus due to the degree of attention given to it (Dallenbach, 1923).

Restle's (1962) model for the learning of cues is consistent with the present point of view. His strategy-sampling model is similar to Estes' (1959) stimulus-sampling model. This concept of a selection of a starting point for the information processing has been emphasized previously in the perceptual task by Harcum (1957a, b), Fudin (1969), and White (1970). Harcum (1957a, b) emphasizes the left-right aspects of the spatial task, as well as the saliency of reference points (Harcum, 1970b). White (1970) proposes that the subject has a tendency to begin his analysis with the elements that produce a stronger trace—ordinarily those closer to fixation. In the case of immediate memory, Hintzman, Block, and Summers (1973) suggest that the "memory strain" increases throughout a given presentation of a list but is lost when the list is to begin again. Jensen (1962a) and many others emphasize the importance of temporal primacy in the serial-learning task.

After the most primattensive item is learned, the remaining items then are likely to be processed in the same sequence as the temporal sequence of presentation. The slope of the function for this effort caused by the subject's set to learn the temporally first items first is probably relatively independent of the degree of bowing in the element-position curve. In Figure 5-3, this slope is arbitrarily adjusted to show a differ-ence between most- and least-distinctive items that is about equal to this difference on the position-distinctiveness curve. Whereas the first component—namely, confusion among syllables—produces a bowed function of increasing difficulty with increasing remoteness of the item from the first and last syllables in the series, the second component—a tendency for the subject to select the items at the beginning of the series to be learned first—produces an increasing number of errors for sylla-bles later in the series. Therefore, if the subject learns faster at the beginning of the list, it is because he is set to learn from the beginning. Such a concept explains why appearance early in a series (primacy) is more beneficial than appearance late in the series (finalcy).

PERSONAL STRATEGY

Since the personal strategies are obviously idiosyncratic to the various subjects, in a properly controlled experiment they would appear at dif-ferent positions. These effects create irregularity in the serial-position curves for individual subjects, but they cancel across subjects, because the subjects are frequently learning different lists, of course, and different subjects see different items as more meaningful. Every veteran researcher in verbal learning has had experience with this phenomenon, usually to his sorrow. An example from my own experience was the use of the so-called nonsense syllable "LUD," which has an associative rating of 58% on Archer's (1960) evaluation. Unfortunately for my experiment, this trigram happens to be the usual abbreviation used at my institution to refer to Ludwell Hall—a dormitory for women. Consequently, the meaningfulness was apparently considerably higher than the expectations based on Archer's data. This, incidentally, is an argument for using "local norms."

When this mechanism of personal attention consistently favors one serial position, as in the above example, it produces what is typically referred to as an "isolation effect" (von Restorff, 1933). To produce this effect, one item is made perceptually or cognitively distinctive by virtually any means. The critical operation seems to be whether or not the experimenter is able to draw the subject's attention to the item (Saltz & Newman, 1959; Coppage & Harcum, 1967).

SPECIFIC EVIDENCE

In his recent book, Kausler (1974) noted that more evidence was needed for the Jensen (1962a) strategy hypothesis. He does not cite all of the available evidence, however, some of which is, in my judgement, rather convincing. Some of the evidence that was obtained specifically to test the Jensen hypothesis will be described now.

Analysis of Error Types

The hypothesis that the bow in the serial-position curve was due to associative interference or confusion, and the asymmetry due to another factor, may be tested by examination of different types of errors. This approach was used by Deese and Kresse (1952).

DEESE-KRESSE STUDY

Deese and Kresse (1952) described the overall distribution of errors in learning 12 nonsense syllables in terms of three different types of component error. The first of these were errors resulting from subjects' failures to emit a response before the succeeding syllable appeared. The second and third categories of errors were the so-called intralist intrusions and extralist intrusions, respectively. In one experiment Deese and Kresse presented CVC trigrams at a fixed rate of 4 seconds, while in two other experiments, they used CVC and CCC (three consonant) trigrams with unpaced presentation. In the unpaced condition the subject was permitted an unlimited amount of time to anticipate each syllable. The unpaced presentation was employed in an attempt to increase the small proportion of errors of commission that had been obtained with paced presentation. Intruding errors would undoubtedly often replace omission errors if the subject had sufficient time to make the overt response. The experimenters believed that the additional information about these potential overt intrusions would bring out more clearly the contribution of the errors of commission to the overall serial-position curve of learning.

Deese and Kresse reported virtually symmetrical distributions of intralist intrusions, with fewest errors for the items at the beginning and end of the series. This result, which occurred for both paced and unpaced presentation of the syllables, they attributed to associative interference among the syllables within the list. This is empirical evidence for the associative interference interpretation, although other writers (e.g., Slamecka, 1964) have attributed the intrusions to position confusion (mislocation) rather than to remote associative bonds.

Deese and Kresse, (1952) concluded that the extralist intrusions, on the other hand, were not distributed differentially among the syllable positions, and thus did not contribute to serial-position effects. Therefore, the type of error of most relevance to the explanation of the skewness of the serial-position effect seemed to be the failures to respond.

Both the overall frequency and the distribution of the failures to respond among serial positions were different for paced and for unpaced presentation. With paced presentation, failures to respond approximated a characteristic serial-position curve—having greater asymmetry among positions than the distribution of intralist intrusions. With unpaced presentation the total number of failures to respond was smaller, as anticipated. The distribution of these errors showed an increase through the first half of the list and then no consistent trend toward change over the later items. Deese and Kresse thought that this distribution of failures to respond with unpaced presentation, apparently the source of the asymmetry in the total curve, was related either to response-induced inhibition or to immediate-memory span.

WILSON-HARTMAN STUDY

The conditions of Deese and Kresse were duplicated by Wilson and Hartman (1960), who used with 12-syllable lists both the unpaced and the 4-second paced presentation, as well as an 8-second rate of presentation. They concluded that all three conditions of presentation produced symmetrical curves of "remote" errors (i.e., intralist intrusions). Wilson and Hartman (1960) found that the failures to respond in their study produced "bowed curves for all rates of presentation although this effect was least pronounced under the unpaced condition" (p. 217). That is, the failures to respond reached a maximum and then decreased toward the end of the list, for unpaced presentation as well as for both conditions of paced presentation.

HARCUM-COPPAGE STUDY

Harcum and Coppage (1969) replicated the Deese-Kresse design with paced and unpaced lists of 12 trigrams and also with 8- and 16-syllable lists. The main question was whether or not an analysis of the different types of errors supports the hypothesis that the serial-position curve results from the subjects' strategies of acquiring items in consistent order (Jensen, 1962a; Harcum & Coppage, 1965b; Coppage & Harcum, 1967). Deese and Kresse's conditions were closely duplicated, using, however, CVC trigrams only and different lengths of lists. Each subject first learned a six-syllable practice list, which was composed of trigrams having no combination of letters in common with any experimental list. The subject was then assigned to one of seven subject groups. Six of the groups learned different 8-, 12-, or 16-item lists under either paced or unpaced presentation. The seventh group of subjects learned the 12-syllable list, but with paced and unpaced presentation on alternate trials. The purpose of this condition was to permit a more direct assessment of the longer response time per se that was available under the unpaced condition. The authors wanted to determine whether the previous difference in results for these two conditions reflected only the greater opportunity for an overt error under the unpaced condition because of the longer time for responding.

Although the various categories of errors are not as distinct as would appear at first consideration, the three general categories of Deese and Kresse (1952) could be distinguished meaningfully. Errors were placed in a failure-to-respond (FTR) category only if they were merely errors of omission. If the subject made just a partial response, an error of failure to respond was scored only if the letters that he said were correct both with respect to item position within the series and to ordinal position within the particular syllable. The intralist intrusion (ILI) errors consisted of incorrect overt responses that could be attributed with confidence to intrusions of syllables that would have been correct at some other position within the series. For such an intrusion to be scored, at least two letters of a syllable that would have been correct elsewhere in the series had to be reproduced correctly with respect to their positions within that syllable. The extralist intrusion (ELI) category of errors consisted of those overt errors that could not be assigned with confidence to intrusions of syllables from other positions within the experimental list. It included errors in which either the first or last consonant would have been correct at some other position within the list, intrusions from the practice list, and corruptions of correct or incorrect syllables. Logically, single-letter responses that would have been correct at other positions could be included in the intralist intrusion category of errors, as intrusions of responses that were less well learned, or in the extralist category, as coincidental correspondences of initial and final letters with other syllables. Since these data appeared empirically more like the extralist intrusion data, they were considered as extralist intrusions in the further analyses of the data.

The results for the different types of errors for the various groups of subjects are shown in Figure 5-4 in which each ordinate represents the mean log errors (plus a constant of 1 to avoid zeros) for errors within a given category for all subjects. The abscissa represents the serial position. In view of the equivalence of the serial-position curves of total errors, along with the mechanical changes of component curves with changes in pacing rate (Harcum & Coppage, 1969), the results are combined in Figure 5-4 for the paced and unpaced conditions.

The significance of serial-position effects was assessed by evaluating in the analysis of variance the linear, quadratic, and cubic orthogonal components of the differences among serial positions (Hays, 1963). A significant linear component, indicating the predicted linear relationship between serial position and errors of reproduction, implies an asymmetry in the distribution of errors. A mechanism that could produce such an effect would be a progressive change in the distribution of effort for the items from beginning to end of the list, as would be implied by a strategy of subjects to learn the items from the beginning of the series—namely, a primattensity effect as in Figure 5-3. A significant quadratic component, on the other hand, would indicate a parabolic relationship between errors and serial position, which would be symmetrical about the central items. Such a factor, if it reflects poorer performance for the syllables at the center of the series, would imply a mechanism of location confusability or associative interference, such as the distinctness factor proposed by Murdock (1960) and others—such as the end-segregation factor described in Figure 5-3. A cubic trend reflects an inflection in the curve, with both a maximum and minimum, which would not be easy to interpret, probably representing some complex in-

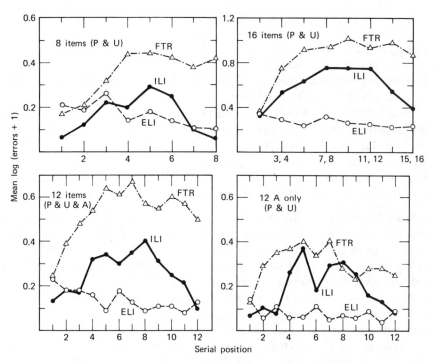

Figure 5-4   Different types of errors per serial position for lists of different lengths, after Harcum and Coppage (1969). Copyright© (1969) by the American Psychological Association. Reprinted by permission.

teraction. Errors in the different categories did contribute differentially to the sums of errors at different positions.

Extralist Intrusions.   The extralist intrusions were more numerous at the beginning of the series than at the end for both paced and unpaced presentations, and for each length of a list, as can be seen in Figure 5-4. This is documented by the significant linear components of position. Thus, the asymmetry of the total curves is produced by the tendency of the subject to make more overt responses at the positions that appear earlier in the series. Since extralist intrusions presumably do not originate from a particular serial position within the list, these errors indicate primattensity—the subject's strategy of attempting to learn first the syllables at the temporal beginning of the series. Although the downward trend of extralist intrusions across serial position was contrary to the conclusion of Deese and Kresse (1952), Harcum and Coppage (1969) concluded, from a reexamination of the Deese and Kresse data, that it did indicate a general downward trend across serial positions with unpaced presentations of both the CVC and CCC trigrams. They also found some positive evidence from the comparable data of Wilson and Hartman (1960). This paradoxical result, which seems to go in the wrong direction, will be interpreted later.

Murdock (1968) found, using position and sequential probes in short-term memory, that beta was greater at the early positions, decreasing and leveling off at about 1.0 for the later positions. This indicated a more relaxed criterion for responding at the beginning of the series. On the other hand, the sensitivity measure, d', showed the typical serial-position curve, with greater recency than primacy effects.

Intralist Intrusions.   The intralist intrusions illustrate the significant quadratic component, which is attributed to element distinctiveness. This is responsible for the bowing of the curve, of course. Although in Figure 5-4 both distributions of intralist intrusions are approximately symmetrical for the completely paced and unpaced series, Harcum and Coppage (1969) pointed out that there were somewhat more errors at the end of the series for the unpaced condition and a few more errors at the beginning of the paced series. This finding of asymmetries in the distributions of intralist intrusions was contrary to the conclusions of both Deese and Kresse (1952) and Wilson and Hartman (1960). However, a specific examination of the data of both previous studies for evidence of this effect did indicate correspondence with the Harcum and Coppage (1969) results. In the Deese and Kresse data there were slightly more intralist intrusions for the last half of the series in both unpaced experiments and the reverse of this for the paced list. The Wilson and Hartman data also revealed small asymmetries that were not in the same direction for each condition of presentation.

The effect of an asymmetry in the distribution of intralist intruding errors was small but consistent. This result did not reflect merely the necessary inverse relationship between failures to respond and intralist intrusions. With completely paced presentation, failures to respond increased at the beginning of the series, but so did the intralist intrusions. Therefore, Harcum and Coppage (1969) concluded that something more than a mere general shift of errors out of the category of failure to respond and into the category of intralist intrusions occurs when presentation is changed from paced to unpaced. Since the subjects take more trials to learn the paced list, the greater number of errors at the beginning of the series is only relative. However, it does emphasize the importance of the decrease for the last half of the series, in which the subjects in fact show a reduction of the total number of overt errors in spite of the increase in trials. One interpretation of this is that the subjects are accumulating more response-induced inhibition in the paced presentation, since there is less chance for the inhibition to dissipate between presentations of the subsequent syllables. In any case, the curves of intralist intrusions are relatively symmetrical.

Conclusions.   The frequencies of intralist intrusions and extralist intrusions were about equal for the completely paced and unpaced conditions for the groups of subjects learning the 12-item lists under the paced conditions (12P), and under the unpaced conditions (12U), respectively. Thus, the primary difference in total errors between paced and unpaced conditions was due to the differences in failures to respond, particularly for items in the last half of the series. The analysis of variance for failures to respond indicated three significant orthogonal components of position. Thus, there was evidence for both the effect of strategy (linear component), and the effect of syllable distinctiveness (quadratic component). There were also significant interactions of the linear and cubic components with rate of presentation. This was consistent with the results of Deese and Kresse (1952) in that the paced and unpaced conditions yielded different distributions of failures to respond. Moreover, the significant interaction of cubic component of position with the pacing condition apparently reflected the flattening of the failures-to-respond curve at the end of the series with unpaced presentation. Since the frequency of failures to respond is greatly reduced at those positions that revealed maximum errors with paced presentation, and also the variability among data points is greater, the determination of the exact shape of the curve in this region is difficult. Harcum and Coppage (1969) concluded that Deese and Kresse (1952) were correct in attributing the shape of failure-to-respond curves with paced and unpaced presentation to differential effects of task-induced inhibition. The paced condition showed greater effects of such inhibition through increasing failures to respond, particularly for the items near the ends of the series. On the other hand, the flattening of the distribution of failures to respond over the later items with unpaced presentation was due to the relative absence of inhibition over the last half of the series, causing a decrease in failures to respond.

The linear component of position for extra-list errors, which was attributed to the subject's consistent tendencies toward learning from the beginning of the list, seems paradoxical, because it represents an inverse causal relation between effort and errors. In reality, however, the emergence of overt errors is one indicator that the subject is making progress in learning. Since the extralist intrusions are the first to intrude, occurring before the subject has learned the population of items very well, they are the ones that he makes while learning the items at the beginning of the list. Later, after the subject has learned the items but not their locations, the number of overt errors increases, but those are now intralist intrusions, which are distributed according to position distinctiveness. This tendency seems to be more pronounced for paced series. One or both of two possible mechanisms could account for this result: (1) the same response-induced inhibition that decreased the relative number of intralist intrusions at the end of the series, and (2) the greater consistency of effort tied to the sheer position of syllables in the case of paced series. Probably both factors are responsible, because both the main effects of the linear component, and the interaction of linear component with pacing, were shown to be significant effects in particular instances.

Deese and Kresse started from the premise that the distribution of total errors in serial learning could be explained as a summation of three components, which would reveal the mechanisms underlying the overall learning process. The reverse of this approach would appear to be more fruitful, however. The mechanisms that determine whether an error will be one of omission or commission are not basic to the overall shape of the serial-position curve. Specifically, a mechanism such as response-induced inhibition or stimulus satiation influences the category of the subject's erroneous response, but it is not of major importance in the process of serial learning per se. On the other hand, a theory about the processes of serial learning has been tested by applying it in an attempt to explain the distribution of component errors.

Thus, both the errors of omission and the errors of commission are bowed because of the element-differentiation factor. The skew in the two distributions is different because of the necessary inverse relation between the errors of omission and commission. The extralist intrusions are greater at the beginning of the list because of the unequal distribution of effort, inducing the opposite skew in the distribution of failures to respond. The failure-to-respond data reflect the significant linear and quadratic components, which are here assumed to be the primary factors contributing to the serial-position effect for total errors. Therefore, of the three categories of error, the failures to respond are the most characteristic of the serial-position phenomenon, showing in each case both linear and quadratic components of position, which is most similar to the results for total errors. The distribution of failures to respond is caused by the same basic factors that produce the intruding errors. They directly correspond to the distribution of intralist intrusions (quadratic component), and they are inversely related to the extralist intrusions (linear component).

Harcum and Coppage (1969) pointed out that their failures-to-respond curve was a bit more skewed than the distribution of intralist intrusions for the unpaced condition because of the inverse contingency with the tendency to make the overt response, as inferred from the distribution of extralist intrusions. The downward trend of the extralist intrusions across the serial positions meant that, of necessity, there must be a bias toward relatively fewer failures to respond at the beginning, and more at the end, than for the intralist intrusions. Presumably the presence of extralist intrusions does not greatly reduce the number of intralist intrusions. With unpaced presentation the subject would presumably give the intralist response overtly if that response were at all available to him.

The analyses of the component errors within the distribution of total errors among serial positions support interpretations in terms of the subject's strategy for processing the individual items (Jensen, 1962a; Coppage & Harcum, 1967). Since the strategy is not basically different for completely paced or unpaced series, the general shapes of the curves of total errors are not greatly different. As expected, the paced conditions produced more total errors than the corresponding unpaced conditions, primarily because of the greater number of failures to respond under the paced condition. Under paced presentation the subject obviously did not have as much time to make those responses that were weaker. Since the unpaced condition adds time between the appearances of successive stimuli, it facilitates dissipation of stimulus-induced or response-induced inhibition from earlier items before the later items are to be reproduced. Significant interactions of pacing-rate and error category were obtained for the 12-, 8-, and 16-item lists. Since this result also appeared for the comparison with the group learning 12-item alternating paced and unpaced trials, it must be attributed at least in part to the additional time per se for the subject to respond in the unpaced conditions.

The sums of all errors per syllable, expressed as a percentage of the totals of errors for each condition, revealed similar shapes between each set of curves for paced and unpaced presentations. The similarity of the serial-position curves of total errors for both pacing conditions corroborated the results of Deese and Kresse (1952) and Wilson and Hartman (1960). This congruence of the total curves is paradoxical in view of the obtained differences between paced and unpaced results for failures to respond and intralist intrusions. The curves of paced presentation are more regular, because the strategy of acquiring syllables is determined more by the structure of the list. With unpaced presentation the associability of the individual syllables has greater importance in the establishment of a strategy. The shapes of the component curves are different for paced and unpaced presentations because of differences in the effects of the strengths of stimulus traces and the amount of response-induced inhibition for the items appearing later in the series. Thus, the types of errors may change with changes in pacing, but the change does not greatly influence the course of learning, except to allow for a greater opportunity for idiosyncratic bases to play a role in the order in which items are acquired. The serial-position effects result from the consistency of the subjects tending to use sheer serial position as a basis for this strategy of acquisition.

Cognitive Anchoring

It is difficult to distinguish between the cognitive selection of an anchor point for serial acquisition and an intrinsic difference in learnability caused by item distinctiveness when the usual method of serial anticipation with larger intertrial interval is used. With this method, the serial-position curve appears after only a single trial (Robinson & Brown, 1926), indicating very early learning for the end items. Voss (1969), using the standard serial anticipation procedure, concluded that the subjects could correctly localize the end items about as soon as the identity of these items was learned. Therefore, the positional cue provided by the temporal space adjacent to the end items causes such rapid learning that it is difficult to analyze the critical basis of the "learnability" of those items.

If the open space adjacent to the end items is omitted, as in the method of continuous presentation (Mitchell, 1933a), then the acquisition of the end items is sufficiently slowed to permit a stage analysis. Such an analysis was performed by Harcum and Coppage (1965a) and Harcum, Pschirrer, and Coppage (1968). The results of Harcum and Coppage's analysis are shown in Figure 5-5, which presents the percentage of the total errors per each serial position during the first and last quarters of the total acquisition process. The critical result of this analysis is the virtual absence of a serial-position effect during the first several trials of learning. Whereas any direct effect of the temporal space—the absence of input or output interference—before the first item is maximal on the very first trial, the marked primacy effect appears only later.

The Harcum et al. (1968) data show a similar result. These analyses therefore both prove crucially, it seems to me, that the so-called primacy effect is not directly due to the fact that the item is first and therefore not preceded by another item. The effect is caused by a cognitive

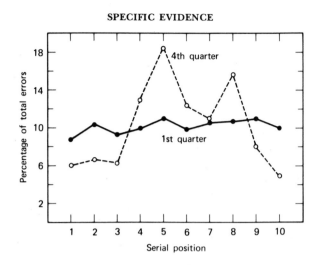

Figure 5-5   Percentages of errors per syllable position in first and fourth quarters of learning, from Harcum and Coppage (1965a). Reprinted by permission of the publisher.

appreciation—coding—of the item as the first in the series, because of its unique first appearance. This is most powerful evidence for the cognitive strategy hypothesis that has been overlooked by Kausler (1974), and by other writers as well (e.g., Farwell & Vitz, 1971).

Order of Learning

Harcum and Coppage (1969) also presented their data plotted a different way, as shown in Figure 5-6. This way of looking at serial-learning results was first suggested by Jensen (1962a). The abscissa represents the rank order of items from low to high in total errors across subjects, expressed as a percentage of the errors across all syllable positions. Therefore, the differences between paced and unpaced presentation in terms of overall totals of errors do not mask the comparisons. Each panel in the figure represents different comparisons of paced and unpaced series. The 12-item data are given in the lower-left panel and reveal one straight line as a satisfactory visual fit to the paced and unpaced data. The same straight line is reproduced with apparent success in the lower-right panel to describe the results for the alternation of paced and unpaced trials with 12-syllable lists.

Whereas one straight line describes the 12-item results, apparently two straight lines are needed to describe the data for the 8-item and

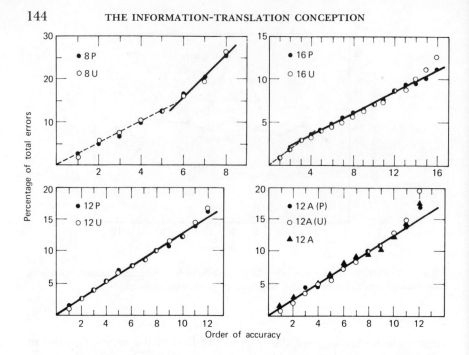

Figure 5-6   Jensen plots of percentage errors under different pacing conditions and lengths of list, from Harcum and Coppage (1969). Copyright © (1969) by the American Psychological Association. Reprinted by permission.

the 16-item series. The 8-item data in the upper-left panel of Figure 5-5 show a break in the function at about the sixth position, with a steeper slope after that point. This break is produced by the fact that the functions of some subjects intersected the abscissa to the right of the origin. This by definition is the effect of a memory span of some finite length.

Although only the 8-item lists show evidence for a memory span in the order-of-learning plots of Figure 5-5, defined as an intersection of the data curve with the abscissa to the right of zero, there was no clear evidence for such spans in the results plotted according to serial-position in Figure 5-4. Moreover, the order-of-learning curves for the paced and unpaced 8-item conditions, showing evidence for a span for some subjects, are virtually identical, but the distributions of errors among serial positions were clearly different. Although there were instances in which some subjects reproduced items correctly on the first trial, these items were frequently not the first items in the list. Therefore, this evidence also argues against the interpretation in terms of memory span for the asymmetry of the serial-position function.

Although the 16-item data may also require a two-line fit, the curve of steeper slope comes at the beginning of the learning process. The result is like that of Harcum and Coppage (1965b) for learning 10-item series before practice. Harcum and Coppage attributed this result to difficulty of the subjects in forming an anchor for the learning. This result is effectively the exact opposite to that predicted from the memory-span argument (e.g., Jensen, 1962a) and thus refutes it.

If a span of memory caused the asymmetry of the serial-position curve, the curve should be more skewed for the unpaced presentation, because the task should be easier. In addition to producing more errors, the paced conditions required more trials to criterion. The relative advantage of unpaced presentation increases slightly as the list becomes longer, and the absolute gain increases substantially. Thus, pacing probably does not affect the shape of total error curves, although it does influence the difficulty of the task and the subject's span of memory.

The strategy argument has been related to the issue of one-trial learning (Jensen, 1963). If the subject learns nothing about, for example, the middle items during the first several trials, it would be most powerful evidence for the strategy interpretation. This approach was used by Bolles (1959), who tested the hypothesis that the subject does not learn the middle items of a serial list until the beginning and end items have been learned. Approximately a third of the way through the learning of a list of nine syllables, he interchanged the fourth and sixth items. The learning was not different for such lists compared to unchanged lists, in terms of errors or trials to various criteria. In a second similar experiment, again the fourth and sixth syllables were interchanged, or these items were replaced with new items. Again there was no significant difference between either experimental condition and the control condition. Actually there were slightly fewer errors toward the end of the list for both changed lists, presumably because of enhanced attention to those items when they were changed. Individual protocols indicated that sometimes the new item was learned even after a single appearance.

Although Bolles (1959) used a within-subjects design, he does not give any indication of what instructions were given to the subjects. He does report, however, that there was no evidence that any subject deliberately chose a strategy of avoiding the learning of the middle items before the change. Even so, this would not contribute to a difference between experimental and control subjects. Actually about a third of the time the subject had already learned the fourth item prior to the change. This contributes to the suspicion that the learning of the changed portion of the list was actually faster than the learning of control items.

A study similar to that of Bolles (1959) was performed by Bean and McCroskery (1973), with the same goal in mind. Using serial-anticipation learning of eight nonsense syllables, they interchanged the middle two or middle four items for experimental subjects after either four or eight trials. Although learning performance after the switch was not significantly inferior for the experimental subjects, it was consistently worse. Although the authors favor a nonassociative interpretation of these results, the data can also be fitted into a two-stage argument (for example, Underwood & Schulz, 1960). The problem for interpretation is to know how far along in the learning process a subject has proceeded before a switch is made. Undoubtedly some subjects had begun associating the middle items before they were switched, even if only after four trials. The most interesting results came from asking the subjects after the experiment whether or not they had noticed the switch. Of the 80 subjects, 48 reported they had not noticed, 6 asked if items had been switched, and 10 reported that they had indeed noticed. This supports the proposition that some subjects had either learned through to the switched items, or they had started with them. This issue will be further discussed in Chapter 9.

CONCLUSIONS

The above separate description in Figure 5-3 of the component factors in serial acquisition of groups of items does not imply that these components are unrelated. On the contrary, the position-saliency function also implies a direction of effort on the part of the subject. The assumption is that the subject will also have a tendency to learn the positionally salient items earlier than he learns the positionally embedded ones. The different amounts of distinctiveness for an item are important, rather than the particular source of the distinctiveness.

Since the suggested components that contribute to the total distinctiveness of individual items are not independent of one another, their effects do not necessarily summate in a simple way. The relative importance of these sources of item saliency for selection of an acquisition strategy would vary with the individual subject and with various experimental conditions.

As can be inferred from the above statement of the hypothesis, the process of serial acquisition looked at in terms of successive trials to some criterion of learning occurs in two general stages (Harcum & Coppage, 1965a, b; Harcum, 1967b). The first stage, called *anchor formation,* consists of the differentiation of items, including the selection of one item to become the cognitive beginning of the series, that is, to form an anchor for the later learning. The second stage, called *serial association,* in which serial learning per se occurs, begins when first-learned items become part of the anchoring configuration to which the other items are associated. These stages are relatively discrete, such that they can be distinguished empirically. Some overlap of stages is permissible by theory, however. For example, one item may be in the hookup phase, while another is being differentiated. This argument assumes that an item is not learned all or none on a selected trial, as some have claimed (e.g., Rock, 1957).

Other data have supported the two-stage conception of serial acquisition. Bugelski (1965) showed that subjects showed a very strong primacy effect, and a relatively weak recency effect, in serial recall of ten words after a single presentation of the series. Frequency in reporting the position correctly, or failures to report an item at all, increased progressively from first to last items. Errors in reporting position, on the other hand, were minimal near either end of the series. Slamecka (1965) points out that the results of Bugelski (1965) show both that item learning is not complete after a single trial for even ten common adjectives and also that position learning has begun. Therefore, the so-called item-differentiation and associative-hookup stages of serial learning overlap in the total acquisition process.

Woodward (1968) argues that probe data from a single trial show differential affects of probe type, because the task is at first associational (cf. Youssef, 1967). Later, the task is integrational, and there is no differential effect of probe type.

Koustaal, Smith, and Panyard (1972) had subjects who were high or low in rating the amount of effort in subvocalizing CVC trigrams learn two lists of nine items of either low and high m' values (Noble, 1961). The rates of learning for the two groups of subjects were not significantly different, suggesting that subvocalization effort does not determine rate of learning. The authors concluded that the difference in rate of learning for low- and high-m' items was determined by the number of processes involved in the learning. Whereas meaningful patterns (e.g., bus, cat) need only be associated or ordered, the patterns of meaningless and unambiguous sounds have also to be learned (response acquisition), whereas meaningless items with ambiguous sound patterns (e.g., qoc, xej) require both a consolidation of sounding and then the response acquisition before they can be ordered.

The key link thus seems to be the effectiveness of the translation process in coding an input into the codification system of the subject. For example, studies by Wood (1969) and Underwood and Zimmerman (1973) show that the associations among items that the subject brings to the serial learning task influence the acquisition of that task. These associations may have been built-in by a previous laboratory-learning task or by experiences with conceptual structures.

The results of Mosher (1969) show that the ordered serial structures of cognitive triads (such as nickel, dime, quarter) interfere with the recall of these triads in some different order. Therefore, an interaction between short-term and long-term learning mechanisms is indicated—an effect that is incompatible with discrete boxlike models of memory. Finally, the study by Mellgren (1967) found the same sort of positional identification problem for a spatial array to be memorized that Harcum (1964b) found for reproduction of tachistoscopic patterns. The positional organization was most difficult in both cases for an array oriented diagonally from lower left to upper right, relative to horizontal, vertical, and the other diagonal. It is difficult in this case to conclude whether the organizational problem was produced by the stimulus configuration, or by the subject's limitations.

A comment is in order about the implied inconsistency in the present theory between a selective strategy of a subject, which implies a discontinuous process of acquisition for individual items, and a differentiation basis for this strategy, which implies a continuous process. The present position is that the subject does attend to each item as it is presented, and he does try to learn it. The subject cannot, however, associate or hook an item to another until it has been sufficiently differentiated. That is to say, the subject typically does not consciously ignore some items in order to concentrate on others. The process is dialectic in that strategy is important for differentiation, but differentiation must necessarily precede association. Following the model of Simon and Feigenbaum (1964), we can say that an image for items must first be formed individually, before these can be differentiated into a new composite image. Alternatively, we can say that one stimulus or stimulus configuration can initiate the formation of a Gestalt, and the associated item can complete it.

The rate of acquisition of individual items in the first stage may be either slower, faster, or equal to that in the second stage of serial learning. With group data the characteristic bowed curve occurs because subjects are consistent in choosing a given item for the cognitive anchor and because of the subject's tendency to make forward associations to this anchor more rapidly than backward associations are formed (Harcum & Coppage, 1965b).

The selection of cognitive anchors may be based on any of a number of attributes of items that can attract the subject's attention, including the physical characteristics of items as well as their relative temporal position (Coppage & Harcum, 1967; Harcum, Pschirrer, & Coppage, 1968). The various bases for selecting a strategy are not mutually exclusive, of course, and the particular basis of a strategy can be idiosyncratic to the different subjects (Lippman & Denny, 1964). According to the present argument the serial-position effect operates because the subjects tend to use, with a substantial degree of consistency, sheer serial position as a basis for their strategy of acquisition, as described in Figure 5-3.

SUMMARY

The distribution of errors in pattern acquisition evolves from the interaction of various bases of organizing the input information. When the organizational strategies based on stimulus attributes, observer sets, and response requirements work together to aid one another, the process is more effective and the distributions of errors are more articulated. When the various bases of organizational strategies are poorly differentiated, or when they tend to conflict, accuracy is poor and the distribution of errors is undifferentiated.

The present argument is that the learning of items within a series is directed by organizational processes for encoding into memory. This process starts with the cognitive designation of some items as first, ordinarily to be reproduced first. Any lack of homogeneity within the stimulus array that helps to differentiate the elements also influences selection for a position in the order of their analysis. In an otherwise homogeneous array, the items at either end of the array would have an intrinsic saliency, which would promote their selection for first processing. This would account for the general superiority of reproduction for items near the ends relative to those near the center of a stimulus configuration, that is, an end-segregation effect.

PART

2

THE PROCESSES

CHAPTER

6

END SEGREGATION

The most salient characteristic of the serial-position effect is the bowing, which remains through many local variations and degrees of asymmetry in the curve. For example, the ubiquitous finding of Murdock (1968) for immediate recall of series of various lengths, and other conditions, was the bowing of the curve. Even though there were changes in relative primacy and recency effects of input, the end items were always more accurately recalled. Typically, this bowing is attributed to some type of interference mechanism, which affects the central items more than the end ones. Schmeidler (1939) obtained parallel results for proactive and retroactive inhibition paradigms. Presumably the early items in a series would exert proactive effects on later items, and later items would produce retroactive effects on the earlier ones. Schmeidler found evidence for both specific task materials and general activity, supporting the interference interpretation. Referring to the importance of interference, McGeoch (1942) concluded that

> it is, for example, one of the major determiners of the common serial-position curve which shows learning to be most rapid at the ends of a series of responses and least rapid at or just past the middle (p. 61).

The evidence points toward some sort of mechanism that adds to the task load for central items. For example, increasing the number of items in the task should add interference. Schulz (1955) thought that his data might show such an increase in the bow of serial-position curves resulting from high intralist similarity, although this was not a clear-cut result. This apparent effect was more noticeable later in learning. Consistent with this conclusion, Horton and Turnage (1970) found that bowing was greater for less meaningful items. Voss (1956) found increased bowing of the serial-position curve as the task difficulty (length) increased. He speculated that any other variable that increased difficulty, such as presentation rate, would add errors differentially to the center of the series.

Delin (1969a), in fact, found that 16-item lists produced more errors per item than 10-item lists. Moreover, Schumsky, Grasha, Trinder, and Richman (1969) found that list length exerted a major detrimental effect on recall, with its greatest effect on the middle syllable. They presented a series of three, five, or seven trigrams to subjects and then requested recall of first, middle, or last items. The middle syllable was about midway between first and last syllables in difficulty of recall for the 3-item list, but dropped to equality with the last syllable for the 7-item series. The first syllable was uniformly best and not strongly affected by the increases in length. This study is notable because there was no effect of a varied retention interval, and the primacy effect was greater than the recency effect. The authors conclude that the reason for both effects was that their data had been obtained from single test trials, rather than from repeated testing. Bousfield, Whitmarsh, and Esterson (1958) also found that curves of free recall of words showed increased bowing as the number of words increased from 5 to 40.

The bowing may also be caused by differential attention favoring the end items. In their article on the "tip of the tongue" phenomenon, Brown and McNeill (1966) suggest that we tend to recall words by attending to the end letters first. This occurs presumably because the end letters carry more information than the middle letters in directing the search of memory.

Although there are obviously a number of different mechanisms proposed for this increased detrimental effect for the middle items, they are not mutually exclusive. In truth, the differences among hypotheses often seem to be more a matter of preference by the theorist for an item-sequence or a position-based conception of the stimulus for serial learning. Thus, the fundamental question of the nature and locus of interference is raised. Does one employ the concept of interference among memory traces, conflicts of strategy, association to some inhibitory process, or ambiguity among retrieval cues? These various theoretical approaches are discussed under the rubrics association to inhibitory processes, response interference, unlearning, stimulus generalization, and position confusion.

ASSOCIATION TO INHIBITORY PROCESSES

One conception of the serial-learning task considers a learned serial response as a conditioned reponse to those items that precede it. This theory is based upon the work of Pavlov (1927).

External Inhibition

James (1931) suggested that interference among responses could be interpreted in terms of Pavlov's (1927) external inhibition, in which a new stimulus in the situation inhibits a correct response. This, he said, was combatted by internal inhibition, which consists of inhibitory unreinforced responses (differentiation). James further said that instructions to the subject caused a set or attitude that acts differentially toward the stimuli and changes from moment to moment. This process, he said, decreases external inhibition, causing less interference, and increases internal inhibition, aiding differentiation. This proposition seems to be a forerunner of the generalization hypothesis, later proposed by Gibson (1940). It also emphasizes the importance of context cues.

Inhibition of Delay

Pavlov (1927) recognized a type of internal inhibition, occurring when an excitatory response was inhibited because it was presented during a delayed conditioned response. He called it inhibition of delay. Items associated with such inhibition assume inhibitory qualities, but the

> inhibitory process (inhibition of delay) is more labile and more easily affected than the excitatory process, being influenced by stimuli of much weaker psychological strength (Pavlov, 1927, p. 99).

Lepley (1932) first proposed that the remote associations reported by Ebbinghaus (1913) had the nature of delayed conditioned responses. He argued that they therefore were like delayed conditioned excitatory tendencies, which conflict with the immediate excitatory tendencies. Ward (1937), noticing anticipatory intrusions in serial learning, supported this idea.

Lepley (1932) explained the extinction and subsequent reappearance of remote associations in serial lists as resulting from the inhibition of remote excitatory tendencies by immediate ones and to more rapid dropping out by the immediate excitatory tendencies, respectively. This explanation is consistent with Lumley's (1932a,b) observations of decreases in irrelevant intrusions or anticipations as learning progresses, and of more rapid extinction for the more remote tendencies. Lepley (1934), too, adduced evidence of the same vein for his theory. Remote excitation was not functional after relatively brief periods of forgetting or after very long periods of forgetting, and overlearning rendered measurement of remote excitations more difficult. Lepley's interpretation of this was that associative inhibition varies with the length of the forgetting interval (namely, it initially rises and then falls) and varies with the degree of original learning. Thus, difficulty within the central portion of a list would be due to conflicting conditioned responses.

Hull (1935a,b) then expanded Lepley's view. He proposed that the delayed conditioned response was due to a stimulus trace, by means of which a stimulus-response relationship could be established even when an appreciable interval had elapsed between overt stimulus and overt response. Each syllable in a series was assumed to have remote excitatory tendencies, which become associated with every other syllable except the one immediately following, with which it has direct excitatory connections. The delay of such a trace-conditioned response, Hull said, can temporarily inhibit the functional strength of an excitatory tendency. Therefore, a remote association inhibits any intermediate excitatory tendency that it spans: the greater degree of remoteness, the weaker the inhibition due to delay. Hull's salient point is that the inhibitions summate, causing a pileup of inhibition in the central portion of a serial list. Since the strength of the excitatory potential is constant for each syllable throughout the list, but more inhibition is attached to those in the center, the learning performance is weaker for middle syllables.

Hull (1935b) provided some evidence for his hypothesis of greater inhibition in the central portion of a series. When the subject took caffeine, learning was generally slower, anticipatory displacements increased 33%, and there was greater oscillation of correct and incorrect responses—taken as a measure of greater interference. In addition, Hull found that whatever was responsible for the serial curve at learning did not show up 20.5 hours later in recall measurements.

Hull's theory was later elaborated and formalized by organization into a rigorous set of postulates and theorems, with logical deductions from them (Hull, Hovland, Ross, Hall, Perkins, & Fitch, 1940). Hull et al. assumed that stimulus traces extend through a syllable presentation cycle, but not through the intertrial interval. Hull and his associates again assumed (1) that both direct and remote excitatory and inhibitory potentials are added to each syllable during each presentation and (2) that these potentials summate, with an excess of excitatory over inhibitory potential necessary for learning and subsequent recall. Excitatory and inhibitory potentials decrease with increased distance from the original syllable, and both decrease with time. The more inhibition acting on a syllable, the more repetitions that are required to raise its effective excitatory potential to the threshold. The reaction threshold varies, or oscillates, from trial to trial in accordance with the normal probability curve. Incidentally, Ebbinghaus himself noticed that memorizing was likely to show small variations in difficulty of short duration "whether they be called oscillations of attention or something else" (1913, p. 27).

According to Hull et al. (1940), at the end of learning the inhibitory potential increases progressively from the ends of the series toward a maximum. In order to account for the skewness of the curve, Hull et al. postulated a more rapid accumulation of the inhibition from the posterior end of the list. Hilgard and Marquis (1940) pointed out, however, that a trace-conditioned response is established very slowly, although the difficulty of the middle of the list is shown very early in learning. They propose that it is more likely that the inhibition is due to interference among response tendencies.

Hull (1952) later modified his theory to make it more applicable to more general classes of behavior. The relevant theorem proposes that when reinforcements follow each response of a chain the overlapping gradients of reinforcement produce an "upward-sloping and upward-arching serial-reinforcement gradient" (p. 168). Although the generalization curve drops off faster toward the end of the series than toward the beginning, the discriminability of differences (d) is greater for items at the beginning of the series. The result with serial reinforcement of heterogeneous response chains, such as learning series of nonsense syllables, is a negatively skewed curve. The idea of a decrease in d values through the series is similar to the later arguments of Murdock (1957) and Harcum and Coppage (1965b).

Evidence for Inhibition

REMINISCENCE

The phenomenon of reminiscence has been used extensively to support the position that there is a buildup of inhibition during learning of a list, on the assumption that greater amounts of inhibition cause greater reminiscence. If increased inhibition (conflict between excitatory and inhibitory potentials) accounts for forgetting, recovery from inhibition accounts for reminiscence. Thus, if the difficulty of the center of a list is due to inhibition, which dissipates more rapidly than excitation, there should be greater reminiscence for the central items.

Lepley (1935) found that there was a relative advantage in retention for central positions at each forgetting interval tested and that factors causing this were evident soon after cessation of learning. According to Hull et al. (1940) there is more reminiscence after massed than distributed practice, and maximum reminiscence occurs later after massed learning because a longer interval is necessary to allow the increased inhibition after massed practice to dissipate. Furthermore, they said, reminiscence is greater for the syllable that required the maximum number of presentations to bring it to the threshold of recall. The longer the list, the more inhibition there is at the maximum point, and the greater the reminiscence.

Ward (1937) proposed that there is an inverse relation between reminiscence and degree of original learning and, therefore, a lesser degree of learning should cause greater reminiscence for a particular syllable. Since, by using completely and partially learned lists, he found the eighth syllable to be the most difficult in a 12-syllable list, and greater reminiscence for syllables 6, 7, 8, and 9 than at 3, 4, 11, and 12 measured by recall, he concluded that these results were due to the overlearning of the end syllables and therefore less reminiscence for them measured by recall. His point was that serial position is related to reminiscence only because end syllables are overlearned.

Patten (1938) achieved results that were positive with respect to greater inhibition in the center of a series. He found that massed practice yielded more errors than distributed practice, mostly in the middle portion, with no difference at the first syllable. He also found more anticipatory errors in the middle of the list. The greater difficulty in recalling the syllables in the middle of the rote series was reduced after ten minutes without practice.

In a series of experiments on reminiscence, Hovland confirmed several deductions from Hull. In the first study Hovland (1938a) concluded that when

> central portions of two lists are equally well learned, in terms of the criterion to recall, one learned by mass practice will show pronounced reminiscence, while one learned by distributed practice will show little improvement (p. 223).

He believed the best explanation of such an effect to be in terms of removal of inhibition. He believed that such explanation is associated with the same factors as the difficulty in the central portion of the series, or "intraserial inhibition," because procedures that decrease serial-position effects reduce reminiscence. Hovland (1938b) also found that the reduction of anticipation failures with a 4-second rate of exposure over a 2-second rate was most pronounced in the middle of the series and less at the ends. With 2-second intervals, moreover, the reminiscence effect following partial learning was most marked in the middle and least at the ends. This was not true with the 4-second presentation.

Later Hovland (1939a) found with paired-associate learning no reminiscence after 2 minutes, although he did find such an effect with a serial list. This indicated that inhibitory tendencies present in the middle of the series were not present in the paired-associates list. He concluded that the best explanation was in terms of the same interference that causes reminiscence.

Shipley (1939) tested Hull's deduction that reminiscence would be greater after a longer series because there would be more remote associations, and thus more inhibition. Using series of 8, 14, and 20 nonsense syllables, he found a general decrease in retention, which he proposed was due to the slow presentation of the syllables, but the decrease was smaller with the longer series.

Hovland (1940a) had subjects learn serial lists to the same criterion by massed and by distributed practice, and found that more trials were required to learn by the former. More syllables were correctly recalled after all of the intervals used between learning and recall after distributed practice (namely, 2 minutes, 10 minutes, and 24 hours). The greater the interval, the greater was the difference between distributed over massed practice. These results, he theorized, could best be explained by altering the mathematicodeductive theory of rote learning (Hull et al., 1940), which assumes that interfering tendencies decrease according to the same general function as the positive tendencies but at a more rapid rate, becoming asymptotic to zero. He proposed that interfering processes decrease rapidly at first, but become asymptotic to a positive value above zero. Inferior retention after massed practice is thus produced because the interference is still present over long periods of time. He further concluded that his results cannot be explained solely on the basis of differential rate of decline of positive learning and an interfering process (which is the classical concept of the advantage of distributed practice). Hovland's explanation is based on the assumption that interferences decline at a rate inversely proportional to their strength; it appears to be the forerunner of generalization theory (Gibson, 1940).

Evidence negative to Hovland's (1940a) hypothesis was presented by Wilson (1943) who hypothesized that remote associations were forgotten faster than correct responses. His subjects learned lists of 16 two-syllable adjectives at 2-second intervals by the anticipation method. He found remote forward and backward associations for all four intervals of rest tested—more forward than backward. Remote associations did not decrease differentially with the increasing length of the interpolated interval.

Melton and Stone (1942), using meaningful material, found, contrary to Hull and Hovland, that the greatest forgetting was in the middle of the list, and it was greater with longer rest intervals (from 2 to 20 minutes). Further, a rest pause was more beneficial with a 2-second rate than at a 1.45-second rate. Also, there was no reminiscence after periods of no practice for as long as 20 minutes, and a faster rate of presentation did not increase reminiscence. The results corroborated Hull and Hovland in that there was greater intraserial inhibition with increased rate of presentation. On the other hand, this resulted in a decrement of recall instead of reminiscence.

Buxton (1949) found that the middle of the 16-item lists of syllables, or adjectives, showed more reminiscence than the end. Buxton and Ross (1949) found that more trials to criterion were required to learn to spell syllables than to pronounce them. The assumption is that greater inhibition is built up if the number of learning trials is greater. Following Hull's hypothesis that there is greater reminiscence after greater inhibition, one could expect greater reminiscence after the spelling of syllables. But the experiment showed more reminiscence after pronunciation of the syllables, even though the bowed curve was more evident with spelling, and there was more oscillation in retention for spelling.

TRANSFER OF GENERAL INHIBITION

Andrews, Shapiro, and Cofer (1954) investigated the transfer of inhibitory potential within a serial list to a derived list of paired associates. They reasoned that the greater inhibition associated with items at the center of the series, to which Hull (1935a) attributed the cause of the serial-position effect, should transfer to a subsequent paired-associate task. Therefore, stimulus items for a paired-associate task taken from the middle of the serial list should be harder to learn than those taken from the ends of the series. This result was in fact obtained when the paired-associate task immediately followed the serial task; in fact the paired-associate results duplicated the serial-position curve from the prior learning. Moreover, when the paired-associate task was delayed

24 hours, the prior effects of serial position were virtually absent, as predicted on the basis of dissipation of the inhibition over time.

MASSED VERSUS DISTRIBUTED LEARNING

Hovland (1938c) found a disproportional increase of difficulty and number of oscillations at the middle syllables in a 2-second rate over a 4-second rate of presentation. The oscillation of responses was taken as an index of interference. Hovland's data are replotted in Figure 6-1 in terms of the oscillation ranges at each serial position. Each data point represents the number of trials between the first correct response and the last failure. The two curves, for 2-second and 4-second rates of presentation, respectively, in general show rather symmetrical bowing, with minima at either end of the series. The two straight-dashed lines drawn through the "Xs," representing the means for first and second halves of each curve, indicate that any asymmetry in the curves actually reflects smaller oscillation ranges at the end of the series. Both rates of presentation show more errors about the middle of the series; the differences

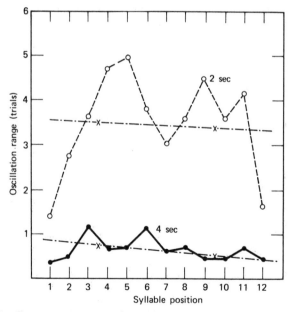

Figure 6-1   Oscillation range per serial position at two presentation rates, after Hovland (1938c). Copyright © (1938) by the American Psychological Association. Reprinted by permission.

between the two curves appear in absolute terms to be larger about the center of the series. This conclusion will be examined critically later in this book, however.

Hull et al. (1940) argued that oscillation increases for increased length of a list. This postulate was confirmed from data by Hovland (1940b) and Shipley (1939). Hovland (1940b) added more information that the serial curve was due to inhibition in the central portion. He found serial-position effects in all lengths of series tested. The efficacy of distributed practice over massed was greater in the central portions. The longer the list, the proportionately greater the difficulty at the central portions. Measuring oscillation as the difference between first success and last failure, he found greater oscillation at the threshold of recall in the central portions of longer lists, more oscillations at every syllable in longer lists, and greater oscillation with massed practice— the rate of increased oscillation to increased length of list being greater with massed than distributed practice.

Underwood and Richardson (1955) also found an effect of distributed practice on recall. For the seventh list learned by subjects, the recall was better for the larger intertrial intervals, but for the first list the recall was better after massed practice.

Keppel and Rehula (1965) found that total learning time was constant for two rates of serial-anticipation learning of 14 adjectives. However, when rates were reversed after selected criteria of learning had been reached, the subsequent performance did not depend upon the presentation rate under which a given criterion was reached. A similar result was obtained by Fischer (1966b), who discovered that the total time required for learning a list of syllables by the anticipation method was constant, regardless of the variation in presentation rate from 2 to 16 seconds. That is, the stimulus-presentation rate multiplied by the number of trials to learning produced a constant. Moreover, the shapes of the serial-position curves were not changed as a function of the rate, when the analysis was performed on an arc-sine transformation of the proportion-correct data.

WEIGHTING OF DIFFERENTIAL PERFORMANCE

Braun and Heymann (1958) varied stimulus meaningfulness, interstimulus interval, and intertrial interval in the same serial-learning experiment. The high-meaningful lists were more easily learned, and both degrees of meaningfulness benefited from the spacing of practice. For raw (absolute) errors, the serial position of items interacted with both meaningfulness of items and interstimulus interval, the latter supporting Hovland's (1938c) finding. However, when performance per serial position was expressed as a percentage of total errors, the serial-position curves for various spacings of items were identical, and the interactions of serial position with spacing of items were not significant. Thus, time that allows dissipation of inhibition of delay does not affect the shape of the serial-position curve, contrary to Hovland's (1938c) theory.

A reexamination of Hovland's (1938c) oscillation-range data, moreover, suggests the same conclusion. His results in relative terms (plotted in Figure 6-2) indicate a different conclusion from the one apparent in the data considered in absolute terms. Namely, the two rates of presentation reveal about equal degrees of bowing when the oscillation range for each presentation rate is weighted in terms of the percentage of the total trials for all ranges under each condition.

Conclusion

These considerations of appropriate weighting of performance seem to be a fatal blow to the concept of a general type of inhibition attached differentially to the items about the center of a series. The evidence favors some type of interference or competition among items or processes.

RESPONSE INTERFERENCE

An alternative to the inhibition of delay idea has been called associative inhibition, or interference. This refers to the difficulty of learning new

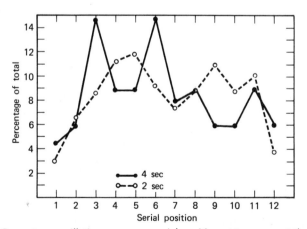

Figure 6-2   Percentage oscillation range per serial position at two presentation rates, after Hovland (1938c). Copyright © (1938) by the American Psychological Association. Reprinted by permission.

associations to items already having associative connections, particularly of moderate strength. As Ladd and Woodworth (1911) pointed out long ago,

> A clear instance of inhibition appears in the fact that lists of words or syllables, up to a certain length, can be recited after one reading, whereas adding one or two more members to the list makes many readings necessary. Perhaps an individual can recite, after one reading, a list of six syllables but, on attempting a list of seven, is unable to give more than one or two of them, or even any at all. The seventh syllable has driven away the others, without becoming fixed in their place (p. 580).

They suggest that the cause of this is the competition among adjacent and remote associations, and imply that this may be the main source of difficulty in learning such lists.

The greater number of errors near the middle of a series to be learned has been attributed to direct interference among response tendencies by, for example, Gibson and Raffel (1936), Gibson (1940), Murdock (1960), and Deese and Kresse (1952). Gibson (1940) attributed the greater difficulty to a problem of discriminating among items. Such a mechanism again would produce a symmetrical distribution of errors, leaving it to another unspecified factor to account for the skewness of the curve. Underwood (1964) points out how "second-order habits" can produce interference in the learning of nonsense letter and word sequences, making them more difficult to learn than would be expected on the basis of no existing prior associations.

Beecroft (1956) found with paired-associate learning that the greater the number of competing associations the more difficult the learning task. The number of competing associations was varied by using differing numbers of synonyms as stimulus items for different lists. Although the number of intruding errors per trial varied directly with the number of competing associations, this effect was not significant. Consistent with Underwood's (1953) earlier result, the greater similarity of stimulus items did not produce a differential effect in recall. McGeoch (1942) suggested that the Ranschburg phenomenon, in which a repeated item, or item adjacent to it, is likely to be omitted or incorrectly reproduced, is due to such intraserial interference. The results of Keppel and Underwood (1962a) on retention loss over time as a function of the number of previous items tested indicate the relevance of proactive interference within a single trial of the serial-learning task.

Jensen (1964, p. 95) devised an index of oscillation, which is proposed as a measure of interference in serial learning (McGeoch & Irion, 1952, p. 118). This index is computed as follows: index of oscillation $= r/R$

(100), where R is the actual number of runs of correct and incorrect responses, and r is the expected number of runs. The formula for calculating r is: $r = 1 + 2EC/(E + C)$, where E is the total number of errors, and C is the total number of correct responses. This index shows, for example, greater oscillation for slow than for fast learners. Although in general the greater the oscillation the slower the learning, this relationship is not simple because factors such as extraexperimental interferences in the case of meaningful words can produce oscillation, but not be associated with greater difficulty. Using a retroactive inhibition paradigm, Jensen found that a condition of low retroactive inhibition produced less oscillation than a condition of high retroactive inhibition. This result supports the contention that greater oscillation is an indication of greater interference in learning. On the other hand, since correlations between total errors and the oscillation index were not all that high (namely, ranging from .47 to .84 for the low interference group under various conditions, and from .38 to .55 for the high interference group under the same conditions), Jensen (1964) concludes "that errors and oscillation are far from being redundant measures" (p. 105).

McGeoch and McGeoch (1936) found greater retroactive inhibition of an interpolated list of synonyms to the original list than for unrelated items. Whether or not the serial position of the interpolated items was changed did not influence the amount of inhibition. Thus, some general factor seemed to be producing the effect, rather than simple chaining or association to position.

Melton and von Lackum (1941) tested the hypothesis that retroactive inhibition was due to two factors: unlearning and competition. They argued that if retroactive inhibition is caused by competition among responses, then the amount of proactive inhibition on interpolated activity should equal the degree of retroactive inhibition on original activity. They found that the inhibition in relearning was greater for the first of two lists than for the second. Thus, they concluded that proactive inhibition results only from the competition of response at the time of retention, whereas retroactive inhibition also involves unlearning. The greater number of intrusions for the first list in tests of retention favors a two-factor theory.

Postman (1952) found evidence for a two-factor theory of retroactive inhibition using a recognition test. Retention was significantly less, relative to a control group, for subjects given a recognition test that did not include items from the interpolated task. Therefore, the retroactive inhibition was present for the case in which response competition was minimal, thus indicating an effect of unlearning. For a group of subjects who had to discriminate between correct and interpolated items on the recognition test, retention was worse than for the recognition without competing responses present, indicating an interference effect for this condition from the competing associations that also were present.

Osgood (1953) concluded that the evidence points to two independent factors in serial learning. The first is a short-term temporal factor that includes a transient form of inhibition and dissipates in time faster than the second. The second is an interference factor, which reduces retention for the items through competing associations. Underwood (1957) summarized evidence that suggested that a major source of interference in retention is the material that has been learned prior to the start of the experimental session.

Primacy-Recency

The terms primacy and recency really define situations rather than describe mechanisms. McGeoch (1942) suggested primacy and recency effects as a possible cause of the serial-position curve, but adds that these effects per se are not the answer. The terms primacy and recency—or finalcy—are primarily descriptive terms. An item that appears first, for example, has an advantage due to the absence of prior learning. It also has the advantage of an emphasis or saliency resulting from the uniqueness of its position. In this subsection, primacy and finalcy data will be considered in terms of the factors of proactive and retroactive inhibition, respectively.

The retroactive and proactive inhibitory effects can cause the serial-position curve, since first items would have reduced effects of proactive inhibition and latter items would have less retroactive inhibition. Those items in the middle would have more of each. And if proactive inhibitory effects are greater than retroactive then the advantage of primacy over finalcy occurs. Foucault (1928) concluded that the serial-position curve was due to "regressive" inhibition, which caused recall failures early in a series, and "progressive" inhibition, which caused response failures at the end of a list. Furthermore, he adds that progressive inhibition is stronger than regressive inhibition.

Gibson and Raffel (1936) obtained correct response scores increasing from the first to the last item, when subjects were asked to draw one of five serially presented forms. This effect of recency, they said, was the result of retroactive inhibition—subsequency, not recency. That proactive inhibition was present—but masked—was deduced, because reproduction was better when one figure was given alone than when the last figure in a series of five was tested. Such "interaction within series" resulting from the interruption of memory-trace formation by traces already or subsequently formed, they conclude, has a possible detrimental effect on retention. Their report that retroactive inhibition is stronger than proactive inhibition conflicts with some evidence (Foucault, 1928; Robinson & Brown, 1926), but also corroborates the conclusion of Welch and Burnett (1924). This may be due to their use of spatial forms instead of the usual verbal material. However, the final conclusion of Gibson and Raffel was that future investigations should be oriented not to primacy and recency per se, but to possible inhibitory influences within the series, as well as "position character" and membership in a temporal group. The relevance of this suggestion to the conceptions of generalization and position confusion, to be discussed later, is obvious.

Murdock (1962b) describes the serial-position curve of free recall as consisting of a primacy effect, a greater recency effect, and an asymptote for the items in between. The asymptote represents the number of items in the series when it is manifested; for shorter series the primacy and recency effects converge to prevent the appearance of the flat asymptote. Murdock concludes that the serial-position effect represents the summation of proactive and retroactive interference effects.

Wing (1967) proposed a trace-interaction model of serial learning, which showed promising parallels to some free-recall data. He predicted that the first task of free recall would produce greater primacy than recency effects, but that subjects on subsequent tasks would switch tactics to take advantage of the stronger traces due to recency; this result was obtained. Wing's theoretical curves showed the appropriate changes in primacy and recency when the effects of backward and forward associations were appropriately weighted.

Glanzer and Cunitz (1966) and Atkinson and Shiffrin (1968a,b) have proposed that primacy effects reflect a long-term memory-storage process, whereas recency effects reflect short-term memory. Evidence for the latter was provided by Postman and Phillips (1965), who did not find a recency effect in free recall when the responding was delayed after the stimulus presentation was completed. Evidence from the so-called continuous presentation in serial learning refutes the interpretation in terms of simple primacy and finalcy (recency) (Mitchell, 1933b; Harcum & Coppage, 1965a). In this method the temporal space between the last item in the series and the first item in the series on the next trial (namely, the intertrial interval) is not greater than any other inter-stimulus interval. Therefore, only on the first trial is the first item not preceded by another item, and only on the final trial, after the series is learned, does the last item fail to have a following item. Presumably, there should be minimal differences among items in retroactive and proactive inhibition if only the number of preceding and following items are considered. Nevertheless, a clear serial-position curve emerges in the continuous-presentation method. Further evidence against the simple item-interference concept is found in the fact that this serial-position curve is not found at the beginning of learning, when any differential effects of proactive inhibition should be maximal (Harcum & Coppage, 1965a). The differential performance among items appears when the differential effects of prior and poststimulation are minimal. This result was discussed in Chapter 5 (Figure 5-5).

Backward Associations

Evidence for backward, as well as forward and remote associations, has been presented in Chapter 2. Since the subject is ordinarily instructed to learn forward associations, backward associations typically are responsible for negative transfer, because they would naturally tend to interfere with the correct forward associations.

McGeoch (1936) required subjects to learn a serial list partially before interrupting them to ask for associations to individual items. Correct responses were most frequent, with forward responses more numerous than backward ones. The frequencies of responses decreased with greater degrees of remoteness, still with greater numbers of forward association.

Primoff (1938), using each item as both a stimulus and response in paired-associate learning—a double-function list—found that the series was much more difficult to learn than a paired-associate task prepared in the usual manner, with a given item used only as "stimulus" or "response." He tested for backward, forward, and remote associations from a serial-learning task after the subjects had transferred the associations to the serial task from prior learning of a double-function paired-associate list, or had become familiar with the items—but not the associations—on a prior paired-associate task. When the subjects were asked to give the prior (stimulus) or succeeding (response) item to a specific (probe) item, the number of correct backward associations was almost equal to the number of correct forward associations. Primoff (1938) argued that the greater difficulty of double-function paired-associate lists, relative to control pairs, was due to the presence of backward associations in the former. After adjustment for the opportunities to make the various kinds of associations, the results in learning a double-function list showed about five times as many forward associations as backward. The reason for this was that the instructions to the subjects had told them to learn the forward associations. Remote associations were relatively rare with respect to the total possible numbers of such errors. Primoff argues that the serial list has cues, such as "rhythmic place," serial position, and logical arrangement, that inhibit backward associations.

Umemoto and Hilgard (1961) also found that backward associations in double-function paired-associate lists typically interfered with performance. If, however, the different pairs were sufficiently similar (e.g., noonday-gid; gid-midday), the learning was facilitated.

Murdock (1958) supported Harcum's (1953) results for negative transfer of backward associations, also finding equivalent degrees of such transfer for forward and backward associations. Murdock (1962a) later provided evidence for the equivalence of forward and backward associations in paired-associate learning, using either a stimulus or a response item as a probe. In four experiments, generally the frequency of correct recall of a member of a pair was equal regardless of whether a stimulus or response term was used as the probe. Murdock is careful to point out that, since both members of the pairs were exposed simultaneously, use of the terms "stimulus" and "response" to refer to the individual members is, strictly speaking, inappropriate. As would be expected, there was a very strong recency effect and a small primacy effect.

The existence of backward associations was verified through positive transfer by Jantz and Underwood (1958), and through a retroactive inhibition paradigm by Keppel and Underwood (1962b). Jantz and Underwood (1958) found significant recall of R-S associations after S-R learning of paired associates, as well as significant transfer from S-R to R-S learning. Both of these effects increased with greater degrees of S-R learning. Feldman and Underwood (1957) found that after learning a list of seven paired-associates to a criterion of two successive correct, the subjects could reproduce 50% of the total simulus members and 61% of the component stimulus letters when given the so-called response terms. These results imply backward associations.

Young and Jennings (1964) found evidence for backward associations in paired-associate learning using the A-B, B-A transfer paradigm. Positive transfer was obtained when the similarity between stimulus and response words was low or medium, but not when this similarity was high (namely, identity), as in a double-function list. When a double-function list was well learned (namely, 40 trials), the transfer was positive at first, but it quickly changed to negative.

Raskin and Cook (1937) suggested that possibly "backward" association is nothing more than remote-forward associative tendencies extending through the end of the list temporally, thus associating a later item to items appearing earlier in the next presentation (trial). They base this hypothesis on data revealing remote excitatory tendencies as strongest closest to the stimulus, gradually decreasing, and then rising again in strength. This rise, which is contrary to Ebbinghaus' idea of the strength of remote associations, they believed resulted from the presence of the opposite kind of remote associations acting across the temporal space between successive presentations of the list. Furthermore, they felt justified in concluding that apparent backward connections were more than remote-forward bonds, since such "backward" associations were stronger (by the method of measuring associative strength used) than could be expected of corresponding remote forward associations.

Postman and Stark (1967) examined intruding errors in the paired-associate task of their study on transfer from serial learning to double-function paired-associate learning. Assuming bidirectional associations in serial learning, they argued that there should be initially greater backward intrusions from the serial learning list on the paired-associate list when the same associations were maintained than when the associations were new. This result was obtained. For the condition of re-pairings of items from the serial learning on the paired-associate list, the number of previously correct intrusions was greater than for the control list for which the items had not been seen by the subject previously. Later Stark (1968) found that intruding backward associations from a prior serial-learning task were not as frequent as forward ones in a double-function paired-associate transfer task.

The study of Young, Milauckas, and Bryan (1963) was described in Chapter 2. They obtained positive evidence for transfer of forward associations on the basis of transfer from a double-function paired-associate task to a serial list. Dolinsky and Juska (1967) repeated the study of Young et al. (1963), but added a fourth condition in which the backward associations of the prior paired-associate learning became the correct specific associations in a continuous serial-learning task. Results supported the Young et al. (1963) finding that the group of subjects learning the same items with new associations was significantly worse in serial learning relative to a control group learning all new items. Neither the transferred forward nor backward associations significantly aided serial learning relative to the control group. Thus, the incompatible forward and backward associations in the prior paired-associate task consequently interfered with the learned forward and backward associations, respectively, and therefore canceled the positive transfer effects in the overall results.

Horton and Grover (1968) found that subjects who learned a double-function paired-associate list revealed positive transfer to a serial list composed of the forward associations. Another group of subjects for whom the serial associations were reversed from the paired-associate learning (namely, backward associations) failed to show a significant difference from the control group. Actually, the empirical difference indicated that the backward associations were more difficult to learn than the new associations learned by the control group.

Schwartz (1970b) found more forward errors than backward errors after the one trial of serial learning, but equal numbers of correct forward and backward associations. The difference in errors may be an artifact of the fact that more commission errors occurred at the end of the list. To test the hypothesis that the differentially greater number of correct forward associations appears only after multiple trials of serial learning, Schwartz used a missing-scan technique. The serial position functions were flat, however, probably because the lists were strongly overlearned.

An issue today is whether the backward response tendency is as strong as the one in the forward direction (Asch & Ebenholtz, 1962; Battig & Koppenaal, 1965; Ekstrand, 1966). Although so-called backward responses clearly do enter into a complete understanding of various verbal-learning tasks (Ekstrand, 1966), there is still some doubt about their origin. For example, Cason (1926a) found evidence of apparent backward association in serial learning, but concluded that it is due to practice "backwards in the forward direction." He concluded that with logical material learning a series in the forward direction forms inhibitory associations against learning in the backward direction. However, it is apparent in most serial-learning experiments that the subject had no time to rehearse or "learn backwards."

Storms (1958) suggested that apparent backward associations in word association might be due to a priming or sensitization effect. This is similar to the proposition of Conrad (1960)—that subjects are merely filling in an unrecalled response with some available response.

Asch and Ebenholtz (1962) provided rational and empirical evidence that associative bonds are formed equally well in forward and backward directions. The empirical results in the typical tasks with nonsense syllables—of stronger forward association—are due to particulars of the research situation. These artifacts of method and situation include precisely the paralearning mechanisms proposed here. Because the subject is set to learn forward associations, and because he verbalizes one term more often than the other, making it more available as a response, the asymmetry of the associative connection is produced.

Remote Associations

Remote associations, it will be remembered, are connections between two items of a series that are not adjacent to one another. There are three lines of evidence: transfer on derived lists, postlearning association tests, and intruding errors during learning.

DERIVED LISTS

Ebbinghaus' (1913) method of derived lists employs items from one list at displaced positions on a second list, but maintaining the same degree of remoteness from one another. He explained positive transfer on the derived list in terms of the previous remote associations.

Cason (1926a) attempted to test the statement of Ebbinghaus that the strength of association decreases with the number of intervening items (i.e., degree of remoteness). His subjects overlearned a prose passage and then immediately learned a list derived from the original material. His conclusions in general were negative to Ebbinghaus' theory of remote associations. He concluded that since overlearning of prose resulted in inhibition of remote associations, then learning was very specific in nature.

Hall (1928) found that remote associations show up only slightly in immediate memory. She had several original lists from which she derived a control list by using syllables from the different lists in the same position as they were in the original lists. The test list consisted of alternating items from one original list with items from the same positions in the other original lists. Remote associations showed up only slightly in immediate memory as would be consistent with Cason's results, but remote associations caused large differences in lists relearned after one week. Her explanation was that immediate associations inhibit remote associations, but with the forgetting of immediate associations the remote associations can function. This implies differential forgetting of immediate and remote associations. Hall's results are amenable to Gibson's idea (1940) of generalization in that a breakdown of differentiation would cause emergence of more remote associative responses.

The derived-list method has come under severe criticism. The reason for this was clearly stated by McGeoch (1936), who argued that this method involves some associative and other types of inhibition that may block overt remote associations. In the derived-list method the items must be reorganized into a new sequence. McGeoch (1936) says of this method:

> It measures, in addition, only the transferred effects of remote associations acquired in the original list and later applied to the learning of the test list. It does not measure either the direct formation of remote associations during the learning of the original list or their individual presence during recall and during the learning of the derived list (p. 222).

Slamecka (1964) also criticized the derived-list method as a technique for demonstrating remote associations. He found that the typical derived-list paradigm produced positive transfer for a familiar alphabetic series, whereas a modified derived list, of equal remoteness of associations but without the regular pattern, produced no transfer effect. Subjects were told that the transfer list contained the same items, but in different order. On the other hand, when the original learning involved 12 nonsense syllables learned to a criterion of two successive correct responses, using the same design, no transfer effects for the derived lists were found. Since none of the subjects detected the patterning in this derived list, subjects' knowledge of the patterning of the items in the derived list seems to be necessary. To test this interpretation, Slamecka then repeated the nonsense-syllable study, but this time fully informed the subjects of the rules for constructing the derived lists. He found significant positive transfer for the traditionally patterned list, and a nonsignificant positive transfer for the modified-derived list.

Bugelski (1965) attacked Slamecka's (1964) assault on derived-list evidence for remote associations on the basis that derived lists classically have not always produced positive transfer, and that Slamecka's modified derivative list effectively prevents subjects from using mediators effectively.

Hakes, James, and Young (1964) used the derived-list paradigm, with certain modifications, to study the role of remote associations in serial learning. Stimuli were 16 two-syllable adjectives. For different groups of subjects the items in a first and a second list were arranged such that the items of the second (test) list had been separated by one, two, or three items on the first list. For control subjects no items were common to both lists. Each of the three derived lists revealed ultimately negative transfer with respect to the control list. This fact of negative transfer, which was contrary to Ebbinghaus' (1913) earlier result, was taken by the authors as very damaging evidence to the notion of remote associations. On the contrary, this evidence is not at all strong. In the first place, the serial position of all items except the first is changed from first to second experimental list. To the extent that the subjects were learning serial positions, the transfer would conform to a negative paradigm. Second, higher interitem associations can produce more intraserial interference when serial-position information must be maintained (e.g., Underwood, 1953; Postman, 1967). Particularly, the interfering tendencies are greatest at the middle of the series, which is precisely where Hakes et al. (1964) obtained the greatest negative effect of the prior associations. Furthermore, the transfer was slightly positive at the beginning of the transfer task for the experimental subjects, consistent with Postman's (1967) earlier results for series in which there had been prior response learning followed by negative influences (interference).

In a later paper, Hakes and Young (1966) recognized this problem and pointed out that the opposite conclusion from that of their earlier study is possible. Namely, the Ebbinghaus finding of apparent positive transfer may be an artifact of his use of a control condition (random-order derived list) that yielded strong negative transfer. The derived lists thus produced apparently positive transfer because they were less negative than the control effects. Hakes and Young go on to point out that the derived-list paradigm must produce negative transfer if one looks at the fate of the adjacent (correct) associations on the first list. In the derived list, these associations are changed, and therefore must produce strong intraserial interference.

Shebilske and Ebenholtz (1971) challenged the conclusion of Hakes and Young (1966) and Young (1968) that the finding of Ebbinghaus (1913) of positive transfer in his derived-list paradigm was due to an inappropriate control condition that did not control for the negative transfer expected from a random rearrangement of the original list. They argued that since Ebbinghaus had used a random arrangement of a number of prior lists, there would be no specific interfering associations. Also, because of the great experience in learning enjoyed by Ebbinghaus, there would be no necessity to control for nonspecific transfer effects. Also, they refuted Slamecka's (1964) contention that the positive transfer was due to Ebbinghaus' knowledge of the derivation paradigm, by pointing out that Ebbinghaus had employed a special experiment with a sufficient time delay to ensure that he would not recognize the particular nature of the derived series. Therefore, they concluded that Ebbinghaus' result of positive transfer stands as valid.

Shebilske and Ebenholtz (1971) cite three possible reasons for the real discrepancy in the results of Ebbinghaus and those of the more recent investigations that found negative transfer in the derived-list paradigm (Hakes, James, & Young, 1964; Young, Hakes, & Hicks, 1965). These are (1) the shorter retention interval used by the modern researchers, (2) the greater frequency of retention tests in current research, and (3) the high level of expertise in rote memorizing of Ebbinghaus relative to the typical unpracticed subjects. This latter point is most interesting in view of the recent research on release from proactive interference (e.g., Wickens, Born, & Allen, 1963) and the stimulus-differentiation interpretation of isolation (Saltz, 1971). Perhaps Ebbinghaus had learned somehow to "isolate" items cognitively, to protect them from the ravages of associative interference.

ASSOCIATION TESTS

When Wohlgemuth (1913) had subjects say the number "ten" each time that a nonsense syllable appeared in a list to be learned, the usual greater frequency of forward to backward associations for nonsense syllables was eliminated. The motor component of verbalization of the syllable was thus suppressed, and this was the component that usually added to the strength of forward associations.

McGeoch (1934) claimed to establish the existence of remote forward and backward associations, but found no large correlation between frequency of association and degree of remoteness. Also, as he pointed out, his use of the association method for determining remote associations produced more remote associations than reported by users of the derived-list method.

The association method was again used by McGeoch (1936) to test for intraserial associations after serial anticipation learning. After the subject had learned a list of ten words, he was given a word from the list and asked to report the first word that came to his mind. About 54% of the responses came from remote positions (i.e., other than the immediately following item). Thus, remote associations are apparent. There appeared to be no relation between frequency and degree of remoteness, however. The difficulty with such an analysis is that the degrees of remoteness are necessarily confounded with serial position of items—only the first and last items have the possibility for the greatest degrees of remoteness, and these items tend to be overlearned. Backward associations were also apparent, with about 59% of them remote. Forward associations were more frequent then backward ones. Results were generally equivalent when nonsense syllables were used as stimuli instead of meaningful adjectives.

Raskin and Cook (1937) found upturns in frequency for the most remote associations. This they attributed to the less-remote associations across the intertrial interval. Raskin and Cook instructed their subjects to respond with the first syllable within the series "that popped into his head." This resulted in some responses of syllables that had not been on the list and even some responses of the stimulus syllable to itself—namely, to repeat the stimulus.

The association method was used by Wilson (1949) to test for remote associations in the learning of 16 two-syllable adjectives by the anticipation method. Remote associations occurred about 32% of the time; it should be noted, however, that adjacent backward associations were counted as remote, and associations between the sixteenth and first items were scored as correct. The numbers of remote associations and the number of extraneous associations decreased with increased degrees of learning. Thus, Wilson concluded that serial learning involves the progressive suppression of remote associations.

Dallett (1959) used the association method to test for remote associations after subjects had learned 14 nonsense syllables to a criterion of

11 out of 14 correct. The test was delayed 30 seconds, 20 minutes, or 48 hours after the completion of learning. Remote associations were scored for all responses other than the forward adjacent (correct) ones. Although the associations of greater remoteness showed greater forgetting at the greater retention intervals, the effects were not significant.

The method of association as a valid indication of remote associations was attacked by Slamecka (1964). He argued that this method was confounded by the differential degrees of learning for the items at different serial positions in original learning. To test this interpretation, he had subjects become differentially familiar with six nonsense syllables by having various frequencies of appearance of each item within a deck of cards each containing one syllable. The frequencies of 25, 10, 3, 1, 3, and 10 approximated the relative "familiarization" that the items would receive in a serial-learning task. The subject was subsequently presented each item and asked to give the one of the other syllables that came to mind as an associate to it. The relative frequency of emission of each item corresponded to the relative frequency of prior experience, supporting the response-availability argument. But, as Wing (1967) points out, these relative frequencies were approximately the same for each probe item, indicating no gradient of remoteness for each item, contrary to the results of McGeoch (1936) after prior serial learning. From these data Slamecka generated artificial gradients of "remoteness" that, when corrected for opportunities for remote associations, revealed some similarity to the results of McGeoch (1936) and Raskin and Cook (1937).

As mentioned above, Slamecka's (1964) association table failed to show the traditional remoteness gradients. Also, the combined gradients did not reveal nearly the steepness of the traditional gradients, and the upturn for the most extreme degrees of remoteness was too exaggerated (e.g., McGeoch, 1936). The point that the upturn is probably an artifact of the differential availability of the end items after serial learning is well taken. As a matter of fact, McGeoch (1936) made this point himself.

Dallett (1965) defends the association method for obtaining remote associations by attacking two of Slamecka's (1964) contentions. First, he points out that logical deductions from the item-position effect of serial learning would indicate a flattening or upturn in the number of remote associations as the degree of remoteness increases, rather than predicting the decrease in frequency with greater remoteness. The logic of this is that the end elements are best learned and are the only ones to enter into the most remote associations—a so-called response bias.

The second objection to Slamecka's argument is that his artificial gradients of remote associations really do not represent a duplication of the traditional data on so-called remote associations by the association method. His data for frequencies of remote associations, corrected for opportunity, are shown in Figure 6-3, along with some classic curves for comparison. The shapes of Slamecka's (1964) gradients are compared in Figure 6-3 to classical ones of McGeoch (1936), Raskin and Cook (1937), and Bugelski (1950). Since the various curves were not based on the same numbers of items in the series, the curves are justified at the left and right extremes. It is obvious that Slamecka's curve is the only one that fails to show greatest frequencies for first-order remote associations. It is closest in shape to the Raskin and Cook (1937) curve, in that the corrected frequencies show a marked upturn for the most remote associations. Although Raskin and Cook concluded that the subjects had made associations between last and first items across the intertrial interval, such an apparent effect could have been produced by the stimulus bias that Slamecka (1964) proposes. Dallett further criticized the simple correction for opportunity used previously (Raskin & Cook, 1937) in evaluating the remoteness gradients, because often a very small empirical frequency is multiplied by a large correction factor, resulting

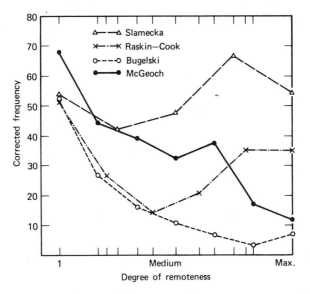

Figure 6-3   Comparison of corrected frequencies of remote associations, after McGeoch (1936, reprinted by permission of the University of Illinois Press), Raskin and Cook (1937, copyright © by the American Psychological Association. Reprinted by permission.), and Bugelski (1950, copyright © by the American Psychological Association. Reprinted by permission.), to Slamecka's (1964) familiarization data (copyright © by the American Psychological Association. Reprinted by permission.).

in the upturn for the most remote associations. Also contributing to the correction for differential opportunity was the fact that the end items were better learned in the original task and, therefore, more likely to appear because of the increased familiarity.

Dallett (1965) showed that Slamecka's (1964) empirical results from the prior familiarization of stimuli (without serial learning), yielded "remote-association" gradients that were actually flatter than the prediction based on the marginal totals of his "association" matrix. Therefore, the simple correction for opportunities, which assumes equally likely choices of the various response alternatives across serial positions, is not adequate. Dallett showed, moreover, that a correction of Slamecka's results for a response bias, in addition to a stimulus-familiarization bias, resulted in a superior prediction for Slamecka's "remoteness-gradient" results than the corrections for stimulus bias alone. Dallett (1965) also presented results from his earlier study (Dallett, 1959), using predictions based on stimulus and opportunity biases, that showed that actual remote-association gradients after serial learning were steeper than the predicted curves. Thus, Dallett concludes that so-called remote-association gradients are not entirely artifactual, although serial-position effects associated with the subject's nonrandom responses contribute to the gradient. It should be noted, however, that Dallett (1959) counted adjacent backward associations as remote. He leaves open the question of whether the nonrandomness of response is the cause, or the effect, of the typical serial-position result.

Slamecka (1965) rejected Dallett's (1965) evidence on the grounds that the statistical significance of the difference between the predicted and empirical curves was not established. In view of the consistency of Dallett's results, this rebuttal is weak.

Bugelski (1965) argued that Slamecka's (1964) familiarization procedure for generating associative data of "remote associations" suffers from the fatal flaw that it reveals in the association matrix equal numbers of backward and forward remote associations. Such a result is inconsistent with usual results from actual serial learning results, although Slamecka (1965) argues that such quantities of backward associations have been obtained in real experiments (Dallett, 1959).

In reply to Bugelski's (1965) critique of his treatment of the remote association issue, Slamecka (1965) replied with a general defense of the position-learning view of serial learning. He did, however, emphasize the learning of relative position, rather than absolute position. For example, one might not indeed be able to report the identity of the seventeenth letter of the alphabet, but one could come reasonably close to it. Moreover, a subject could report, with very few errors, which of two letters appears later in the alphabet. Such a feat would be more difficult to explain in terms of remote associations; as Bugelski (1965) suggested, however, knowledge of position could be the result of a "confluence" of remote-associative effects.

Bugelski (1965) performed an experiment to test predictions from Slamecka's theory that the piling up of short-range remote associations was due to earlier learning of the items (usually near the ends) that contribute to the most remote associations, and that items whose position is learned should not appear as remote associations. Accordingly he presented a series of ten four-letter adjectives only once to a group of subjects. Subjects were asked first to reproduce the word following a probe item (which had been the third in the series). Then they were asked to reproduce the entire list in serial order. Bugelski's subjects revealed decreasing gradients of associations, even though each item was presumably still available as an associate, presumably contrary to the prediction from Slamecka's interpretation. Slamecka (1965) did not agree with this conclusion, however. He argued that response overlearning, which creates a response bias favoring "remote associations" in the association technique, does inhibit so-called anticipatory and perservatory errors in serial learning. The reason for this involves the task facing the subject and the instructions given to him. Contrary to the association technique, in which the subject is usually asked to give the first item that pops into his head and, consequently, does not censor the items according to their correctness of the degree of remoteness, in the serial-learning task the subject attempts to get the greatest possible score for accuracy. He therefore tends to inhibit the overt expressions of items that he has just seen, which may be strong in his mind, and other items that may be clear to him but that he knows to be incorrect because he knows their positions. In such a case, only the items that have not been learned—either through association to position or to prior items—are available to become "remote associations."

Slamecka (1965) argued, therefore, that Bugelski's (1965) data from the one-trial experiment actually supported his position-learning argument. Since Bugelski's subjects obviously had not learned all of the responses in one trial, then the Slamecka argument would not predict equal frequencies of associations across all serial positions. On the contrary, the distribution of remote associations would have to conform to the distribution of items whose identity had been learned.

In Bugelski's (1965) serial-recall task there was a positive correlation between the frequency of recall of an item and its frequency as a remote associate, which he interpreted as contrary to Slamecka's argument. Bugelski pointed out that the tenth item was learned better than the ninth item, but also it appeared more often as an associate. On the other hand, as Slamecka (1965) pointed out, the first two items were learned very well, but appeared infrequently as (backward) associates. Since Bugelski's data indicated in several places that position-learning occurred, even on the first trial, but obviously all items were not equally available as intrusions, then according to Slamecka's position, a positive correlation should have appeared between correct positionings and frequency of intrusions. Therefore, Slamecka argued that Bugelski's data supported the Slamecka argument against remote associations, rather than rebutting it.

Other data from serial recall in Bugelski's (1965) experiment had bearing on the way that a serial list was learned—what stimuli were used in a single trial. In the first place, there was a very strong primacy effect, consistent with the fact that failures to respond tended to increase from first to last positions, as did the number of correct position placements when the prior (stimulus) item was not correct. The correct-position placements could have come about through position learning or through remote associative effects. Correct responses to the proper stimulus, but placed in the wrong position, revealed a rather symmetrical serial-position function with a broad maximum over Positions Four to Seven, supporting the idea of interitem associations. Finally, responses given neither to the correct stimulus nor in the correct position revealed a typical bowed serial-position curve in terms of the positions that would have been correct.

INTRUDING ERRORS

The appearance of overt errors, which intrude from either earlier or later positions in a serial list, is a usual phenomenon of serial learning (e.g., Lumley, 1932a,b; Ward, 1937). It is tempting to consider such intrusions as prima facie evidence of competition among response tendencies at the various serial positions. Lumley (1932a,b) reported that subjects tended to anticipate responses that would be correct later in the series, that responses correct in the near future were anticipated more often than those correct in the distant future, and that advanced learning increased the proportion of near to remote anticipations.

Bugelski (1948), using a list of eight nonsense syllables, found remote forward associations diminishing with negative acceleration from the first to the sixth remote syllable. This supports Hull's theoretical analysis and description of the diminishing stimulus trace. In an attempt to explain the skewness of the serial curve, after observing more frequent first-order associations for stimuli late in the list than for earlier stimuli,

Bugelski suggested that the important thing was not the number of associations spanning an item, as earlier hypothesized by Hull (1935a), but the strength of the associations. Thus, he proposed that Hull's theory should be modified to include a differential weighting for the remote associations spanning an item. Such a weighting, he reported, would add asymmetry to the curve in the proper way.

An additional difficulty is pointed out by McGeoch (1942). Hull assumes that remote association is due to stimulus trace and that the more remote associations are weaker because the trace is weaker. It is not proved, however, that there is any clear relation between degree of remoteness and latency of response, which may be taken as a measure of strength of response. In fact, Raskin and Cook (1937) and Hertzman and Neff (1939) found a U-shaped relation between remoteness and strength of association with slight and varying degrees of overlearning, respectively. The experimenters in both studies concluded that this result was due to the circularity of associations through the temporal interval between presentations. When Hertzman and Neff (1939) increased mastery of a list and eliminated circularity, they found a steeper remoteness curve from the test syllable. Hertzman and Neff concluded that greater mastery of a list increased the tendency for forward responses. This indicates that the method of learning is influenced by the direction in which the associations are being formed. The gradient of remote association found by Hertzman and Neff showed more near intrusions than far intrusions, and the proportion of near intrusions increased with increased learning. There was an absolute tendency for all syllables to be given with the same frequency as the degree of mastery increased. Maintaining that these results cannot be explained by contiguity principles alone, they invoked other intangible causes.

Bugelski (1950) modified Hull's (1935a) position by assuming differential weighting of remote associations spanning an item. The interfering traces are stronger at the end of the series, because there are fewer traces left for interference. Thus, the interfering effect of a remote association is greater toward the end of the series, producing the asymmetry. Bugelski (1950) repeated Raskin and Cook's (1937) study of remote-association gradients, but with appropriate counterbalancing for differences in difficulty of syllables. Eight CVC nonsense syllables were learned by the anticipation method for eight trials, with the subject instructed to anticipate each syllable with some response, even if he knew that the response was incorrect. Although Bugelski's weighting scheme added asymmetry to the serial-position curve, and thus was a closer approximation than Hull's (1935a) deduction, it still did not produce as much asymmetry as was obtained in his empirical data. The results revealed more forward intrusions than backward ones. Whereas the backward intrusions increased progressively from beginning to end of the series, as would be expected in line with increased opportunities for backward associations at positions later in the series, the forward associations do not mirror this result. Actually the first-item position shows fewest anticipatory errors. Therefore, a serial-position effect within the anticipatory errors occurs and must therefore confound the calculation of remoteness gradients. As Bugelski points out, only the first and eighth items contribute to the greatest (seventh) degree of remoteness; the items toward the middle of the series, which reveal most anticipatory errors, contribute to the lesser degree of remoteness only.

Wickelgren (1966) investigated what he called associative intrusions in short-term serial recall. Such intrusions are scored when correct responses are given to repeated stimulus items, but at the wrong position. Wickelgren aurally presented lists of nine letters, including eight different letters and one repeated letter, under instructions to subjects to recall the letters in order. The position of the repeated item (at beginning or middle of list), the number of items separating the same (repeated) item, and the phonemic similarity of the items following the repeated item were varied. If the associative-intrusion effect were influenced by the position or separation of the repeated letter, Wickelgren would argue that the effect is determined by the subject's acquisition strategies, rather than associative interference. Since the existence of the associative intrusion effect was verified, and it showed no differential effect caused by the various experimental conditions, Wickelgren concluded that his evidence supports an associative-interference theory of short-term memory.

Mitchell (1933b) noticed that a similar number following a number tended to obstruct its learning. This so-called Ranschburg effect is discussed later under the heading Output Interference.

Conrad (1960) suggested that intruding errors are not a manifestation of interference of other incorrect responses with the correct response. He argued that the subject first fails to recall an item and then selects some alternative item to fill in the recall. To test this hypothesis he varied the time interval between successive tests of immediate memory. Increased time between tests should allow memory for potential serial-order intrusions of items to fade. The interference theory would, therefore, predict fewer errors in recall, whereas the memory-decay theory would predict no change in performance. Conrad found that, in fact, the shorter intervals between successive messages produced more overt intruding errors, but the number of messages correctly recalled did not vary as a function of interval between messages. Thus, his hypothesis was supported.

Peterson, Brewer, and Bertucco (1963) investigated the guessing strategies of subjects in a serial-anticipation task in which subjects could learn the population of items but not their order. The task was like serial-anticipation learning except that the order of the items within a series of nine words was varied from trial to trial. Since the same words appeared on each trial, after the subject learned all of the words, he could theoretically be perfectly accurate in "guessing" the final item on a trial through a process of elimination. His guessing would be progressively less accurate as the items were further removed from the final item, of course. This guessing strategy could account for the so-called recency effect both in serial anticipation learning and in immediate free recall. The results showed that an item was emitted as a guess with increasing frequency as the time interval increased since it had appeared. The highest frequency of guesses was for words that had not appeared as yet on the trial; the subjects divided their guesses evenly among them. Guessed items were designated as forward and backward responses if they were given too early or too late, respectively. The means of forward responses at each position, weighted according to the number of opportunities to make such errors, progressively increased from first to last serial position. On the other hand, the backward responses, similarly weighted, were far more numerous. The proportions of omission errors increased across serial positions, consistent with the previous results of Deese and Kresse (1952). Peterson et al. suggest that the recency effect in serial-learning experiments may be attributable largely to the obtained guessing effect. They point out that the "recency" effect that they obtained compares favorably with the so-called recency effects in serial-learning experiments.

Peterson et al. (1963) checked out the guessing hypothesis in a second experiment, this time using paired-associate learning. The results were the same as for the serial anticipation task, except that the backward responses increased throughout a trial. They concluded from both studies that subjects do not always emit a response, even if it occurs to them, when they know that it is incorrect. Moreover, the number of correct anticipations in serial learning reflects guessing strategies as well as learned associations, thus inflating the number of correct responses at the end of the list. As they point out, however, the magnitude of this effect is not easily calculated. Also, in the case of the serial-learning task the definition of a correct guess and a correct association becomes blurred. In the absence of a certain knowledge about the functional stimulus in serial learning, how can we say that a subject who has learned all of the stimuli, remembers which ones of them have appeared and correctly deduces the final item has not made a correct association but a correct guess? Actually, if the stimulus for the serial learning is a configuration into which the subject fits or constructs (associates) the correct response, we would have to say that the fruit of a successful strategy was a correct association—and not a correct guess.

Postman (1967) found, in serial learning of word lists of high or low intralist associability, that the range of intruding associations was broader and the frequency of backward associations was greater for the high-association items. He concluded that the interference from natural (preexperimental) associations was greater for these items.

Postman (1968b), in his commemorative address on Hermann Ebbinghaus, points out the complexity of the serial-learning task and stresses current doubt about the validity of the remote association concept. He referred to the arguments of Slamecka (1964). In his criticism of the evidence from anticipatory and perseverating errors in serial learning for the existence of remote associations, Slamecka offers an explanation of these errors in terms of position confusion. He proposes that at first the subject learns only the end items and is uncertain about the identity and the position of the items in the central region. At this stage, when the subject guesses he produces any of the items he knows except those he has just seen and those whose position he also knows. Thus, Slamecka concludes:

> At this early stage he is more likely to emit remote associations of higher degree than later, since his ignorance of the list is maximal, and his guesses are less constrained. As learning proceeds, the uncertain region of the list shrinks in extent, leaving fewer unplaced items to be guessed, thus logically insuring that the resulting total errors, as well as their degree of remoteness, will be smaller (1964, p. 72).

Slamecka (1964) supports the contention that the region of uncertainty from which unattached responses are drawn progressively shrinks as learning progresses by showing that the variability of intralist associations is reduced toward the most difficult position as learning progresses. This argument is certainly consistent with the present position. In view of the discussions in Chapters 2 and 3, however, it seems clear that the position-learning and sequential-association conceptions of serial learning are not mutually exclusive. It would seem that with progressive serial learning the immediate, adjacent (correct) association would become sufficiently strong to inhibit the appearance of that item as a remote association—namely, Dallett's (1965) proposition of a response bias. Therefore, the possibility of remote associations as coexistent with position confusion remains.

Underwood (1952a) failed to find a relationship between intralist similarity and the number of commission errors. He concluded that high intralist similarity promoted an increase in tendencies for such errors, but that the subject would "tolerate" the emission of such errors only so often and would thereafter withhold uncertain responses.

Underwood and Goad (1951) found that the frequency of remote errors decreased from first to second halves of learning. Slamecka (1964) also pointed out the decrease in so-called remote associations as learning progressed. He denied, however, that these were actual remote associations but, rather, emitted responses from a decreasing pool of learned but unlocalized items.

The study by Deese and Kresse (1952) of various types of intruding, as well as omission, errors in serial learning has been discussed previously. Harcum and Coppage (1969) classified intruding errors as so-called anticipatory or perseveratory errors, although these results were not presented in their paper. Their data for paced and unpaced presentation of 12-item series are shown for each category of error in Figure 6-4. This figure shows clearly that the change in the shape of the distribution of intruding errors for paced and unpaced presentation is not due to a difference in the proportions of anticipatory and perseveratory errors. Actually, this proportion is about six to one under both conditions. The distribution of perseverative errors changes in the same direction as the distribution of anticipation errors for paced and unpaced presentation, although the number of errors of this type is small. These errors may be conceptualized as forward or backward remote associations (Ebbinghaus, 1913), respectively, or as differentiated but mislocalized responses that are emitted according to the opportunity for such errors (Slamecka, 1964). Although the numbers of such errors are about the same for paced and unpaced presentation, it should be recalled that the number of trials is greater in the case of the paced condition. Consequently, the proportion of intralist intruding errors is greater in the unpaced condition. The subjects have more time to make overt errors with unpaced presentation, but fewer trials in which to add to the total. This suggests that the number of overt errors is being depressed by some factor in the paced condition, but the implication of the change in the shapes of the curves in Figure 6-4 is that the number of intralist intruding errors is being depressed differentially for different syllable positions. Specifically, the number of intralist intruding errors at the end of the list with paced presentation is depressed below the absolute number of errors for the unpaced condition, which accumulated in fewer trials.

Perseveration errors are very few, and thus the curve of intralist intrusions is essentially a curve of anticipation errors. The few perseverative errors are distributed about as one would expect—the frequency is

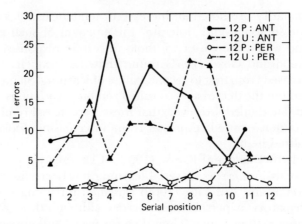

Figure 6-4   Anticipation and perseverating errors with paced or unpaced 12-item lists, after Harcum and Coppage (1969). Copyright © (1969) by the American Psychological Association. Reprinted by permission.

greater at the end of the list where the opportunity for such errors is greater. With paced presentation, however, there is a trend toward the emission of a greater number of these errors in the first half of the list, compared to unpaced presentation, and fewer such errors in the second half of the list. The direction of this difference is the same as that for the anticipation errors, suggesting a response-related mechanism of inhibition, rather than a difference in the progress of learning.

The direction of the skew in the distributions is different for the anticipation and the perseveration curves, as would be expected in terms of the numbers of opportunities for such errors across serial positions. A second difference is that the anticipation errors for both paced and unpaced presentation dip markedly for the items near the beginning of the list, whereas the perseveration errors continue to rise to the end of the list for the unpaced condition. Both types of intralist intrusions reflect the fact that the subject has learned syllables, in whole or in part, but produces them at the incorrect position. The lingering traces of the stimuli at the beginning of the series interfere with the tendencies of the subject to give them again—either through a stimulus satiation effect, or because the subject remembers them well enough to know that they had already appeared earlier in the series. The functions of anticipation errors reflect the changing opportunities for such errors to occur; the dip at the beginning is probably due to the fact that these first items are learned early, thus eliminating these positions as possible loci of intralist intruding errors. The drop in anticipatory errors at the end of the series probably reflects the fact that there are fewer items to anticipate. With unpaced presentation more anticipatory errors appear in the last half than in the first half. This seeming paradox probably reflects the fact that the last positions are the later learned, although the spelling of the syllables is learned much earlier so that they become available as overt intrusions for positions that have not been mastered.

For the condition of alternating paced and unpaced trials with 12-item lists, used by Harcum and Coppage (1969), the curves of intralist intruding errors were nearly symmetrical. The breakdown of intralist intruding errors into the categories of anticipation and perseveration errors for the alternating paced and unpaced conditions is shown in Figure 6-5. Perseveration errors are again scarce, and thus the absolute differences between the results are small; these results are, however, consistent in direction with the completely paced and unpaced data. The anticipatory errors do show the shift with paced presentation toward fewer errors at the end. Under this condition of learning, performance changes on paced trials can reveal only momentary availability effects and, thus, one would expect that the distribution of the alternate trials would not be markedly different.

In Figure 6-5 there is a tendency toward an interactive effect between the relative numbers of perseverative versus anticipation errors and the pacing of the trials. Whereas perseverative errors are more frequent under the paced than the unpaced trials, the anticipatory errors are

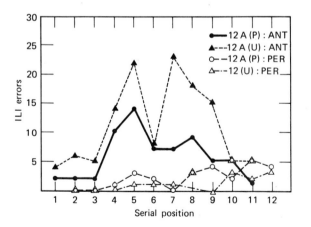

Figure 6-5 Anticipation and perseverating errors with alternating paced and unpaced trials of 12-item lists, after Harcum and Coppage (1969). Copyright © (1969) by the American Psychological Association. Reprinted by permission.

more frequent for the unpaced trials. This result strengthens the argument for the importance of a stimulus trace. Such a trace should be stronger at the end of the series with the paced trials, because the time between the appearances of the stimuli is shorter. One possible interpretation of the above interactive effect is that the subject merely emits the stimuli with the strongest trace when he does not know the correct response. Thus, a stronger trace for the stimuli at the beginning of the list would tend to increase the probability that an earlier syllable would be given. The tendency for the greater number of errors to appear for the second half of the series with unpaced presentation, and for the beginning of the list with the paced trials, in the alternating condition corresponds to the noted difference between completely paced and unpaced series. Therefore, this indicates that the pacing condition has a momentary "mechanical" effect upon performance rather than a long-range effect upon the learning process as Deese and Kresse (1952) imply.

The stimulus-trace concept is relevant to the arguments for and against the existence of so-called remote associations. However, it would be a moot argument whether the actual overt response was given to the immediately preceding syllable—that is, a direct forward association (Ebbinghaus, 1913)—or whether it was given as a deducible response to constraints on the number of possible responses at a general location within the list (Slamecka, 1964). Of course, the strength of previous traces within the series would be a significant factor in the determination of which responses were available.

Harcum and Coppage also obtained intruding errors for 8-item lists that are comparable to those obtained with the 12-item lists. Whereas the unpaced curve shows more errors at the end of the series, the paced condition reveals more errors at the beginning of the list. However, both curves are generally symmetrical, so that overall only the quadratic component of position is significant. The anticipation and perseveration errors of the 8-item conditions are shown in Figure 6-6. The errors in both categories show the difference between paced and unpaced presentation; both anticipation and perseveration errors show the greater frequency of errors toward the end of the list with the unpaced presentation.

For 16-item lists Harcum and Coppage (1969) found that the absolute numbers of overt errors do not differ greatly for paced and unpaced conditions. The basic shape of intralist intruding functions is bowed. However, the intralist intrusions again show the change in skewness for the two conditions of pacing. The magnitude of the difference is not great, but the difference is apparent, particularly for the items at the

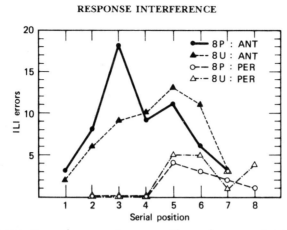

Figure 6-6   Anticipation and perseverating errors with paced or unpaced eight-item lists, after Harcum and Coppage (1969). Copyright (1969) by the American Psychological Association. Reprinted by permission.

very beginning and end of the series. This is reflected in a significant interaction between the linear component of position with the rate of presentation. The usual trend in the direction of change in the asymmetry of paced and unpaced series for the anticipation and perseveration errors can be seen in Figure 6-7. The curves are not greatly different, but again both classes of errors show the same direction of change.

The Kimble and Dufort (1955) study of serial learning revealed generally symmetrical distribution of intruding errors. This, again, is consistent with the Deese and Kresse (1952) and the Harcum and Coppage (1969) results.

DISCUSSION

One problem for the theory of remote associations is that the remote associations of greatest degree are necessarily between the first and last items, which are better reproduced. Therefore, the responses are more available, possibly accounting for the upswing of the most remote associations. Another possibility is that the last and first items are associated across the intertrial interval, which actually is temporally closer than the "remote" interval. This again would produce an upswing of the remoteness gradient.

Remote associations undoubtedly contribute to the interference within a serial list. Probably the analytic techniques, of either intruding errors or association gradients, do not describe the full complexity of the mechanism.

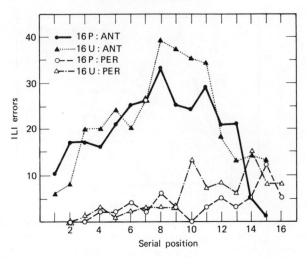

Figure 6-7 Anticipation and perseverating errors with paced or unpaced trials of 16-item lists, after Harcum and Coppage (1969). Copyright (1969) by the American Psychological Association. Reprinted by permission.

Mediated Association

Peters (1935) suggested that two items could be associated by their mutual association to a third item, as in an A-B, C-B paradigm, in which the subject is afterward presented with a list of Λ items and asked to name the corresponding C items. In several experiments, he found some positive evidence for indirect or mediate associations; the awareness of the subject about the connection between lists was important. There was no difference between mediated associations in the backward or forward direction (namely, whether the common item in the two lists was stimulus or response). McGeoch (1942) also suggested that a possible cause of apparent remote association is that the two items are associated with each other by means of mutual association with a third, or mediate, item.

Russell and Storms (1955) provided evidence that the natural, preexperimental word associations of the subjects could serve as mediators in paired-associate learning. The subjects who had learned to associate a nonsense syllable to a word could later show facilitative effects of this in learning a new response item that was associated with the prior response through a mediational chain of frequent normal associations (e.g., stem, flower, smell). Cramer and Cofer (1960) also obtained positive results for paired-associate learning mediated by natural (preexperimental) associations. Positive transfer was obtained both for mediation between stimuli and between responses, when the associations were in the forward direction and also when they were in the backward direction.

Mandler and Earhard (1964) have shown how a pseudomediation effect can appear in paired-associate learning. They show how unlearning of the original backward associations (B-A) by the second task (B-C) in the A-B, B-C, A-C paradigm can decrease the interfering effect of the association between B and A when the A-C pairs are to be learned.

Conclusion

Evidence has thus been presented for interference in response selection or production processes. The specific mechanism or mechanisms by which this occurs are not known, however. Ceraso (1967) suggests that interference operates through a "crowding" of items from different categories. Therefore, the subject has to search his memory for items belonging to a larger population, which decreases the availability of that item. Postman, Stark, and Fraser (1968) go further to suggest that the competition in interference may not be between specific associations but between responding systems.

OUTPUT INTERFERENCE

The competition that produces interference in serial learning may be between the correct response and the response that the subject has emitted or been tempted to emit previously. Two rather general categories of such interference are, first, the more specific interference of prior responses in a series and, second, the broader category of all responses that have tendencies that could compete with the correct one. This second category is similar to the position-confusion interpretation to be discussed later in this chapter.

Specific Competition

Scheible and Underwood (1954) investigated the effects of the proportion of overt errors in serial learning on the time to learn. Three groups of subjects learned serial lists under three different instructions. The control condition did not instruct the subject about the proportion of overt errors to be produced, whereas the "high" instructions told the subject to guess on every occasion, and the "low" instructions told the subject to withhold a response unless he were sure of the correct response. An independent check did reveal that high-guessing groups did, in fact, make more overt errors. An analysis of variance failed to reveal a significant difference between the three groups in terms of trials to criterion. Therefore, Scheible and Underwood concluded that the tendency of the subject to make or inhibit the overt response did not affect total learning time. Although the results of the statistical test were negative, the results were, in fact, positive. No matter which subjects were receiving which instructions, the control condition produced the best learning at each stage of practice, and the low-responding condition produced poorest learning. The failure to find a significant difference was probably due to the use of trials to criterion as the measure of learning, with the criterion of learning taken as one errorless trial.

Another example of specific output inhibition comes from Jahnke's (1969b) study of the Ranschburg effect, which describes the decrease in serial recall for a group of disconnected items when one of the items is repeated in the series. His results, and those which he obtained later (Jahnke, 1969a), support the conclusion that the Ranschburg effect is very much dependent upon a variety of experimental conditions. Two important contributing factors seem to be that the repeated items are not too close to one another in the series and that recall is serial—with output interference contributing to the inhibitory effect.

Underwood and Goad (1951) found that distributed practice aided learning for a high-similarity list, but not for a list of low similarity, although the distributed practice did produce more overt errors. This is inconsistent with the arguments and data of several researchers. For example, Conrad (1960, 1965) argues that overt intrusions are not the result of interference, but the cause of it. Montague (1953) similarly proposes that the emission of incorrect responses produces the interference; the subject confuses what he overtly responded with what he should have responded. The data of Scheible and Underwood (1954) support this argument. Therefore, once the subject has experienced an item in the incorrect position, through an overt intruding error, this incorrect association can compete in some manner with learning it in the correct position.

Goggin (1967) found, with a retroactive inhibition paradigm in paired-associate learning, that procedures that increase the number of intruding errors will exert a greater retroactive effect. This was attributed to the greater opportunities for unlearning when an overt intrusion is made.

Peterson, Brewer, and Bertucco (1963) indicated that the subjects did not always make a response they knew to be wrong—for example, from just having seen that item. Thus, the number of intrusion errors is not necessarily inversely correlated with the accuracy of serial-learning performance (Slamecka, 1964). The Deese and Kresse (1952) and Harcum and Coppage (1969) data on intralist intrusions support this finding. The subjects can build up a responding inhibition that can inhibit overt responding and decrease intrusions without affecting the actual learning.

Buschke and Hinrichs (1968) instructed subjects to rehearse series of ten numbers, cumulating the rehearsal from first to last items. Recall was tested by one of four output orders: forward serial, backward serial, free, and natural sequence. Since the subjects typically used the natural sequence of the numbers as the basis for free recall, results for these two conditions were generally equivalent. Serial recall was generally the same overall for the two directions of ordering, and less accurate than for the meaningful organization. Examination of the recall attempts during rehearsal learning showed that the ordinal position of the recall attempt was directly related to the proportion of correct recalls. The first five recalls were almost perfectly accurate for all four experimental conditions. Thereafter, the drop for both of the serial-recall conditions proceeded at a faster rate than for meaningfully organized recall. Thus, the forgetting (output interference) increased more rapidly for the strings that were ordered in terms of nonmeaningful temporal sequence.

General Competition

Deese and Hardman (1954) analyzed the types of errors in retention of serial-anticipation learning, paired-associate learning, and serial association of connected discourse. In serial relearning most errors were either within-list errors or failures to respond. For both paired-associate and connected-discourse learning, the errors were primarily due to intrusions of items from interpolated learning, with an associated reduction of within-list errors. The difference between the different types of learning seems to be that the item in serial learning is more firmly embedded in a stable context than is the item in paired-associate learning. The passages of connected discourse were deliberately designed to be similar and thus to promote between-list confusions. These results support the conclusion that the source of errors in retroactive inhibition depends upon the contextual cues.

Deese and Marder (1957) tested recall of original serial learning after an interpolated serial-learning task, by an unpaced anticipation test after

4 minutes, 2 hours, 24 hours, or 48 hours. Within-list errors decreased and between-list errors increased. Since the total number of items retained did not vary over time, the authors concluded that the context (list membership) of items was forgotten faster than the items themselves.

On the basis of Hull's (1943) theory, a number of studies have predicted that increased drive would facilitate response evocation. For example, Taylor (1951) showed that subjects categorized as high anxious on her Manifest Anxiety Scale learned a conditioned eyeblink response much more easily. The argument is that high-anxious subjects have a higher general drive level than less anxious subjects. Rosenbaum (1956) found that high-anxious subjects not only gave larger amplitude of a motor response to a visual stimulus, they also showed greater response amplitude to similar (untrained) stimuli.

If the task given to the subject requires a discrimination among possible responses, however, instead of a simple increase in the strength of one response, as in the case of the eyeblink, then the task is more difficult for the subjects under higher drive. Direct support of this difference was obtained by Farber and Spence (1953) and by Beam (1955).

Farber and Spence (1953) had the same subjects, categorized as anxious or nonanxious, learn a stylus maze. The nonanxious subjects performed with greater accuracy on the maze, as predicted from the Taylor-Spence hypothesis (Taylor & Spence, 1952). Farber and Spence also predicted that the difference between subject groups would be most different where the task was most difficult. Therefore they examined the relative performances at the various choice points and discovered that the difference was greater for the more difficult items. Farber and Spence reported a rank-order correlation of .74 between overall difficulty rank, as determined from a pretest, and rank according to the magnitude of difference between groups. Actually a calculation of the correlation in terms of the total errors combined for both groups of subjects on the experimental tasks with the absolute difference between groups at each choice point increases this correlation to .85. Since such a result could be an artifact of the different overall totals of errors for the different groups, given the character of the serial-position curve, the proper comparison should however be in terms of the level of performance. Reanalysis of these Farber and Spence data fails to support their conclusion. When the serial positions are ranked according to the percentage of difference in errors, in ascending order, the rank-order correlation was −.52, using the pretest criterion of difficulty, and −.43 using the task-performance criterion. This difference is not due to a gross difference in definition of relative difficulty, since the two orders correlate significantly ($\rho = + .83, p < .01$). The percentage rankings and the absolute rankings of the differences between groups fail to correlate significantly ($\rho = .058$). This analysis means that in percentage terms the advantage of the nonanxious subjects decreased as the task became more difficult. This argument is not simple, however, because it is not always clear whether or not differences between serial-position curves should be evaluated in absolute or relative terms (Harcum, 1970a).

Rather convincing evidence that the difference was not an artifact of intellectual differences between groups was the finding by Farber and Spence (1953) that high- and low-anxious subjects matched for total errors produced differential performance at easy and difficult positions. While the anxious subjects performed better than nonanxious for the five easiest positions, the reverse was true for the five most difficult positions. Farber and Spence ran the same low- and high-anxious subjects that had been used in their stylus-maze experiment in a conditioned eyeblink experiment. The low-anxious subjects that had been superior in maze learning were now less easily conditioned. The difference was that there were fewer competing response tendencies in the classical-learning paradigm.

Beam (1955) found that subjects in real-life stressful situations required more trials to master a serial list and made more errors. The serial-learning stimuli were three-letter nonsense syllables of unspecified difficulty. On the other hand, galvanic skin responses were conditioned by shock to a light stimulus significantly faster for these same subjects under stress. Presumably, responses were energized by the anxiety, facilitating conditioning of the galvanic skin responses, but inhibiting performance when there were interfering responses in the serial-learning task.

Taylor and Spence (1952) tested subjects who scored at extremes on the Manifest Anxiety Scale (Taylor, 1951), using a verbal T maze for the task. The subject had to anticipate in a serial-learning situation whether the next response on the memory drum would be a "left" or a "right." There were 20 choices in the series. Since the task involved the trial and error learning of correct responses from competing ones, the authors predicted and obtained faster learning for the low-anxious groups, because the increased drive also strengthens the incorrect response tendencies as well as the correct ones (Hull, 1943).

Hughes, Sprague, and Bendig (1954) obtained negative results from a repetition of the Taylor and Spence (1952) study with two modifications in method; they used a slower presentation rate and varied the number of alternations at successive choices in the verbal T maze (i.e., runs of the same choice). The high- and low-anxious subjects did not differ significantly in terms of trials to criterion or errors, and the interactions between subject groups and type of list were not significant. Learning curves were plotted in the manner of Vincent (1912), in which the total number of learning trials was divided into tenths of learning in order to compensate for individual differences in learning ability. These curves were not different for anxious and nonanxious subjects.

A number of studies, reviewed by Jones (1961), support the prediction of Taylor and Spence (1952) that anxiety level inhibits performance when response competition is high. For example, Jensen (1962b) investigated serial learning of colored forms for groups of subjects categorized according to performance on the Maudsley Personality Inventory (Eysenck, 1962) as extroverted or introverted and high or low neurotic. As predicted, an increase in presentation rate degraded performance significantly more for the high-neurotic subjects. The deleterious effect of increased presentation rates for the extroversion-introversion dimension was not significant. The shapes of the serial-position curves were all equivalent, representing the typical skewed, bowed result.

Willet (1958) found that subjects with high neuroticism scores on the Maudsley Personality Inventory (Eysenck, 1962) took more trials to learn a serial list and made more oscillations. These differences produced greater bowing of the serial-position curves, presumably because of the greater interference at the central item-positions.

Lazarus, Deese, and Osler (1952) point out that stress exerts an energizing effect on performance and thus results in an increased output. Therefore, the subject under stress may increase his speed of performance at the expense of accuracy. If this occurs in serial learning, the subject is likely to increase the proportion of commission errors. Since commission errors are more prevalent about the middle of a series, the bowing of the total curve of errors is consequently increased.

Montague (1953) found a significant interaction between intralist similarity in serial learning and the anxiety level of the subjects. This was predicted from the Taylor-Spence (1952) theory. Whereas the high-anxious subjects performed better than low-anxious ones on low-similarity lists, in which intralist competition was presumably low, they were inferior to the low-anxious subjects in learning lists with high intralist similarity.

Lucas (1952) employed immediate serial recall for ten consonants, using subjects classified as anxious and nonanxious according to Taylor's test (Taylor, 1951). Test series contained zero, two, or five duplications of letters. Subgroups of subjects were given various numbers of false reports of failure. The nonanxious subjects were superior overall, because their performance increased with increased failure-feedback, whereas the anxious subjects deteriorated with successive failure experiences. The advantage of nonanxious subjects increased as the number of duplications increased.

Deese, Lazarus, and Keenan (1953) found that anxious subjects performed better under all conditions of a serial-learning task consisting of 12 anticipation trials for 12 three-consonant nonsense syllables. Since the items were highly dissimilar, the results seemed to be largely motivationally determined. The smallest difference between the high- and low-anxious subjects was for a control (neutral) condition, followed by a condition in which the subjects were given random electric shocks (i.e., unrelated to performance). The greatest difference occurred when the subjects were given the shocks for failures to give correct anticipations.

In order to resolve the discrepancy between the results of Lucas (1952) and Montague (1953), which found poorer performance for anxious subjects under some conditions, and those of Deese, Lazarus, and Keenan (1953) which found superior performance for anxious subjects, Lazarus, Deese, and Hamilton (1954) repeated the Deese et al. (1953) study with a different population of stimuli. Instead of the dissimilar items used previously, they used a list with extremely high intralist similarity (namely, duplication). Although none of the differences was significant, they were all in the direction predicted by the Taylor-Spence hypothesis (Taylor & Spence, 1952)—namely, the nonanxious subjects performed more accurately. Therefore, the anxiety appears to add to the difficulty of differentiating the items within the series and thus to the overall difficulty of the task.

Saltz and Hoehn (1957) pointed out the problem of distinguishing between competition of responses and difficulty of the task, arguing that these are not the same but that they have often been treated so. Their procedure was to select nine high-association (easy) items from Glaze's (1928) list, and build in formal similarity (i.e., competition). These items were matched with an equal group of low-association items in which precautions were taken to eliminate formal intralist similarity. Subjects were high- or low-anxious according to the Taylor (1951) scale. The differences between list types for both anxious and nonanxious groups in terms of trials to criterion were small and not significant. Nevertheless, the interaction between type of list and subject group, although tiny, was in the direction of the Taylor-Spence hypothesis. The interaction itself was not tested. Considering the unreliability of trials-to-criterion measures, the failure of the significance test is not very damaging to the hypothesis.

In a second experiment, Saltz and Hoehn (1957) constructed by similar means a low-competition list that was actually higher in difficulty than the high-competition list that was used in the first experiment.

Here the result is truly damaging to the Taylor-Spence hypothesis if one accepts the Saltz-Hoehn definition of competition in terms of formal similarity. Since the presentation rate was 2 seconds, and the noncompeting items were of zero association value, the task was very difficult. In fact, for a nine-item list the means of about 30 and 45 trials to a criterion of one perfect recitation for nonanxious and anxious subjects, respectively, represent poor performance indeed. Saltz and Hoehn suggest that the great overall difficulty of the difficult, noncompeting list becomes stressful and therefore potentiates or triggers additional anxiety that contributes to further detriment in performance. This would be predicted on the basis of the alleged U-shaped function (Yerkes & Dodson, 1908), relating high arousal and performance. Perhaps the resolution of this problem in terms of the Taylor-Spence hypothesis is that with extreme levels of anxiety the discrimination is so poor that all alternative responses are highly competitive.

The conclusion of Saltz and Hoehn's (1957) second experiment was supported by some results of Matarazzo, Ulett, and Saslow (1955). Subjects were assigned to one of seven anxiety levels on the basis of the Manifest Anxiety Scale (Taylor, 1951), and tested on a stylus maze. The authors predicted a U-shaped function of performance, with subjects of intermediate anxiety level showing best performance. The performance was assessed in terms of the learning time to three consecutive perfect runs and the number of trials to reach the criterion. The time measure showed the predicted U-shaped result. The trials-to-criterion measure did not produce the clear relative advantage for the low-anxious subjects, however. Although the minimum still fell at an intermediate level of anxiety, and the highest levels revealed marked deterioration, the lowest levels did not show the marked disadvantage.

Silverman and Blitz (1956) found that high- and low-anxious subjects did not yield different numbers of errors in serial learning of eight low-association syllables. However, they did respond differently to the threat of avoidable and nonavoidable shock. The high-anxious subjects appeared to be less responsive to threats and also less likely to learn the concurrent incidental stimuli that were irrelevant to the main learning task.

In two studies of serial learning of nonsense syllables, Sarason (1956, 1957) supported the conclusion that high- and low-anxious subjects did not differ in learning ability, but they did respond differently to failure experiences and ego-involvement instructions. Therefore, task differences and situational factors that affect the subject's strategies are important in determining relative performances of anxious and nonanxious subjects.

Krishna and Varma (1972) also found that high-anxious subjects took longer and made more errors than the low-anxious in learning a series of 15 low-association nonsense syllables. The test, which was used to distinguish subjects of high and low anxiety, purported to be a test of clinical "free-floating" anxiety.

Conclusion

Evidence for both types of output interference has been presented. It is difficult to state specifically the nature of this mechanism. The critical factor may be the selector (retrieval) mechanism by which a response was chosen for overt emission, or it may be a general inability to inhibit incorrect responding tendencies.

Farber (1955) distinguishes between the motivational (drive) properties of variables and their associative properties. He argues that often the effects of so-called motivational variables are effective because of their associational cues instead of their drive value. Thus they would aid retrieval. This further complicates the problem of predicting effects of increased arousal.

UNLEARNING

Associative inhibition may not be due to competition between responses, but to unlearning of the original response. Melton and Irwin (1940) had 24 subjects learn a list of 18 nonsense syllables for 5 trials and rest 30 minutes or learn a second list for 5, 10, 20, or 40 trials. Then the subjects relearned the original list to a criterion of 2 successive errorless trials. Since the anticipatory method was used, with the subjects spelling the responses, overt interlist intrusions of responses could be recorded. The results showed an increase of retroactive inhibition with early increase of original learning and a decrease in retroactive inhibition with very high degrees of interpolated learning. Intrusions from the interpolated list occurred in general proportion to the degree of retroactive inhibition measured. The intrusions were attributed to similar syllable positions or to identity of letters in the two syllables. This interpretation is interesting in view of the controversy between association and position-learning hypotheses of serial learning. Since there were overt signs of proactive inhibition from the test list within the interpolated list, Melton and Irwin concluded that the results favored a transfer theory of proactive inhibition. Retroactive inhibition includes, in addition to competition of responses, however, an unlearning of the original responses. This conclusion was supported by Melton and von Lackum (1941), who found less proactive inhibition on interpolated material than retroactive effect on the original material.

Other studies of paired-associate learning have supported the argument for unlearning as a component of retroactive inhibition (e.g., Barnes & Underwood, 1959; McGovern, 1964; Goggin, 1967). McGovern (1964), using four transfer paradigms, concluded that the subject unlearned both forward and backward associations, as well as the response itself—which was presumed to be unlearning of the connections between stimulus context and the items. Goggin (1967) tested and supported the "response elicitation theory," which proposed that responses were extinguished by being overtly or covertly made during the acquisition of an interpolated learning task.

Keppel (1968) has been a major proponent of the unlearning conception, emphasizing unlearning as the major process in forgetting. Keppel and Zavortink (1968) investigated the relative contribution of unlearning and response competition on serial learning by an immediate recall test of retroactive inhibition from an interpolated serial-learning task. A paced-recall test involved five additional anticipation trials on the original list, which is presumably affected by both unlearning of original associations and competition among responses. An unpaced recall of the first list presumably involved only the unlearning of prior associations. Therefore, differences between the two tests should reflect the competition component of retroactive inhibition in serial learning. For the paced recall, the investigators obtained results duplicating those of Hovland (1940a), and Postman and Riley (1959). Namely, on the first relearning trial the serial-position curve for experimental subjects was very flat, whereas the usual bowed curve was obtained for the control subjects. However, on the second relearning trial both primacy and recency effects were reinstated for the experimental subjects—with the primacy effects the stronger. This could be attributed to a generalized response competition—a set to respond from the incorrect, interpolated list, or to specific competition between responses, or to unlearning.

Keppel and Zavortink's (1968) comparison of results from the paced serial-anticipation relearning test with the unpaced modified free-recall test presented some procedural problems, since the free-recall test did not require correct position association as did the anticipation test. A position-dependent scoring was made possible by use of data obtained after the unpaced subjects had completed their recall task. They had then been given the items in scrambled order and asked to re-order them as on the original list. An item correctly recalled on the free-recall test was scored as associatively correct if it also had been given in the correct absolute or relative position on the re-ordering test. This re-ordering showed clear primacy and recency effects for both control and experimental groups. Since the position-associated (adjusted) results for the paced and unpaced tests were equivalent, the additional factor of competition in the paced task was presumably of minimal effect. There-fore, the results for the paced test were produced primarily by unlearn-ing. Thus, by this argument, the missing primacy effect in the free-recall test was not basically due to a loss of set, but primarily to the unavailabili-ty of the items at the ends of the series. Keppel and Zavortink caution that the validity of their results rests on several unproved assumptions about the equivalence of mechanisms and functional stimuli of the paced and unpaced tasks, however.

Since Keppel and Zavortink's results appear to show the differential unlearning of first and last items, the reason for this provides an interest-ing basis for speculations. They suggest that perhaps the answer lies in the functional stimuli for end items versus middle items. If end items are associated to positions, then the paradigm for strong negative transf-er is invoked by the interpolated learning (namely, A-B, A-C). If middle items are associated to other items, then the paradigm for weaker nega-tive transfer is involved (namely, A-B, C-D). There are some problems with this interpretation, too, since the subjects were able to re-order the end items with greater accuracy than the middle items.

STIMULUS GENERALIZATION

Generalization theory (Gibson, 1940) considers learning a series as re-quiring a differentiation of each item from others within the list. This hypothesis has obvious relevance to competition of responses. Gibson proposes that generalization occurs between not only stimulus items but response items as well. She points out that the Gestalt concept—that homogeneous items suffer "aggregation" of traces and therefore lose their identity and are more difficult to retain—is similar to her proposed theory. Also, Deese (1958) asserts that "anticipatory and perservatory errors are attributable to stimulus generalization" (p. 171).

Explanation of Cason's (1926a, b) associative results of greater difficul-ty for longer lists can be explained by the generalization hypothesis; more items cause more difficulty in discrimination. Since the degree of generalization between items is unpredictable, the number of trials necessary for learning is also unpredictable. Gibson proposes that the extent of differentiation depends on the time that has elapsed since differential reinforcement, because spontaneous recovery will occur with a longer latency the further differentiation has progressed.

Using paired-associate learning, Gibson (1942) found that a high-generalization list is harder to learn than a low-generalization list, and it is less well retained. She found more overt intruding errors for more similar (high-generalization) items. Her data show that the learning of a second list is inhibited less if the first list is slightly learned or well learned, and the interference is greatest when the first list is moderately well learned. In another experiment by Gibson (1942), generalization first increased and then decreased with increasing degrees of learning for paired associates. The stimulus-differentiation study of Gagné and Foster (1949) also showed an initial increase and then decrease of intruding errors as the degree of pretraining on the task components increased. Confusion is apparently maximal when alternatives have about the same response strength.

Gibson (1941) extended her theory to include retroactive inhibition, proposing that gradients of generalization within a list correspond to gradients of perceptual similarity. Gibson (1940) suggests that a recognition-memory task would perhaps require a Gestalt-type perceptual analysis. Since the elements at the ends of a homogeneous array are ordinarily the most identifiable because of their unique positions, they would enjoy an advantage for storage in the memory system over the elements embedded within the group of elements. For example, the learning of the beginning and ending syllables, which separate figure from ground, provides a basis for localizing individual items within the series. Such aggregation or lack of differentiation interferes with memory for the items (Gibson, 1942; Underwood & Schulz, 1960)—a point that is particularly relevant to the present thesis.

Gibson (1942) concludes that the serial-position effect cannot be deduced from the generalization hypothesis alone. But, if the difficulty of certain portions of the serial task is due to conflicting excitatory potentials, as many have suggested, the concepts of generalization and differentiation can be used to explain the intraserial effects. Apparently factors influencing the course of differentiation, such as set, vividness, configuration, and so forth, indirectly cause the serial-position curve.

Phillip and Peixotto (1943a, b) found evidence for Gibson's theory. They defined generalization as the assigning of the correct response to inappropriate stimulus (i.e., incorrectly localizing response), and discrimination as the correct localizing of the correct response. In incomplete paired-associate learning, they found generalization gradients (Phillip & Peixotto, 1943a). In a series of 12 paired associates (but not in shorter series), Phillip and Peixotto (1943b) showed a generalization curve for inadequate responses as a function of distance from the base syllable. They also reported that generalized responses were more frequent than discriminated responses during most of the learning, but discriminated responses increased while generalized responses decreased toward the end of learning.

The generalization hypothesis is supported by many other studies that show faster learning for the series of lower intralist similarity (e.g., Underwood, 1952a; 1953; Underwood & Goad, 1951; Underwood & Richardson, 1956). However, as Underwood (1954) points out, intralist similarity does not affect recall of the series, contrary to Gibson's (1940) hypothesis, whereas interlist similarity does produce a decrement in recall. The difference according to Underwood (1954) is that interference in learning and recall can come not only from other items within a list but also from different lists. In serial learning and relearning, higher intralist similarity promotes intralist interference, but reduces extralist interference, because the lists are more differentiable. Since intralist interference is a greater influence in serial learning, the learning and relearning should be affected by similarity. For recall, however, the advantage of similarity for interlist differentiation, and the disadvantage of similarity for intralist differentiation, tend to cancel, producing no overall effect of similarity in recall. The intralist interference is less in serial learning, because the constant starting item provides a cue to identify each list—the first items provide gross differentiation cues for the various lists. As Underwood (1954) puts it:

> By gross differentiation is meant that there are cues, especially the cues provided by the first syllable of the list, which allow S to identify the list as a list. Phenomenologically speaking, these cues allow S to say in effect, "Oh, yes, *this* list." (p. 164).

Schwartz (1970b) calculated generalization gradients of errors after one-trial serial learning of ten words, using probes for recall of position, immediate forward associations, and immediate backward associations. He used three methods. The first was to compute the distance between actual response and correct response, in terms of serial positions, subtract this from the expected distance due to chance, and weight according to the expected distances, which vary according to the serial position. Virtually all values for each probe were positive, indicating a grouping of errors closer to the position of the correct response. Moreover, these values increased progressively from first to last serial positions, indicating sharper generalization gradients around the terminal items. The second method employed a rather complicated correction for the greater frequency of guessing at the end of the list and revealed about the same degree of response generalization at each serial position. A third method permitted a description of the shape of the generalization gradient over adjacent positions, but lost specific position identification by collapsing over the various serial positions. Each probe type revealed a negatively accelerated gradient, with greater than chance values at distances of one and two positions, and less than chance for greater distances. The slopes of the curves showed apparent slight differences, with the position probe showing steepest slope, and backward associations the least slope.

Number of Alternatives

Jahnke (1963) investigated serial-position effects in immediate serial recall of strings of consonant letters of length five through nine. The results yielded typical serial-position curves with greater primacy than recency effects. Bowing was greater for the longer series; this was attributed to the greater interference with the longer series. In spite of the greater interference in recall of the later items of longer series, the first item was reproduced with almost perfect accuracy for each length of list, therefore showing some sort of insulation—presumably cognitive in origin—from the increased interference. Jahnke points out that the serial recall of immediate memory is like a single unpaced trial of serial-anticipation learning, which also shows greater primacy than recency effects. Jahnke (1965) later investigated in one study both serial and free immediate recall of word lists of various lengths. Again, the bowing was greater for the longer series.

Miller (1965), in two experiments, presented items of different categories and arrangements for repeated trials of presentation and serial recall. In the first experiment, lists of 12 consonant letters were more difficult to learn than 12 digits, but 6 digits followed by 6 letters were easier than the numbers alone. However, four groups of items (namely, digits, letters, names of months, and color names) were easiest. To account for these results, Miller proposed a "weighted alternatives" score, which is the sum across all items of a list of the product of the number of alternative items at a given position and the number of positions occupied by items of the same category. Thus, the learnability of a list is related to the number of possible alternatives competing with the items to be learned. This idea is similar to the item-differentiation component proposed by Gibson (1942) and Saltz (1971).

In a second similar experiment, Miller (1965) showed that grouping items of a similar category together was more advantageous to learning than when the items were not so grouped. This is consistent with the reduction-of-alternatives idea.

Intralist Similarity

Presumably, the more rapid learning of easily differentiable items (Underwood & Richardson, 1956) is due to the fewer numbers of intruding associations. Since Noble's (1952a, b) measure of meaning, m, was based on the mean number of associations produced on demand by a subject, a paradox is produced. Although learning is presumably inhibited by increasing the number of possible associations, the number of associations is greater for meaningful items, which are learned faster. This paradox was pointed out by Postman (1963a), as one of the principles of conservation that reduced the amount of interference effects to be expected from the number of preexisting associations. Moreover, high similarity of responses facilitates the response-learning phase of verbal learning (Underwood, Rundquist, & Schulz, 1959).

Underwood and Richardson (1956) found that both low intralist similarity and high meaningfulness of the items facilitated serial learning by the anticipation method. They emphasized the importance of interference in serial learning from items learned in previous lists. Also, verbal experiences from everyday life would interfere particularly with high-meaningful items. But they also emphasized the "transitoriness" of such interference (cf., Wickens, Born, & Allen, 1963). Underwood and Richardson (1956) found that meaningfulness of items facilitated serial learning and reduced the interfering effect of intralist similarity. However, recall was not influenced by meaningfulness when allowance was made for the degree of original learning. A similar result appeared from serial-position differences—once degree of original learning was taken into account there were no differences among serial positions. Schulz and Kasschau (1966) also failed to find a difference in the shapes of serial-position curves for items of various degrees of meaningfulness when the results were plotted in the manner of McCrary and Hunter (1953).

Postman and Goggin (1964) supported the conclusion of Underwood and Richardson (1956, 1958) that meaningfulness aided serial learning, whereas intralist similarity of items hindered serial learning. Moreover, meaningfulness decreased the deleterious effects of high similarity. In comparing part learning of halves with whole learning of ten-item lists, they found an advantage due to the length-difficulty relationship. The overall advantage was small, however, because of a partly compensating loss caused by the combination phase of learning and the interference caused by conflicting cues when the items had different relative positions in the part-learning task (of five items) and in the total learning task (of ten items); in the combination phase, one of the first items in the five-item part lists had to become the sixth item of the ten-item list. The array of primacy and recency effects within list parts on the first trial of the total-list combination supported this interpretation in terms of losses of initial or terminal anchor points. Moreover, the serial-position curves for total learning were flatter for the part learning, primarily because there were dips about the middle of the series (namely, isolation effects) caused by the differences between the two original parts.

Brewer (1967) and Smith and Brown (1968) also showed that serial learning of high-meaningful words is faster than the learning of low-meaningful words. Presumably the differentiation afforded by the high meaning overcompensates for the greater number of associations.

Familiarization

Noble (1955) found that increased frequency of prior exposure for nonsense syllables facilitated their subsequent learning. Presumably the familiarization process aided in the response acquisition phase of learning. Hovland and Kurtz (1952) found that the effect of stimulus familiarization on trials to criterion was the same for lists of 6, 12, and 24 items. Therefore, the associative hookup phase is more important in learning the longer lists; the advantage of familiarization is lost after a few trials of the longer lists.

Riley and Phillips (1959) investigated the effects of prior familiarization of nonsense syllables on later serial learning and the types of intruding errors made. Serial learning was facilitated. Although the frequency of inventions and partial responses decreased, the frequency of intralist intrusions per trial increased. The reason for the former was that the subjects learned the population of stimuli via the familiarization and thus knew what items were not on the list and also how to spell the ones that were. The reason for the latter was that the frequency of intruding errors was maintained, and therefore the actual items on the list were the only ones available for intrusions. Thus, familiarization increases knowledge of list membership, but does not reduce intralist generalization. Although the conclusion that intralist intrusions increase for familiarized series is at variance with the earlier conclusion of Hovland and Kurtz (1952), Riley and Phillips (1959) suggest that the difference is due to a difference in measurement. Whereas they used a weighting of errors per trial, Hovland and Kurtz (1952) did not take the differences in trials between familiar and unfamiliar series into account.

Added Cues

Lippman and Lippman (1970) had third-grade children learn to arrange seven-item series of forms or colors in the proper relative position after each of three study trials. For a control group the stimuli were colored squares presented temporally. For one experimental group the stimuli were of the same stimulus colors but also represented various geometric shapes, still presented temporally; for another the same color squares were presented spatially. Although the total exposure time per item was equated across conditions as closely as possible, both of the experimental conditions produced superior performance, with the spatial cues producing a greater advantage than the form cues. All conditions produced similar serial-position curves except that the curves came together for the first temporal position or, presumably, the left-most spatial position. This convergence of the curve was possibly a ceiling effect, since each group of subjects exhibited almost perfect performance for that first item.

Kausler and Trapp (1962) had subjects learn lists of eight nonsense syllables, with two-digit numbers appearing as irrelevant cues. The irrelevant cues were either close to the stimulus syllables (i.e., "central") or displaced farther to the side (i.e., "peripheral"); presentation rates of 2 per second and 4 per second were used. One-half of the subjects were given bonus-incentive instructions. There was a significant serial-position effect and a significant quadruple interaction of incentive instructions, irrelevant-cue position, presentation rate, and serial position. From this interaction, Kausler and Trapp speculate that the cue conditions affect the distinctiveness of the items within the list, thus influencing the performance on the relevant serial-learning task, possibly differentially at the various serial positions.

Brown and Rubin (1967) found that presenting each of 12 trigrams of a serial list on a different distinctive color background increased errors for low-meaningful lists and decreased errors for high-meaningful lists. For a transfer task, paired-associate lists of six pairs were constructed as follows: (1) successive pairs of syllables with the even item the response and the odd item the stimulus; (2) the odd-item stimulus trigram plus its background color; or (3) the background color alone on which the odd item had appeared. The color-only pairs showed superior learning to either the color-trigram combination or the no-color pairs. This indicated that subjects were learning colors in the serial-learning task, and this interfered with paired-associate transfer. A serial-position effect was found for paired-associate pairs according to serial position in original learning. For the control, no-color stimuli, the errors were greatest about the middle positions, but the reverse was true for the color-only pairs.

These results imply that the effects of added color cues in serial learning depend upon the part of the serial list in question. Either color cues are used more effectively in the middle of the series, or else they add some greater interference resultant to the ends. The correct interpretation cannot be made confidently. The color did add difficulty to the serial-learning task, possibly because of the added information, which could produce conflicting associations between trigram and its color background as well as between color and succeeding and other trigrams.

Young and Parker (1970) found that items associated with high-meaningful items on a previous paired-associate task were learned faster than the same items previously paired with low-meaningful stimuli. This associated-confusion effect is similar to that obtained by Mewhort (1967) in tachistoscopic perception of words. The subject is not always able to ignore unnecessary and distracting stimuli (e.g., Harcum & Shaw, 1974).

Stimulus Isolation

In a classic study, von Restorff (1933) found positive effects on recall for an item in a series that had been made perceptually distinct. This so-called isolation, or von Restorff, effect has been subsequently obtained many times under a variety of tasks and conditions. The isolated item thus is more distinct and differentiable than the other, embedded items.

Smith and Stearns (1949) studied the effect of isolating the eighth item in a 13-word list on the trials to criterion and on performance for the items preceding and following the isolated item. In two experiments each subject served as his own control, with appropriate counterbalancing for practice effects. Although the unisolated series generally required fewer trials, the differences were not significant. The isolated item revealed substantially more correct responses, as did the item following it. Most of the other items in the isolated list fell below control performance, accounting for the general lack of difference in overall learning efficiency. Thus, Smith and Stearns (1949) attribute the positive effect of isolation, and the spread of that effect, to "the use made of the isolated item in the organization of the list by the learner" (p. 381).

Kimble and Dufort (1955) had subjects learn 13-item lists of high-meaningful words, except that an experimental group learned less meaningful words at the seventh position. The typical bowed curves of total errors and the symmetrical curve of intruding errors were obtained, but with only the least meaningful item (a nonsense paralog) showing the predicted dip in errors at the seventh position. The authors explain this result in terms of competing associations, but in a rather inverse way. They suggest that the meaningful words tend to invoke multiple associations that interfere with the overt emission of the correct response. But it seems that such logic, carried to the extreme, would imply that lists of more meaningful items should be learned with greater difficulty than less meaningful lists. This is, of course, contrary to their own results for lists of different levels of meaningfulness. This paradox has been discussed previously in this chapter. A better interpretation is that the isolated item is perceptually differentiated, and therefore more insulated from confusion with other items.

Some studies have, in fact, found overall facilitation for an isolated list. Raskin, Hattle, and Rubel (1967) found not only an isolation effect for the seventh item of a 12-item list when that item was paired with an electric shock, but also found overall facilitation for the entire list. Control groups were either unshocked or they received shocks during the intertrial interval. The authors attributed the isolation effect to an orienting response (i.e., differential attention) to the shocked item.

The study of Sen, Clarke, and Cooper (1968) was exceptional in two respects. First, the subjects were severely retarded adults; second, the isolated series were learned faster than the unisolated ones. The population of subjects was probably not important except in relation to the difficulty of the task. The task was serial-anticipation learning of eight projected outline forms, except that two isolated items were completely colored slides. The potency of the isolation technique, in the context of the length of the series, may have created the impression of several smaller lists of different kinds of stimuli, since the so-called isolated stimuli were actually a different kind of stimulus than the unisolated ones. The result was interpreted by the authors in terms of increased arousal brought about by the very different nature of the isolated items. In another experiment, when the isolated stimuli were merely red outlines, in contrast to the black-outline unisolated stimuli, an isolation effect again appeared, but this time there was no overall difference in rate of learning.

INSULATION HYPOTHESIS

The prediction of Newman and Saltz (1958) from the differentiation hypothesis, that an isolated series would be learned faster than an unisolated series, was not confirmed in their study. Indeed the usual equivalence of learning for such series has been well documented (e.g., Jones & Jones, 1942; Jensen, 1962e, g), although some exceptions were mentioned above. Therefore, Newman and Saltz attribute the isolation effect to more rapid learning of the response item that has been isolated. They rejected the idea of stimulus generalization and response generalization as complete explanations of the isolation effect in serial learning. The reason for this was that the isolated item did not show fewer overt intrusions elsewhere in the list than a control item, and the isolated list was not easier to learn.

Saltz (1971) proposes a "stimulus-isolation" argument to account for the effect of stimulus differentiation. This states that familiarization with a stimulus tends to isolate or insulate it from associative interference from other stimuli. This isolation is achieved by two processes: attention to cues (Lawrence, 1949) and generalization reduction (Gibson, 1940). Instead of involving the formation of associations, it consists of pure stimulus learning, in which the subject learns to discriminate the item from other stimuli. Thus, meaningful verbal material has already achieved a high level of differentiation which the subject can bring to the task. Since these items exert less internal interference, overall learning is rapid. The insulation hypothesis predicts therefore two specific effects of isolation: (1) the effects will be greater in series of high intralist similarity; and (2) the effects will be greater when presentation rate is faster, because there is less time for the differentiation processes.

Kintz, Kirk, Miller, Regester, and Zupnick (1965) used a random ordering of Kimble and Dufort's (1955) 13 high-meaningful words, with low-meaningful paralogs at Positions Four, Seven, and Ten for the experimental subjects. Isolation effects were found at each of the three positions, but the difference from control data was significant only at the fourth position.

Wiener (1970) tested the differentiation interpretation (Newman & Saltz, 1958) by manipulating presentation rate—and thereby familiarity—in isolated and unisolated lists. He predicted that the isolation variable would be less effective in a list that had been more differentiated by the greater familiarity with the items. Also he predicted from the differentiation hypothesis that the isolated item would be emitted as an intrusion less often, and that the item following it would be learned sooner than the comparable item on the control list. For ten CVC trigrams learned by the anticipation technique, the sixth item was isolated for the experimental subjects. Presentation rate was 2 seconds or 4 seconds for different groups of subjects. As predicted, the isolation effect was significantly greater for the faster presentation. The results with respect to intruding errors were mixed, however. The isolated item did intrude less often at the slow rate, but there was no difference at the fast rate, which should have shown this effect even more than the slow rate. The author suggests that the fast rate did not permit many intrusions, and thus did not provide a good test for the hypothesis. The item following the isolated item was learned faster under the fast-rate condition, but not for the slow rate. This result is consistent with the differentiation hypothesis.

In two studies R. E. Johnson (1971, 1972) duplicated the isolation effect caused by meaningfulness differential, but only for the case of low-meaningful items inserted in lists of higher meaningfulness. In general, the greater the isolation effect, the greater number of intrusions of the isolate into surrounding positions. When the number of isolates increased (R. E. Johnson, 1972), the degree of isolation effect decreased.

Rosen, Richardson, and Saltz (1962) tested the hypothesis that structural isolation of an item would be more effective in a list of low intralist similarity than in one of high intralist similarity. For lists of either high- or low-meaningful items (Noble, 1952a,b), all items were typed in black ink, except for the fifth item for the experimental subjects. The isolation effect was assessed in terms of the relative number of correct anticipations in learning at the fifth position for 15 trials and in terms of relative rank of correct responses for that position. As predicted, for both measures the effect of isolation was greater in the low-meaningful list. An analysis of the intruding errors was confusing, however, since the high-meaningful list showed more intruding errors than the low-meaningful condition. For the low-meaningful series the isolated item produced significantly more intruding errors than the control item, in line with the Saltz and Newman (1959) argument for increased attention to that item, but contrary to what would be expected for a better differentiated item.

McManis (1967) tested the differentiation hypothesis of Newman and Saltz (1958) by perceptually isolating an item for serial learning in lists of differing formal intralist similarity. The differences in similarity were produced by having the second and third letters of items shared (repeated) by the nonisolated items within a list of seven-item CVC trigrams, to produce a high-similarity list, and by having no letters duplicated (except for two of the vowels) in a high-differentiation list. The middle item was typed in red for the isolated list, whereas all other items were typed in black. Each subject learned either high- or low-differentiation lists, but under both the isolated or unisolated conditions in counterbalanced order. Learning was by the anticipation method. As predicted, the subjects made a greater percentage of correct responses on the isolated items, and this difference was greater for the less differentiated (high-similarity) list. The number of intruding errors was also less for the isolated item, and this difference was again greater for the low-differentiation list. Since similar results were obtained for the item following the isolated one, the isolated item is also more effective as a stimulus on the low-differentiation list, as predicted from the differentiation hypothesis. The number of intrusions from the isolated position and from the position following it was greater in the control list than for the isolated list, and this difference was greater for the low-differentiation series. This result is consistent with the differentiation hypothesis, but contrasts with the findings of Newman and Saltz (1958).

Jensen (1962g) asked whether or not the isolation effect was present in the serial-learning (association) phase of the serial-learning task, as well as in the response-learning phase, as suggested by Newman and Saltz (1958). Accordingly, he had subjects learn by the anticipation method a series of nine known items (colored geometric forms). The item at Position Six (a blue triangle for the control subjects) was replaced by the words "blue triangle" for the experimental subjects. Although the two lists were learned with equal facility, the number of errors at Position Six was significantly smaller for the experimental subjects. The number of intruding errors at this position was also smaller for the experimental subjects, but not significantly so.

Jensen's (1962g) results support those of McManis (1967), and conflict with those of Newman and Saltz (1958). The difference may have something to do with task difficulty and the relative lengths of the response-learning and serial-association stages. Presumably the subjects would emit the isolated item more frequently as a guess during the early stages of learning, and consequently learn it earlier. Jensen (1962g) showed that the order of learning the isolated item was in fact earlier than the rank for the comparable control item. Thus, the isolated item would remain unlearned over fewer trials and thus be available as an intrusion for fewer trials.

Lively (1972) used a probe technique in short-term memory to test certain predictions from generalization theory (Gibson, 1942; Newman & Saltz, 1958). With one digit and nine consonants, or one consonant and nine digits, with ten-item homogeneous control series, the isolated item was at the first, third, fifth, seventh, ninth, or tenth position. There was no overall isolation effect in frequency of correct responses at isolated positions, contrary to prediction from generalization theory.

On the other hand, using the isolated items as probes, the following items were significantly better recalled. This included the first item, for which the last item on the list was the probe. Again contrary to prediction from generalization theory, the isolated lists were not better recalled than control lists, even in regions about the isolated position. As predicted from generalization theory, the isolated item appeared less often as an intrusion error. Lively interpreted his obtained stimulus effects in terms of a hypothesis, closely related to the generalization hypothesis, that he called the recognition hypothesis. This hypothesis states that correct recognition is related to the extent to which the different stimulus items can be differentially encoded; it emphasizes stimulus differentiation, rather than confusion among responses.

SURPRISE HYPOTHESIS

The surprise hypothesis (Green, 1956) states that the subject is "surprised" by the first different item. Green found that only the first isolated item in a series produced a significant isolation effect at recall. The surprise variable must necessarily be confounded with the absence of a proactive interference effect from prior similar items, however, as Green points out.

Saul and Osgood (1950) repeated an earlier experiment of Siegel (1943), which employed isolated and homogeneous items but added delayed recall conditions of 1 and 24 hours. They pointed out that there is really no theoretical argument between Gestalt theories and behavioristic (generalization) theories of learning, in that both would predict faster learning for material which could be better organized. On the other hand, the Gestalt theory proposes autonomous changes in the memory traces, whereas the behavioristic approach attributes changes in the memory traces to interference. The results of the experiment were rather ambiguous, primarily because the results of the original learning did not faithfully duplicate Siegel's (1943) results. The first isolated item showed enhanced recall but probably, as Saul and Osgood suggest, because of a "surprise" effect (Green, 1956) of the first change in stimulus type. The remaining effects in both studies could be attributed to an artifact of run lengths. The two control (embedded) items (Positions Six and Sixteen in the series) both showed dips in correct responses, but they were the only items falling at the end of a run of three items. Thus, subjects' guessing strategies could reflect a tendency to avoid such a response. The same argument could account for the large jump in correct responses for the second isolated item in Siegel's (1943) data. This item, the thirteenth one, is the first one following a run of two items from the category that had never shown a run length greater than one previously.

Thus subjects' strategies of predicting run lengths could account for both the Siegel (1943) and Saul and Osgood (1950) data—except for the first isolated item, of course. Since the degree of homogeneity must be at least partially confounded with run length, the slight downward trend relating accuracy of immediate recall and degree of homogeneity could be accounted for by errors in anticipating the lengths of runs; as the runs of one type became shorter, the runs of the other type became longer. If the subject forgot the cues provided by run length, then the delayed recalls should fail to show a relation between memory loss and homogeneity—which was the result obtained by Saul and Osgood. Actually the percentage-of-loss figures they report imply a constant loss as each serial position, since the percentage of loss seems to be inversely related to the number of correct responses in original learning.

Roberts (1962) used 15-item lists of either high or low meaningfulness (Noble, 1952a), and embedded items of different meaningfulness for experimental subjects in both types of list at Positions Five, Eight, and Eleven. The isolation effects were significant only for the high-meaningful items embedded in the low-meaningful series. There was no effect for the items following the isolated items. The difference in intrinsic meaningfulness of the isolated items contributes to an isolation effect in the first case, of course, and operates against it in the second condition. Contrary to the generalization hypothesis, however, the isolated series were not learned faster than the unisolated ones. An interpretation of these results in terms of response generalization was supported by the fact that the isolated items revealed more intruding errors among the three positions of isolation than did the unisolated items at those same serial positions. Also, the isolated items tended not to be given as intrusions at the surrounding (nonisolated) positions as often as the control items. Thus, the isolated character of the different items was noted as a basis for categorization, and the intrusion within categories was greater than that across categories.

Gibbons and Leicht (1970) found greater isolation effects for the seventh item in a 10-item list of high-meaningful items (words) than for low-meaningful material (trigrams), although the difference was not significant. This seems contrary to the generalization hypothesis but, again, the prediction is not unambiguous.

Discussion

The cognitive basis of the isolation effect is illustrated by a number of experiments. For example, Kimble and Dufort (1955) found an isolation effect for a word of different meaningfulness, without a perceptually differentiating factor, such as a different color. On the other hand, Gumenik and Slak (1969) failed to find an effect of isolation caused by a difference in evaluative meaning for words in serial-anticipation learning. A word judged to have a good affective meaning was placed at the eighth position of a 15-item series of good (control) words or bad (experimental) words. The mean number of errors at the eighth position was not different for experimental and control groups. Since the results were negative, one cannot tell whether the absence of an isolation effect was due to the general ineffectiveness of evaluative meaning as an isolating agent, or that the subjects just did not notice the difference. Some cognitive appreciation of the isolation seems critical.

Conclusion

Underwood (1961) points out that the effects of stimulus differentiation are essentially equivalent to those of a lack of generalization. He further argues that response generalization must also be incorporated, along with stimulus generalization, into a theory of verbal learning. The lack of discrimination among items is indigenous to serial learning. In the EPAM model simulation of cognitive processes (Feigenbaum, 1963), oscillation and interference are the natural consequence of learning new items, which may interfere with the cue functions of an item.

Several lines of evidence support the conclusion that the subject's cognitions and strategies of learning influence the differentiation of items. For example, Jenkins and Postman (1948) concluded that their failure to find a spread of effect was due to the subject's "preoccupation" with the key response and thus his failure to learn the adjacent items. The Wickens, Born, and Allen (1963) results on removal of proactive inhibition support the notion of a cognitive insulation of interference effects.

The generalization-differentiation hypothesis has some obvious similarities to other hypotheses, such as, for example, position confusion and retrieval codes. An item identified by position should be thereby more differentiated than one not so associated to position, and therefore easier to become associated with other items. Speaking more broadly, an item can become associated with a total context, thus gaining distinctiveness. As Anderson and Bower (1972) suggest, contextual cues provide one basis for so-called time tags.

POSITION CONFUSION

The position-confusion conception of interference in serial learning argues that the position identification is more accurate for items near either end of a series. The subject is less able to localize an otherwise available response when the proper position of that response is farther removed from the end positions. This conception has gained greater favor as the evidence has mounted that subjects learn serial position, but it is not new.

Bugelski (1974) instructed some subjects to learn the serial order of 20 words presented aurally by using their normal procedure for learning; he instructed other subjects to form associations between the images of succeeding pairs. Whereas the normal instructions produced a typical bowed serial-position curve with stronger primacy than recency effects, the instructions to form imaged pairs produced a general decline in accuracy for items from beginning to end of the series. Specifically, the usual bowing was not observed when the subjects had been instructed to learn the series as a sequential chain of pairs, without regard to position cues.

The position-learning alternative to remote associations proposed by Slamecka (1964) was anticipated by Lumley (1932b) who argued that some errors in serial-maze learning were due to position mislocalization. He argued that the subject at first gains only part knowledge of the location of an item:

> On the contrary, units are first localized as being in the middle, near the beginning, or near the end. Also certain letters are localized with respect to other letters, and groups are formed. As learning progresses, localization in the series becomes more specific until the series can be given in its right order (p. 196).

Therefore, an anticipation error occurs when the subject has only an imprecise knowledge of item location. Lumley found that subjects learning a typewriter-keyboard maze increased the ratio of near to far anticipatory errors as learning progressed.

McGeoch (1942) also suggested that serial items may be associated to their position. He states:

> The first and last items are the ones most likely to be associated with their ordinal numbers. To some extent the other early and late items share in this association with position, but the middle ones are much less likely to do so because the intermediate serial positions are less clearly identified and discriminated during practice. The serial positions, coming in an order already known to the subject, act, presumably, by providing a ready-made mnemonic system into which to fit the new items (p. 114).

Position Learning

Schulz (1955) concluded that the serial-position effect reflects the discriminability of the various serial positions. He pointed out that the middle of the serial list suffers from the greatest "position confusion," which he equates with generalization. Schulz found that the higher the criterion of learning, the more accurate were the subjects in reporting the relative position of items after serial learning. Also, the subjects were more accurate in positioning items of lower intralist similarity. This latter conclusion was supported by results of Keppel and Zavortink (1968).

Postman (1967) investigated the effect of high and low interitem associative strength on serial-anticipation learning and recall. Using lists of high frequency associates to a key word (Deese, 1959), or unassociated items, he found that the original learning was not significantly different for high- versus low-associated items, although the difference favored the low items. There was a significant interaction in terms of serial position, however, with no difference for end items, and a significant difference favoring the unassociated items at the center of the lists. Presumably the items at the center suffer more interference, particularly from natural associations existing before the experiment began. Supporting this interpretation was the greater diversity of intruding errors for the high-associable series, as well as the greater proportion of backward errors. The subject loses both the list-membership identification and the time tag indicating the recency of a stimulus. The recall data were especially interesting in that immediate (30-second delay) serial recall produced the same serial-position interaction between high- and low-association series, but the delayed recall revealed greater loss of retention for the unassociated items. The superior retention for high-associated items was attributed to superior recall of responses; this interpretation was supported by a greater percentage of intralist errors at recall for these items. On five trials of relearning after recall, the immediate-recall condition showed continued superiority of the unassociated items. In the delayed-recall condition, however, the high associates began better, but were soon surpassed by the unassociated items. These results again support the argument that high association facilitates response recall, but thereby fosters greater intralist interference in serial learning. Thus, in free-recall situations, in which reproduction of serial position is not required, the response learning shows unopposed facilitation. On the other hand, when reproduction of serial order is required, the response facilitation also fosters intraserial interference.

The study of Hicks, Hakes, and Young (1966) shows that subjects were learning serial position, as tested by immediate testing of association between item and position. The learning was superior at both ends of the ten-item lists and better for items at the beginning than at the terminus.

Woodward's (1968) study of sequential and positional probes in immediate memory indicated, by the d' measure of signal detectability (Swets,

Tanner, & Birdsall, 1961), greater retention of position information than sequential information for end items. Schwartz (1970a), using the d' measure, also found greater bowing of the serial-position curve for positional relative to sequential probes.

In their study of position learning in serial learning, Ahmed and Voss (1969) used two special control groups that provided data of special interest here. One group of subjects was asked to place items within the serial dimension even though they had never seen the items before. The resultant deviations from the "correct" placements did not show differences among serial position except that the values for the end positions were greater. This would be expected on an artifactual basis because of the greater range of possible deviations for the end items. Another special control group of subjects was actually told the position of an item and asked to reproduce that position along a line representing the entire series. Here the results were in striking contrast—a symmetrically bowed curve with very small errors at the ends. This shape of curve would be expected on the basis of position confusion. The experimental subjects after a single trial of serial learning revealed a monotonic function, with few inversions, showing a marked reduction in size of deviations at the initial serial positions. The deviations for the terminal items were equal to those of the subjects with no prior experience with the items or knowledge of their location.

Peterson, Meagher, and Ellsbury (1970) had subjects read aloud five-, six-, or seven-digit messages, presented simultaneously in a memory drum. A position probe for recall of the proper digit was indicated on the next turn of the drum. Performance was virtually perfect for five- and six-digit messages; the seven-digit series produced a skewed serial-position result, with poorest performance at Positions Four and Five. Contrary to the conclusion of the authors, an examination of the results shows that the sixth and seventh positions produced more correct responses than the second and first, respectively, lending some support to a greater recency effect due to readout from short-term memory.

To test the notion that the large effect of primacy with the seven-digit series was due to differential encoding of the earlier items into a longer-term storage, Peterson et al. (1970) evaluated the effects of inserting a repetition of a digit into the sequences of seven-digit numbers. According to trace-strength theory (Wickelgren, 1966, 1970), the first items would have stronger traces, resulting from the adjacent repetition of an item, and would thus exert a stronger proactive interference effect. A retroactive inhibitory effect would occur for probes preceding the repeated items. An information-encoding point of view would argue for the inhibitory effect on recall of a repeated item prior to the probe position, because a chunking phenomenon would cause loss of one item position, displacing the following digits and thus resulting in an error when position of a subsequent item was probed. On the other hand, Peterson et al. argue that results determined by sensory memory would increase the performance for the other items, because the chunking or vividness of the repeated digit would reduce the memory load for the remaining digits—effectively shorten the series. This facilitory effect would occur whether the position of the repeated items preceded or followed the probe position. The subsequent results were entirely in accordance with this latter prediction; repeated digits facilitated recall to an equal degree whether they preceded or followed the probe position. Thus, predictions based on associative interferences were not supported.

To determine whether or not their earlier results were due to the fact that the repeated digits had been adjacent, Peterson et al. (1970), in a similar experiment, varied the distance between repetitions of an item by interposing zero, one, three, or five unique digits. The advantage of repeated digits was present only when they were separated by one or no items. Otherwise they were recalled with accuracy equal to that for items from the control sequence that contained no repeated items. Thus, there was no substantial evidence for an effect of associative interference.

The "distinctiveness function" of Murdock (1960) was successfully used by Detterman and Ellis (1971) to fit short-term memory data. For this it was necessary, however, for them to reverse Murdock's functions (i.e., assign best performance to the last rather than the first position). Presumably the reason for this was that Murdock (1960) was fitting his curves to serial-learning data obtained by the anticipation procedure (Bugelski, 1950), which typically show a stronger primacy than recency effect. In contrast, the Detterman and Ellis data employed a probe technique in which the subject was asked to report the original position of a probe item, a procedure more likely to show a recency effect (e.g., Waugh & Norman, 1965; Murdock, 1968). Although Detterman and Ellis were able to fit the data from normal subjects rather well, they were less successful with data of retarded subjects. Since the results for the retarded subjects show consistently greater recency effects and smaller primacy effects than predicted, these investigators suggest that the retarded subjects are different in rehearsal strategies or in retention of memory traces. The problem of the relative strengths of primacy and recency effects in short-term memory is difficult to solve by an invariant distinctiveness function because, as Murdock (1968, Experiment 7) showed, the relative strengths change depending upon the subject's prior cognition of the responding order to be used.

Melton and von Lackum (1941) found that intruding errors from one list to the next tended to come from the same serial position, implying associations to serial position. Conrad (1959) used immediate memory for digits to duplicate their results. Subjects heard a series of three to six digits and were later asked to recall them. Substitution errors from a previous message strongly tended to come from the serial position that was correct on the earlier message.

The same conclusion was reported by Dey (1970). In Dey's study, interlist intrusions were obtained from two serial lists learned in haphazard alternations. These intruding errors formed a regular generalization gradient around the correct position. The results are shown in Figure 6-8, somewhat modified from the report of Dey. Not only did the majority of the intrusions come from the corresponding serial position within the other list, the remaining intrusions tended to cluster about the correct position. Therefore, the subject has a knowledge of the general location of the item, even if he does not know its correct position. The intralist intrusions were more likely to be from anterior than posterior directions. Nevertheless, the interlist intrusions were greater for the items about the middle of the series.

The argument for the position-based origin of intruding errors was bolstered through an analysis by Harcum (1969) of earlier data of Harcum, Pschirrer, and Coppage (1968). The data were obtained from serial

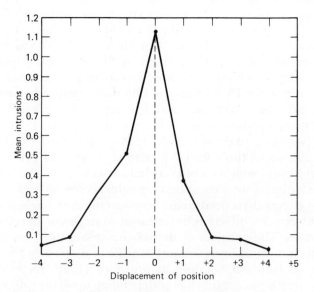

Figure 6-8   Gradients of intruding errors, after Dey (1970). Reprinted by permission of University of Illinois Press.

anticipation of nonsense syllables in continuous presentation. Errors of omission, intralist intruding errors, and extralist intrusions were tabulated in terms of the subjects' cognitive serial positions. That is, serial position was identified relative to the item that the subject said was cognitively for him the first in the series. These results, shown in Figure 6-9, indicate a symmetrical curve of intralist intrusions (ILI), a slightly skewed curve of extralist intrusions (ELI) favoring the end of the series, and the usual bowed curve for the failures to respond (FTR). These results duplicate the results of Harcum and Coppage (1969) for serial learning with the usual intertrial gap and again suggest that the cognitive identification (encoding) of the items, and not the rest pause between trials, is the determinant of the positional bowing.

Other evidence was obtained by Lippman (1968) that the bowing occurs because the unique location of the end elements permits more accurate localization within the overall pattern. He had five groups of subjects begin learning 12-item lists of nonsense syllables under the usual conditions of greater intertrial interval than interstimulus interval. For four of the groups, designated the experimental groups, the greater temporal gap of the intertrial interval was then interchanged with the regular interstimulus interval between the sixth and seventh item. This was done after criteria of, respectively, 1, 4, 7, and 10 items had been correctly anticipated on one trial. On the assumption that very early

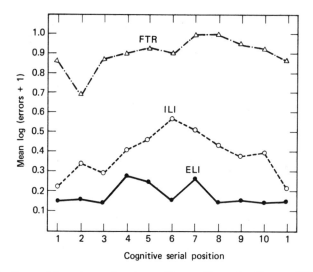

Figure 6-9 Errors of three types at each cognitive position, after Harcum (1969). Reprinted with permission of publisher.

in the acquisition process the larger intertrial interval served as a strong cue for learning the ends of the list, Lippman reasoned that the early displacement of the larger gap would produce an extended performance decrement, whereas the same operation performed later, after the ends of the list had been learned, would not substantially affect the progress of learning. This hypothesis was supported. Although the groups did not differ on the measure of trials to the criterion of one perfect recitation, the serial-position curve was virtually unaffected when the shift came after the criterion of ten correct had been reached. The earlier the change, the greater the magnitude of the "isolation effect" about the seventh syllable. Even with the shift after the criterion of one item correct, the overall structure of the series was obviously determined by the first temporal item with respect to the original location of the differential intertrial interval. Thus, consistent with the conclusion of Lippman and Denny (1964) and Coppage and Harcum (1967), the first experience of a temporally first item was sufficient to establish a mnemonic structure for the list.

Transfer Studies

A substantial amount of evidence from transfer studies for position learning was presented in Chapter 3. Consequently, only a few studies will be mentioned here.

Sisson (1938) argued that a serially ordered list would be less susceptible to retroactive interference because the items would be more differentiated due to their association to serial position. Experimental subjects saw five presentations of a ten-item list of adjectives in serial order or in randomized order, followed by another list of the same type, and then they recalled the original list. Control subjects read jokes instead of learning the second list. Although the original learning of the serial-ordered list was slightly—but not significantly—better, the recall for the rest condition was slightly better after the jumbled presentation. The percentage of retroactive inhibition was greater for the jumbled list, and the number of intruding errors was greater for the jumbled list, supporting the hypothesis.

Keppel (1964) provided some evidence for positional mediation of retroactive inhibition. Subjects learning an interpolated serial list had difficulty in recalling the original serial list when the serial position of the items had remained constant. On the other hand, subjects for whom the serial position of items in original learning had not remained constant did not encounter the retroactive inhibition from the interpolated task.

In Ebenholtz' (1965) study of the transfer of position learning from one paired-associate task to another, the interfering information of changed position was much more deleterious for the middle items of the series. Ebenholtz generalizes that the distinctiveness of positions is the factor that accounts for the bowed serial-position curves, both in his paired-associate study as well as in serial-learning studies. He suggests that relative position may be used as a cue for discrimination among items whenever other bases are not available.

The study of Young, Hakes, and Hicks (1965) produced conflicting evidence about the direction of transfer from one serial list to a second one derived from prior first-order remote associations. List length was an important variable, with 8-, 12-, and 16-item lists all showing initially negative transfer, but the shortest list reversing later to produce slight positive transfer overall. This result for the 8-item series is puzzling, particularly in view of the serial-position results, which reveal the positive effects for the end items, although these items were undoubtedly learned first. The resolution of this paradox probably lies in the weakness of the method of plotting the learning curves. Young, Hakes, and Hicks used Melton's (1936) method of plotting the acquisition of items; deficiencies of this method will be discussed in Chapter 9. The general tenor of results for each length of list is therefore that the negative transfer tendency was greatest for the middle items, where confusion among item positions was greatest.

Free Recall

Waugh (1960) pointed out the common observation that as the length of a series increases, the number of items correctly reported first rises to a maximum and then decreases. Her subjects in one experiment saw a series of digits and were asked to write down a designated number of them from the terminal end of the series in any order. When there had been at least five items prior to the number required in the reproduction, the reproduction accuracy for a given number of items was independent of the actual number that the subject was required to reproduce. On the other hand, if no other digits preceded the recall series, the accuracy was much greater when the subject had only to recall a given number; thus, primacy and recency effects complemented one another. In a second experiment, Waugh (1960) showed that both the initial and terminal span results across serial positions could be predicted from the conditional probabilities obtained from 18-digit series. That is, performance was predictable on the basis of the joint probabilities in terms of proximity to beginning and to terminus of the series.

Bruce and Papay (1970) provided evidence against the proactive inhibition interpretation of the primacy effect in free recall. They inserted a forget cue in the series to indicate that all preceding items would not have to be recalled. Not only was there a "primacy effect" for items following the forget cue, contrary to the proactive inhibition hypothesis, but also a depression in recall for the item preceding it. A forget-cue condition produced different results from an isolation condition for the same item. Whereas the isolation of an item improved performance for that item only, without changing the results for the other items, the forget cue produced also a retrograde loss for the prior item and a general facilitation for the subsequent items. The preceding item probably suffered from inaccessibility to retrieval because it was so strongly encoded with a forget tag because of its proximity to the forget cue. Since the forget cue and the isolation stimulation were identical, obviously the difference was in the instructions to the subjects. Perhaps the critical difference was not the instructions to forget, but that these instructions marked cognitive boundaries between two groups of words. In any case, the forget cue insulated the following items from a proactive-interference effect.

In a free-recall task Tulving and Patterson (1968) found that a cluster of related words within a series of unrelated words tended to be recalled from long-term memory as a functional unit; if one item of the cluster were recalled, all of the related items would be recalled. This functional relatedness was more important than input order in determining the probability of recall. Recall within such a unit was independent of the number of units recalled. The related items in short-term memory— those at the end of the list—tended to be recalled as individual items rather than as one functional unit. Thus, Tulving and Patterson conclude that the end items are coded and retrieved on the basis of the temporal-position cue, which does not make use of the relatedness, whereas the items from middle positions of the series were coded according to a higher-order organizational unit represented by the relation.

Evidence for two factors comes from the results of Seamon (1972) who recorded reaction time in probed recall of individual items after serial-recall learning. The stimulus series consisted of four stimulus categories with three examples blocked under each category. Practice eliminated the serial-position effects, but not the within-categories differences, for categories. Thus, primacy and recency effects are due to differential rehearsal, whereas the greater difficulty of middle members of the categories is caused by decreased accessibility of the traces of those items.

Conclusion

In memorizing a series of items, the subjects use position cues as an aid to memory, to a degree that depends upon the conditions of the task. For example, Horowitz (1961) showed that high intralist similarity facilitated response learning, and thus free recall, of 12 trigram series. On the other hand, such high item-similarity hindered item-placement in the series, and thus interfered with serial learning. Schmeck (1970) evaluated this conclusion of Horowitz (1961) by testing retention of ten CVC syllables of high and low intralist similarity by serial anticipation or paced free recall after a single paced presentation. Results supported the prediction that high similarity facilitated free recall, but hindered serial learning.

Jensen (1964) found that his subjects were more consistent in terms of relative performance among serial positions for color-form stimuli than for lists of trigrams and words. Words showed less consistency than trigrams. These results can be inferred from Figure 6-10, which shows the serial-position results plotted in percentage terms for the lists of words, trigrams, and color forms, respectively. The serial-position curve is least peaked for the more meaningful items. The reason for this is that the intralist similarity for the least meaningful material was greater; the subjects would be more likely to use idiosyncratic associations to the words as a basis for learning. The curve for the color forms is more asymmetrical, indicating greatest primacy effects for this material, presumably because the memory span for this material was greater. As a measure of the consistency of the subjects, Jensen used the average correlation between serial-position curves for all pairs of subjects within a condition. Whereas the average product-moment correlation was .32 for the word lists, it was .41 and .63 for the trigrams and forms, respectively. Therefore, the greater the intralist similarity the more relevant was relative position as the stimulus for learning.

An illustration of the above points can be taken from unpublished data of Postman and Jensen for serial learning of children in grades 4, 7, and 10 and college students.* They obtained a greater skew in the serial-position curve for word series than for trigrams, and more for college students than children. Presumably, the words were more

*I am indebted to Professors Postman and Jensen for a copy of this paper.

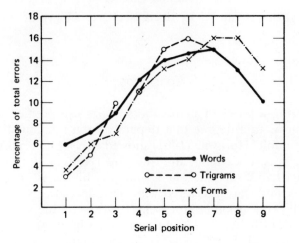

Figure 6-10   Errors per serial position for three types of stimuli, after Jensen (1964). Used with author's permission.

influenced by the directional meaningful associations, which conflicted with the sheer positional basis of organization. The college students would be more practiced in memorization, and thus more consistent in the choice of the temporally first item as the anchor for learning.

DISCUSSION

The bowing of the serial-position curve has been attributed to interference that may come from several sources that are not mutually exclusive. It has been described in such terms as competition of responses, lack of discrimination, or ambiguity about the best order of acquisition. Shiffrin (1970) discusses interference in terms of memory search. Thus, the issues involve the kind or source of interference rather than whether or not such a mechanism exists.

Crowder (1969) has used the designation of *passive theories* and *active theories* to refer to the different conceptions of the mechanisms in immediate memory. The former refer to essentially inhibitory effects resulting from the multiplicity of elements to be recalled. The latter refer to strategies of codification and rehearsal imposed upon the task by the subject. These two approaches reduce to essentially differences in terms of response interference and rehearsal factors in memory. Also, Johansson (1970) concludes from a study of isolation effects in recall of digit and letter series that the evidence favors either attentional or interference interpretations, dependent upon the specific conditions.

Atkinson and Shiffrin (1968a) argue, therefore, that interference is a descriptive rather than an explanatory term. They point out that the term interference can mean not only structural features of memory that are not under the control of the subject, as well as search mechanisms that are actually control processes. Harcum's (1975) comparison of serial learning of homogeneous and mixed items supports this position. The mixed series was learned faster or slower than the homogeneous series depending upon whether or not the heterogeneous items were arranged in an order that supplemented or conflicted with a strategy based on the temporal order of items. Whereas the structural features of the mixed items reduced interference due to item discriminability, they added interference by providing a viable alternative to the strategy based on temporal serial positions.

The evidence points to a response-related mechanism as the most important factor. For example, Nachmias, Gleitman, and McKenna (1961) argued that the stimulus-generalization conception of the isolation effect would produce a greater effect of stimulus-term than response-term isolation in paired-associate learning. Isolation effects were equal for stimulus and response terms, however. Moreover, the intruding errors were greater within isolated or unisolated categories than across categories, suggesting a cognitive-encoding interpretation of retrieval cues.

Other evidence was provided by Shuell and Keppel (1967b) that retroactive interference was greater on the response side than on the stimulus side of the recall process. When two lists of words were learned in succession by the same method, either free recall or serial recall, the interference effect was greater than when the method changed from first to second list. But there was no difference for the free-recall test whether or not the input was in constant or variable sequence. Apparently the interference was in terms of position as encoded by the subject for recall, rather than in terms of stimulus relations. This conclusion was supported by the finding that list membership was less well differentiated in recall for the subjects tested under free recall for both lists. This is consistent with Ceraso's (1967) conclusion that the interference is due to less availability for items whose list membership is less well retained.

Cognitive confusion has been cited as a source of internal interference (e.g., Saltz, 1971). In immediate memory the so-called prefix and suffix effects (e.g., Crowder, 1967) are examples of inhibition produced by adding extraneous material to be processed and remembered, either before or after the test material, respectively. Neisser, Hoenig, and Goldstein (1969) found that when a redundant prefix was presented in a speaking voice from a different sex of speaker than that used for the target series, the prefix effect was essentially eliminated. Therefore, the cognitive break between the prefix and the target string made it possible for the subject to differentiate between target and prefix easily, and thus to exclude the prefix from his active construction of the unit to be recalled. This is consistent with Saltz's (1971) suggestion that cognitive barriers can insulate verbal material from inhibitory interference effects by aiding in their differentiation. Harcum's (1969) analysis, and that of Harcum and Shaw (1974), also supports this argument.

Bewley, Nelson, and Brogden (1968) had subjects learn two or three serial lists by alternating trials of different lists, by learning the lists in succession, or by combining the items into one list. The successive condition, which essentially was learning by parts, produced the fastest learning by far. Each alternating or successive condition produced individual similar, typical serial-position curves, whereas the items learned as one series produced one overall, typical serial-position curve. Generally, the items learned as just one list were learned about as fast as in the alternating condition. Therefore, the effect is much like that of the Wishner, Shipley, and Hurvich (1957) study, with a strong effect of isolation at the demarcation between lists, but no gross change in overall learning.

Lester (1932) showed that the subject's intention to avoid retroactive inhibition and his knowledge of the experimental paradigm decreased the inhibitory effects. She attributed this to "mental set," which maintained the learning conditions when recall was tested, resisting the disruptive force of the interpolated material.

> In other words, preparation for a future contingency greatly lessens the startling or upsetting effect of its actuality (1932, p. 697).

Nagge (1935) found that dissociation of learning and interpolated states by way of changes in sensory mode, hypnotic state, or motor responses significantly decreased retroactive inhibition, whereas a gross change in room environment did not.

Postman and Underwood (1973) discuss the theory of interference in the context of the retroactive-inhibition paradigm with paired-associate learning. Nevertheless, many of their points are relevant to the acquisition of a serial list. For example, a single list can be thought of as two or more composite lists, as in the manner of Bewley, Nelson, and Brogden (1968). Instead of thinking of items as components of different lists, they can be thought of as components of list segments—

such as beginning, middle, and end. Postman and Underwood (1973) argued that the traditional conception of retroactive interference—unlearning and response competition (Melton & Irwin, 1940)—is still viable in spite of attempts to substitute encoding for it (Martin, 1971; Greeno, James, & DaPolito, 1971). A critical issue is that there are general components of unlearning in addition to the unlearning of specific associations (McGovern, 1964). Postman and Underwood (1973) propose response-set interference (Postman, Stark, & Fraser, 1968) as an extension of the unlearning component of two-factor theory. This involves a selector mechanism that suppresses the responses from one list. Postman and Underwood do not deny the relevance of encoding processes as explanatory principles, but they are chary of expecting such processes to account for all of the phenomena of retroactive inhibition.

Postman (1963a) listed several "principles of conservation" by which the ravages of interference among habits are mitigated. The first is that an item having multiple associations is also more meaningful in that it has a greater base of discrimination than other items caused by converging associations. In the context of serial learning, the items of high interitem associations are facilitated during the response-learning stage, but inhibited during the serial ordering or associative hookup stage. The second conservation factor is the differentiation of items caused by list membership. The cognition of an item as a member of a different list enables the subject to reject it as a correct response at the time of recall. The third is a selector mechanism by which the subject tends to limit the population of the potential responses to those that are relevant to the task. For example, he does not import nonsense-syllable responses when he is learning a list of adjectives. The fourth principle of conservation is that the subject often uses as functional stimuli, and thence the mediators of transfer, something other than the nominal stimuli of the task. Therefore, the subject can use strategies of learning and practice or mediation that reduce the effective competition. As Postman says:

> Strategies such as recoding and systematic rehearsal are designed to increase resistance to interference and to conserve the effects of training. As we have seen, strategies of learning can radically alter the functional conditions of transfer from these predictable on the basis of the formal experimental paradigms (1963a, p. 47).

The final mechanism is recoding of stimuli to reduce interference. The subject is able to discover or construct different codes and rules that reduce the number of possible alternatives. In summary, Postman points out that performance factors can contribute to the retention measures and thus contaminate the apparent effects of interference among habits.

Postman's (1963a) point is illustrated by a study of Garrett and Hartman (1926). They had subjects learn lists of 12 nonsense syllables, and then relearn the same list in the same or reversed order, or with successive pairs only in reversed order. The same order was learned most quickly, of course, followed by the completely reversed list. The series with reversal only of pairs was most difficult, probably because this construction rule was less obvious to the subjects. Of the ten subjects per group, only three of them could perceive immediately that the pairs had been reversed; but all subjects with the completely reversed list immediately perceived the rule that determined the new arrangement. Whereas the reversed-pairs list was composed of smaller changes in the position of items, some of the adjacent associations were new, and the whole arrangement appeared to be haphazard to most of the subjects. A simple cognitive correction was apparently effective for the subjects learning the reversed list, making the previous learning relevant and helpful.

Conrad (1965) suggests that subject's so-called transposition errors are not due to order or position confusion, but to failures of memory (decay) plus the subject's strategy of avoiding repetition of an item when the test series (individual messages) are constructed without repeating items. After a series of six items, selected from ten letters, was presented visually in sequence, the subject wrote down his recall. Substitution errors tended to come from acoustically similar letters. Repetition of letters in the reproductions was more frequent as the separation from the first emission of the item in the sequence was greater. Repetitions increased across serial positions. Therefore, the probability of transposition errors is correlated with the probability of confusion among items. Conrad illustrates his theory by a model consisting of a fixed number of boxes, each representing the serial position of an item. The name of each item is stored in the box and read out by the subject in an order determined by instructions. The identity of the boxes depends upon the temporal ordering of the filling of the boxes. There is no way that the contents of the boxes can interchange. The recall of an item in a box depends upon its strength; if the strength is insufficient for recall, the subject either fails to respond or he guesses. There is a separate storage, determined by the instructions and by other experimental conditions, of the available responses for subjects to make in the situation. Since this store of available responses is small, the subject will tend to select his guesses from it, creating the illusion of an error in ordering.

Conrad cautions that this model, as presently developed, should be restricted to relatively short sequences and immediate report. Longer intervals would disrupt the simple organization proposed by the model. However, it would seem that spatial tags applied to the boxes would provide a more stable organization that would persist longer than a purely temporal identity. This perhaps explains why in serial learning the position coding of temporally presented items is important, as documented in Chapter 3.

Spear (1970) points out that the concepts of response competition and unlearning were at first applied to single responses or associations, whereas more recent emphasis has been placed on membership in a list. Thus, an item may be learned through a convergence of multiple cues. Bugelski (1965) argues, in fact, that serial learning can involve both position learning and sequential associations. For short sequences he conceded that subjects can learn positions of first and last item, and, by association to them, can deduce the position of other items. On the other hand, for long sequences—even well-learned ones such as the English alphabet—the subject ordinarily cannot report the ordinal position of a letter embedded about the middle of the series. In such cases, he must go back to some known reference point, and then reestablish the necessary sequential cues. Thus the reestablishment of the proper context appears necessary for the use of the retrieval cues.

Evidence for the cue-dependent forgetting hypothesis was summarized by Tulving (1974). This hypothesis proposed that forgetting is caused by the failure of the recall cues to permit retrieval of intact information from memory; it does, however, permit the possibility of forgetting caused by a change in the memory trace. As Tulving admits, one fault with this hypothesis is that it cannot be refuted, since the only way of proving that an effective cue was present would be for the correct recall to be obtained.

Tulving and Thomson (1971) found that a change or removal of a word paired with an experimental word at the time of a recognition test impaired performance for that item. Thus, there is a retrieval problem in recognition memory also. Hovland (1940a) found no serial-position effects on a recall trial (first relearning trial) 24 hours after massed practice to a criterion of one perfect recitation. The serial-position effect was, however, reinstated on the second relearning trial, most likely because of the reinstatement of the necessary retrieval cues by recall of context from experience with the first relearning trial. This result was also obtained by Postman and Riley (1959) and Keppel and Zavortink (1968).

The reference points are cognitive. On the basis of such references the subject can categorize even a single list into components of, for example, beginning, middle, and end. Thus, the coding problems of response-set interference (Postman, Stark, & Fraser, 1968) would be relevant. The coding could, in fact, employ a purely cognitive dimension. Mosher (1969), for example, had subjects recall triads taken from the same cognitive structure, using a short-term memory paradigm similar to that of Peterson and Peterson (1959). The members of the triad were presented in the natural serial order (e.g., nickel, dime, quarter) or in a scrambled order (e.g., Thursday, Tuesday, Wednesday), and recall was either in serial (forward), backward, or free order. Since item retention was extremely high, it was possible to examine the retention of order information, assuming perfect retention of items. In free recall, the subjects tended to use the natural sequence, even with unordered input. For serial recall, the position information was almost perfectly retained, whether or not the input had been ordered. For backwards recall, however, the retention with unordered input was poor across all trials. For backwards recall of ordered input, the retention was almost perfect for the first two trials, but it declined for the remaining six trials. Therefore, it appears that simple temporal position information is vulnerable to the effects of prior tests.

Presumed interference in cognitive coding can generate bowed performance curves in tasks other than learning. For example, Harcum and Shaw (1974) showed that accuracy of reading-out the information in tachistoscopic patterns was affected by the cognitive confusion produced by adding elements to the original array. The greatest effects were for the end items that were now flanked by the extra items. Also, Jensen (1962d) found a serial-position effect in spelling errors for words. Thomas (1971) showed that a serial-position curve was generated by interference between a cognitive process, which makes decisions about relative points along a continuum, and a coding process used by psychiatrists in defining the mental state of patients. Specifically, the coding uncertainty of the judgment formed a bowed relationship with a factor-analytic score representing the diagnostic evaluation. Thus, the closer the rating of a patient was to either extreme of the rating dimension, the less the uncertainty of the rating.

The above argument supports the hypothesis that the distribution of intralist intruding errors reflects the combined effects of the constraint imposed by a bowed function of item discriminability, plus the tendencies to make or inhibit the overt response. That is, the syllables in the positions at either end of the list are more discriminable because of their uniqueness and, therefore, they are less likely to be localized incorrectly. The probability of confusion of position is greatest for the central items, with the total distribution of location confusability assumed to be similar to that proposed by Murdock (1960) for the distinctiveness of the items in a series. As Murdock points out, the shape of the serial-position curve does not change with changes in certain stimulus attributes, such as meaningfulness or familiarity, which do affect the rate of learning to criterion for the complete task. Thus, he argues, "Distinctiveness is a function of the ordinal position in the series rather than of the intrinsic characteristics of items" (p. 24). It might be added, parenthetically, that the intrinsic characteristics of items are more important in sequential associations, which are more important for the middle items.

The distribution of intralist intrusions generally conforms to this symmetrical function, but the exact distribution is modulated by the tendency for the subject to make the overt response. The symmetrical curve of discriminability determines the availability of possible responses from within the list at each position, whereas the asymmetry is determined by the strategy of the subject in selecting items to be attempted in terms of overt response, and by the response inhibition or stimulus satiation that is associated with the direct, "mechanical" effect of responding rate.

Harcum (1957a, 1964b, 1967b) has proposed that the end-segregation effect in tachistoscopic pattern perception is like the associative interference effect in serial learning. Harcum (1964a) and Harcum and Shaw (1974) found, with tachistoscopic perception of patterns, that performance at a given element position was hindered by the addition of elements at either end of the pattern. Also, the perceptual accuracy is related to the relative position of the elements within the pattern rather than to absolute retinal position. In some cases the elements near fixation show most errors instead of minima of errors (Harcum, 1964a). According to Harcum's (1967b) information-translation theory, the two ends of a uniform spatial or temporal series provide the reference points for an organizational process that gives the basic bow in the curve, with fewer errors near the ends. The end-segregation effect could be the result of the absence of spatial inhibition or masking effect from other elements from one direction. The mechanism in vision may be considered as lateral inhibition (Ratliff, 1961) or spatial masking (Woodworth & Schlosberg, 1954).

This similarity of results suggests common mechanisms in the two tasks and puts limitations on the range of possible mechanisms if one admits the reality of common mechanisms. The generality of the results points to a higher, cognitive mechanism accounting for the end-segregation result. This would most likely be the organizational processes of memory.

The variations in physical characteristics of a task thus seem to be less important than the subject's paralearning strategies. For example,

Keenan (1967) found no significant difference in learning time among five conditions of serial presentation for 12 three-letter words. These included, in addition to the standard serial-learning procedure, procedures in which single items were added cumulatively on successive trials; the subject paced the presentation himself; a "time-out" procedure blanked out certain stimulus exposures on some trials; and—a variation of the time-out method with the blanking-out of items—the subject was forced to overlearn the items that would presumably be overlearned if the subject followed the usual order of acquisition for items (Jensen, 1962a). Total learning time was held constant for all procedures. A sixth procedure—called whole-list learning—presented the entire list simultaneously in a spatial array, but allowed the same amount of time to study as before. This procedure produced much better immediate serial recall, as well as a different serial-position distribution of errors; the usual primacy effect was missing. Therefore, this method obviously involved somewhat different mechanisms, one of which could be a strategy of scanning the total array in different directions and a spatial basis for differentiating items. Harcum and Friedman (1963) obtained a similar result from the comparison of simultaneous and sequential tachistoscopic spatial arrays. Although simultaneous presentation of all items yielded greatly superior reproduction, the spatial distribution of errors was more skewed with the simultaneous presentation, with fewer errors on the left.

In summary, the best interpretation of the end-segregation phenomenon seems to be in terms of reduced alternatives. Any operation that fosters a reduction in the number of alternative retrieval cues (codes)—not necessarily in the number of possible responses—will facilitate performance in learning and memory. For example, Bower and Bolton (1969) argue that rhymes are easy to learn because rhyming of responses provides a rule that permits a restriction in the number of response alternatives. In the same way, end items are facilitated because the retrieval cues for them are less ambiguous. Whereas the end items are associated virtually exclusively with position, the middle items also tend to be retrieved on the basis of sequential associations.

SUMMARY

The bowed function of end segregation has been attributed to complex interconnections among items, to errors of localization, or to a lack of discrimination among items or codes. Whether or not the bowed function is more related to position confusion or to interference among items is determined by the moot answer to the question of whether the subject is learning positions or interitem associations. The critical factor is that the number of alternative retrieval cues is less for end items and, thus, the choice of the proper retrieval cue is less ambiguous.

CHAPTER

$$\boxed{7}$$

PRIMATTENSITY

Although early theories were successful in accounting for the aggregation of errors near the middle of a serial list, as discussed in the previous chapter, the attempted explanations for the skewness of the curve were less satisfying theoretically. The cause of the asymmetry is more labile than the cause of the symmetrical bowing in the serial-position effect. Therefore, it is more attractive to relate the mechanism of asymmetry to the more transient mechanisms of psychological strategy or differential attention.

This chapter deals with the subject's direction of attention and intention to learn the items in an order corresponding to the expected temporal order of reproduction. It assumes that learning is an active process facilitated by such direction of attention; there is little doubt that learning is facilitated by intention to learn (Smith & McDougall, 1920). The real problem with intentional learning in experiments with verbal lists is the determination of just what the subject is intending to learn first. The reasoning is circular unless an independent check on the subject's strategy is made.

The term "strategy" is used because it connotes a cognitive mechanism and because it has been used for this purpose previously (Feigenbaum & Simon, 1962; Harcum & Coppage, 1965b). This use of the word "strategy" has disadvantages because, for some investigators, it connotes

236

only the use of a conscious plan of attack—a deliberate, reportable manipulation of conditions to solve a problem. To be sure, many subjects cannot give a report of how they go about a serial-acquisition task. As I use the term, it could also include unconscious habits transferred to a new task.

The selective aspect of attention would be affected by what Atkinson and Shiffrin (1968b) called cognitive "control processes." Several lines of evidence suggest that these control mechanisms are primarily central in origin, rather than peripheral (Harcum, 1967c; Harcum & Smith, 1966). As Harcum (1957a, 1964a) points out, primacy effects are not exclusive attributes of specific receptive systems since they have been found in various tasks, including visual (Harcum, 1957b) and aural (Pollack, 1953). Also, Glanzer and Clark (1963a, b) showed that the reproducibility of a visual pattern was related to the number of words that the observer had to use in describing it. The more difficult the encoding, the more difficult the perception.

RELEVANT VARIABLES

Before going into a more detailed description of the possible mechanisms of this strategy, which typically favors the first items, it is instructive to examine the types of variables that influence the so-called primacy and recency effects. The categories of variables are not mutually exclusive, and they frequently interact. The range of variables includes organismic as well as input and output factors.

Stimulus Isolation

As mentioned previously, any departure from homogeneity in the stimulus array that would be helpful in identifying and differentiating elements would also be likely to influence the selection of the order for their analysis in the information-processing mechanism. When there is no departure from uniformity of items and conditions, the items at either end would stand out because of their intrinsic characteristics as boundaries of the series. Thus, either end item could be selected as a first anchor in the organization process. The important and difficult problem is to discover the factors that determine which end of the stimulus array will win out as the item to be reproduced first.

Miller (1963) pointed out how the isolation effect in serial learning could be accounted for by the macroprocess (strategy) postulates of Feigenbaum and Simon (1962). Harcum (1965a,b) applied the notion of strategy in perceiving also to the isolation effect in pattern perception. With visual patterns the observers tend to encode the element at the left as the first item, apparently because the spatial dispersion of stimuli provides a strong organizational basis.

In the case of continuous serial presentation, in which the intertrial interval is temporally equivalent to the interstimulus interval, the "isolation effect" becomes, in some cases, a "primacy effect." Lack of homogeneity about an item increases the likelihood that the subject will perceive that item as the "first" item in the series.

The study by Glanzer and Peters (1962) strongly suggests that the usual larger temporal gap between successive presentations of a series ordinarily determines the perception of a "first" syllable. The spacing would presumably affect the attensity of the first and last syllables—that is, facilitate their serving as anchor points in learning. Other studies of serial learning with continuous presentation of items support this argument (Bowman & Thurlow, 1963; Glanzer & Dolinsky, 1965; Lippman & Denny, 1964; Breckenridge, Hakes, & Young, 1965b).

With no temporal space at all between the last and first syllables, Mitchell (1933b) still obtained the serial-position effect, however. Apparently the mere fact of beginning with a certain syllable marked that syllable as the beginning. Such data support a theory of mnemonic organization, since apparently equalized proactive and retroactive inhibitory effects do not destroy the usual shape of the curve. Mitchell concluded that both primacy and finalcy facilitate learning, but the primacy effect is greater and extends farther than the finalcy effect. This conclusion corroborates Foucault (1928) and Robinson and Brown (1926); nevertheless, the results of Mitchell are contrary to the hypothesis that the serial curve is caused by retroactive and proactive inhibition. Although proactive effects, as well as retroactive effects from the end of the list, could be assumed to be acting on the beginning of the list, the serial-position curve was still present.

Fischer (1966b) used different presentation rates without an intertrial interval and discovered that the serial-position curve was typical except that the "origin" was displaced from first to second item. This result was explained by later results of Harcum (1973). Harcum argued that, if the intertrial interval was effective for its cue value and not its provision for dissipation of inhibition, a shorter intertrial interval than interstimulus interval should also be effective. His results showed serial-position curves organized around the temporally first item, whether or not it was preceded by a differentially shorter interval. This occurred presumably because the temporal primacy effect was a stronger cue than the short-interval one. Positive evidence for the cognitive-set hypothesis was inferred from the fact that the short interval degraded performance more for the following item when that item was perceived as first in the series. Harcum concluded that the subject needed more time at this point to shift coding of items from "end items" to "beginning items."

Other studies have employed physical isolation of items with the usual larger intertrial gap. Amelang and Scholl (1971) provided evidence that the subject used some strategy in order to structure a series for recall. Isolation in terms of word meanings produced different effects depending upon the location of the isolated word (namely, first or ninth in a ten-item list) and upon whether instructions produced intentional or incidental learning. Under intentional instructions the subject showed a positive isolation effect, but only at the ninth position. Under incidental instructions a negative isolation effect appeared, but only at the first position. Order of recall correlated with order of presentation positively under intentional learning and negatively under incidental learning. Apparently there was a greater tendency for the subject to organize the intentional material from temporal beginning to end, but the reverse for incidental learning. The critical difference seems to be that the semantic isolation required the development of an appreciation of the categories. This would provide isolation for the later items in the intentional series, since the subject would be more likely to have developed a concept of the category of homogeneous words. But this would hinder recall of the initial item in the incidental series because it was of a different category; it could not have been isolated until the later items had been perceived and their meanings interpreted. In free recall the first item would suffer because it was not a member of the more frequent category, which was therefore less likely to be recalled.

Rabinowitz and Andrews (1973) found isolation effects in both intentional serial learning of 11 items by fifth- and sixth- grade children and in free recall of incidental learning of items appearing with the items to be learned. Instead of a spread of effect there was a compensatory decrease for other items, producing no overall difference for the isolated and unisolated lists of words. This suggests an effect through redistribution of attention.

Huang and Hynum (1970) used an 11-item series of nonsense syllables with a study-recall method. Isolation at the middle of the list was achieved by varying the number of dimensions of difference for the isolated item and by varying the number of isolated items. The isolation effect increased by degrees as the degree of isolation increased. For the single highly discriminable isolate, there was a spread of effect to the following item. The isolation effect decreased as the number of isolates increased, with five isolates producing a serial-position curve equivalent to the control curve. There was no overall facilitation of performance. Steil and Hynum (1970) isolated the middle word, or the three middle words, of a 13-word list of meaningful nouns by printing these items in red. An isolation effect was obtained only for the isolation of the single word. As usual, overall learning was not facilitated. Thus, the strength or power of the isolation variable is important. This conclusion is consistent with the argument that many variables compete with one another as determinants of primacy (Harcum, Pschirrer, & Coppage, 1968).

Instructions

Pollack, Johnson, and Knaff (1959) and Waugh (1960) emphasized the importance of the instructions given to the subjects in immediate-memory tasks. Krueger (1932) showed that directed attention facilitates learning the material regardless of its position, and that constant attention equates learning. When the subject directed his attention to the center of a list, the center was easiest to learn, and the curve was symmetrical. The study of Wing (1964) indicated that the subjects' set was more important than the structural differentiation of a series in determining the distribution of errors.

Fischer (1967) discovered, incidentally to a study done for another purpose, that the distribution of errors in serial learning of nonsense syllables, aurally presented, was dependent upon the subject's intention to learn or not to learn the stimuli. Subjects heard nine items and then were asked to recall them in any sequence. Those subjects instructed to learn the items showed a serial-position curve with greater primacy than recency effects. The subjects merely told that they would hear nonsense syllables, and therefore, who did not intend to learn them, showed reduced both primacy and recency effects. Subjects given an irrelevant task to perform showed the typical result of free recall—namely, greater recency than primacy effects. Fischer concludes that the irrelevant task focused the subject's attention away from aspects of the stimuli that would be relevant later. Nevertheless, there was no difference between the three learning groups in terms of the proportion of subjects correctly recalling syllables.

Bartz, Lewis, and Swinton (1972) showed that the primacy and recency effects in free recall could be influenced by the subject's expectancies about what items would be tested in recall, and thus, apparently, their strategies in transferring different items into long-term memory.

Rehearsal

Although experimenters frequently assume that subjects learn in a manner prescribed by the instructions given them in the experiment, this is not always true. Buxton and Bakan (1949) had subjects memorize nonsense syllables with instructions not to correct errors in anticipation before attempting to anticipate the next correct response, and not to rehearse during the interpolated rest interval. However, one-half of them admitted correcting wrong responses, and the majority of them admitted rehearsal during the rest interval.

Substantial evidence has been presented that supports the hypothesis that subjects, if allowed to rehearse, will tend to rehearse from the beginning of the series. Reynolds and Houston (1964) varied instructions to subjects learning a list of 12 common nouns by serial anticipation for a single trial, tested on the second trial. One group of subjects was instructed to rehearse cumulatively from the beginning of the list as each new item appeared. This group was equivalent to the control group, which was given no instructions, in that the primacy effect was large and there was no recency effect. Groups of subjects instructed to rehearse pairs of items or single items did not reveal significant primacy effects. These results imply that uninstructed subjects nevertheless adopt the self-instructed strategy of rehearsing from the beginning of the series. Jung (1964) found that the serial-position curve showed a monotonic increase of errors from beginning to end for the cumulative method of serial learning.

Palmer and Ornstein (1971) studied free recall of nine-word stimuli with instructions to the subjects to rehearse cumulatively from the beginning of the series or to rehearse successive pairs as paired associates. Testing by a prior-item probe revealed no primacy effect and a strong recency effect from the paired-associate rehearsal technique, and a strong primacy effect for the cumulative-rehearsal method. This latter, however, was not as strong as the recency effect. In a second experiment, groups were given the cumulative-rehearsal instructions or instructions not to rehearse (namely, rehearse only the items currently being presented), and the probed-recall test was given immediately or delayed for 15 seconds, during which time rehearsal was prevented. The rehearsal instructions produced greatest accuracy of performance, including the greatest effect of input primacy. For immediate recall the no-rehearsal group revealed a strong recency effect and no primacy effect, while the rehearsal group revealed both strong primacy effects and strong recency effects. With delayed recall, the no-rehearsal group showed no serial-position effects, whereas the rehearsal group revealed only a weak primacy effect. Thus, the recency effect appears to be entirely the result of short-term memory, since it was absent when the delay was inserted. The primacy effect, on the other hand, with immediate recall was a joint function of short- and long-term memory, since only a portion of it was lost when the recall was delayed. Therefore, these results support the contention of several researchers (e.g., Glanzer & Cunitz, 1966; Atkinson & Shiffrin, 1968a, b), that rehearsal facilitates the transfer of information into long-term memory. The results further imply that the primacy effect is attributable, at least in part, to differential rehearsal of the initial items.

Buschke and Hinricks (1968) had subjects cumulatively rehearse ten-number series for recall in different orders. Control subjects were not instructed to rehearse. For recall in the forward direction, both rehearsal and control subjects produced the usual bowed serial-position curve, with greater primacy than recency effects. For recall in the backward sequence, however, the serial-position curves were quite different for rehearsing and nonrehearsing subjects. The rehearsal subjects again revealed a greater primacy than recency effect, although the performance for the last item alone was about perfect. The nonrehearsing subjects, however, revealed a strong recency effect and no effect of input primacy. When retention was measured by free recall, there were slight asymmetries in the curve, favoring primacy for rehearsing subjects, and recency for nonrehearsing subjects. The serial-position effects for free recall were minimal because the subjects under this condition tended to emit the numbers in their natural serial order, rather than on the basis of the temporal order of presentation. Therefore, the free-recall results were about the same as when the subjects were instructed to recall in the natural serial order.

Corballis (1969) recorded the overt rehearsal of subjects prior to immediate recall of eight visually presented digits. Whether or not the subjects were instructed for ordered recall, some of the ten subjects rehearsed cumulatively from the beginning, and others tended to rehearse items in groups. One subject who had not been instructed to recall in order used no strategy other than merely to repeat the presented digit. The cumulative rehearsers showed strong primacy effects and little recency effects in recall. The rehearsers of grouped items revealed generally symmetrical serial-position curves.

Voss (1956) found that the position of maximum difficulty moved closer to the center of the series as the length of pattern increased from 8 to 24 items with unpaced responding. He suggested that with paced responding the advantage of primacy would probably be reduced because the subjects would have less opportunity to rehearse from the beginning.

Ellis and Dugas (1968) found that subjects shown nine CVC syllables at nine horizontal locations, under paced or unpaced sequences, revealed typical serial-position effects for probed recall of single items. Although the recency effect was generally greater, the subjects showing generally longer latencies of response relative to subjects revealing short latencies were superior in correct choices for the initial items, but not for the end ones. The authors conclude that the subjects with longer latencies were rehearsing, and the rehearsal favored the beginning items.

Ellis and Hope (1968) obtained evidence supporting a dual-process theory of the serial-position effect in free recall. They presented a series of digits or letters visually and later asked the subjects to indicate the position of a probe item. Variables such as a delay of recall, which reduced the presumed short-term clarity of the traces of the items, tended to reduce the recency effect. On the other hand, variables such as slower presentation rate, which permitted rehearsal and thus facilitated long-term memory, tended to increase the primacy effect. Presumably the subjects during rehearsal selectively favored the items at the beginning of the series in the transfer of the information into long-term memory. Ellis (1969) again concluded from a probe-type memory task that a primacy effect is facilitated by opportunity for the subject to rehearse.

Leicht (1968) tested the hypothesis that the primacy effect in free-recall learning of 20-noun lists was due to differential rehearsal for the initial items. Although instructions to the subject designed to inhibit rehearsal did not affect the primacy effect, an increase in presentation rate did reduce it. The slowest rate (namely, 3 seconds) produced about equal primacy and recency effects, presumably because the additional time allowed more rehearsal, which favored the items at the beginning of the series.

Results of Koffman and Weinstock (1974) for serial learning of low-meaningful syllables by children and adults supported the proposition of a tendency for subjects to favor the initial items through rehearsal. Verbalization of the stimuli decreased the primacy effect, presumably because it hindered this differential rehearsal.

SUMMARY

The results clearly show that rehearsal facilitates selective effects in learning and recall. But, as Underwood (1949) points out, if rehearsing is ruled out then the curve is still bowed. Therefore, the critical factor in determining the primacy or recency effects is not the rehearsal per se, but the factor that determines what is rehearsed. Some other factor causes the subject to favor some items by greater attention to them.

Practice

This section is concerned with the development of the subject's approach to the serial-acquisition task. It asks whether or not the subject changes his strategy of learning in order to make his learning more efficient. Murdock (1964) has shown that the serial-position curve for the recall of paired associates reveals a greater recency effect after practice, without a change in the overall level of performance. Thus, the shape of the curve seemed to be determined not by the amount of proactive inhibition present, but by a redirection of attention.

Concepts like memory span or encoding efficiency are relevant because the asymmetry of the serial-position curve has been attributed to them. To be sure, the relevance of a concept of span assumes that subjects consistently favor some items to be included in the span, if there are so many items that some must be left out. Seamon (1972) was able, with practice, to eliminate significant serial-position effects among categories for reaction time to probed recall of single items in lists composed of four blocks of three categorized items. This suggests that ordinarily primacy and recency effects are produced by selective effort, made necessary by the difficulty of the task.

If the asymmetry of the serial-learning curve is produced by a span of memory for items at the beginning of the series, the skewness of the curve should therefore increase with practice. Murdock (1960) points out that his distinctiveness curve is fixed for series of a given length and, therefore, may not be applicable to all data in which various different levels of practice are represented. He points out that serial-learning data obviously vary as a function of practice and, therefore, would present this difficulty to his theory. Detterman and Ellis (1971) reversed first and last serial positions and used Murdock's (1960) distinctiveness model to fit short-term memory data. They also found differences between retarded and normal subjects, which they attributed to differences in rehearsal strategies. The retarded subjects had much stronger recency effects.

Jahnke (1963) showed that serial recall produced greater primacy than recency effects, but the reverse was true for free recall. Thus, the relative strengths of primacy and recency may change depending upon the subject's prior cognition of responding order (cf. Harcum, Hartman, & Smith, 1963).

Presumably, the size of the span increases with practice. Lepley (1934) found that practice did increase the asymmetry of the curve. Also, the asymmetry was greater for the subjects at a higher educational level. As possible explanations for this he proposes an increase in the memory span with practice, and a progressive change in the order with which the subjects learned the items, with more items learned from the beginning of the list. In free recall of word pairs, Friedrich (1974) similarly observed less overall accuracy for younger children relative to adolescents, because of specific depression of the beginning and middle serial positions.

The results of Jensen and Roden (1963) for lists of nine colored geometric forms supported Lepley (1934). They did not, however, find typical serial-learning curves. There were essentially no errors for the first three items, presumably because their subjects were highly intelligent and the task relatively easy.

Waugh (1960) noted that practiced subjects had a longer "initial span" in both 18-item and 12-item digit series, whereas the "terminal spans" were not different from those of unpracticed subjects. Thus, practice promoted primacy effects more than recency effects. Moreover, for the 12-digit series the practiced subjects tended to write down the beginning items first.

Harcum and Coppage (1965b) attempted to verify Lepley's (1934) results of practice in serial learning. Thirteen subjects learned a different serial list of ten nonsense syllables each day for 12 days by the anticipation method. Two subjects continued for totals of 34 and 42 days, respectively. The position of maximum errors was obtained by ranking each syllable position from least to most total errors. Results are shown in Figure 7-1 for four blocks of three sessions, in which the abscissa was thus labeled "order of group learning" to distinguish it from the Jensen (1962a) method of plotting the ranks for items for each subject individually before summing. The maximum of errors shifts from Item Six in the first block of sessions to Item Eight in the last two blocks of sessions. This change in the rank order of items seems to occur progressively with practice. Presumably, this ranking of items is highly correlated with the order in which the items are learned. Thus, with practice, the subjects show an increase in the tendency to learn the items from the beginning of the series progressively toward the end. This change in order of items can account for the increased skewness in the serial-position curve because it produces a greater similarity in the rank order of items for individual subjects.

A change in the shape of the group-learning curves also supports the conclusion that the order of learning items is more consistent after practice. The consistency among subjects in the order of learning the items is given by the slope of the curve; the steeper the slope between adjacent pairs of data points, the more consistent the subjects in order of learning those items. The basis for this relation between shape of

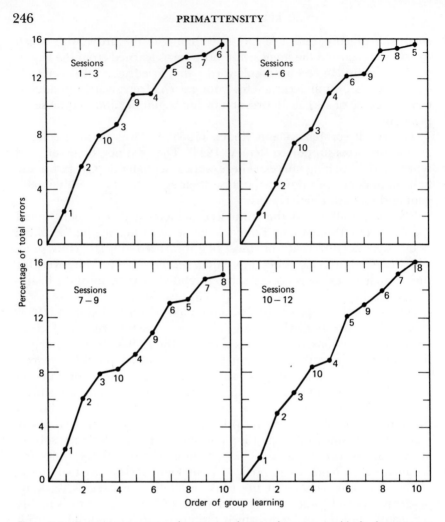

Figure 7-1   Percentage error according to group learning for successive blocks, from Harcum and Coppage (1965b). Reprinted with permission of publisher.

the curve and consistency of learning the items is that the functions are linear when the averages are for the rankings for individual subjects (Jensen, 1962a). If all subjects were perfectly consistent—the order of items were identical—the group learning and the Jensen plot of individual learning would be identical. As can be seen in Figure 7-1, the subjects were most consistent for items at the beginning and end of the list. The number of errors is smaller and the curve is steeper. When subjects become less consistent with one another, the group-learning curves become flatter. A complete absence of consistency would result in literally horizontal functions (i.e., all tied ranks). The change to a flatter slope as the later items are acquired produces a bow in the group-learning curve. Since the curves become progressively less bowed as the subjects become more practiced, the subjects were becoming more consistent in learning the items in a given order. The consistency among subjects necessarily accounts for the appearance of the classical serial-position curve. Obviously, if the subjects were completely inconsistent in the order of acquisition for the various items, there would be no serial-position effects in grouped data.

The data for the two subjects who served for the many additional sessions give added weight to the argument for consistency. For the last block of five sessions the data according to order of group learning produced virtually linear plots. In these plots the consistency was for the same subject over five lists, rather than for different subjects on the same list. The near linearity of these plots indicates that each of the subjects is learning the items in virtually identical orders from one day to the next.

Figure 7-2 shows the results for the four successive blocks of sessions in terms of the order of learning the items, after the manner of Jensen (1962a); the abscissa is the rank order of items from fewest to most errors for the individual subject, and the ordinate is the percentage of total errors for all items. Most of the data in each of the four blocks of sessions are apparently well described by a single solid line. For the first three blocks, however, these solid lines fit nine of the data points, but not the data point for the first item. Therefore, the dashed lines are used to connect the point of origin with the solid lines where they cross the position of the syllable that was second in order of learning. These dashed lines are drawn because a y intercept above zero does not make sense—namely, indicating some errors before the task has begun. Also, these lines tend to describe the results for the first and second items. This difference between dashed and solid lines means that the first-learned items are more difficult to acquire than the later ones.

The slopes of dashed and solid curves incline toward one another with practice. This increase in relative slope of the solid curve with practice in Figure 7-2 means that more errors are made for these items relative to the first two items. At the end of practice, when the asymptotic level of performance has been reached, one function, similar to that of Jensen (1963) for the easier task, is obtained.

A memory span, by definition, means perfect accuracy for at least one item after a single trial. The memory span can be measured from the order-of-learning data as the distance from origin to the intercept

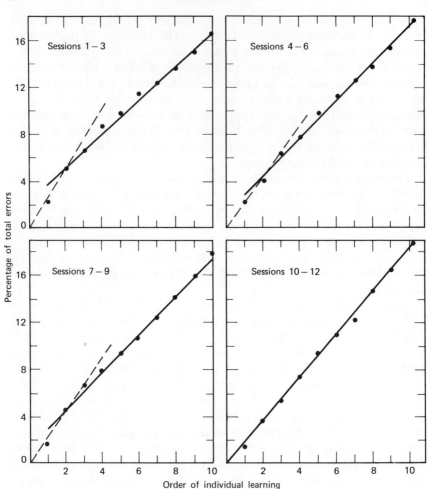

Figure 7-2 Percentage error according to individual learning for successive sessions, from Harcum and Coppage (1965b). Reprinted with permission of publisher.

of the data function on the abscissa. If the size of the span fluctuates for different subjects or for different sessions, there should be at least a flattening of the function at the beginning of learning. The opposite result, in fact, occurs in these data; the first-learned items often are the most difficult to acquire. After the first-learned items have been acquired, to provide an anchor, the remaining are easier to learn. This supports the results of Robinson and Brown (1926), who found that items near the middle of longer serial lists exhibit positive acceleration of learning curves.

The above argument does not deny that a memory span can appear in serial-learning data to affect the distribution of errors among serial positions. The subject who learned 34 lists did show a span in the later sessions. Over the last five sessions this span included the items at the first two serial positions. On the other hand, the subject who continued practice for 42 days never did reveal a span. For the last five lists his data still gave evidence for the slower acquisition of an anchor.

Jensen and Roden (1963) found almost errorless reproduction of the first three items within the nine-item series. Moreover, a typical bowed serial-position curve appeared for the remaining six items, just as it would have for a seven-item list of more difficult items. Therefore, if there is a span, the addition of the remaining items occurs in an *order* that produces the skewed serial-position curve. Thus, it appears that an anchor for learning may be a group of items acquired simultaneously as part of a span, or a single item acquired with great difficulty. The skewed serial-position curve is generated for the items as they are added to this anchor. If the serial task is relatively easy, there will be a "span" at the beginning of the series. The items of the span then become the anchor for the subsequent "serial learning."

Response Order

The effect of responding sequence has three aspects: the temporal characteristics of the overt response, inducing in recall tasks a differential delay in reproduction of the various items; encoding and response selector mechanisms that determine which responses are to be favored in output; and determination of whether or not a response is to be given at all. The first two of these are not important in the typical serial-anticipation task because the timing and ordering of the responses are constrained. The third is important because of potential interference effects of overt intruding errors.

Broadbent (1958) related the effects of recall order, and knowledge about recall order, to two possible processes of memory. In a storage-first process, information is transmitted into permanent memory through an "S" or temporary storage system before it enters a "P" or perceiving system. In an overload process, the information can go into either the "S" system or the "P" system first, with the "S" system used only for overloads. The "S" system can pass information successively only (sequential processing). Very brief exposures of familiar tasks would not require an extensive storage in the "S" system, and the process would tend toward the latter mechanisms. Serial-order effects may be found even with simultaneous stimulation in the storage-first process, even though instructions concerning order of report are delayed until after stimulation. In the overload process, if the order of input does not coincide with the order of the "P" system, then it may have to be transposed before the information enters the "P" system. In such a case, the element-position effects may be abolished when the instructions about order of recall are given only after stimulation. For example, Kay and Poulton (1951) required subjects to recall the last half of a serial list first. When the subjects knew in advance the recall condition to be required, with ordered recall the ordinary serial-position curve was obtained. However, with the displaced order of recall, a dip in the serial-position curve was found at the first item of the second half of the list. When the subject did not know the order of recall in advance, the usual serial-position curve was still obtained when the items were recalled in order of presentation, but a symmetrical curve of errors was obtained with the displaced order of recall.

Jahnke (1963) pointed out that serial recall in immediate memory produces greater primacy than recency effects, whereas free recall produces greater recency effects. He subsequently examined this relationship in a single study (Jahnke, 1965), using lists of 6, 10, and 15 words. The analysis showed that recency effects are greater than primacy effects for free recall, and for longer lists. The evidence from the overt orders of reproduction was interesting with respect to the subjects' strategy of responding. The accuracy of recall was significantly correlated with the order of recall under every condition except for free recall of the six-item list, for which recall order was significantly correlated with presentation order. For free recall, the subjects tended to recall in the order of presentation only when the lists were short; with the longer lists, the subjects tended to recall the last items first, and then the first items. These data thus support the argument for subjective organization of series in free recall, with response ordering more important than input ordering.

Postman and Jenkins (1948) showed that a disparity between what the subject thought would be the method of testing recall, and was presumably preparing for, and the actual test used caused less than maximum retention. Results of Jahnke (1965) and Bruder (1970) indicate that subjects' cognitive set for free or serial recall influenced their relative strengths of primacy and recency effects. If recall is free, the subject often shifts the order of output of items from initial items first to final items first. Bruder (1970) found, on the other hand, that subjects not instructed until after stimulus presentation performed the same as subjects instructed prior to stimulus presentation. One interesting aspect of these results, however, was the almost complete absence of recency effects for serial recall, and the superiority of recall of first over last items in the free-recall conditions. Apparently the length of the series (namely, 15 and 20 words) contributed to this effect.

Cermak (1972) found that the subject's expectation about whether or not each of several series of items would be tested at the end of the experiment influenced his organization of the material for free recall. Subjects who had been tested continuously trial-by-trial tended to emit the items from the final position first in the free recall, and to show a very strong recency effect. On the other hand, subjects who did not have to respond on each trial revealed a substantial tendency to emit the items from the first series first, and to show a substantial primacy effect across the series.

Hinrichs (1968) used pre- and poststimulus cuing of recall order—either forward or backwards—for nine-digit sequences. Forward recall was superior to backward recall, and precuing was superior to postcuing. The cuing-by-recall-order interaction was significant, because the recall orders were not significantly different for postcuing, but significantly different for precuing. Although the serial-position curves were not greatly different for pre- and postcuing, indicating no effect of the subject's knowledge on the strategy of rehearsing, there were some differences. Paradoxically, for example, the advantage of recency with forward reporting was greater with prior knowledge. Perhaps the task was easy enough so that all traces of items were available to the subject when he received information about the required recall order. The recency effect of input was greater for forward reporting than was the primacy effect of input with backward reporting, probably reflecting the greater efficiency of the forward reporting order.

Battig (1965a) reported evidence that the items with the strongest mnemonic trace are not always reproduced first in free recall. Sometimes the subject attempts first the items of weaker strength that he may not remember if he delays until after the well-learned items are recited.

Postman (1964) also has emphasized the importance of whether or not the subject is told to recall in a prescribed sequence. These conditions of ordered recall and free recall, respectively, may produce the same results under some conditions. In free recall, the items that are reproduced first are favored. These are likely to be the items that were the last to be presented, however. If responding conditions are not specified, then the observers tend to reproduce their responses in their habitual, easiest ways. The order of meaningful verbal responses would be constructed according to the syntax of the language, for example (Deese, 1961; Schlosberg, 1965). With meaningless binary patterns, the observer consistently responds from left to right when given an option (Harcum, Hartman, & Smith, 1963); this result is the same as actually instructing him to respond from left to right.

When Murdock (1968) instructed subjects to recall items for an immediate-memory test in either a "first-item-first" or "last-item-first" order, the results were a bit different depending upon whether the instructions about recall were given before or after the stimulus presentation. For precuing, the end of the list reported first showed the greater effect—either "primacy" or "recency." For postcuing, the recency effect was the stronger when the last items were reported first, with about equal primacy and recency effects when the beginning was reported first. These results were quite similar to those of Harcum, Hartman, and Smith (1963) for left-to-right and right-to-left reporting of tachistoscopic patterns, if one accepts the equivalence of a left-to-right spatial order to a temporal sequence from beginning to terminal items.

Battig (1966) showed that forcing subjects to recall items in a serial order that did not conform to a natural order based on item similarity was detrimental to recall. He concluded that recall order was a "performance" rather than a learning factor, because on a subsequent recognition test the method of recall used previously (free or serial) was not a significant variable.

Maisto and Ward (1973) found a smaller recency effect for serial recall than for serial anticipation. Perhaps the reason for this was a greater reliance on sequential-chain cues in the serial-recall task, fostering a beginning-to-end organization.

SUMMARY

Practice affects the serial-position distribution by providing feedback to the coding mechanisms. The ordinal code that is most effective in promoting retrieval for a given output requirement will be the one that is developed. If the subject prepares for an output procedure that is not, in fact, subsequently required, the performance is hampered because the retrieval code is inappropriate.

POSSIBLE MECHANISMS

Several suggestions for the explanatory mechanism or mechanisms behind the asymmetry of the serial-position curve are now discussed. They will be grouped under four rubrics, although the various categories are not discrete or mutually exclusive.

Differential Inhibition

The first category is somewhat distinct from the rest. It involves the differentially greater buildup of inhibitory influences from the end of the series (Hull, Hovland, Ross, Hall, Perkins, & Fitch, 1940). Since this early formulation involved nothing more than a postulate, it is not very helpful as an explanation. Later, Hull (1952) modified this position to include stronger anticipatory influences. The evidence points, however, to stronger effects of cognitive variables.

Associative Asymmetry

A corollary principle to the "primattensity" effect is that "forward associations" are easier to establish than "backward associations." That is, the subject is also set to form associations in the "forward" direction, which is to say, from the beginning of the series to the end (Harcum & Coppage, 1965b). A similar idea is Bugelski's (1948) method of assigning greater weights to remote forward associations.

PAIRED-ASSOCIATIVE EVIDENCE

There is considerable evidence for stronger forward associations, from paired-associate as well as serial learning. The evidence is not unambiguous, however. The difficulty is to assess the strength of the associative bond independent of retrieval considerations.

Harcum (1953) provided evidence for the learning of backward associations using a transfer paradigm, but the negative transfer attributed to backward associations was about equal to that for forward associations. Murdock (1958) repeated Harcum's (1953) experiment and discovered about equal amounts of negative transfer in the A-C and B-C paired-associate learning paradigms.

Using mediation paradigms, Horton and Hartman (1963) investigated the effect of a B-C mediator after A-B learning on the acquisition of A-C and C-A associations. The forward associations were superior.

Schild and Battig (1966) found, using bidirectional as well as unidirectional training of paired associates, that the unidirectional associations were more often correct. Since the bidirectional condition equated stimulus and response availability, the associative asymmetry was not due to this factor. In another experiment, after a pair in bidirectional learning had been given correctly once, its directionality was kept constant, either in the same direction as the correct response, or in the reverse of that direction. The prior unidirectional responses were learned fastest, with the bidirectional training slowest, and the shifted bidirectional to unidirectional pairs intermediate in speed of learning.

Gallup and Wollen (1968) controlled for item availability and direction of recall in testing the hypothesis of associative symmetry in paired-associate learning. Since R-S recall was superior to S-R recall under some conditions, the principle of associative asymmetry was upheld, but the direction of the asymmetry was not consistent.

Although Murdock (1958) found equivalent transfer effects of forward and backward associations in paired-associate learning, he did not, however, generalize this result to serial learning because of the fundamental differences in procedures. He concluded:

> Serial learning in a forward order does occur; this is attested to by everything from the fact that the alphabet is notoriously difficult to recite backward to the fact that following serial learning forward associations are almost always considerably stronger than backward associations. However, the method of serial learning very definitely imposes a set to learn in the forward direction since the items are always presented in the same order (p. 113).

Battig (1968) also concluded that the issue of associative symmetry cannot be resolved at present because of artifacts associated with "the fundamentally different learning processes involved with stimulus and response terms within the paired-associate task" (p. 156).

SERIAL-LEARNING EVIDENCE

That directional set was possibly the cause of primacy is supported by Wohlgemuth's (1913) finding of both forward and backward associations, but more in the direction that the subject was directed to look for them. Probably the subject is set to learn the forward associations. Wohlgemuth conceived the idea that the strength and direction of associations were dependent upon the subject's "unconscious bias" to react in a certain direction. He presented lists of ten syllables and ten diagrams, and measured the associations formed by the method of recall. When the subject was instructed to form associations in the forward direction, more forward associations were formed both for syllable and for diagram lists. However, when the subject was instructed to form association of each item to the one preceding it, then more backward associations were formed. Backward set in general reversed the relative strengths of backward and forward associations with diagrams and reduced the relative strength of forward to backward associations with verbal material from 3.4 to 1 to 1.6 to 1. Evidently there is a strong set to learn verbal material in the forward direction. Wohlgemuth, at any rate, concluded that associative tendencies are equally strong in both directions and overt response tendencies may be reversed by the proper set.

Further evidence was offered by Hermans (1936). He photographed on movie film 11 pairs of nonsense syllables so that each pair was followed by every other pair once, but within the pair the order was always the same. Testing by the association method, eliminating those cases where the subject made both a forward and backward response within the same pair, he found that approximately 30% of the time the subject gave the first syllable of a pair when the second number was given as the stimulus. Approximately 70% of the time the subject gave the second syllable of a pair when the first number was given as the stimulus.

Wilson's (1943) subjects learned lists of 16 two-syllable adjectives to a criterion of 12 correct anticipations and were tested after rest periods of various lengths. Although he found associations in all degrees of remoteness in both backward and forward directions after all rest intervals, the forward remote associations outnumbered the backward ones.

Using the association method, McGeoch (1934) established the empirical existence of remote forward and backward associations. McGeoch had his subjects learn serial lists to complete mastery, and then tested them immediately using the associative method. About one-third of the associations were backward. He reported that over one-half of the recalls in the forward direction were remote, and 60% of those in the backward direction were remote. He concluded that the associative method produced stronger evidence for remote associations than did the derived-lists method.

Ribback and Underwood (1950) stated that a bowed serial curve implies that the items are learned from both ends toward the middle. The front end is learned more rapidly than the back end because the curve is skewed toward the end, and equal learning rates would cause the most difficult portions to be at the exact middle. They attempted to excerpt positions of the beginning and end of the lists and compare their learning rates. Their results showed empirically that the skewness of the curve was due to a faster rate of learning forward then backward.

Postman and Adams (1957) found that intentional learners gave more correct forward associations than incidental learners after serial anticipation learning, and they also gave fewer backward and remote associations. Schwarz (1970b) found equal numbers of correct forward and backward associations after one trial of serial learning, although more forward errors appeared than backward ones.

SUMMARY

The foregoing results indicate that the generally greater tendency for forward association rather than backward is due to the subject's intention to learn in the forward direction. The preceding item becomes the cue for the retrieval of the following one if this is the way the subject expects to be tested. Therefore, the temporal order is not as important as the expected retrieval requirement.

Perceptual Enhancement

Some theorists have argued that the first item is favored through its perceptual saliency. Thus, it stands out because of its intrinsic distinctiveness, or because the context of the task tends to direct attention toward it. This is usually the first item in an ordered-recall task, and the final one in a free-recall task. For example, Tulving and Patterson (1968) account for the recency effect in free recall on the basis of the effectiveness of the retrieval cue provided by the temporal input.

Rosner (1972) used a position probe to test retention of series of four pictures in immediate memory for preschool children. When the pictures were all from the same pool of items, the performance across blocks of trials deteriorated, whereas unrelated items showed a slight proactive effect. When some control subjects were shifted to a new pool of items, a large primacy effect was obtained for the first items after the shift, and the first postshift series of items was facilitated by a more general primacy effect. These results indicate that these young children could gain release from proactive interference by a cognitive insulation of the new, different items from the old, producing the primacy effect across serial positions for the first items of the postshift series.

DISTINCTIVENESS

Robinson and Brown (1926) found primacy effects more pronounced and spread farther than finalcy effects. Further evidence indicated that these effects, moreover, were due to interference. In plotting learning curves for individual items in the list, they observed items in central portions of longer lists exhibiting early positive acceleration. This was interpreted to mean that more difficult items in long lists could not be learned until the easier ones had been acquired.

Hull's (1952) notion of decreasing d (distinctiveness) of items throughout the serial list is an alternative to the notion of initial set. He argued that, particularly with homogeneous items, the first item was most distinctive because it was preceded by different activity from the rest of the items; the remaining items lost in distinctiveness as they were more removed temporally from this different activity. Murdock's (1960) treatment was similar to this, except that he considered the temporal series as a sensory scale of increasing intensity, and thus took the logarithm of serial position for theoretical weighting.

Workman (1951) described three prerequisites for eliminating the advantages of temporal primacy and finalcy in serial learning. The first is to make the intertrial interval equal to the interstimulus interval. The second is to use a "precursor" list before the first presentation of the list to be learned, and the third is to repeat some items within the precursor list. Workman predicted that for such a series the perceived first item would be learned first, with a gradient of difficulty around it. Arguing from the work of Smith and Stearns (1949), he predicted that the gradient would show faster learning for succeeding items than for the preceding items. Thus the serial-position curve should be asymmetrically bowed relative to the perceived-first item. Furthermore, Workman predicted that there would be no serial-position curve if the subjects did not consistently select some item as first. The results for 12-syllable lists, plotted relative to the first temporal response-term—the item that followed the temporally first item—failed to show a coherent serial-position curve, as predicted. These plots in terms of the first item following the perceived-first, or in terms of the first-learned item, showed the typical serial-position result, as predicted. Usually the first-learned item was the one following the item that was perceived as first. Also as predicted, the items following the first-learned one showed slightly greater correct anticipations than the preceding items, but with decreasing gradients of correct responses in each case.

Lieury (1973) eliminated a primacy effect in free recall of words by presenting, for incidental learning beforehand, a different group of words or pseudowords. For one of the experimental conditions the overall transfer was positive, and for another it was negative.

Schumsky, Grasha, Trinder, and Richman (1969) found that the first syllable of a series of three, five, or seven items presented just once was not influenced by the series length. Therefore, there was minimal proactive inhibition on the first item and very little retroactive inhibition.

Underwood (1972, 1973) has been a recent proponent of the perceptual distinctiveness argument. In two studies, Underwood (1972, 1973) found bowed serial-position curves in serial recall when differential attention to parts of the series was controlled. Therefore, he attributed the primacy effect to perceptual enhancement, rather than to differential rehearsal. The main argument against the perceptual differentiation argument is that one can get a cognitive judgment of a "first item" without a built-in perceptual difference (e.g., Lippman & Denny, 1964; Harcum & Coppage, 1965a). Moreover, it is also possible to install a perceptual difference and fail to produce a position effect (e.g., Glanzer & Dolinsky, 1965; Harcum & Smith, 1966).

CONTEXT

Underwood and Richardson (1956) found only about 1.3% forgetting in the recall of the first and second items in a serial list when the subject had learned only one list. Therefore, they concluded that inadequate set or absence of warmup accounts for only a small part in the retention loss of a serial list.

Melton (1963a) pointed out that the results of Postman and Riley (1959) on the first recall of an original serial list after interpolated learning showed a reduced primacy effect. However, for the second recall trial the primacy effect was reinstated. This may be attributed to the reinstatement of the context for first and last items of the original list by the first recall trial (Melton, 1963a), by the subject's regaining his set to respond with items from the original list, or by the first recall trial's serving as a cue to reactivate the appropriate traces, although not sufficiently for a complete recall of the list.

Keppel (1968) concludes that the evidence verifies the existence of the unlearning of forward, backward, and contextual associations in retroactive and proactive inhibition of paired-associate learning. He suggests that the results of Postman and Riley (1959), showing a flatter serial-position curve on relearning that they attributed to generalized response competition, may also be explained in terms of unlearning contextual associations.

Hintzman and Block (1971) found that accuracy of position judgments was best at the beginning of a long series and poorest at the end. They suggest that contextual information may possibly be the cause of these strong primacy effects in position judgments. Hintzman, Block, and Summers (1973) later supported this view. Under some conditions their subjects were able to reproduce information about the relative position of items within a series, even if they made errors with respect to which series the item was a member. When several lists were used, with immediate recall there was a large recency effect for the end items of the last list. With delayed recall this recency effect was reduced, although primacy effects were not affected. Thus the primacy effect appears to be a recognition of the "differential cognitive strain" experienced by the subject as he encountered items at greater distance from the beginning item. This contextual cue aids the identification of the items at the beginning of a series. This notion is similar to the propositions of Postman and Riley (1959) and Peterson (1963).

In discussing organizational factors within free-recall learning, Tulving (1968) considered the special problem of accounting for the learning of the first item. He argued that there was no compelling need to account for trial-by-trial increments in free recall in terms of the strengthening of contextual associations. This function is served by the secondary organization or strengthening of interitem associations. He concluded, however:

> This is not to say that contextual associations—which I would like to define as associations between different aspects of the subject's total experience in an experimental situation and the to-be-remembered items— play no role at all in free recall. It is logically necessary that at least one item—and psychologically plausible that a small but fixed number of items—be initially associated with the context to make later recall of the list possible (1968, p. 24).

SUMMARY

The perceptual enhancement of an initial item obviously affects its retention. This effect is accomplished through attraction of the subject's attention to that item and his active use of it in a retrieval plan.

Initial Set

A postulate for theories of serial acquisition in terms of a selective strategy of acquisition for the different items is that the subject is ordinarily set to begin the learning at the item which he perceives is the beginning of the series (Harcum, 1967b). This component explains why the temporally defined beginning of a series is ordinarily learned faster than the end.

Ebbinghaus (1902) essentially expressed the idea of a set toward learning the first item first. The wording that he used to describe the serial-position effect, in the number of promptings required to learn a list of 12 syllables, implies a sequential order in acquiring a serial list. He found that most promptings were required about the middle items. Ebbinghaus reported that the subject's attention, if left alone, was directed to the beginning of the list. He concluded that the stamping in begins at the beginning and at the end of the series and finally reaches the later middle members.

Müller and Schumann (1894) investigated whether or not two successive syllables of a series, which are learned in a prescribed trochaic rhythm to the first errorless reproduction, are associated more strongly if they are component parts of the same measure than if they belong to two different successive measures. They predicted that the association would be stronger in the first case than in the latter. The results verified this prediction. Müller and Pilzecker (1900) supported Müller and Schumann's conclusion. They also claimed to show that the end syllable of a measure has a noticeable tendency to produce the beginning syllable. This tendency, they believed, was not as strong as the tendency of the beginning syllable to reproduce the end syllable, but it was still of the same order of magnitude. They called it the "initial reproduction tendency" and concluded that it was not mere backward association. Also, they concluded that this was not as strong as the tendency of beginning syllable to produce the final syllable. Such a process might explain the advantage of temporal primacy.

Welch and Burnett (1924) had their subjects write down syllables immediately after learning and in any order, eliminating rehearsal. They found a large recency effect and no effect of primacy. Their conclusion was that primacy was ordinarily due to more frequent repetitions of initial items. Jenkins and Dallenbach (1927) put a different interpretation on these findings, however. Such results, they say, are due to the direction of the subjects' attention toward the final item. They thus explain primacy in terms of a mediating set:

> The serial mode of presentation will suffice, we believe, to arouse an 'initial set' toward the first syllable, and thus accent it and cause it to be reported more frequently than any other syllable within the stimulus-series (pp. 290–291).

Support for the existence of such an initial-set tendency was offered by Meyer (1939). Meyer attempted to test the finding of Müller and Pilzecker (1900) that when one syllable is accented in learning a complex of syllables in a series, then presentation of one member of the complex calls forth the first member, and then the rest of the syllables in sequence. The existence of such an initial reproductive tendency was supported. He stated that the explanation of it was not in terms of simple association, because this would necessitate stronger backward than forward associations. The underlying factor, he said, was "temporal organization."

The results of Ahmed and Voss (1969) indicate early learning of position identity for initial items. After a single trial of serial learning the subjects could very accurately reproduce the location of the first items in the series, but this ability decreased steadily over serial positions such that the final items were localized no better than the performance of the control subjects.

Malmo and Amsel (1948), comparing serial learning of anxious and control subjects, found that the anxious patients not only made more errors in learning, because of presumed discrimination deficits, they also were apparently less consistent in their ordering strategy. This can be inferred from Figure 7-3, from Malmo and Amsel, which shows a more nearly symmetrical serial-position distribution of errors for the patients. According to the present orientation, the patients had a deficit in organizational strategy and thus did not consistently begin the acquisition with the first item. Hence, the primacy effect was greatly reduced.

RECALL MEASURES

Raffel (1936) found a diminution in the advantage caused by primacy when decreased emphasis was placed on serial position in recall. If no

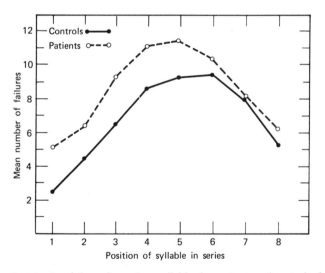

Figure 7-3 Anticipation failures for various syllables by patients and controls, from Malmo and Amsel (1948). Copyright © (1948) by the American Psychological Association. Reprinted with permission.

restrictions are placed on recall, learning is more rapid, and the end of the list is learned best. This agrees with the findings of Welch and Burnett (1924) and Jenkins and Dallenbach (1927). Raffel suggests that the primacy effect is due to rehearsal, and that with instructions to learn the list in order the subject has a set to learn the beginning.

Sampson (1969) supported the argument that subjects set to learn a series show a stronger primacy than recency effect in free recall. For subjects without such a set there was no primacy effect—only a recency effect. These results are attributed to a tendency of subjects who are set to learn actively to rehearse the series from the beginning.

The hypothesis of initial set was supported by evidence from the comparison of the learning of series having built-in directional characteristics. For sequentially organized material, such as verbal items with a close approximation to written English, the primacy effect was greater than the recency effect, even in free recall (Deese & Kaufman, 1957). In other words, the subject apparently sees in the preorganized material an intrinsic beginning, which he sets out to learn first. The set to learn first the beginning appears itself to be a product of learning.

Roberts and Lewis (1968) compared serial-position curves of free recall of eight-item lists of words or nonsense syllables for subjects categorized on the basis of performance accuracy. The word lists showed significant differences among serial-position curves for subjects of different ability. Presumably the primacy effects were greater than recency effects for this material because the subjects were more likely to construct meaningful sequences. Actually, for the subjects showing best recall there was little evidence for recency effects. For the nonsense materials all subject groups showed greater recency effects than primacy effects, with the untransformed data showing parallel curves. The serial-position differences were apparently due to the differences in materials, since the subjects tended to fall into the same groups on each task.

Crowder (1969) found that ordered recall of nine digits was better when the subject knew the length of the series to be recalled. The results of a serial-position analysis, reproduced in Figure 7-4, show that this advantage was limited to the first half of the series. These results were attributed to the differential greater rehearsal of the initial items by the subject, on the presumption that known length facilitated rehearsal. Support for this was obtained by comparison of the results for subjects having good recall with those having poor recall. The subjects having good recall revealed a much greater primacy effect with the material of known length, but the serial-position curves of good-recall and poor-recall subjects did not differ when length of the series was not known.

McHugh, Turnage, and Horton (1973) tested the hypothesis that ini-

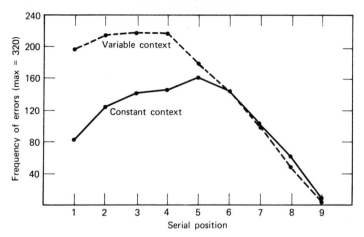

Figure 7-4   Errors per serial position with variable or constant context, from Crowder (1969). Reprinted with permission of the Academic Press.

tial items in serial recall are coded into long-term memory, whereas final items may not be. Accordingly they interpolated tasks of varying similarity to the original word list during the delay of recall. The long-term memory store should respond to differences in similarity of the interpolated task, whereas items in temporary store should be uniformly lost regardless of the similarity variable. The recall scores for each condition revealed strong primacy effects, and no recency effects, as would be expected on the basis of the delay of recall. Interpolated items of greatest similarity (namely, identity) showed greatest retention, followed by the items of least similarity (namely, digits instead of words). High- and low-similarity items were next, followed by the medium-similarity condition, that was worst of all. The ordering of conditions was about the same across all serial positions, although the differences were greater for the terminal items. These results indicate that items at each serial position have been encoded in long-term memory; they are consistent with the hypothesis that the subject organizes the list about the initial items and differentially rehearses the initial items.

Bousfield, Whitmarsh, and Esterson (1958) found that the order in which items in free recall were reproduced was directly related to the frequency of recall. In general, the serial-position curves showed slightly greater primacy than recency effects. The authors attributed this to the use of words as stimuli, which increased the probability of rehearsal from beginning to end. They concluded:

We offer the conjecture that the extent of the primacy effect varies directly with the amount of rehearsal of the stimulus-items during learning. We must assume, however, that there is a tendency for rehearsal to take place in the forward direction starting with the initial items. It appears reasonable to suppose that within limits there should be some correspondence between the order of rehearsal and the order of recall of the items (1958, p. 260).

Postman and Phillips (1954) found in two experiments that free recall of 20-item series produced both primacy effects and recency effects for intentional learners, but only a recency effect for incidental learners. Marshall and Werder (1972) found strong recency and no primacy effects in free recall of 18 nouns when the subject had been told there would be no recall, and rehearsal had been prevented by a distractor task. On the other hand, intentional learners under otherwise the same conditions showed about equal primacy and recency effects. Finally, intentional learners who were allowed to rehearse revealed greater primacy than recency effects. Overall performance was best for the rehearsing, intentional learners, and poorest for the nonrehearsing, incidental learners.

Postman and Adams (1957) studied intentional and incidental learning of serial lists of high and low intralist similarity. One experiment employed free recall and found greater recency than primacy effects for incidental learners, more so for low-similarity material. On the other hand, intentional learners revealed about equal primacy and recency effects for low-similarity lists, but strong primacy for the high-similarity items. Postman and Adams attributed the greater primacy tendencies for intentional learners to rehearsal from the beginning of the series. The differential in performance between intentional and incidental learners was greater for the low-similarity items. This latter conclusion was supported for serial anticipation learning in another experiment. In that experiment, using serial-anticipation learning, they determined the frequency of associations to a probe word. Intentional subjects gave more correct forward associations and fewer backward and remote associations, with the difference increasing with practice.

Bugelski's (1965) results, with a single presentation of ten items followed by free recall, were mentioned previously in Chapter 5. Both failures to report correctly the position of an item given correctly after its preceding (stimulus) items, as well as failures to respond at all, show progressive increases from first to last items. Since the subject was unaware that there would be only a single trial, he may be presumed to be attempting to learn first the items at the beginning of the series. Similarly, the effectiveness of the learning would be enhanced the closer the item to the beginning of the series.

The primacy effect in free recall is attributed to an attentional enhancement, which may therefore foster selective rehearsal. The selective rehearsal may, therefore, enhance a primacy effect, but it is not in itself the cause of it.

DIRECT EVIDENCE

Brown (1937), on the assumption that the galvanic skin response measures alertness of attention, used this device to determine whether or not subjects gave greater attention to first and last parts of a serial list, thus accounting for primacy and finalcy effects. He presented lists of 19 nonsense syllables at an 8-second rate, without a larger intertrial interval. A mark on the drum indicated the beginning of the list. The slow rate was used in order to allow for the latency of the galvanic response. For each subject each serial position was ranked according to greatest values of summated galvanic skin response and also according to total number of correct anticipations. Correlations varied from + .67 to + .14 for individual subjects. When ranks were computed from total performance across all subjects, the correlation between galvanic responses and correct anticipations was + .80, a significant result. These results are shown graphically in Figure 7-5, indicating a very close parallel between the physiological response and the performance measure. Thus, Brown concluded that subjects learn the first items first because they attend to them more than the middle or last items. The explanation of primacy and finalcy effects in terms of the absence of proactive and retroactive interference is ruled out by the use of intertrial intervals that were equal to interstimulus intervals.

Underwood (1941) also found evidence for a relation between intentional effort and learning performance. He found product-moment correlations of .55 to .70 between the frequency of correct anticipations in serial learning lists of 16 two-syllable adjectives and the frequency of galvanic skin response during the anticipation intervals.

Obrist (1950) used the galvanic skin response as an indicator of attention to a task, arguing that this response results when a subject mobilizes his energy to adapt to some situation that confronts him. Obrist argued that the serial-position curve was the result of differential attention or arousal as the list is presented, and his results supported this position. In general, he found that the galvanic skin response was greater during learning of nonsense syllables than during mere passive repetition of the same items. Moreover, the magnitudes of the responses were greater for the subjects who were the faster learners. For 15 subjects, the rank-order correlations between summated magnitudes of the galvanic skin response to a syllable and the number of correct anticipations for the following syllable ranged from + .83 to + .31—eight of them significant

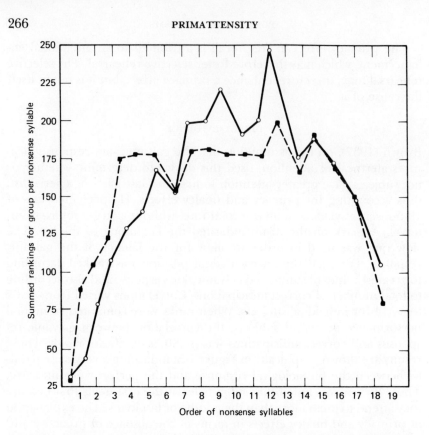

Figure 7-5   Positional correspondence for all subjects of galvanic responses (solid squares) and correct anticipations (open circles), from Brown (1937). Copyright © (1937) by the American Psychological Association. Reprinted by permission.

at the 5% level of confidence or better. These response magnitudes were also significantly correlated with correct anticipations per serial position ($\rho = +.62$). This result is illustrated in Figure 7-6, which shows the data for the entire group of subjects. Obrist also gave an example of the results for an individual subject, which is shown in Figure 7-7. This figure shows clearly that the peaks and dips of the galvanic-skin-response data and the performance data matched very well at the various serial positions.

Obrist (1950) noted that the galvanic skin response is much higher for the item at the first serial position relative to the items at the other positions. This can be easily seen in Figures 7-6 and 7-7. He concludes:

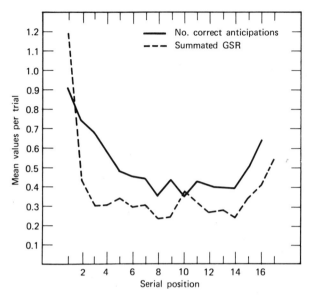

Figure 7-6   Positional correspondence of galvanic responses and correct anticipations for a group of subjects, from Obrist (1950). Used with author's permission.

Part of the large reaction obtained here is probably attributable to factors other than those associated with the anticipation of the first syllable. Respiratory irregularities, which are known to produce GSR's, are particularly common at the beginning of the list. Changes in the attitude or mental set of the subject are also more likely to occur here (p. 23).

Although Obrist does not document his last statement, it does seem reasonable, and it is consistent with the present approach. It should be noted that the successive presentations of a series were accomplished without an intertrial interval except for the time required for presentation of the word to cue the first item which was the same as the interstimulus interval.

Obrist (1950) also noted that the galvanic skin responses tended to decrease over the four quarters of learning trials. Most of this effect occurred during the first two quarters of learning, primarily resulting from the decrease for the first-learned syllables. The later-learned syllables, in fact, showed a progressive increase across the four quarters. These results are illustrated in Figure 7-8. Curve A in this figure represents the syllables learned fastest, and Curve Ac represents these data

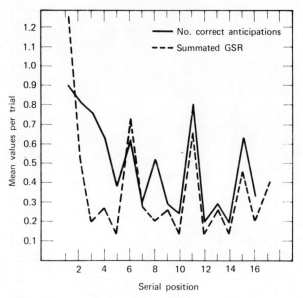

Figure 7-7 Positional correspondence of galvanic responses and correct anticipations for one subject, from Obrist (1950). Used with author's permission.

excluding the syllable at the first position, which was noted above as showing relative extreme responses, and which was always among the first learned. Curves B, C, and D represent groups of four syllables that were learned progressively later in the acquisition process. The curves obviously show progressively smaller decreases for syllables learned later, with a slight increase for curve C, and finally a greater increase for curve D. Obrist offers a tentative explanation for these results: namely, that there is a shift of attention from one part of the series to another part as learning progresses. He points out that the largest response magnitudes occur for given syllables during the quarter of learning in which these syllables show the greatest gains in acquisition. He goes on to speculate:

> This shift in attention may possibly explain serial position effects, the idea being that, for some reason, perceptual or otherwise, attention is focused upon the beginning and end of a list first and is shifted to the middle after the ends are learned (Obrist, 1950, p. 38).

Obrist (1950) bolsters this conclusion by citing several subjects who indicated, by introspective report at the end of the experiment, that they

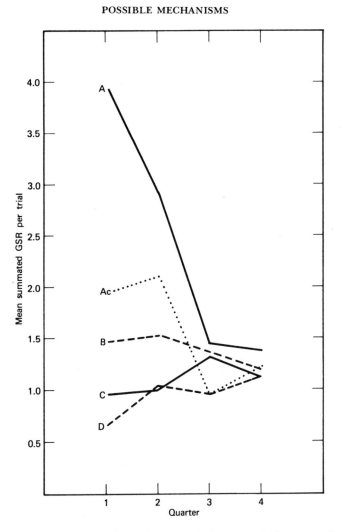

Figure 7-8 Relation between galvanic responses for items acquired at successive quarters of learning, from Obrist (1950). Used with author's permission.

did exactly this in spite of specific instructions to distribute attention equally.

The conclusions of Obrist (1950) were supported by Thompson and Obrist (1964), who found decreased alpha and increased beta and super-imposed EEG waves relative to control conditions during learning and overlearning. The hypersynchrony was taken as an indicator of effort in learning. There was a very close correspondence between the EEG responses and the items that were learned in successive quarters of learning. For example, during the first quarter of learning, alpha responses were least for the items for which the criterion of learning was reached during that quarter. The response was progressively greater during the first quarter for items which were subsequently learned in second, third, and fourth quarters. In each case, alpha responses during a quarter of learning were least for those items for which the criterion of learning was reached during that quarter.

Murdock (1966) showed that a measure of response strength (d') did not show variation in performance over serial positions in a probe test of short-term memory for five paired associates, although the typical recency effect in terms of probability of recall was obtained. The difference was that a measure of the subject's criterion for responding (beta) revealed a stricter criterion for the initial items, favoring a recency, rather than primacy, effect. Moreover, latency of responding was shorter for the terminal items; confidence judgments were highly correlated with the response latencies. These results suggest that the usual recency effect in short-term memory is due to the subject's strategies that favor the terminal items.

Woodward's (1968) study has been previously described in Chapter 2. He used sequential and positional probes, or both, to investigate potential cues for short-term memory. His results indicate, generally, a progressive increased stringency in responding from beginning to end of the series, a paradox in view of greater recency effects.

Bernbach (1969) described a study in which differential payoffs were used in probed recall of digit series to differentially reward rehearsal of beginning or end items. Accordingly, primacy effects were increased when the payoff rewarded reproduction of the initial items, and recency effects were increased when the payoff rewarded the final items.

OTHER EVIDENCE

Murdock (1968) found that the sensitivity measure, d', revealed the typical serial-position curve, with greater recency than primacy effects. Thus, the presumed greater perseveratory stimulus traces for the last items in immediate free recall would presumably produce a greater recency effect. Wing (1967) showed that subjects, as predicted, showed shifts on subsequent tasks of free recall from relatively greater primacy effects to greater recency effects. He argued that subjects learned to take advantage of the stronger traces for the later items in the free-recall task, and thus changed from a forward-recall strategy to a backward-recall strategy.

Data negative to a theory in terms of set was offered by Zeigler (1939). He found no consistent relation between time spent by the subject on syllables at various positions and the order of learning them. However, as would be predicted, most subjects took more time in the middle of the series to learn to the criterion. Therefore, it is not possible to assign cause-and-effect relationships.

Asch, Hay, and Diamond (1960) studied the distributions of errors for items arranged in various spatial configurations. They concluded:

> The learner's knowledge of the ends of the series constitutes one condition of the serial gradient. It seems necessary to conclude that the gradient requires, as one condition, a particular cognitive operation, namely the identification of the beginning and end of the series and the location of items with respect to these boundaries (p. 196).

The previous experiments in serial learning lead to the conclusion that the total process involves a mechanism of "anchor learning," plus a mechanism of "serial learning per se" (Harcum & Coppage, 1965b). Harcum and Coppage (1965b) concurred with the conclusion of Asch et al. (1960), on the basis of alleged primacy effects in serial learning with continuous temporal presentation of syllables, all of which appeared at the same spatial position. The syllables that were perceptually isolated from the others by either temporal or structural differences were more likely to be learned first.

Harcum and Coppage (1965a) have shown that the primacy effect in serial learning with continuous presentation appears only when the second (i.e., serial-association) stage of the process is reached. This further supports the argument for a cognitive basis for controlling the so-called primacy effect. Certain control data from the Coppage and Harcum (1967) study were subsequently analyzed to show that the serial-position curve of errors in continuous serial learning does not appear at the early stages of learning. Thus, the data from learning, by the anticipation method, ten homogeneous nonsense syllables, presented without an intertrial gap, show that temporal primacy and recency per se are not involved in the production of the classical serial-position curve of rote learning. Only negligible differences among item positions appeared early in learning, when differential effects of proactive inhibition among the individual items should have been maximal. But a primacy effect did appear later. This primacy effect was attributed to the subject's strategy in selecting a syllable, differentiated on the basis of being temporally first, as a reference point around which the complete list was finally learned.

Harcum and Coppage (1969) provided evidence for the selective-effort hypothesis by analysis of the different types of errors in serial-anticipation learning. The extralist intrusions support the argument for a greater initial effort expended toward learning the temporally first items. A later similar analysis of serial-learning data obtained from continuous presentation also supported this conclusion.

Later data of Harcum (1973) obtained from serial-anticipation learning with a smaller intertrial than interstimulus interval supported the set idea. Harcum concluded that the subject must reset the code of items from "end-of-series" to "beginning-of-series" each time a trial is completed and a new one begins. He used this interpretation to explain why the shorter interval was more deleterious to performance for the following item when it occurred before the beginning of the series than when it occurred in the middle of the series.

SUMMARY

The subject given a group of items to learn will establish an order in which the items will be acquired. Typically the temporally first item is coded as "first," and therefore becomes the cognitive anchor for the subsequent learning.

CONCLUSION

Attentional set may be the reason that the serial-position curve is skewed toward the end of the list—that primacy is more potent than finalcy. But to hypothesize set by itself to explain the serial-position curve does not add much. The important goal is to find out how this factor operates through other processes of information analysis.

A number of parameters of the task influence the strategies of information analysis of the subjects. Relevant variables may be associated with the stimulus configuration, or with response characteristics, or with the interaction of either of these with the central processes of mnemonic organization. Some variables, such as instructions to the subject, will potentially affect all three categories of factors, although the effect might be more pronounced for, say, the so-called central processes. For example, Mitchell (1933b) instructed her subjects that they should study the numbers during the first trial and then on succeeding trials attempt to anticipate. She explicitly stated that there would "be no time between successive lists" (p. 2). Therefore, the task was structured to emphasize, at least implicitly, the ends of the series, even though the list was continuous.

In Krueger's (1932) experiment it was immaterial as far as total learning was concerned whether the subject's attention was first directed to the difficult or easy items. Results from this experiment may well be compared to others (Smith, 1949; Smith & Stearns, 1949) in relation to isolation effects.

Of great significance for the present thesis is the finding of Jensen (1962g) that the linear relation between rank-order of learning an item in serial learning and mean of errors per item was unchanged for series containing an isolated item, although the order for learning individual items was changed. As Jensen (1962a, g) concludes from the fact that a series containing an isolated member is no easier to learn than an unisolated one, the isolation effect merely reflects the changed order of learning individual items. It is not the result of making the isolated item inherently easier to learn. The isolation effect is apparently caused by the strategy of the subject in using the heterogeneous item as an anchor point, attending to it and thus moving it up in the order of items to be learned.

Feigenbaum and Simon (1962) and Jensen (1962a,g) propose that the subjects tend to select the first item of a series as an anchor point for the later learning. The immediate memory span, if it is large enough, thus tends to include this item. The serial-position curve is generated by successive additions to this anchor in both forward and backward directions. This model considers serial learning as "information-processing strategy" in which a central mechanism processes the items serially. Since immediate memory has a limited capacity to store information, the information-processing mechanism makes the memorizing task easier by using "anchor points" in systematizing the information. Feigenbaum and Simon assume that the subjects used the ends of the series as such anchor points in order to reduce "cognitive strain."

In the usual serial-learning conditions, the greater distinctiveness of first and last temporal items produced by their proximity to the intertrial interval causes their selection as such anchor points. The subjects tend to add other items systematically to the anchors, with equal probability on both ends because it is easier to learn items adjacent to items already learned. Since the subjects first learn two items at the ordinal beginning of the list, before adding items from the end anchor position, the skewness of the curve is produced.

The shape of the serial-learning curve is thus produced by the choice of the anchor points by the subject and by the breadth of his immediate memory span. The high degree of consistency among subjects in the shape of the curve is due to the usual tendency to select the first item as the anchor point.

Jensen's (1962a) theory of serial learning also is based upon the subject's strategy of learning. However, Jensen proposes a span of memory to which items are added with equal facility at either end during the course of learning. Thus, the size of the memory span for the items at the beginning of the series determines the degree of skewness of the curve. Subjects possessing longer spans exhibit greater skewness in the distribution of errors. Thus, as Jensen (1962a) proposes, the serial curve is produced by successive addition to a base provided by the immediate memory span at the beginning of the series. However, as Feigenbaum and Simon concluded, the memory span probably does not encompass more than one syllable pair. Associations between items within a span should occur more easily than the association of subsequent syllables as additions to the span. Since the association between the first- and second-learned items of a series to be learned (ordinarily the first and second items in the series, respectively) is as difficult as each subsequent addition (Jensen, 1962a), this initial association between items is not formed more easily than others outside a supposed immediate memory span. More likely, therefore, the asymmetry is caused by differences in the order with which different items are added subsequently.

The results of the Harcum and Coppage (1965b) experiment indicate that the subject adopts a strategy for the order in which the items will be learned. The subject usually starts with the first and last temporal items. The associations to these anchors are formed faster in the forward direction, because the subject is set to make forward associations. With continued practice in a serial-learning task, the subject becomes more consistent in using the first item as the anchor.

Harcum and Coppage (1965b) distinguish two processes in serial learning—a differentiation component and serial learning proper. The latter component involves the actual association between items, and it is the one that is influenced by the strategy of forming associations. It determines the order in which items are processed and, as a consequence, the direction of associations. Presumably this primattensity is produced by the learner's past experience with similar tasks (Deese & Kresse, 1952; Lepley, 1932). This factor accounts for the skewness of the distribution of errors. Harcum and Coppage (1965b) propose that, after the subject learns the temporally first item, he then acquires the list by adding other items to this first-learned one. The items following the previously learned items are added to the learned base faster than items preceding the learned base. That is, forward associations are made faster than backward associations. Thus, this component in the process of information handling involves a selective mechanism that directs the focusing of attention, in sequence, to parts within the group of stimulus elements. This process involves a strategy of information analysis, chosen by the individual to be the most effective for the specific task. The more detailed analysis of the Harcum and Coppage (1965b) data, as it related to effects of practice, was given in a previous section of this chapter.

The difficulty of evaluating shapes of serial-position curves is further demonstrated by the results of Noble and Fuchs (1959). To test the conclusion of McCrary and Hunter (1953), that the shape of the serial-position curve was invariant if the values at each serial-position were converted to percentages of total errors, Noble and Fuchs tested groups of subjects who were categorized according to initial learning ability. The serial-position curves for the fast learners in percentage terms were more peaked than those for the slow learners. That is, the differences between the positions showing fewest errors and those showing maximum errors were greater for the faster learners. These results must be interpreted with caution, however, because this apparent difference in shape can be an artifact of the difference in efficiency of learning, as Jensen (1962c) and Harcum (1970a) have suggested. The apparent differences among serial positions can be exaggerated for the fast learners because the number of total errors in the denominator for the percentage calculations is smaller. These subjects have been much more efficient in terms of the number of correct items per trial.

Noble and Fuchs (1959) do not make a suggestion about what mechanism would produce the different results for the different subject groups. Harcum and Coppage (1965b) have offered a proposition which covers this situation. In fact, the Harcum and Coppage data are quite consistent with the Noble and Fuchs data if one accepts the reasonable assumption that learners of high ability on the task behave about the same as learners who have practiced extensively on the task. Harcum and Coppage propose that subjects more consistently use serial position as a basis for the selection strategy for acquiring the items as they become more practiced. As evidence for this they plotted the results shown previously in Figure 7-1, called the "order of group learning" for the subjects before and after practice. These results are merely the serial-position data for the group of subjects reordered in terms of rank from low to high totals of errors. Since the ordering of serial positions for individual subjects in terms of ascending numbers of errors is virtually linear, the plot of the group results approaches linearity as the subjects are more consistent in their ordering. Fortunately, Noble and Fuchs (1959) gave complete data so that the plots of group-ordered data could be made for each group of subjects according to learning skill. These plots are shown in Figure 7-9. Whereas the faster learners show relatively linear plots, like the practiced subjects of Harcum and Coppage (1965b), the slower learners tend to show bowed curves, flattening out toward the end of learning, like the unpracticed subjects of Harcum and Coppage. The actual serial-position identification is given next to the data points for the fastest and slowest learners. Therefore, the superior learners more consistently select the temporal basis of organization for acquiring the serial list.

A closer comparison of the results for slow and fast learners in the Noble and Fuchs (1959) experiment is shown in Figure 7-10. In this figure, the number of errors for two slow groups was adjusted downward to produce an equal total number to that of two groups of fast learners. Clearly, the fast learners show an approximately linear trend, whereas the data for slow learners bow, with a relatively flattened function toward the end of learning.

Mechanism of Primattensity

Primattensity implies not only that the subject has his attention drawn to some item that he cognizes as the first, or anchor, item, but also that he uses this item as a reference point to define and thus retrieve the other items in the array. Therefore, this item becomes the corner-

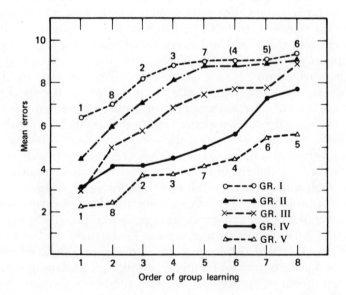

Figure 7-9 Errors per items ranked for five groups of subjects exhibiting different learning rates, after Noble and Fuchs (1959). Reprinted from *Science*, 27 February 1959, **129**, 570–571.

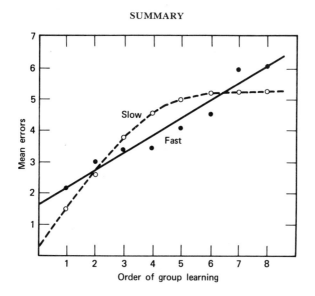

Figure 7-10   Errors per items for slowest and fastest subjects, after Noble and Fuchs (1959). Reprinted from *Science*, 27 February 1959, **129**, 570–571.

stone of an active construction of an organizational system that represents the task when it has been learned.

The mechanism of primattensity does not distinguish between the possibilities of perceptual enhancement as a means for attracting attention as opposed to the direction of attention as a means for enhancing perceptual saliency. Such mechanisms should produce the same result: differentially greater effort toward acquisition of those items so favored. There is no generally applicable rule that would describe which factor is first or more important. According to the configurational-hierarchy hypothesis, the context of the task could change with each trial and would, of necessity, change as each new item is learned. The configuration of the task, as organized by the subject, would reflect the interaction of subjects' expectancies and the physical attributes of the stimuli.

SUMMARY

This chapter considered the factors that influenced an inferred facilitating set to learn a serial list from temporal beginning to end. These included stimulus factors such as physical isolation of items, central factors such as rehearsal and instructions, and response factors such as the required output order. In the typical serial-anticipation technique all of these factors would imply the selection of the temporally first item. When techniques such as free recall are used, the focus of attention tends to shift to the most recent items. Which basis of organization is more influential is a relative question and often requires an empirical answer.

CHAPTER

$$\boxed{8}$$

PERSONAL STRATEGY

Much of the evidence on organizational factors in learning and memory, summarized in Chapter 4, is relevant here. A conclusion reached in that chapter was that in serial learning the subject makes fewer errors for those items that are favored by the internal structure of the series (e.g., Mandler & Mandler, 1964; Weingartner, 1963). The important point for present purposes is that this internal structure may be fabricated by the particular attitude, set, experience, and cognitive style of the learner. Eckstrand and Wickens (1954) documented this point. Their subjects transferred, from a pretraining task to a test task, a set to use a particular stimulus dimension. Transfer was positive or negative depending upon whether the transferred set could or could not be used for the solution of the new task, respectively. They argued for the transfer of set, as follows:

> In fact, it is probable that in everyday life the most considerable portion of the significant positive transfer which occurs is between tasks for which no simple dimensional analysis of the stimulus and response similarity is possible. In other words, we learn how to solve problems much more frequently than solutions to problems (1954, p. 274).

Moore (1936) argued not only for a transfer of set, but also for the influence of the transferred set in an active organization of the material of the new task. Moore showed how the subjects' "determining tendencies" (set), established by instructions, controlled both what he perceived and remembered. He concluded that his results supported an "organismic" and "configurational" theory of learning, as follows:

> The old Law of Temporal Contiguity no longer adequately describes learning. Items of experience, presented together, may not be recalled together. On the other hand, items of experience not presented together may be recalled together. An organism's experiencing two stimuli at the same time does not guarantee a linkage of the stimuli. The organism must cooperate functionally in the enterprise of connection forming. There must be a set which organizes the events into a unified pattern. Only when the sensory and motor responses fit into a pattern do they tend to persist for future use or reference (1936, p. 570).

Thus, the prior experience of each subject would establish idiosyncratic determining tendencies for him to perceive certain things and to remember them selectively. To the extent that these influential sets are idiosyncratic to individual subjects, they would produce particular alterations, peculiar to each subject, in the shape of the serial-position curve.

The structure established by such sets would determine which item was perceived as first, and which order of acquisition for items would be followed. For example, Workman (1951) noticed that the syllables varied greatly in terms of the frequency with which they were seen as first, even though they had been chosen to have equal association value. He concluded that, when the beginning and end of the series are hidden by some experimental manipulation, even slight differences of association value become important. Under such conditions, the actual final choice becomes highly idiosyncratic. Therefore, even an item without temporal primacy may be made very easy to learn by other extrinsic factors.

Underwood (1966) scaled the difficulty of 27 trigrams and correlated these values with free-recall measures for these items; the product-moment correlations between scaled difficulty and learning performance per item were about .90. The correlation for individual subjects was estimated to be at least .63. Evidence for an idiosyncratic factor in learnability of items was obtained by computing a subject's correlation between his rating of the learnability of an item and his learning of it, and comparing this correlation to the correlation between his rating and the learning of that item by another subject. Since the correlations for the subject of his own rating with his own learning data were consistently higher, presumably a portion of the learnability of an item is in the eye—or mind—of the beholder. Thus, the present position is that item difficulty is primarily in the mind of the learner. To the extent that these differences are idiosyncratic, they do not affect the differential performance among item positions for the groups of subjects.

If intrinsic interitem associations are strong enough, the subject will use them instead of his own idiosyncratic bases for organization, in the organization of a free-recall task (Cofer, 1965). Cofer (1968) asks,

> Does it not make sense to find experimenter-defined materials which provide the subject with his "hypothesis" of his "strategy" and then systematically to observe how behavior changes as we manipulate materials in such a way as to deprive them of compellingness and salience? Would not a theory of how the subject functions with compelling experimenter-defined materials, if successful have a great deal of carry-over to the processes involved in the case of materials where the subject has to find relationships (hypotheses? strategies?) on the basis of which he can accomplish his task? It is difficult at the moment for me to see how the procedures of paired-associate and serial-anticipation learning can be modified to permit the observation of hypotheses and strategies, but it should be possible (1968, pp. 530–531).

Schulz (1955) found that high intralist similarity increased asymmetry of the curve, especially late in learning. The reason for this is that heterogeneous items increase the likelihood that the subject might discover, for him, an item that was more learnable than the beginning item. Without the differential meaningfulness cue, the subjects would be more likely to begin with the temporally first item. Therefore, as Harcum and Coppage (1965b) argue, the increased tendency to anchor the task on the first item increases the asymmetry of the curve. Thus, the variable of intralist similarity affects the coding strategy of the subject. As the items become more similar, and therefore less easy to differentiate on the basis of their intrinsic characteristics, the relative position becomes more important as a cue. This argument is supported by Jensen's (1964) results comparing the consistency of subjects in learning words, trigrams, and color forms, which were described in Chapter 6. The more meaningful the items, the less consistent the subjects were in showing similar serial-position effects.

Brewer (1967) found that high-meaningful lists were learned faster than low-meaningful lists, as would be expected. The meaningful series presumably gives subjects a better or easier basis for mnemonic organization of the items. Reports of subjects about their learning strategies led Brewer to suggest that there should be consideration of what the subject is actually doing during a learning trial. This supports the present argument—that we should examine how a subject makes use of the meaningfulness of items to organize and learn a serial list. Spear (1970), in discussing the research on learning-to-learn, concludes that:

> Taken as a whole, this work emphasizes the wide variety of means by which Ss may improve their verbal learning performance, means considerably more subtle and complex than simply strengthening an associative bond between verbal units. To understand verbal learning, one certainly must gain control over these many ways in which S may operate on verbal material (p. 597).

MNEMONIC AIDS

The learning of a list is easier if the items can be fitted into meaningful categories or codes, as discussed in Chapter 4. Ebbinghaus (1902) was the first to point out the advantage of meaningful wholes in verbal learning. He observed that meaningful sentences or poetry were learned faster than comparable lists of nonsense syllables.

Müller and Schumann (1894) tested the hypothesis that associations are stronger when learned to one correct repetition in accented rhythm rather than without such rhythm. Each subject learned four lists of 12 syllables in trochaic rhythm (accented odd numbers). The experimenters then transposed the lists, but kept the rhythmic feet the same. This required much less time to learn than when the syllables were put in different feet. Müller and Schumann also found that the learning was easier when certain extra bases for association were included in the series. For example, learning was easier when the adjacent syllables possessed the same beginning consonant, rhymed with one another, or formed a word or phrase.

Guilford (1927) attempted to show the effectiveness for memory of a large degree of "formal character" within a series. In both his syllable and number lists he employed hidden schemes that, if discovered, speeded learning of the list. He concluded that in serial learning form takes precedence over individual members of the list, and that this form appears step by step. This interpretation appears questionable, but might be more meaningful when considered in the light of the intralist differentiation processes hypothesized by Gibson (1940, 1941, 1942).

As McGeoch (1930) has shown, the ease of learning varies directly as the meaningfulness of the material. Three-letter words are learned even faster than nonsense syllables of 100% association value. On the basis of this information, it follows that organization into meaningful groups facilitates learning.

Dashiell (1942) studied free recall of monosyllabic words, emphasizing the number to be recalled but not their order. Eight of the nine subjects tended to regroup the words into "sequences that represented separate thought-contexts." He concluded that the evidence supported an organization factor in memory, in addition to an associational factor.

Weingartner (1963) showed that serial learning is faster if the order of items is consonant with the associative structure of the items in the series. Gardner, Nappe, and Wallace (1968) had subjects arrange 12 words in a sequence that they thought would be easy to learn. Then different subjects were given either their own arrangement to learn, someone else's arrangement, or a random arrangement of the words. As expected, the random arrangement was most difficult to learn. Although there was a slight advantage to learning one's own preferred arrangement, the difference was not significant. Therefore, some orderings are easier than others, and there is a substantial agreement by subjects about which orders are easiest. Earhard (1967) also found that her subjects could recall in serial order more accurately when the items were arranged in an order that had been the output order for those items by previous learners in free recall. For subjects that were classified as poor subjective organizers, this preferred serial order also aided the free recall of those items.

Delin (1969a) had subjects learn serial lists of 16 nouns, either by "standard" instructions or by instructions to construct a mnemonic image for pairs of items. The mnemonically instructed subjects made fewer errors and reached a one-errorless-trial criterion in fewer trials. Moreover, the errors of the mnemonic subjects included a higher proportion of omissions. The response latency on the first anticipation trial was slower for the mnemonic subjects, indicating greater retrieval time from the mnemonic code.

Hovland and Kurtz (1952) assessed the importance of item familiarity in serial learning. They found that familiarization aided learning for shorter lists and for initial stages of longer lists. Familiarization did not reduce intralist intrusions, but it did reduce extralist intrusions.

According to Deese (1961), the free recall of sequentially organized material involves an underlying process including first an associative framework based on organization implied by the interword associations. To this the subject adds sequences constructed according to his own verbal habits of organization. The serial-position curve of learning exhibits a greater primacy than recency effect with "free" recall of sequentially organized material (Deese & Kaufman, 1957). Deese (1957) similarly showed "primacy" effects in the serial lists with serial recall and "recency" effects with free recall, with the order of reporting syllables in free recall being related to the accuracy of report. Thus, a recency effect is the result of the subject's translating the learned information into a free-recall situation.

Deese (1968) argued for an analysis of free-recall learning that does not presume association by contiguity. He proposes that organizational processes are at work and that both organizational and associational processes are determined by some more basic mechanisms. He concludes that associations are just the indices of underlying patterns of relation, and not the organization itself or the cause of it. Deese (1968) prefers to explain the deeper structures of organization in recall in terms of a distinctive feature analysis to describe the organization in associations and memory retrieval. Retrieval of an element in memory results from the intersection of some set of distinctive source features that generate the production of the single item. This conception is an alternative to classical associationism, which Deese considers inadequate to account for organization in recall.

Johnson (1968) points out that the serial-position curves of Deese and Kaufman (1957) for English-like sentences appeared more irregular than those usually obtained from unstructured serial lists. Also, the results of Mandler and Mandler (1964) show evidence of a greater effect of the grammatical structure of the sentence than the serial position of the words. Apparently, grammatical structure competes with the serial-position structure as a basis for learning.

DeSoto and Bosley (1962) found anchor points in memory when there was a purely cognitive structure organization of stimulus items. They had subjects learn four men's names as stimuli to each of the responses "freshman," "sophomore," "junior," and "senior." Even though stimuli were not presented in a consistent temporal or spatial order, a serial-position curve was found, with apparent anchoring at the beginning and end of the cognitive structure provided by the college-class distinction. Moreover, there were generalization gradients of errors in the cognitive structure with fewer errors for the greater degrees of remoteness.

Pollio and Deitchman (1964) had subjects learn the responses "beautiful," "pretty," "fair," "homely," and "ugly" as the responses to groups of stimulus words. A serial-position effect was found for the logical ordering of these adjectives, with pairs involving the response "beautiful" being learned first and those using the word "ugly" learned last. They also found that with the same design a response series of "hot," "warm," "mild," "cool," and "cold" produced the same result. Interestingly enough, the results varied somewhat according to the season of the year that the experiment was conducted. Responses of "hot" were learned first during the summer, whereas responses of "cold" were learned first in the winter, while a group tested in the spring showed relative equality of learning the "hot" and "cold" reponses. From such data, Pollio (1968) concludes:

> These data provide us with an extremely good demonstration of the sensitivity of this procedure to gross changes in input to particular points on the structure as a function of extra-experimental events and clearly reveal the effects of such input on the operational characteristics of relevant items in associative structure (p. 55).

Pollio (1968) argues that interitem associative strength has both faciliatory and interfering effects on the process of serial learning. The facilitation comes from the increasing availability of responses, and the inhibitory effect comes from the probability that the existing interitem associations will interfere with the new arbitrary associations to be required in the serial-learning task. Postman (1963a), in fact, found that there was no difference in serial-learning performance for a series of high interitem association and one of low interitem association.

Thus, the evidence points to the effectiveness of mnemonic aids in learning and to the experiential factors that determine which aids will be useful to a subject. Each subject will presumably use the aids that will make the material most meaningful to him while at the same time minimizing effects of interference.

NONCONTINUITY OF LEARNING

The issue of the continuity-noncontinuity of learning is involved in the differential strategy conception of serial learning. The strategy argument proposes that the subject is more likely to learn the items attended to, and that the remaining items are not learned—or at least not as efficiently learned—until their turn comes up in the strategy. Discussing Postman's (1963b) paper on one-trial learning, Miller (1963) concludes:

> Notice, incidentally, that the Feigenbaum and Simon theory assumes that the subjects will rehearse a few items and let the others go unnoticed on each trial. Postman's experimental demonstration that if you interfere with a rehearsal strategy, you destroy the Rock effect is strong evidence that many people do follow an EPAM 1 strategy of memorization. Postman refers to this rehearsal strategy as an artifact, but if Feigenbaum and Simon are on the right track it may be the most important fact of all (p. 326).

Ordering Strategy

Shephard (1963) discusses the inadequacy of the S-R associative model for tasks in which selective attention to some stimuli is a factor. He described instances of differential analysis of the responses of single subjects to individual stimuli within a complex array (Shephard, Hovland, & Jenkins, 1961). Whereas some cumulative curves indicate smooth progression of the sort that would be expected according to S-R laws, other curves show discontinuities for different tasks at different times for different subjects. Average curves would not do justice to the underlying processes.

Shephard (1963) suggests, furthermore, that the subjects may establish a "cognitive map," or a recoding of the series (Miller, Galanter, & Pribram, 1960). Therefore, even in so-called "rote learning" there is the need for concepts like hypotheses, strategies, and plans. Shephard concludes that there has been uncritical acceptance of a research methodology in this area that consists entirely of isolating "gross factors that affect overall performance." This approach is limited in the following way, however:

> No matter how many such factors have been isolated, however, the question is seldom raised as to whether it is possible to proceed in the reverse direction and show that the factors isolated in this way are sufficient to provide a complete and detailed account of the trial-by-trial performance of any one subject (Shephard, 1963, p. 63).

To counter this deficiency he proposes the use of behavior synthesis by computer that combines basic assumptions into predictions of behavior that can be compared to the empirical behavior of an experimental subject. For simpler theories the computer is not necessary.

Eagle (1967) showed the relevance of strategies of learning and instructions about strategies of learning to free recall of word lists. Subjects verbally reporting a simple rehearsal strategy recalled fewer words than those reporting use of an associative structure. Instructions to use either rehearsal or organizational strategies did increase the use of the instructed strategies, but not all subjects reported using the instructed strategy, and overall the instructions did not influence performance. Therefore, the significant variable was what the subject reported he did, rather than what he was instructed to do. This study, therefore, also provides evidence for the validity of subject's reports of their learning strategies.

Relative to Young's (1968) suggestion about the possible effect of Ebbinghaus' (1913) experience in learning on the attainment of positive transfer in the derived-list paradigm, the results of Harcum and Coppage (1965b) for very well practiced subjects suggests that the learning process is somewhat different. Specifically, the strategy is more consistent, and oscillation in retention is virtually nonexistent.

Farwell and Vitz (1971), apparently unaware of the earlier relevant work of Harcum and Coppage (1965a, b), designed an experiment to test the model of Feigenbaum and Simon (1962). They had subjects learn lists of 8, 12, and 16 nonsense syllables to a criterion of one errorless trial. The researchers observed that substantial numbers of the subjects did not learn the first and second serial items first, and that, even exclusive of the first two items, there was a tendency for the subjects to learn items toward the beginning of the series before those at the end (namely, in the eight-item lists, a Three before Eight; Four before Seven; and so on). Also, the subjects frequently learned items that were not adjacent to some previously learned item. Each of these three results is contrary to a postulate of Feigenbaum and Simon (1962), but is consistent with the present configurational-hierarchy hypothesis.

In a study by Bolles (1959), middle items were changed before they had been learned, but there was no effect on overall learning relative to a control list without the changed items. This appears to provide evidence for noncontinuity (strategy effects) in serial learning. However, a possible deficit in learning the changed middle items could have been offset by the increased saliency of the new items when they appeared.

Pacing

The results of Harcum and Coppage's (1969) analyses of the component errors of the serial distribution of total errors among positions support interpretations in terms of the subject's strategy for learning the individual items. Since the strategy appears to be basically the same for paced or unpaced series, the general shape of the curves of total errors is not greatly different. In order to permit a visual comparison of the shapes of the distributions with paced and unpaced presentation, the sums of errors per syllable were expressed as a percentage of the totals of errors for each condition. The results revealed very close similarity between each set of curves for paced and unpaced presentation, except for the lists of eight syllables. Since the interaction of serial position and pacing rate was not significant for a group of subjects who alternated paced and unpaced trials with 12-item lists, it seems unlikely that the pacing variable affects the shape of the total curve of errors, although the unpaced series generally produce less regular curves than the paced lists. The greater irregularity is probably caused by the greater possibility, with the increased time for making the response, for the subject to develop idiosyncratic bases for association of the syllables rather than to use merely the serial position of the item. This conclusion is supported by the results of coefficients of concordance, W (Siegel, 1956), for the rankings of items in terms of order of learning by individual subjects. Although for the subjects learning 12-item lists the concordance among subjects was significant for both pacing conditions ($W = .193, p < .01$ for unpaced; $W = .305, p < .001$ for paced), the degree of relationship as measured by this statistic was greater for the paced condition. Thus, the effect of subject-determined pacing is to add variability among subjects, but without changing the shape of the final serial-position curve for the combined group of subjects. Other variables such as the opportunity for the subject to select a more efficient strategy of learning in the unpaced situation may affect comparisons between paced and unpaced conditions for different groups of subjects.

The similarity of the curves of total errors for the two pacing conditions corroborates previous results. The curves of Deese and Kresse (1952) for CVC trigrams with paced and unpaced presentation are virtually identical when the data are converted into percentage plots. Moreover, the points on the curve for paced presentation seemed a bit more regular. The percentage plots for the three conditions of Wilson and Hartman (1960) were also essentially identical, but the regularity of the curves was about the same for each condition. Thus, the evidence points to generally equivalent shapes of total errors for paced and unpaced conditions, at least for the 12-syllable lists.

The category of errors with unpaced trials may change in some cases from failures-to-respond to intralist intrusions, but the evidence is that the change does not greatly influence the course of learning—except to allow greater opportunity for idiosyncratic bases for the modification of the order in which the items would be acquired. The appearance of serial-position effects means that the subjects tend to use sheer serial position as a basis for this strategy of acquisition with a substantial degree of consistency.

Factors Controlling Order

Since the order of acquisition of individual items is multifariously determined, each basis is pitted against the others as each item is to be added. The system is dynamic, resulting in possible changing of learning cues from item to item. This could be systematic, as in changing from position cues to intrinsic item-discriminability as one learns the end items and progresses toward the embedded items. The strategy could also change with practice, showing greater primacy effects (Harcum & Coppage, 1965b). The total cognitive structures of the series may change as each item is acquired. For example, a learned item lends discriminability to an item that is adjacent or close to it.

One would expect that the evidence would show more item association with meaningful material and more position learning with nonsense material. Noble (1952a) found an inverse relationship between errors in serial learning of words and their meaningfulness, m, defined as the number of associations written in response to the word for one minute. There was, however, about the same shape of serial-position curves for items of different m. In fact, Jensen (1964) found that subjects were most consistent across serial positions in learning color forms, and progressively less consistent for trigrams and words, respectively. This result is further supported by unpublished data of Jensen and Postman, mentioned in Chapter 7. There was less consistency in the order of acquisition for the more meaningful stimuli. The correlation among subjects for order of learning color forms was $r = .8$, whereas for highly meaningful material this correlation was $r = .3$. Presumably, for the meaningful stimuli there is greater likelihood for idiosyncratic bases of association. A similar result was obtained for a comparison of subjects of different ages; the older subjects showed less consistency in order of learning for items at the various serial positions.

McKenna and Harcum (1967) studied unpaced serial learning of word lists and reproduction of tachistoscopically presented binary patterns in the same group of aged subjects. An analysis of individual differences in frequency of errors of "primacy," "recency," and "bowedness" effects revealed some consistency across tasks. The major contributor to this consistency was relative primacy, measured by the tendency to err on the first (or left-most) two items of each task ($r = .44, p < .05$). Primacy in tachistoscopic perception predicted total errors in serial learning ($r = .52, p < .05$). The correlation between total errors on the two tasks was not significant ($r = .36$), however. In the serial-learning task, a disorganization score (D) differentiated between the "good learners" and "poor learners." This measure is similar to that of Tulving's (1962) "subjective organization" (S.O.) measure.

The results of Robinson and Brown (1926) and Mitchell (1933a) further support the strategy idea. The learning curve for the more difficult items, near the middle of the series, did not show positive acceleration until the easier items, near the ends, had been acquired.

Bugelski (1950) pointed out that different syllables within a series could be learned with differing numbers of errors, even when serial-position differences were controlled. Thus, studies such as the one by Raskin and Cook (1937), which confound item-characteristics with serial position, suffer from the problem of not separating intrinsic item differences from differences due to their relative positions. Bugelski used the same eight items as Raskin and Cook, but arranged them in eight different orders for different subjects such that each item appeared once at each serial position. There were significant differences among items at each serial position, with overall variation among items from 49% accuracy over all positions for the easiest item to 22% for the most difficult item. The situation is further complicated when these learnability figures are compared to the associability norms of Archer (1960); the ranks of these items show a positive correlation, but not a significant one ($\rho = +.262; p > .05$).

Bugelski's (1950) data also show an interaction between the learnability of the item and the serial position. The easier items are less affected by serial position; that is, the difference in anticipation accuracy at the best location (almost always the first position) and at the poorest location is greater for the easiest items than for the most difficult items. These differences weighted according to the totals at the most favorable serial positions show a positive rank-order correlation to the relative difficulty of the items ($\rho = +.905, p < .01$). This effect may be inferred from Figure 8-1, which compares the serial-position curves for the most- and least-difficult items. The curve for the easiest item is flatter. The absolute drop in errors from best to worst serial positions was less, and also the denominator for the weighted score was greater. Actually the drop in actual numbers of correct responses from best to worst syllables was approximately the same at each serial position, but at Serial Position One the most difficult item produced 71% as many correct responses as the easiest item, whereas at the least favorable position for either syllable the most difficult item produced only 20% as many correct responses as the easiest syllable.

Bugelski's (1950) data also support the strategy argument in a slightly different way. He used lists of eight-syllables of varying difficulty, learned by the anticipation method for eight trials. Eight different groups of subjects learned different orders of syllables, such that each item appeared once at each serial position. He obtained the classic serial-position curve of correct responses. These results are plotted in Figure 8-2, in the manner of Harcum and Coppage (1965b), who rearranged the abscissa such that the serial positions are ranked from best to poorest in terms of performance. The figures next to each data point indicate the serial position represented by that point. The steeper slope for the

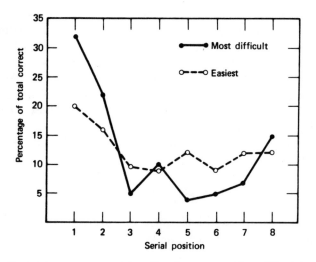

Figure 8-1 Correct responses per serial position for most- and least-difficult items, after Bugelski (1950). Copyright © (1950) by the American Psychological Association. Reprinted by permission.

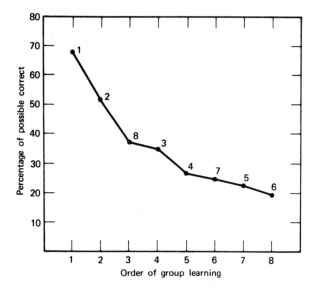

Figure 8-2 Correct responses for items ranked for the group of subjects, after Bugelski (1950). Copyright © (1950) by the American Psychological Association. Reprinted by permission.

best-performance items at the left indicates greater consistency of subjects in the order in which these items are acquired. The flattening of the curve for the most difficult positions indicates less consistency in the order of acquisition at those positions. This conclusion is supported by coefficients of concordance among the eight different items, computed separately for the first and second group of the four serial positions learned. Thus, the analysis will consider the consistency across positions for the various syllables, regardless of the fact that eight groups of subjects were involved, each learning that syllable at a different serial position. Although the order of acquisition for the first four positions was not significantly consistent among the various items ($W = .404$; $p > .05$), the consistency was greater than for the second group of four positions ($W = .100$; $p > .05$). The lack of significance of the consistency measures is not disturbing, since different groups of subjects learned the item at the various choice points so that subject group was confounded with serial position.

It is interesting to note, also, that the order of acquisition for the eight positions shows only one departure from the order predicted by Jensen (1962a), and that this departure occurred in the second of the two groups of four positions. Therefore, these data support the argument that the shape of the serial-position curve is produced by the consistency of the strategies of subjects in learning some serial positions before others.

The results of a different analysis of the Bugelski (1950) results shown in Figure 8-1 reflect the more typical way of looking at such data. This way looks at the consistency of subject groups in the order of acquiring syllables at the different positions, with, of course, different syllables at each position for each group of subjects. For the first four serial positions to be learned (namely, One, Two, Three and Eight), the subject groups were not significantly consistent in the order of acquisition ($W = .314$, $p > .05$). For the second block of four serial positions the subjects were less consistent ($W = .029$; $p > .05$). Therefore, both in terms of the consistency analysis for syllables (even with different subjects), and for subject groups (even with different syllables), the results show greater consistency for the first four serial positions learned than for the last four serial positions. These results support the argument of Harcum and Coppage (1965b) for a strategy interpretation for the shape of the serial-position effect in serial learning.

Brown (1964) investigated the relationship between stylistic characteristics of subjects and their learning on a serial-anticipation and a free-recall task. The cognitive style, called "M," reflected the extent to which the subject chose to organize or structure a nonstructured situation in terms of "isolated manifest properties of the stimuli." That is, the measure reflected whether the subject, given some plastic pieces to play with, merely sorted them according to some physical attribute (namely, high M), or whether he responded in a creative way. Low-M responses, therefore, indicated that the subject was more likely to organize or categorize in terms of meaningful abstractions. Interestingly enough, the distribution of M scores was bimodal, with subjects scoring at either mode performing better on serial learning than subjects of intermediate creativity. The low-M subjects learned faster, increasing their advantage with additional numbers of trials. Therefore, this cognitive style of creative organization was related to serial acquisition, although in a way that is not clear.

Brown (1964) suggests that perhaps the subjects of intermediate M do not have, by definition, a set way to organize a task, and that either plan of organization—by manifest isolated stimulus characteristics or conceptual abstractions—is better than no plan at all. Unfortunately for present purposes, Brown did not relate the M style of the subjects to the types of errors made, or to possible differences in tendencies to learn sequence or positions. Also, an interpretational problem is involved when one considers the possibility for a confounding of intellectual differences with scores along the M dimension. Presumably, the low-M style, with the greater tendency for meaningful abstractions, would be more characteristic of the more intelligent student.

The sheer temporal characteristic of a sequence can also be the basis for recall. Asch (1964) presented eight-syllable lists in different orders on each trial, permitting the subject free recall. He found that the syllables that were the first and last items for the particular presentation were the first ones that the subject tended to recall with greatest accuracy. Since there could be no consistent temporal bonds among syllables, only the temporal position in the immediately preceding series could become the basis for the sequence in which they were recalled.

Battig, Allen, and Jensen (1965) found that subjects in a free-recall situation tended to give the newest acquisitions first, instead of items that had been correctly recalled on previous trials. A possible explanation for this is that the subjects may adopt this strategy in the knowledge that a weaker response habit may be forgotten if it is postponed until later in the recall sequence. On the other hand, Postman (1968a) proposes that this effect is an artifact of the fact that in free recall the subject is prone to recall the most recent items first. Because the series is randomized on successive trials, the most recent item on a given trial is not likely to have appeared at that position previously to have been correctly reported.

Conclusion

The studies cited in this section support an argument for subject strategies and hypotheses in serial learning. Thus, the factors of belonging and similarity relations are more important than simple frequency of association. The course of learning proceeds therefore at an irregular pace, depending upon the organizational factors. The progression of learning curves is the topic of the next chapter.

ISOLATION STUDIES

A number of studies have altered the vividness of restricted portions of a serial list and compared the errors per syllable position with control items that have not been differentiated from the others. Items thus isolated are usually learned more quickly than the corresponding ones in control lists. Wallace (1965) has reviewed the literature on isolation effects.

Miller (1963) pointed out how the phenomenon of isolation in serial learning could be accounted for by the macroprocesses postulated by Feigenbaum and Simon (1962). The evidence indicates that the saliency of the isolated item draws attention to it and, to a lesser extent, to the items near it. This mechanism is an alternative to the concept of a gradient of effect (Zirkle, 1946). Martens (1946) found that by saying "right" after random numbers from one to ten he achieved a backward and forward positive gradient of effect. Stone (1946) found a spread of negative effect to syllables adjoining rewarded responses, but Jenkins and Postman (1948) found they were learned significantly more quickly. Zirkle's (1946) explanation was that the frequency of correct responses was proportional to the isolation of the syllable and that syllables adjacent to an isolated syllable take on a degree of isolation, and therefore attract attention to themselves.

Magne (1952) found that a stimulus pattern containing a perceptually isolated item had to be exposed for several seconds before an isolation effect was obtained. This he interpreted to mean that the subject must have time to experience the isolation cognitively before it can be effective in ordering perception and memory. Harcum (1965b) supported this interpretation for immediate recall of tachistoscopic patterns. Thus, isolation seems to achieve the effect through attracting attention and, consequently, serving as an anchor for the organizational processes of memory.

Strictly speaking, an isolation effect is not a manifestation of a personal strategy, because such an effect is demonstrated only if a substantial number of subjects consistently respond to the different item. It is discussed here as an analog of the personal strategy mechanism. A structurally isolated item should affect behavioral strategy in the same way as does an item that owes its saliency to some adventitious relation between its structure and the idiosyncracies of the subject. For example, in a meaningless array, a "meaningless" item that stands out for a subject merely because it happens to represent his brother's initials should be responded to in much the same way as if it were truly meaningless but, for example, printed in red ink.

Recall

Apparently the first study to manipulate item vividness and to determine the effects on associations was done by Calkins (1895-1897). In a series of ten items, each the pairing of a color to a numeral, one item was made more vivid than the others. All numbers except the vivid ones consisted of two digits in black print. The vivid number was paired with the same color paired to a normal (control) response, similar to the other items. The vivid item consisted of three digits printed in red. When the color that was stimulus for both a normal numeral and a vivid numeral was presented, the frequency of vivid responses was compared to the frequency of normal responses. The vividly associated numerals were given more than twice as often as normally associated ones. Calkins also reported that the effect of vividness was more noticeable in the middle of a series than at the ends.

Van Buskirk (1932) increased the speed of learning a syllable within a series by isolating it. This was achieved by printing the syllable to be isolated in red letters on a green background, whereas the other syllables in the list were printed in black letters on a white background. This effect persisted over time. Also the usually difficult areas of the list displayed a relative gain over those usually easily learned, consistent with Calkins' (1895-1897) result. Perhaps the items at the beginning and end are normally easier to learn because they already have a degree of vividness due to their unique positions.

Using a list of ten items, von Restorff (1933) achieved isolation by presenting a series including one number and nine nonsense syllables, or one syllable and nine numbers. The control list was a series of various items. After only one presentation and ten minutes of learning a sensible text, the subject recalled the isolated items approximately 70% of the time, compared to approximately 22% for the aggregated items.

Siegel (1943) attempted to test von Restorff's principle of "isolation and homogeneity" by studying the role of spatial and temporal organization in mnemonic systems. He concluded that learning was faster for items that were different from adjacent items. Postman and Phillips (1954) performed an experiment similar to that of Siegel (1943) and Saul and Osgood (1950), using incidental and intentional learners, and items isolated both at Position Three and Thirteen in a 20-item list. Only the intentional learners revealed isolation effects. Thus, the isolation is important only insofar as it is helpful for the subject's task, in which case he uses it to develop an organization for the series. Nevertheless, Postman and Phillips argue that the mechanism is one of aiding discrimination, and thus reducing intraserial interference. They argued, on the assumption that Gestalt psychology would predict more isolation (organization) for incidental learners, that their results were contrary to Gestalt organizational principles.

In discussing the Postman and Phillips (1954) paper, Köhler (1958) argued that the results of Postman and Phillips were consistent with Gestalt principles, rather than contrary to them. He argued that the isolation must be noticed for it to be effective in organization. Presumably, only for the intentional learners was it important for the subjects to pay attention to cues, such as the isolation, that would aid the organization, and thus the learning.

Fischer (1966a) subsequently tested the hypothesis that the subject's awareness of structural differences was necessary for suborganization of series, and thus superior recall. Groups of incidental or intentional learners were given series of nine syllables of 100% association value (Glaze, 1928), with isolation either at the fifth position, or at the second, fifth, and ninth positions, or at the fourth, fifth, and sixth positions. For a control condition there was no isolation. Free-recall performance failed to reveal overall differences among groups. Upon questioning, the subjects did not often report using the isolation variable as a basis of describing the series. When they did show such grouping according to the isolation variable, the recall of the syllables was less frequent. Moreover, some subjects in the incidental learning groups revealed isolation effects in recall performance. Therefore, Fischer argued that the subject's attention to structure may detract from his attention to content, thus inhibiting his performance, contrary to Gestalt principles.

Smith (1949) later again pointed out how the presence of an isolated item in a 13-item series improved both recognition and recall of that item but failed to influence overall performance for the total series. An isolated item at Position Eight resulted in a deficit for the following items, and an isolated item at Position Thirteen produced a deficit for the preceding items. Smith pointed out that the isolated syllable is speeded in learning, but learning of other items in the series is depressed as "compensation" so that the list taken as a whole is not learned any more quickly. This suggests that a reorganization of learning has occurred. On the other hand, McLaughlin (1968) found that isolation of an item facilitated free recall of the item but did not affect recognition. His results support the Saltz and Newman (1959) contention that isolation facilitates response learning but not association between items.

Gibbons and Leicht (1970) presented evidence against the differential rehearsal conception of an isolation effect. Subjects instructed to distribute rehearsal evenly over the entire series did not perform differently from subjects given "conventional" instructions. Although across all experimental conditions there was no overall difference between entire isolated and unisolated lists, there was a significant triple interaction between meaningfulness of items, isolation condition, and instructions condition. Whereas the isolation condition was slightly inferior for the high-meaningful list under both types of instructions, the low-meaningful conditions produced differences. With conventional instructions these items revealed substantially better recall for the unisolated series, but the reverse for the equalized rehearsal. These results present difficulty for the selective rehearsal conception, but apparently also for any other theory.

Cimbalo and Pelonero (1970) exposed complete ten-item series for 2.5, 10, or 20 seconds. The authors predicted that there would not be an isolation effect in serial recall for the shorter exposures (namely, short-term memory). Apparently they were unaware of several experiments that had shown isolation effects even with tachistoscopic exposures of 0.1 second (Harcum, 1965a, b; 1968). The results of Cimbalo and Pelonero, in fact, supported the earlier results in that an isolation effect appeared for each stimulus duration. Contrary to previous results, however, the isolated series were reproduced with greater accuracy overall. Cimbalo and Pelonero suggest that the isolated item effectively reduced the length of list, possibly aiding codification and retrieval of the items.

Serial Anticipation

Isolation effects have also been obtained in serial-anticipation learning. These effects were obtained under both continuous presentation and with the usual intertrial gap.

TEMPORAL DISCONTINUITY

McGourty (1940) reported a very important study in which she altered the serial-position curve by manipulating the homogeneity of the syllables in the list. Her control condition consisted of ten dissimilar three-letter consonants. In one experimental condition the formal similarity (homogeneity) was maximal at the two ends of the series. This was achieved by constructing the three syllables at either end of the list to have letters in common. In a third condition the formal similarity was greatest for the middle four syllables. Although the control list showed the usual serial-position curve, the experimental lists revealed greater difficulty for the homogeneous syllables. This experiment is particularly interesting because it has bearing on several theories. McGourty designed it to test Foucault's (1928) hypothesis that the curve was due to progressive (proactive) and regressive (retroactive) inhibition. She predicted that the greater homogeneity would create more internal inhibition (intraserial inhibition), which, in accordance with Foucault's hypothesis, would alter the curve. She concluded that intraserial inhibition was greatest for similar items and that her altered curve could best be explained by Foucault's theory of retroactive and proactive inhibition—proactive inhibition being more potent than the retroactive. However, the same results can be used, as here, to support the theory that vividness is a factor in the serial-position curve, with the assumption that homogeneity decreases vividness or isolation. This experiment can also be used to support the theories of Hull et al. (1940), Hovland (1938a, b, 1939a, b), and Gibson (1940, 1941, 1942).

Jones and Jones (1942) tested the hypothesis that increased emphasis on, or vividness of, a syllable for serial learning would change the subject's strategy of learning—if the isolation would "serve as a reference point and result in a new pattern of learning, rather than being merely learned more readily itself, as a specific item" (p. 96). Lists of ten nonsense syllables were learned by the anticipation technique and then relearned one week later. The seventh syllable was typed in red on the experimental lists, and all other items were typed in black. For both learning and relearning, the isolated seventh item, as well as the sixth and eighth items, was learned faster than the controls, with most of the remaining items showing superiority for the control items.

Since the general shapes of the two serial-position curves were approximately equivalent, Jones and Jones (1942) concluded that the evidence was negative relative to a reorganization of the task for the isolated condition. Subjects generally did not report different strategies for the isolated list. However, as the authors point out, the formal isolation of a single item may not be sufficient to change the overall strategy drastically with respect to serial position. Nevertheless, the relative flattening of the isolated curve, because of the superior performance in the region of isolation and inferior performance elsewhere, does suggest a different distribution of attention. The variables that determine the basic serial-position distribution of errors are too powerful to be completely overcome by mere isolation of a single item. Since the authors found no statistically significant difference in the total learning time of the isolated list and the normal list, their conclusion was that specific aids show their effect on specific items and it is "not justified to conclude that all aids necessarily reorganize the learning of the entire task" (p. 100).

Smith (1948) reported a facilitative effect of item isolation, with a spread of the isolation effect to adjacent items. Nevertheless, the more remote items were reproduced with less accuracy than the control items. Thus, he concludes that:

> isolation by virtue of adventitious factors, such as the color of the isolated item, seems to produce a redistribution of effort on the part of the subject, without any appreciable change in the overall learning (p. 235).

Smith and Stearns (1949) also reported a spread of effect from the isolated item, evidenced by enhanced recall for syllables near it, and postulated the spread of a degree of isolation by other syllables in accordance with their proximity to the isolation. If the first and last syllables of any series may be considered as thus isolated from the others, a spread of isolation effect could explain the gradients of difficulty rising from end syllables toward the middle.

Another interesting observation on the second and third days of the Smith and Stearns (1949) experiment revealed a sharp rise in correct anticipations at the position in the control list corresponding to the one employed for the isolated syllable in the experimental list on the first day. They interpreted this as due to the direction of the subject's attention toward that syllable by the isolation technique of the first day. This was probably the case. Thus, the serial-position curve can be altered by calling attention to one of the syllables, causing it to be learned faster than would ordinarily be the case.

Wishner, Shipley, and Hurvich (1957) used a 14-item list composed of two adjacent 7-item lists printed in different colors. A dip in errors at the eighth-item position indicated that most subjects learned the total list as two shorter lists. The interpretation of this was that the change between lists added an anchor point in the middle.

Fischer (1964) was concerned with the fact that Wishner, Shipley, and Hurvich (1957) had found superior learning of an isolated list, whereas other researchers (e.g., Jensen, 1962g) had found an isolation effect but no overall facilitation of learning the isolated list. She hypothesized that the difference was that Wishner et al. had instructed the subjects that the isolation variable demarcated two lists. Therefore, she repeated the Wishner et al. experiment, independently varying the structural isolation and instructions to learn one or two lists. The isolated lists were learned in fewer trials, but there was no effect of instructions on overall learning. Instructions did, however, produce an isolation effect at the change of lists consistent with the typical isolation effect—superiority about isolation but a compensatory detriment elsewhere. Possibly with the different colors the subject is able to reduce confusion between items of the two lists (list membership), but the gain from two-list coding is lost by confusion of sublists when the color coding is absent.

Saltz and Newman (1959) did, in fact, find more frequent emission of the isolated element after only a single trial—indicating enhanced attention to that item during the subsequent trials. The above arguments imply that the isolation effect would not have to be some all-or-none phenomenon. The empirical results of Saltz and Newman (1960) with serial learning do, in fact, show an isolation effect occurring in different degrees depending upon the degree of isolation.

Kasschau (1972) observed differential rates of serial learning for words varying in semantic meaningfulness (i.e., departures from neutral ratings of 4.00 on the semantic differential, or D_4), but with associative meaningfulness, m (Noble, 1952a), held constant. The polarized words were learned faster, also with the negatively accelerated rate observed by Noble (1952a) for words of differing values of m. Kasschau (1972) also attempted to reproduce the same isolation effects with the D_4 measure that Rosen, Richardson, and Saltz (1962) had produced with lists of varying m. Rosen et al. had found an isolation effect of printing the fifth word of a nine-word list in red, with the remaining items printed in black, but only for lists of low-m words, and not for high-m words. Presumably, the high-meaningful items were already sufficiently discriminable. The isolation effect was present for both high- and low-D_4 lists to an equal degree. Kasschau suggested that the difference from the Rosen et al. result was that the semantic differences took longer to become manifest, and that the isolation effect had been set in motion before the semantic differences were appreciated by the subjects. This does not seem likely, however, because his earlier data (Experiment 1) showed differences in the lists of varying D_4 right from the start of learning. The present interpretation is merely that subjects tend to use slightly different weightings of the components of their overall strategies for associative and semantic meaning of items.

McLaughlin (1966) varied length of list and the position of an isolated item. Since the total isolation effect for items other than the isolated item itself was greater for later locations in the series, McLaughlin concluded that the results cannot be completely explained by Gibson's (1940) generalization hypothesis. Bone and Goulet (1968) found that the greatest change in ordering of items occurs when the middle item of a ten-item list is isolated, in comparison to isolation at the first or tenth positions. The absolute effect is also greatest for the middle item but, on the other hand, the percentage of facilitation is equal at all three positions. Thus, a ceiling effect influences the absolute magnitudes of isolation effect.

Lippman (1968) argued that if, early in learning, the larger intertrial interval becomes a strong cue for learning the ends of the series, then displacement of this gap early in learning would interfere with performance. Five groups of subjects began learning lists of 12 nonsense syllables in the usual way. For four experimental groups, after criteria of one, four, seven, or ten items correct had been reached, the larger gap was then moved to the interval between sixth and seventh items. As predicted, the serial-position curve was not affected when the change came after ten correct anticipations had been reached, but for the earlier changes an isolation effect appeared about the seventh syllable.

By using the spin technique of presentation, Saufley (1967) discovered that a serial-position curve was generated when the most accurately reproduced item was taken as the first serial position. This is consistent with the results of Lippman and Denny (1964), and suggests the use of idiosyncratic anchor points for those subjects for whom temporal position cues were minimized. This conclusion is further supported by other results with continuous presentation.

CONTINUOUS PRESENTATION

Several theories of serial learning propose that the skewness of the curve arises from the subject's tendency to learn the temporally first item first. The role of the spacing between successive presentations of a list, which presumably calls attention to the fact that the list is beginning again, is thus emphasized. However, the first syllable exposed is apparently taken as the first syllable of the list, and the usual serial curve is generated, even though the syllables are presented continuously (i.e., with no gap at all).

A study by Coppage and Harcum (1967) employed continuous presentation of nonsense syllables in a serial-anticipation task, with careful attention to an effort to avoid the mention of a list of syllables. The reasoning behind this was that the mere mention of a list might imply to the subject that there is a beginning and an end to the series. The study was designed to test hypotheses derived from theories that account for the serial-position curve of rote learning in terms of the subject's strategy in organizing the task for learning. The approach was to investigate the subject's basis of selecting anchor points for learning lists in continuous presentation. Two hypotheses were tested: (1) the subjects organize their learning about the first and last temporal items when no structural cues within the series are provided; and (2) the subject selects a structurally isolated item within the series, regardless of its temporal position, to be learned first. It was predicted that in a control series the subjects would not strongly agree in use of the first-presented syllable, or any other individual certain syllable, as the first-learned syllable. An experimental series was identical to the control series except that one syllable was perceptually isolated. It was predicted that the isolated syllable would consistently be learned first, and the bowed curve of learning would be derived when that syllable was defined as the first in the series. In other words, the isolated syllable would serve as the anchor point for learning the entire list. Both hypotheses were verified, except that the effect of the structural isolation depended upon its position in the temporal series. These results indicate that temporal primacy, or any other basis for differentiating items of a serial list, is only important insofar as it affects the subject's cognition of which items constitute beginning and end of the series. Typically the subject's strategy is to learn the cognitively first item of the series first.

The above study was corroborated and extended by Harcum, Pschirrer, and Coppage (1968). Results supported the conclusion that both temporal primacy and structural saliency of items facilitate learning of a continuous ten-syllable series because they affect the subject's cognition of beginning and end of the series. Since, in the previous experiment, the same item was structurally isolated in each of the five temporal positions, there was a confounding of structural isolation with syllable difficulty. To eliminate this confounding, a Latin-Square design was used so that each of ten CVC trigrams was structurally isolated once in each of the five temporal positions (Positions One, Three, Five, Seven, and Nine) over a total of 60 subjects. The hypotheses were: (1) the subjects organize their learning around the first and last temporal items when no structural cues are given; (2) the subject selects a structurally isolated item within a list, regardless of its temporal position, to be learned first; and (3) an assimilation of the two anchoring tendencies occurs when the temporally and the structurally isolated items are close together in the series, producing the greatest primacy effect under this condition. All hypotheses were supported.

At the end of their experiment which employed continuous presentation of ten-syllable lists, Harcum, Pschirrer, and Coppage (1968) asked the subjects if they had used any particular strategy or approach in learning and, if so, to describe it in their own words. The subjects' report of which syllable was learned first frequently corresponded with the "primacy effect" in their distribution of errors. These data from subjective reports directly measure the variable that Harcum and Coppage (1965b) proposed is the critical intervening variable in the establishment of the serial-position curve of learning—namely, the subject's cognition of a "first" item. This independent measure of which item is cognitively first removes the potential circularity of the argument that predicts a correlation between an idiosyncratic choice of a cognitively first item and an idiosyncratic location of a so-called primacy effect.

Goulet, Bone, and Barker (1967) isolated the first, fifth, or eighth item of an eight-item series of words in continuous presentation, with presentations beginning on either the first or fifth words. The structurally first word was marked by an asterisk, and the isolated word was printed in red ink. It is not clear from the report whether or not the subjects were told that the asterisk marked the beginning of the list, or whether it was just another isolation device. In any case the isolation treatments did affect the order in which the items were learned.

Lippman (1971b) isolated the seventh syllable of a 12-item series for serial-anticipation learning. For control subjects no item was isolated. For one category of subjects, the usual intertrial interval was employed, but for another the beginning of the series was disguised by the addition of four items prior to the first trial, and by using continuous presentation. List demarcation improved overall performance, but isolation did not. The series with the disguised starting point showed a marked attenuation of the serial-position effect. The isolation effects were found in both list structures, being superimposed upon the conventionally organized series and generating a clear-cut serial-position curve for the continuous list.

With continuous presentation the serial-position curve is less marked because the first item is less salient. Thus, as Harcum, Pschirrer, and Coppage (1968) argue, the subject has a weaker tendency to anchor the learning on the temporally first item. If the list is structured by other means—even by instructions, for example—an isolation effect may not be obtained, even with continuous presentation (Glanzer & Dolinsky, 1965). These results thus support the proposition that various bases of item differentiation compete for the subject's attention as learning begins. If one item consistently wins out as a consistent attention getter, then an isolation effect is obtained.

Conclusion

The influence of vividness or isolation upon the serial-position curve is difficult to consider apart from the effect of the other theories. In particular, it is likely that its effects can be subsumed under generalization and differentiation—that isolation aids in differentiation. It is probable that vividness in and of itself is not a primary factor in the serial-position curve but that its importance accrues from its effect on other causal factors. Specifically, the vividness of an item draws attention to it and causes the subject to use it as a reference point in the organization of the series. Ordinarily this entails only a selective distribution of attention, but occasionally the subject can use the additional cue to improve the efficiency of retrieval coding, and thence improve performance on the learning task.

INSTRUCTIONS

The importance of instructions to the subject on the relative importance of different cues for serial learning, as discussed in Chapter 2, is evidence for the relevance of the subject's strategy in approaching the task. Asch (1968) points out that the importance of instructions in transfer studies indicates the importance of cognitive processes in serial learning.

Nevertheless, as in the case of isolation cues, there is no reason to believe that the subject will in fact pay attention to them. Mandler (1968) points out:

> But giving a subject a rule, for example by instructions, does not necessarily mean that he will use it, nor is the report of a rule any guarantee that it has been used (p. 118).

DISCUSSION

The evidence that has been summarized indicates that cognitive factors such as set, attention, and mnemonic strategies determine performance in serial learning. Therefore, sheer frequency of stimulus and response pairings is of less importance. As Asch (1968) concludes:

> Finally the evidence increasingly points to the conclusion that the serial learning gradient is a relationally determined effect of position along a dimension, not a standard associative effect (Murdock, 1960; Jensen, 1962; Ebenholtz, 1963) (1968, p. 223).

The results of Young, Patterson, and Benson (1963), described in Chapter 2, further support the strategy argument. The re-learning of an 11-item list in reversed order revealed facilitation for middle items for which the position was least changed by the reversal. The last two items of the reversed list also seemed to show some facilitation, possibly because they had been learned better in original learning. These results do not seem too different from those of Bredenkamp and Bredenkamp (1970), who in a similar study with 10-item lists reported no difference in positive transfer at the first two serial positions, but significant differences thereafter. The serial-position results for the experimental (transfer) group was attributed primarily to the superior general learnability of items at the end positions. It is of particular interest that in the Young et al. study the first three positions of the transfer list were actually inferior for the experimental subjects. Therefore it appears that a sort of isolation effect was operating, which generally favored the middle items, with a compensatory inhibition for the first items. Thus, as Young et al. suggest, the middle items might have become more differentiated—presumably because of superior association to position in the prior learning. This differentiation could have moved these items up in the order of acquisition, along with the end items that presumably had been overlearned during the acquisition of the first task.

It does not seem to matter how the subject's attention is directed toward a particular item. It could be due to some intrinsic structural characteristics of the item, to some aspect of the response requirement, or to some preexperimental set or habit of the subject. Since all that seems to matter is the fact of the directed attention, the choice of the first item may be highly idiosyncratic.

The bow in the serial-position curve is produced in terms of perceived position in spite of the other factors that compete for attention because the temporal primacy is typically a stronger determinant of the direction of attention than intrinsic differences among syllables for an individual subject. Moreover, the positional cues exert a consistent effect for all subjects that guarantees a temporal-position primacy effect in the combined data across subjects when the population of items is relatively homogeneous.

SUMMARY

The foregoing results show that the subjects, when presented with a serial task to learn, may use any source of heterogeneity of items or conditions within the series as a reference point. When other aids are missing, the two ends of a series alone apparently provide the basis for its mnemonic organization. Later, items adjacent to learned items have an advantage. Since the order of acquisition does not always proceed in order of adjacent items, however, other factors such as association to position and association to some meaningful context are also important to the order of acquisition. This interpretation is consistent with the conclusion of Battig, Brown, and Schild (1964), that position learning is less important for items about the middle of the series.

By definition, the idiosyncratic bases of associative ordering cancel out when the results for all subjects are combined. Thus, only the effects of the consistent, position-based cues remain.

3

EVIDENCE
AND
CONCLUSIONS

CHAPTER

$$\boxed{9}$$

THE REAL
SERIAL-LEARNING
CURVE

The present thesis is that the traditional curve relating item position and error probability, in spite of its generality as a research result, is not the most meaningful way to describe the process of serial learning. The serial-position curve is a convenient final description of the outcome of serial learning, but that is all it is; it fails to reveal much about the process of acquisition. An effective and satisfactory scientific analysis must also give a correct picture of the process or processes, as well as the outcome (Werner, 1937).

Following this approach, this chapter focuses on an analysis of the mechanisms in the serial-learning process, rather than upon the outcome with respect to relative performance per serial position. The purpose of this chapter is to establish that the best method to describe the results of the serial-learning process is to describe the temporal progression of learning, rather than to show the distribution of the errors among the various items at the end of practice—namely, the serial-

309

position curve. This goal inevitably leads, therefore, into a discussion of learning curves in general, what they mean, and how they are best plotted to reveal the underlying mechanisms. Tulving (1964) emphasized the distinction between correct responses in free recall that were attributable to short-term memory from the immediately preceding trial (namely, intratrial retention) and the correct responses caused by recall of the item from experience with it on a prior trial (intertrial retention). Thus the so-called learning curve is a composite of both acquisition and memory processes. With respect to the intratrial retention, an item is always learned as it is exposed, although later it becomes unavailable because it is followed by a group of similar items that perhaps destroy the proper cues for retrieval.

Melton (1941), in his review of learning theory and principles, argued that all learning is not the same, and that it should be analyzed in terms of different dimensions or relations among factors. For example, rote learning and reasoning are similar because they require verbal and ideational activity, but they are not similar in terms of the different requirements for discovery of the correct response.

Thus, the effects of selected variables could depend upon the type or phase of learning that was involved. For example, Underwood (1961) points out that in paired-associate learning highly similar responses should facilitate response learning but inhibit the association phase—granted that these two phases may never be distinct. Deese (1968) argues further that it is not necessary to assume that strength (response learning) and organization (associative learning) go on successively. Underwood, Rundquist, and Schulz (1959) also argued that the integrative and associative phases can overlap. For example, the subject can use the first letter alone as the functional stimulus for the associated response.

LEARNING CURVES

The progression of learning is of course inferred from the learning curves. Therefore, different methods of plotting the course of learning one task are not valid if they produce different shapes of the learning curve. Melton (1941) points out the central importance of the shape of the learning curve, as follows:

> The form of the relationship between practice and performance has been extensively investigated, presumably because it represents the basic quantitative description of any learning process and because it is of considerable practical value to be able to predict whether improvement with prac-

tice will be, for example, rapid at first but with continuous diminishing returns from added practice, or slow at first with more rapid improvement in the middle or terminal portions of the practice period (p. 681).

He goes on to say that in spite of efforts to find a typical learning curve, these efforts have not been successful because of the many variables which influence this shape. These include such factors as the amount of transfer from previous learning, the measure of performance, and the unit of practice (McGeoch, 1942). Melton (1941) lists some other factors that influence learning curves, such as the length, meaningfulness, and difficulty of the material.

Thurstone (1930), relying heavily on the data of Lyon (1914, 1917), argued that learning time varies approximately as the 3/2 power of the number of items to be learned, whereas the necessary number of repetitions varies approximately as the square root of the number of items to be learned. Thus, depending upon whether or not the exponent is greater or less than one, the function shows positive or negative acceleration, respectively. Similarly, Stevens and Savin (1962) fitted power functions through cumulative learning curves based on many different learning tasks, including serial learning. Although the exponents were typically between 1 and 2—indicating a negatively accelerated learning curve—they point out that an exponent larger than 2 would produce a positive acceleration, making both positive and negative acceleration possible by a change in the size of the exponent.

Culler (1928) predicted an S-shaped function relating learning performance as a function of frequency of repetitions (trials). The typical learning curves of positive, zero, and negative acceleration represent stages in the progress of learning, when it starts near zero. Culler further points out that the sigmoid curve may have more than a superficial similarity to the psychometric function of sensory response. For example, he asks, if time of stimulus exposure is sigmoidally related to sensory performance, should not increased time in terms of repeated trials be similarly related to the learning of a response? Hull (1934) pointed out that the sigmoid learning curve appears where the learning starts from zero. He proposed a theoretical interpretation for the S-shape (Hull, 1943).

Krueger (1946) had subjects learn lists of 5, 15, or 100 nonsense syllables having different degrees of difficulty. For the easy lists, the curves were negatively accelerated, but the performance was already high on the first test. The list of 100 easy items showed the classical sigmoidal curve, with early positive acceleration, and then negative acceleration. For the more difficult material, the curves were positively accelerated, starting, of course, from a relatively low level of performance.

The conclusions were the same when easy and hard items were used in a mixed list (Peterson, 1928).

Woodworth and Schlosberg (1954) discuss the fact that the unit of measurement for performance can influence the obtained shape of the learning curve. They use the example of learning to shoot a rifle. If the target is very small the subject may require much practice before he achieves the first hit, ensuring an initial positive acceleration and thus an S-shaped curve. If the target is very large, the subject will start off with many hits, and thus show only the negatively accelerated curve. Such an analysis of the effect of target size was undertaken by Bahrick, Fitts, and Briggs (1957), showing such an artifact in the obtained shape of the acquisition curve. Woodworth and Schlosberg (1954) conclude:

> There are dozens of different ways in which one may plot learning curves, and an almost infinite variety of shapes that the curves may take (p. 537).

Woodworth and Schlosberg point out, however, that one feature of the curve that almost always appears is a gradual leveling off of performance as the final level of practice is reached. Therefore, the one generalization that can be made about a typical learning curve is that it shows decreasing gains as a subject approaches his limit of learning, as long as the sensitivity of the scale of performance permits scores beyond this limit of his ability. Osgood (1953) supports this interpretation; perhaps an initial positive acceleration will occur, but limitations on the subject's ability will eventually lead to negative acceleration.

Waugh (1961) found that the slope of the learning curve for lists of words was linear under serial recall when scored without regard to order, but was negatively accelerated under conditions of free recall. Waugh (1962) argued that serial recall of lists of digits was independent of list length and number of trials. The negative acceleration often observed in learning was attributed to the approach to the ceiling on performance imposed by a length of series that might be completely recalled. Her data supported the contention that each exposure of a series added a constant number of new items to the number that could already be recalled, thus producing the linear acquisition function.

Fischer (1968) found that trials to criterion and serial-recall performance, for 7-syllable lists learned by serial anticipation, did not vary for several proportions of stimulus presentation times with a numeral 2-second presentation rate. The lists contained no intertrial interval. This total-time constancy implies a constant acquisiton rate for each item.

The serial-learning curves of Deese, Lazarus, and Keenan (1953) for serial anticipation of 12 consonant nonsense syllables, under several con-

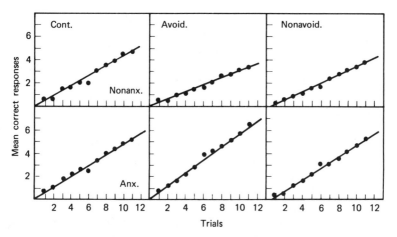

Figure 9-1   Serial-learning curves for anxious and nonanxious subjects under three conditions, after Deese, Lazarus, and Keenan (1953). Copyright © (1953) by the American Psychological Association. Reprinted by permission.

ditions, were all approximately linear, as can be seen in Figure 9-1. The curves, reproduced separately in the six panels of the figure, represent respectively the results for groups of anxious and nonanxious subjects tested under neutral control conditions, avoidable shock for incorrect performance, and random (unavoidable) shock unrelated to performance.

Melton (1941) points out the problems of pooling data from different subjects. Estes (1956) also discussed the propriety of making inferences from averaged curves in order to understand the function for the individual subjects. He pointed out that the function of group means is not necessarily different from that of the individual subject. He does urge the use of the same degree of caution, however, in the treatment of averaged curves as one would employ for making statistical inferences in such familiar cases as uses of analysis of variance and chi-square tests:

> Just as any mean score for a group of organisms could have arisen from sampling any of an infinite variety of populations of scores, so also could any given mean curve have arisen from any of an infinite variety of populations of individual curves. Therefore no "inductive" inference from mean curves even for such purposes as determining the effect of an experimental treatment upon rate of learning or rate of extinction is not attended by considerable risk. These considerations set rather severe limitations upon the use of mean curves in the study of learning (Estes, 1956, p. 134).

Estes does go on to say that some forms of individual curves are not distorted by the averaging, and others can be made amenable to such group analysis by appropriate transformations of the data. In other cases, the individual curves can be examined to determine whether or not a mean curve could be expected to conform closely to the shape for individuals. The same argument holds for repeated measures on the same subject.

Noble (1961) argues for the fruitfulness of looking for the interaction of stimulus and organismic variables in attempting to discover psychological laws. He concluded from the evidence on selective learning that predictions from Hull's (1952) postulate, that the rate of acquisition is a positive function of initial level of ability, was supported.

Ellis, Pryer, Distefano, and Pryer (1960) compared serial learning by the anticipation method for ten-noun lists by children of various measured intelligence levels. Although the more intelligent subjects learned faster, the shapes of the learning curves were generally the same. The Vincentized curves were, however, unusual in that they showed essentially a reverse-S shape; the first part of the curve was negatively accelerated, and the final part was positively accelerated. The authors do not describe their method for calculating Vincent curves. Perhaps an "end-spurt" artifact is present (Melton, 1936). The serial-position distribution of errors did not reveal important differences in the shapes of these curves as a function of intelligence. However, Barnett, Ellis, and Pryer (1960) later selected the data of 46 retardates and 47 normal subjects from this study and analyzed the serial-position curves by the method popularized by McCrary and Hunter (1953). The resulting curves were very similar, although slightly more bowed for the more intelligent subjects. This difference in curves undoubtedly reflects the difference in "efficiency" that Jensen (1962c) also describes; the more intelligent subjects would have made fewer errors per trial, as well as shown fewer trials to criterion.

Thus, the variety of factors that can influence the shape of the learning curve has been shown to be substantial. Some of the differences depend on the method of plotting, however, instead of on true differences in the progression of learning. For this purpose it will first be necessary to examine certain differences in the shapes of serial-acquisition curves in order to understand how those differences depend on the way the curves are plotted.

The Vincent Plot

The Vincent curve (Vincent, 1912) basically converts the number of trials into tenths of learning. In this manner a subject who has completed the learning does not contribute inappropriately to a flattening of the curve for the later trials. Jensen has found that the Vincentized curve for errors as a function of trials is approximately linear, using the modification which was suggested by Hilgard and Campbell (1937). An illustration of a plot of his unpublished data is given in Figure 9-2, showing the mean percentage of total learning occurring in successive fifths of the learning process. Granted that these data are adequately described by the straight line, there is a slight downward bend of the array. Waugh (1963), on the other hand, obtained slight bowing in the opposite direction for correct serial-anticipation responses and for serial recalls. Also, Spielberger and Smith (1966) found negatively accelerated curves of correct responses in serial-anticipation learning for both high- and low-anxious subjects, under both neutral and stress conditions.

The Melton Plot

Another method for plotting learning curves for the serial-learning task produces a different shape of curve. It shows decreasing efficiency of performance with advancing trials as illustrated in Figures 9-3 and 9-4. This plot, suggested by Melton (1936), shows the number of trials re-

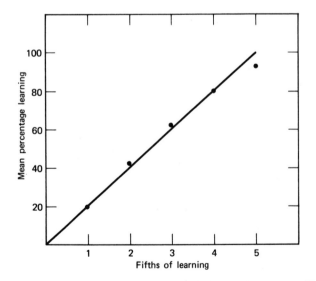

Figure 9-2   Vincent plot of serial learning from unpublished data of Jensen. Used by author's permission.

quired for the subject to reach selected criteria of performance. Figure 9-3 represents the comparison of proactive and retroactive inhibitory effects in relearning a serial list, as well as the results for a rest (control) group (Melton & von Lackum, 1941). Each curve shows decreasing gains with additional learning, as do data from original learning from Postman and Schwartz (1964) in Figure 9-4.

The difference between this method, hereafter called the Melton plot, and the Jensen plot provides the central issue and starting point for the present discussion. Does the course of serial learning proceed in constant increments, as the Jensen results would imply (Jensen, 1962a), or is progress made at a decreasing rate, as the Melton curve of results for serial learning would imply (Postman & Schwartz, 1964)? Underwood and Goad (1951) present serial-learning curves, using the Melton plot, that also show the negatively accelerated gains with increased trials.

Although inversions in performance, or oscillations of correct and incorrect trials, are a common feature of the progression of learning, the Melton plot does not show such inversions. This plot merely records trials on which the subject reaches given criteria for the first time. If the subject falls below a previously attained criterion on a subsequent

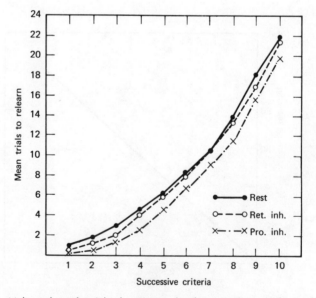

Figure 9-3   Melton plots of serial relearning under three conditions, after Melton and von Lackum (1941). Reprinted with permission of University of Illinois Press.

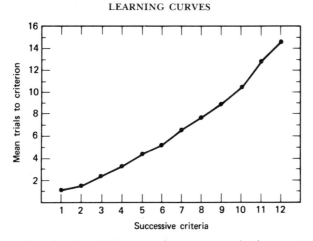

Figure 9-4   Melton plot of serial learning, after Postman and Schwartz (1964). Reprinted by permission of the Academic Press.

trial, this fact is not reflected in the curve. Therefore, the Melton curve is ambiguous in the respect that it does not show whether or not, or on which items, the subject faltered on the subsequent trials. A precipitous leap ahead in accuracy of performance cannot possibly be mitigated by a later poorer level of performance. This problem, which produces the "end-spurt" of learning (Hilgard & Campbell, 1937), is actually present at each stage of learning. This problem is reduced, to be sure, by using the criterion of two successive correct achievements of a level of accuracy before the subject is given credit for achieving that level of learning. Nevertheless, it creates difficulty in interpreting the meaning of the curve.

There is another related problem with the interpretation of the Melton curve of learning. Since the Melton plot is not item-specific, the meaning is not clear, when, for example, three of the items are "learned" (i.e., reproduced correctly) on two successive trials, but these are not the same three items for the two trials.

A third ambiguity in the portrayal of learning by the Melton plot is its intersection with the ordinate above zero. Underwood and Goad (1951) found for lists of 14 words with two degrees of intralist similarity, and three intertrial intervals, that the Melton plot intersected the *y* axis at about two trials. This artifact of method is not a great concern because its source is known. It occurs because some subjects at the beginning of learning actually achieve the criterion level for several items in the same trial (Melton, 1936).

The Hayes Plot

The Hayes plot (Hayes, 1953) attempts to capture the nature of the acquisition process for the learning of individual items that is masked by the conventional methods of plotting the changes in performance as a result of experience. This masking occurs because the data are combined for groups of items, or subjects, each of which may show learning at a different stage of the total acquisition process for the complete group of items or subjects. Therefore a smooth curve of performance with respect to ordinal learning trials is achieved, in contrast to the possible all-or-nothing character of the process for individual items, or for individual subjects. Hayes' original data was shown previously in Chapter 1 (Figure 1-2).

Restle's (1962) mathematical model of cue-learning strategies implies a discontinuous, insightful curve of learning for individual subjects. This curve is typically blurred into an S-shaped curve in the averages for different subjects because of variations in exact solution times. Moreover, other factors, such as a subject's irrational perseveration on incorrect responses or an incorrect strategy and complexity of possible correct strategies, add variability to the empirical data. The rate of learning depends on the proportion of the possible strategies or cues that will produce a correct response.

To avoid such blurring due to individual differences in achieving criterion trials, the Hayes plot recasts the results for each item, or subject, with respect to the trial of attainment of the learning criterion. In this way the precriterial performance can be examined for better-than-chance success. Similarly, the postcriterial performance can be examined for evidence of retention that is less than perfect. Hayes plots of serial-learning data are illustrated in Figures 9-5 and 9-6, taken respectively from paced learning of 12- and 16-item nonsense syllable lists by the anticipation method in the Harcum and Coppage (1969) experiment. Criterion for learning an item was two successive correct anticipations. These criterion trials, labeled as C_1 and C_2, must show 100% accuracy, of course, just as the immediately preceding trial $(C-1)$ must show 0% accuracy. The precriterial trials $(C-3$ and $C-2)$ which precede the last precriterial trial indicate that some learning has occurred, and the post-criterial trials $(C + 1, C + 2$, etc.) indicate that retention is not perfect. Nevertheless, the general picture is of a rapid change in performance at the time the criterion is reached. The change appears more nearly continuous for the more difficult (16-item) list because the points prior to and subsequent to the precriterial trials generally show ascending performance. On the other hand, the easier (12-item) list shows a general downward trend for the postcriterial trials.

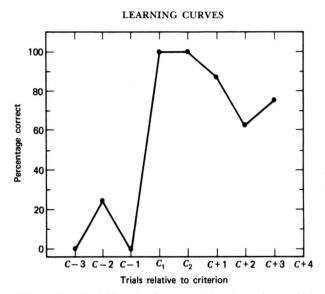

Figure 9-7 Hayes plot of serial learning for one subject. From *The Psychology of Learning* by James Deese. Copyright (1958) by the McGraw-Hill Book Company, Inc. Used with permission of McGraw-Hill Book Company.

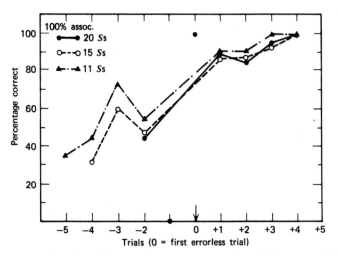

Figure 9-8 Hayes plot of serial learning to a stringent criterion of high-meaningful items.

for one-trial learning, but it still indicates something better than chance performance before the criterion trial, and something less than perfection afterward. Figure 9-9, showing data for low-associability items, makes a strong case for the continuity argument. In both figures the results are given for the total group of 20 subjects, and for subgroups of the slower learners. The faster learners do not have as many data points because the number of trials to learning was fewer.

CONCLUSION

The problem of arriving at a definitive conclusion to this question precludes an easy answer (Miller, 1963). The Teghtsoonians take a middle-of-the-road view with respect to recognition learning (Teghtsoonian, 1964; Teghtsoonian & Teghtsoonian, 1971). They find evidence for both incremental and discontinuous learning—a general increase plus a sudden jump about the critical trial.

Underwood and Keppel (1962) concluded that the evidence for or against one-trial learning was not crucial. The problems of resolving this issue include the definition of a single trial. As they point out, for example, a slow rate of presentation may mask several covert trials. On the other hand, the subject may ignore some items for several trials in order to concentrate on one or two items. Underwood and Keppel

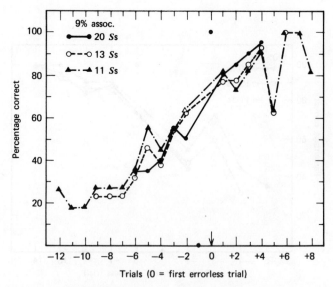

Figure 9-9   Hayes plot of serial learning to a stringent criterion of low-meaningful items.

(1962) point out that a crucial test of the one-trial learning controversy is not likely. In addition to problems relating to thresholds of performance and item selection, there is evidence that subjects adopt strategies in learning which would cloud that issue. As they suggest, if a subject decides to concentrate on one or two items on a given trial, and ignores all of the others, then the arbitrary definition of one trial makes the theoretical issue meaningless.

Restle (1965) argues that no classical theoretical issue can be decided by the all-or-none learning phenomenon. The various theories can handle all-or-none data as a special case. Gregg and Simon (1967) conclude that not only the conditions of the experiment, but also the predilections of the subjects, influence whether their strategy produces data in the all-or-none or incremental form. The subjects may adopt a one-at-a-time strategy, or an all-at-once strategy, and thereby control the form of the results.

Postman (1964) points out the relevance of the distinction between principles of performance and principles of association to the issue of one-trial learning. The increments of associative strength may be smaller than the sensitivity of the performance measure. Also, the contextual conditions of testing may not be adequate to elicit the learned response, as Miller (1963) suggests in his "junk-box theory." The present hierarchical-configuration hypothesis of the functional stimulus offers a similar interpretation. The confluence or configuration of stimuli may not be adequate to establish the availability of the learned response. Therefore, the present position is that this theoretical issue is not critical, although the evidence does favor the incremental approach. The present view is that learning of all items is continuous on successive trials, and that the serial-position curve reflects the cumulative effects of interference processes in serial learning.

This issue has nevertheless focused new attention to the analysis of processes which deal with the acquisition of particular responses by individual subjects. Cofer (1961b) commented as follows in the proceedings of the Office of Naval Research conference on verbal learning and behavior at New York University:

> Another point, which would probably have puzzled Ebbinghaus and perhaps McGeoch, is that frequency of pairing as a factor in associative strength or frequency of usage as a factor making for differential learnability of words has been questioned by at least some of the participants here. This is a complex issue, and in a sense, the phenomenon of single-trial acquisition of associations is not new. It has been known for many years that subjects are able to anticipate one or two paired associates correctly after a single learning trial. But the reorientation which some

of the participants seem to be undergoing concerning this problem is that single-trial association of well-integrated units is the rule and that the slow acquisition of serial or paired-associates lists perhaps represents interference or other processes not typical of the formation of single associations. It is clear that not all workers in this field share this persuasion or would conclude that list learning does not permit the observation of the formation of simple associations (p. 225).

The Jensen Plot

One of the most powerful lines of evidence for the strategy hypothesis of serial learning is what Jensen (1962a) calls the order-of-learning plot. Jensen (1962a) has shown that typically there is a linear relationship between the rank order of the items with respect to frequencies of failures to anticipate items in serial learning, and the actual number of errors for each item. For this plot the items are ranked for each individual subject in terms of the total errors per item, and then these errors are averaged across subjects within each rank. Such a plot, hereafter called the Jensen plot, was illustrated in Chapter 5 (Figure 5-5), with data from Harcum and Coppage (1969). It may be recalled that Harcum and Coppage presented lists of 8, 12, or 16 nonsense syllables with intertrial intervals of 6 seconds, and at a rate of 4 seconds per item, or at an unpaced rate in which the subject could take as long as he wished before responding. Another condition with 12-item lists employed paced and unpaced presentation on alternate trials. Learning proceeded until a criterion of two consecutive errorless trials of correct anticipatory spelling of each syllable was reached. These Jensen plots of the Harcum and Coppage results in Figure 5-5 reveal functions starting at the origin, as usual for 12-item lists. In that figure, the data are shown in the lower-left graph for completely paced and unpaced trials (12P and 12U), and in the lower-right graph for alternating paced and unpaced trials (12A).

The data for the 8-item lists, in the upper-left panel of Figure 5-5, and for the 16-item lists, in the upper-right graph, apparently need two straight lines to describe all of the data. The ubiquity of linear functions for each condition of pacing and for each length of list, but with different slopes and intercepts, leads to further speculations about the extent of individual differences on this task. Thus, Jensen plots have been made for each subject who learned the 12-item list under paced presentation (the 12P condition). This condition is used because it probably is the most typical of the serial-learning task. Although the basic function of each subject appeared to be approximately linear, there were clear indications of individual differences in two respects: the locus of the intersection of the basic function with the ordinate, and the slope of this function. These two attributes of the functions had been offered by Harcum and Coppage (1965b) as, respectively, measures of a subject's ability to form anchors for the subsequent associations of new items, and measures of his associative skills.

The abscissa in Figure 5-5 is labeled "order of accuracy" because it does not literally represent the order of learning for the items. Admittedly, this ranking should very closely parallel the order in which the items are learned. The Jensen plot, because of a methodological constraint, does not permit inversions in the function; the items are actually ranked in terms of relative accuracy. This procedure leaves the true meaning of the scale in the abscissa open to question, however. As pointed out above, this ranking must be highly correlated with the order of learning, but is not identical to it.

According to Jensen, this linear function of errors for individual items, identified in terms of their order in learning, means that other items are added to a first-learned item at a constant rate in a consistent, progressive sequence. This result supports the interpretation of serial-position effects in terms of strategies of information processing (Feigenbaum & Simon, 1962; Harcum & Coppage, 1965b). It is the consistency of the subjects, in terms of the ordinal position in the sequence in which the items are learned, that produces the characteristic curve of errors per item-position. The asymmetry in the distribution of errors among serial positions occurs because the subjects typically learn the temporally first item first. The adjacent items in forward and backward directions are added alternately in turn, in such a way that the item just after the middle of the series is the last one added. Thus, the serial-position curve with the basic bowed shape, and with a slight degree of asymmetry, is generated.

The linear Jensen plot has been shown to be applicable to many sets of learning data. The further generality of the Jensen (1962a) order-of-learning concept is suggested by its applicability to the results of tachistoscopic pattern perception (Harcum, 1967a). Just as the spatial distribution of errors within tachistoscopic patterns is parallel to the temporal distribution of errors within the serial-learning task, the Jensen plots also are parallel (Harcum, 1966a).

VALIDITY OF JENSEN HYPOTHESIS

Evidence for the validity of the Jensen plot would favor the present interpretation that the strategy of the subject determines the distribution of errors. However it should be emphasized that the strategy hypothesis would not be restricted to predicting a linear function of acquisition. Although the Jensen plot ordinarily shows a straight line from the origin of the graph, the plot does not have to be linear. The function may be curvilinear, as Jensen has found in unpublished data from learning a finite set of familiar stimuli, such as a particular order for a known group of letters from the alphabet. Moreover, the function may intersect the abscissa, indicating a memory span, or it may intersect the ordinate, indicating a greater difficulty of forming an anchor for the subsequent serial association (Harcum & Coppage, 1965b). It may indicate greater difficulty of the discriminative phase, as it does for meaningless material.

The results for the individual subjects in the Harcum and Coppage (1969) study are illustrated in Figures 9-10, 9-11, 9-12, and 9-13. The straight lines are visually fitted to the data points. The numbers in parentheses indicate the order of acquisition for the various serial positions, with tied positions underlined. As would be expected, the faster learners revealed flatter slopes of the serial-association curve. Moreover, one of the slower learners (No. 1) showed evidence for a higher intercept on the y axis—indicating slower formation of the anchor for learning. The functions for these subjects seem to represent linear functions with a

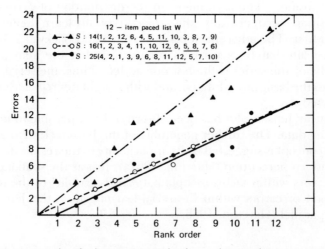

Figure 9-10   Jensen plots for learning List W by three subjects, after Harcum and Coppage (1969). Copyright © (1969) by the American Psychological Associaion. Reprinted by permission.

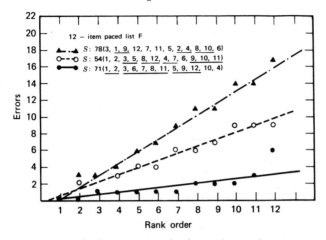

Figure 9-11 Jensen plots for learning List F by three subjects after Harcum and Coppage (1969). Copyright © (1969) by the American Psychological Association. Reprinted by permission.

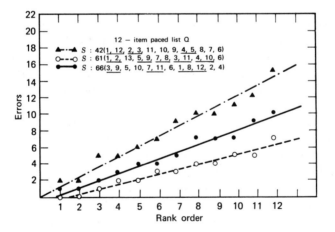

Figure 9-12 Jensen plots for learning List Q by three subjects, after Harcum and Coppage (1969). Copyright © (1969) by the American Psychological Association. Reprinted by permission.

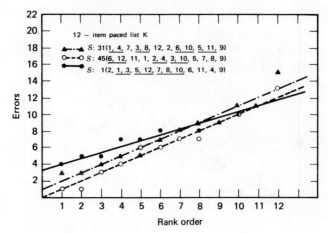

Figure 9-13   Jensen plots for learning List K by three subjects, after Harcum and Coppage (1969). Copyright © (1969) by the American Psychological Association. Reprinted by permission.

relatively high degree of regularity, but the data of one subject (No. 71), a fast learner, may not exhibit this basic linear function. Although the last point for this subject is obviously very high with respect to a linear extrapolation from the other points, the absolute deviation of this point from the linear progression amounts to only about three errors.

The Jensen plots of the results for individual subjects, as shown in Figures 9-10, 9-11, 9-12, and 9-13, obviously should reveal greater regularity than plots in terms of serial position, because these Jensen functions are forced to be monotonic, and without inversions of data points. Nevertheless, the similarity of the near-linear plots for each subject suggests that the linear function for the group of subjects is not the result of averaging nonlinear functions from different subjects. It is also consistent with the assumption of stages in the acquisition of items for individual subjects. Both these stages may involve linear progress of acquisition, but at different rates for the two stages.

There are several problems with Jensen's (1962a) interpretation, however. The most important problem is that it does not require the right degree of consistency among subjects in the order of acquisition for the various items. Paradoxically, the serial-position curve requires consistency among subjects for its typical appearance, but also a measure of inconsistency. This point can be illustrated by reference to Figures 9-14 and 9-15.

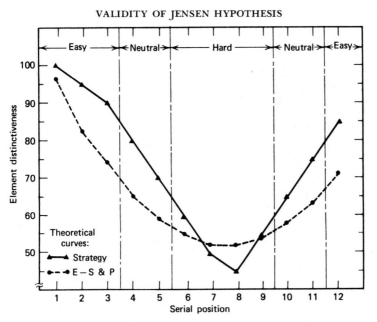

Figure 9-14   Comparison of predicted serial-position curves from the theory in Figure 5-3 with the strategy hypothesis of Jensen (1962a).

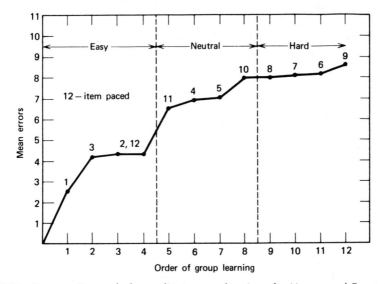

Figure 9-15   Errors per item ranked according to group learning, after Harcum and Coppage (1969). Copyright © (1969) by the American Psychological Association. Reprinted by permission.

In Figure 9-14 the abscissa represents serial position, and the ordinate represents item distinctiveness, in the Murdock units which were used in Figure 5-3. The greater distinctiveness implies fewer errors in learning. The "strategy" curve gives the results to be expected on the basis of Jensen's (1962a) position, with a linear drop in errors from Position One until Position Eight is learned at the last. The curve labeled "E-S & P" refers to the end-segregation and primattensity proposed in Figure 5-3. Thus predictions of Jensen's (1962a) theory and those of the information-translation hypothesis are contrasted in Figure 9-14. E-S & P results are predicted from the theoretical argument illustrated in Figure 5-3, with the addition of the strategy hypothesis of Jensen (1962a) to determine the order of acquisition of items. Although "goodness" of the shape of serial-position curves has never been operationally defined, obviously the strategy curve is too peaked to be a typical serial-position curve. Therefore, a typical serial-position curve, in which the differences between items become smaller as the totals of errors are greater, implies departures from the consistent ("idealized") strategy that was proposed by Jensen (1962a) for individual subjects.

For convenience, the various items at different positions in Figure 9-14 are designated as easy, neutral, and hard according to the number of errors per item required before it would be learned. Thus, the items at Positions One, Two, Three and Twelve would be easiest; those at Positions Four, Five, Ten, and Eleven would be neutral; and the items at Positions Six, Seven, Eight and Nine would be hardest. It should be noted, of course, that this classification is for the overall group of subjects, without necessarily implying that this particular categorization would apply to each subject. However, we can assume that these same data in Jensen plots would have produced the typical straight line relating errors and rank-order of items in terms of errors.

Figure 9-15 gives a plotting of the actual data points obtained by Harcum and Coppage (1969) for a 12-item serial list learned in the usual way. However, the abscissa is changed so that the items are now identified according to the rank order of each item at the given serial position, in terms of the totals of errors for the group of subjects. We have been calling this plot the "order of group learning." Note that in Figure 9-15 the rank on the abscissa retains the identity of the item, because it indicates the ranking for the group. The digit beside each data point indicates the actual ordinal position in the series of the item for which the performance is represented by that data point. The Jensen plot, on the other hand, would not retain the identity of the item because the ranking is made for each subject before the summation and averaging procedure.

As Harcum and Coppage (1965b) have pointed out, the order of individual performance (Jensen plot), and the order of group performance are not identical, because the subjects were not completely consistent in their order of performance. Otherwise, the ranking for individual performance would be item-specific also, and the order of group performance would be linear. In other words, the two plots would be identical. The difference is that the subjects tend to become less and less consistent as the items get harder and harder. Thus, Jensen's (1962a) idea of a perfectly consistent strategy predicts a curve that is too peaked.

The problem remains of squaring up the valid results of the Jensen plot with the invalid appearance in Figure 9-15 of the prediction from the idealized strategy in Figure 9-14. The answer is that the idealized strategy may well represent the results of a single subject, but the end-segregation and primattensity curve is not likely to do so. A number of subjects showing an idealized strategy can produce variation in the location of the item showing maximum errors, tending to wash out the differences in difficulty among "hard" items in the combined data.

The above argument suggests that a "good" (smooth) serial-position curve cannot be obtained from the data of a single subject. Assuming that the Jensen plot is the typical result, the serial-position data would always be too peaked if the subject employed an ideal strategy. The inconsistency of a subject in following an "ideal" strategy results in an irregular serial-position curve. The smoothing of the function gives the illusion of a good serial-position curve for the individual subject.

The Jensen plots of item rank, and even more so the item-specific Melton curves of learning, would imply a serial-position curve of errors that would be too peaked. Even a linear course of acquisition would imply that the last-learned item would be as different in performance from the second-last-learned item as that item was from the third-last item to be learned, and so forth. The typical appearance of the serial-position curve, showing smallest differences among items with the largest error scores, appears to be due to one or both of two factors: variation among subjects, and inconsistency within a single subject. The variation among subjects consists of individual differences in the exact location of the item that is learned last. The variation within a subject involves departures from the coherent order of acquisition of items; for example, the next-learned item is not immediately adjacent to the just-learned item. Thus, the serial-position curve may vary in slope near the maximum, but remain compatible with a linear Jensen plot.

It is my opinion that smoothing the data obscures the true character of the function. For example, the serial-position data of two of the subjects, Nos. 61 and 78, from the Harcum and Coppage (1969) study are shown in Figure 9-16. The data are irregular when plotted according to serial position, but they yield linear Jensen plots. Also shown in Figure 9-16 is an illustration of what the serial-position curve would look like in terms of the actual data if the order of acquisition were strictly in accord with the Jensen hypothesis. A smoothed curve through the actual data would obviously produce a much flatter curve in the region of

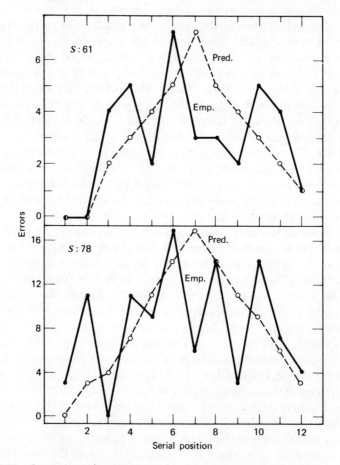

Figure 9-16   Comparison of errors per serial position to Jensen's predictions for two subjects of Harcum and Coppage (1969). Copyright © (1969) by the American Psychological Association. Reprinted by permission.

the peak errors than is revealed by the function predicted by the Jensen plot.

It would appear that the above argument is not testable since it depends upon the moot definition of a "good" serial-position function. Moreover, one rarely obtains an ideal, "textbook" manifestation of the idealized case in the data of a single subject in tasks of this sort. The conclusion is logically inescapable, however. If the data of a single subject was found to produce a smooth curve typical of the average of a group of subjects, then it of necessity could not conform to the linear outcome of the Jensen plot. Specifically, the curve would flatten out (bend down) as the end of learning was reached. This argument points out that the strategy interpretation of serial learning provides more insight into the processes than does an analysis in terms of serial position.

Discussion

One obvious difference between the Jensen and the Melton plots is that in the former the ordinate is plotted in terms of errors, and in the latter it is plotted in terms of trials. Since the performance per item is evaluated on the basis of one possible error per trial, this difference in measures probably would not account for a change in the shape of the curve. A more probable explanation for the difference between plots is that the ranks on the abscissa in the Jensen plot represent specific syllables for each subject, even though this identity is lost in the averaging. The Melton plot is not item-specific even for the individual subject. As mentioned above, the early acquisition curve in the Melton plot may intersect the ordinate above zero because the curve capitalizes on the first attainment of correct responses. Such correct responses can be made as a result of an increase of overt emissions of the item, after item differentiation has progressed, before the item is correctly associated to the specific position within the series, or to the preceding items. The penalties for subsequent failures, in the form of additional errors, which add to the Jensen totals, may account for the rectification of the data in the Jensen plot. This possibility can only be tested, however, for a modification of the Melton plot in which specific items are considered.

The present approach is to calculate both Jensen and Melton plots for given sets of data, while keeping the procedures as comparable as possible, and then to examine the differences which remain. The specific intent will be to determine whether the differences in shape merely reflect artifacts of measurement or reflect fundamentally different views of the same or different aspects of the serial-learning process. Finally, the implications for a theory of serial learning will be discussed.

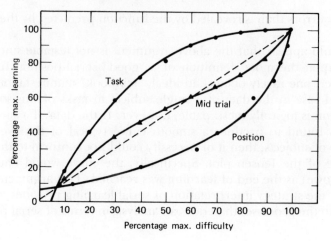

A POSSIBLE RESOLUTION

A possible solution to the problem of the true shape of the serial-learning curve is illustrated in Figure 9-17. The rationale of this theoretical interpretation is that the underlying processes of serial acquisition are not ordinarily linear, and that the usual apparent linearity of the plot of errors is the result of the averaging of processes which themselves are not linear. The apparent linear trend occurs because the curvature produced by one process largely compensates for an opposite curvature in another process.

The difference in shapes of curves may be attributable to differences in performance criteria. Weitz (1961) has discussed the need for understanding our criteria of performance. He cited instances in which different experimental conclusions could be traced to the use of different criteria of performance. Therefore, different criteria of performance may reflect the progression of change in different processes.

In Figure 9-17 the abscissa represents the order of difficulty in which various items are acquired by each subject. In the ideal case, this would result in a monotonic function, regardless of the measure of performance that is used. The ordinate in Figure 9-17 represents the number of trials that are required for the subject to reach selected criteria of performance. Thus, these theoretical curves are similar to Melton curves; but there is an important difference. Namely, these curves are item-specific; the abscissa refers to the order in which the appropriate criterion was reached for a specific item. The item that is plotted for a given order of acquisition is the same for all curves that are plotted on the graph. Both coordinates are converted to percentage of final value.

The lower curve in Figure 9-17 illustrates the results for the trial in which the first correct response (FCR) was reached. Often in practice when actual data are used, the criteria of two successive correct (TSC) trials are used instead of the FCR curve, because the latter criterion is less reliable. Obviously it is less risky to assume that a subject has learned an item if he reproduces it twice on successive trials than if he has merely reproduced it once. The FCR curve, like the Melton plot in Figures 9-3 and 9-4, shows a decreasing rate of acquisition as the subject progresses through the task. The number of trials to achieve the TSC criterion would be greater than for the FCR criterion, of course, but presumably the shape of the curve would be essentially the same. This curve is attributed to the strategy of subjects in approaching the task; it reflects the attempts of the subject to learn the syllables in a given order. The general shape of this curve is derived from the theoretical curves in Figure 5-3 of Chapter 5. Thus, by position alone, total distinctiveness of the items, on the basis of both factors, is highest for the temporally first item. The discriminability then decreases progressively for the other items, as shown in Figure 9-17, until the item just after the center of the series is reached. As can be seen in Figures 5-3 and 9-14, the difference in degree of distinctiveness decreases in ever smaller amounts as the item is delayed to later and later in the learning sequence. The subject is then getting the hardest items, in terms of serial position. As a consequence the difficulty of learning increases in ever larger increments.

The upper curve in Figure 9-17, with the bowing in the direction opposite to that of the FCR curve, designates the criterion of no further errors (NFE)—the trials after which the subject made no more errors for the particular item. The shape of the NFE curve was obtained by calculating the total possible number of associations between dyads of items for lists of length 12, 11, 10, and so forth. The rationale was that as an item is learned the number of competing associations for the next correct association becomes smaller. This gain as each additional item is learned also increases in a geometric progression. As each item is learned, the number of possible associations decreases, because the learned item is removed from the pool of items to be learned. Thus, as the task proceeds, it becomes less and less likely that an association from an unlearned item will intrude to disrupt the performance of a learned item. The learning of an item effectively insulates it from interference with unlearned items, and the task becomes easier.

General support for this relationship can be inferred from the length-difficulty relationship in verbal learning. In several experiments, Derks (1974) studied effects of list length on immediate serial recall. In general, as arrays doubled in size, the apparent difficulty increased by a factor of six. Derks emphasizes, however, that the mix of revelant psychological processes seems to change as the series lengthens, and that individual subjects may be adopting somewhat different approaches to cope with the longer series. Whatever the precise function, the amount of material to be learned becomes easier with positive acceleration as the subject reaches progressive criteria of learning.

The shape of the FCR curve follows therefore the ranks of progressively less discriminable items in the order of acquisition. The lack of discriminability may result from the disadvantage of the relative serial position, from the proactive interference of the previously learned items, or both. Although there is no proof of it, I favor the proactive interference interpretation. The theory seems a bit more logically consistent if we consider that the position influences the strategy, whereas the proactive interference determines the difficulty. As the subject makes progress in learning, the task of remembering what he has learned increases; these items must be sufficiently well learned to allow attention to the acquisition of new items. Since the number of possible competing associations goes up geometrically as items are added, the difficulty similarly increases geometrically.

The NFE curve represents, on the other hand, the task facing the process for hooking-on new items. This task is getting progressively easier as the number of potential associations between items yet to be learned decreases geometrically. The above interpretation is supported by some data from learning of series of different lengths. The rationale for this is that the longer lists make each item of that list more difficult because the number of possible associations to compete with the correct association is greater. Lyon (1917) showed that the time required to learn lists of nonsense syllables by the "continuous method," at the rate of two syllables per second, increased from 9 minutes for 16 items, to 16 minutes for 24 items, to 43 minutes for 48 items, and 138 minutes for 72 items. Thurstone (1930) concluded that the time per item in learning lists of varying length increases as the square root of the number of items beyond the memory span. Hull et al. (1940) summarized the results of several studies on the effect of list length on the number of repetitions required for learning. The curves appear to show positive acceleration up to about 15 items, and thereafter to show negative acceleration. Shurrager (1940) used a scaling technique to measure the perceived difficulty of nonsense-syllable lists of different lengths. The functions were negatively accelerated, becoming asymptotic at about 20 items. Brogden and Schmidt (1954a, b) found a nearly linear relation between the number of errors to criterion in 16- and 24-unit verbal mazes and the number of alternative choices per choice point. The function for the 16-unit maze showed consistently fewer errors than for the 24-unit maze. Lloyd, Reid, and Feallock (1960) found that in recall of paired associates the errors increased with the average number of items subjects had to recall from a sequence.

A number of other studies using different types of tasks have found increased difficulty per item as the length of the task becomes greater. For example, Hovland and Kurtz (1952) found a linear length-difficulty relationship in serial learning of nonsense syllables. Pollack (1953) showed that in absolute terms the number of errors in immediate recall of letter-number sequences increased as the length of the message increased and the number of alternatives per message unit increased. Miller (1965) also argued that the number of alternatives per serial position, as well as the number of serial positions occupied by items of the same category, was a major determinant of task difficulty. Phillips, Shiffrin, and Atkinson (1967) found that the accuracy of probed recall in immediate memory was progressively worse for the item of poorest recall as the length of the series increased.

Leonard and Blick (1970) argued that the usual positive acceleration of the curve relating task length and difficulty was due to the usual confounding of a change in the nature of the task with the change in length. Accordingly, in a card-sorting task, the number of alternative responses were kept constant for one group of subjects regardless of the length of task—namely, number of cards to be sorted. The length-difficulty relationship for this group was linear. For a group in which the number of alternatives increased as the number of cards increased, the length-difficulty function showed positive acceleration. Therefore, the bowing was produced by adding alternatives, rather than by adding length alone.

Krueger (1947) had subjects practice a psychomotor task of various degrees of difficulty—namely, different distances for a ring toss. The easiest task initially revealed a high level of accuracy of performance with negative acceleration and early mastery. Subjects serving in the task of intermediate difficulty showed curves of early positive acceleration, followed by negative acceleration. The subjects with the greatest difficulty of task showed only a positive acceleration. Krueger concluded that each of his experimental conditions represented a different phase of a more general learning curve, showing first positive and then negative acceleration.

The results of Kimble and Dufort (1955) show clearly that the learnability of an item is not intrinsic to the item itself. Whereas the meaningfulness of an item, in terms of Noble's (1952a) m, was inversely related to the difficulty of learning it in both paired-associate and serial-learning tasks, an item of extremely low association value (actually a meaningless paralog) was learned significantly faster than words of much higher meaningfulness when both were embedded in a list of highly meaningful words. Therefore, some mediating cognitive operation is suggested as a determinant of the relative learnability of items. Green's (1956) study of the surprise effect of isolation shows the importance of the subject's appraisal of the stimulus, rather than the intrinsic differentiation by virtue of its different formal character.

Gross and Cady (1970) suggested that the items learned later in a list of paired associates are intrinsically more difficult. This effect is comparable to what has been frequently reported (namely, Williams, 1961). Items empirically classified as easy for one group of subjects, on the basis of relative order of acquisition, were in fact learned more easily by a different group of subjects.

The differences between FCR and NFE curves produce an interval between the two criteria of learning, hereafter called the intercriterial range (ICR), in which the subject may or may not be correct on a given trial. Within this region the items are exhibiting what Hull (1951) had called "behavioral oscillation." Hovland's (1940b) analysis indicated that this oscillation at the threshold of recall should be greater for the items about the middle of the series; this expectation was confirmed for the longer series.

Underwood and Richardson (1956) reported that Vincent curves for four lists of high and low meaningfulness, and high and low intralist similarity, each revealed curves that showed "somewhat" increased frequencies of errors during the first third of learning, a constant increase for the next third, and a decrease for the last third of learning. Gibson (1942) found that curves relating number of overt errors—taken as a measure of generalization—first rise and then decrease as learning progresses. On the other hand, the frequency of correct responses reveals a monotonic increase that does not depart very much from linearity.

This argument for an oval envelope of intercriterial ranges is supported by some previous data of Underwood and Goad (1951). The data were obtained from serial-anticipation learning of 14-adjective lists of high or low intralist similarity under varying degrees of distribution of practice (namely, 2-second, 15-second, or 30-second intertrial intervals). The learning proceeded to a criterion of one perfect recitation. Melton plots of the results yielded the typical progressive increases in the number of trials required to reach successive criteria of learning. Underwood and Goad also examined "mean errors per trial;" the results are reproduced in Figure 9-18. Apparently "errors" refer only to errors of commission—overt incorrect intrusions—and exclude failures of correct anticipation. Thus, the results in Figure 9-18 refer to the mean number of intruding errors that the subjects made in progressing from a previous criterion of learning to the successive one. These values were weighted according to overall differences among conditions by dividing the number of errors by the number of trials required to reach that next criterion. These data are obviously not the same as the intercriterial range, but these two measures must by their nature be highly correlated. Each of the six conditions produced the bowed curve as predicted from the present hypothesis. The relative number of intruding errors first increased and then decreased. Underwood and Goad do not discuss this result further except to point out that this finding corroborates other results (e.g., Gibson, 1942), and that the curve is somewhat more peaked

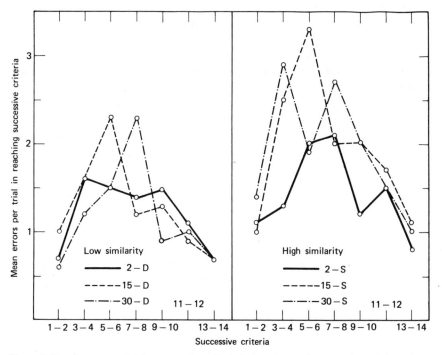

Figure 9-18   Errors per trial for successive criteria in learning under several conditions, from Underwood and Goad (1951). Copyright © (1951) by the American Psychological Association. Reprinted by permission.

for the distributed practice. They demonstrate the paradox of a possible positive correlation between trials to criterion and the number of commission errors that they obtained under some conditions.

Another possible explanation for the shape of the NFE curve is that the NFE is close to the FCR curve for the first-learned items because those items are obviously easier for the subject to learn. Therefore, the subject learns such an easy item early, and he is likely to continue to reproduce that item correctly over subsequent trials. As the items to be learned become those which the subjects find more difficult, the FCR and NFE curves tend to diverge. The ICR becomes smaller again as the end of learning is approached, however. The overlearning of some items results in a concentration of effort on remaining items. As mentioned above, this may occur because the task of achieving a perfect performance for an item becomes easier as the end of learning is approached. It also may be because the opportunities for additional errors for these items are fewer as the learning task nears the end. Often the reaching of the TSC criterion for the last-learned item means that the entire list has been reproduced correctly on two successive trials, which is usually established by the experimenter as the criterion for learning the complete list. Since learning trials are terminated at that point, there are no further opportunities for the subject to make errors in reproducing the items that reached the criterion last. Evidence for the former of these two interpretations will be presented later.

The dotted line in Figure 9-17 represents the vertical average of the NFE and FCR curves. It is labeled the middle-trial curve because it represents a learning curve of trials to criterion which is midway between the FCR and NFE trials. The middle-trial (dotted) function is not completely straight, as can be seen from comparison to the straight line that is drawn for reference purposes. Nevertheless, this average of the theoretical FCR and NFE curves is sufficiently close to a straight line that an empirical test would require much data to determine whether the departure from linearity were significant. The question of whether or not the resultant of the two curves is literally linear provides some interesting speculations. First of all, a nonlinear resultant implies an inequality of acceleration and deceleration of the two outside (limiting) curves. The reason for this inequality provides open avenues for additional investigation.

Doubtless there will be some investigators who will be concerned about the particular form of these curves. It would be nice, for example, to discover that these curves were simple examples of a family of curves, in which merely a change of sign, for example, or size of exponent, produces the difference in shape. This exercise is left for those with the talent and interest to answer such questions. For present purposes, all that concerns us, however, is that the curves show opposite bowing, with inequalities of acceleration that produce a nearly linear, slightly sigmoidal resultant. The sigmoidal shape is consistent with the generally accepted sigmoidal shape of the generalized learning curve (e.g., Culler, 1928). As Osgood (1953) points out, the S-shaped curve may be descriptive of a complex task, in which there are many competing response tendencies from which the subject must select the correct response. On the other hand, other curves, such as Hull's (1943) growth function, are based on the acquisition of isolated habits. It is tempting to make the speculation that the FCR curve represents the acquisition of items, and the NFE curve represents the integration of them into a place in an organized whole.

If one assumes that the errors within the envelope enclosed by the NFE and FCR curves are uniformly distributed over trials, with errors on one-half of these trials, then the middle trial, which is halfway between the FCR and the NFE trials, would give exactly the same result as the total of errors, except that the number would have to be reduced by one because the subjects could not make errors on criterion trials.

Although the curves in Figure 9-17 give specific results to be predicted in serial-learning experiments, it would be overly optimistic to expect that each subject would produce the complete configuration of results. Specifically, the ends of the envelope may be truncated for particular subjects. The beginning may be missing for the slowest subjects and the final portion for the faster subjects. In all probability, the fastest learners would not show an intercriterial range at all. Thus, it is necessary first to examine results for individual subjects and different independent variables. The easier tasks should have minimal differences between NFE and FCR curves. Shorter lists of easily differentiated items should have beginning closure of the envelope, but a truncated end. Longer lists of difficult items should have an open beginning but a closed end of the envelope.

Hull et al. (1940) and McGeoch (1942) conclude that the oscillations in learning an item are a measure of the interference on that item from other items. The data of Hovland (1938c) and Shipley (1939) seem to show fewer such oscillations at the ends than at about the middle of the series. Hovland (1938c) plotted serial-position curves of the averages across the subjects of the number of presentations (trials) required to reach the criterion of "first success" and "last failure." For the individual subject the criterion of first success is what I have been referring to here as the FCR criterion. The criterion of last failure is, of course, one error (trial) fewer than what I have called the NFE criterion. Obviously, the first successes were ordinarily reached on earlier trials than the last successes. The differences between these criteria were smaller for the items at serial positions near the ends of the series than for items about the middle. However, this difference may be nothing more than a recapitulation of the serial-position function; the oscillation may merely be more extensive where learning the item is most difficult. To assess this possibility, serial-position results from Hovland (1940b) for distributed practice were recast in terms of percentages of the total errors and illustrated in Figure 9-19. The two curves show results for the two extremes of criteria; the FCR data are based on trials preceding (but not including) the first success, and the NFE data are trials up to and including the last failure. These are called "Group" curves because they are averaged for the group of subjects across serial positions, instead of according to order of acquisition for individual subjects.

The curves for the two criteria are obviously equivalent in shape in this plot, showing the classical bowed and asymmetrical shape. Moreover, data for massed practice were equivalent when an adjustment for differences in totals of errors was made—a point previously made by McCrary and Hunter (1953). The similarity of Group NFE and Group FCR curves indicates that the apparently greater oscillation about the middle of the series is an artifact of the procedure of averaging across serial positions.

Evidence for the above statement can be derived from the data in Figure 9-19 plotted in a different way. This different plot, shown in

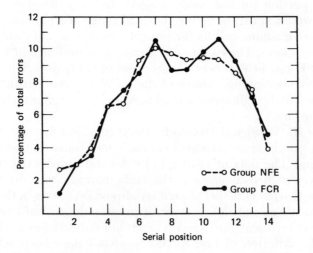

Figure 9-19   Serial-position curves for two criteria of learning, after Hovland (1940b). Copyright © (1940) by the American Psychological Association. Reprinted by permission.

Figure 9-20, merely involves a change in the ordering of the data points from low to higher in terms of relative difficulty. Therefore, the abscissa in Figure 9-20 is labeled "order of group learning." Although the general curvature of the NFE plot is about as predicted for the individual subjects, the FCR curve is clearly bowing in the wrong direction. Thus, the inferred change in rate of acquisition in these FCR data is backwards with respect to the true acquisition process as inferred from the individual curves for the FCR criterion. The curves in Figure 9-20 merely show the progressive change in consistency among subjects as learning progresses, as Harcum and Coppage (1965b) maintain. As the subjects become less consistent, the group-learning curve bends down. The lack of consistency among subjects with respect to the order of learning for the last-learned items washes out the larger differences among these items on the FCR curve for individual subjects. The serial-position of the items provides the only consistent basis for the order of learning, and thus shows up in averaging for all subjects across serial positions. This is evidence that serial position is one basis for the differentiation of items to be learned, and thus a factor in the selection of a serial order for acquisition.

In Workman's study (1951), the oscillation range between first correct response and last failure did not yield much helpful information because the subject frequently became frustrated and upset late in learning and

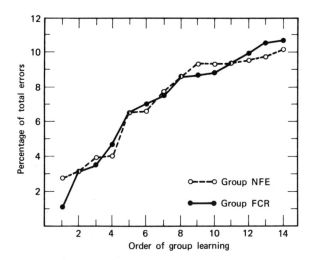

Figure 9-20   Errors by two criteria for items ranked by groups, after Hovland (1940b). Copyright © (1940) by the American Psychological Association. Reprinted by permission.

stopped responding altogether for several seconds—sometimes for a complete trial. When this happened, the subject sometimes made no attempt to anticipate syllables which had been given correctly for 30 or more consecutive previous presentations. Since such a pause in responding would often be followed almost immediately by attainment of list criterion, all items would appear to have been learned on the same trial. In such cases, the measure of oscillation range obviously merely reflected the order of first correct responses, with its wider range for the items learned first.

DISCUSSION

The sigmoidal shape of the resultant curve in Figure 9-17 was not expected. It was the natural result of the theoretical curves which, it was originally assumed, would produce a straight line when averaged. Although *post facto* examination revealed the departures from linearity in existing data, these departures had been universally overlooked, and thus did not enter into the prediction. Therefore, these curves were not contrived to fit the data, but were derived on theoretical grounds.

The serial-learning task seems to be peculiar in that the learning curve is approximately linear. The reason for this probably lies in the peculiarities of the serial-learning task discussed in Chapter 1. Specifically, the discovery of cues to associate to an item becomes more difficult as the task progresses, but the number of items to be associated to those cues is less.

SUMMARY

The main thesis of this chapter has been that the real serial-learning curve is a family of curves like those in Figure 9-17. These curves take into consideration what is happening to the individual item within the list. According to this line of argument, the classical distribution of errors among item positions merely shows that the sheer serial position of items is frequently a major determinant of their order of acquisition. The primary information concerns the order in which the item is attempted by the subject. The present proposition is that more informative indicants of the actual process of serial learning are obtained by studying the performance for each item in relation to the characteristic order in which the items are acquired. The macroprocesses of serial learning can best be described as subject strategies. This includes the general choice of possible bases for associating items, and also the selection of the sequence in which the various items will be learned.

The second area of information concerns the degree of oscillation in performance for that item. That is, the overall level of performance for an item is also determined by the degree to which the item, when it is attempted, is acquired in continuous increments or in a relatively all-or-none fashion.

CHAPTER

10

FURTHER EVIDENCE

A serial-learning theory, such as the one presented in the previous chapters, probably cannot be established or destroyed by a single critical test. The theory begins with the hierarchical-configuration hypothesis, which says that the stimulus for serial learning is a configuration or confluence of stimuli. This configuration is changing dynamically with each trial in a hierarchical structure. The configurations are first simpler, with possibly dyadic associations of an item to a particular position or preceding item. As learning progresses, the configuration becomes more complex so that an item may be given correctly even if the original single stimulus to which it was learned is not present. By the same token, any change in the perceptual configuration could cause a failure to give the correct response, producing oscillations in performance.

As the configuration becomes more complex, it becomes easier for any part of it to evoke another segment—thus increasing the interference among learned response tendencies. This creates the classical negatively accelerated learning curve. Later the possibility for gross changes from a single trial is decreased, reducing the probability of oscillations. Therefore, the items learned later are associated to more stable configurations and learning is faster. This produces a positively accelerated learning curve. The combination of positive and negative acceleration of these two tendencies produces a generally linear, although slightly sigmoid, shape of learning curve over trials when overall accuracy of performance is assessed.

The choice of items for learning is determined by many factors. Together all these factors determine the particular structure of the configurational stimulus. These may include intrinsic structures within the series, such as differential item-associability, perceptual isolation cues, or intertrial intervals. They may also include the effects of differential set for each subject, causing him to emphasize some items in the development of the configuration.

EFFECTS OF SOME VARIABLES

The evidence for the present theory will come from a compilation of instances of its generality and applicability to different sets of data. These are derived from investigations of different variables which already exist in the literature. In a number of cases the published data were re-analyzed, and in others analyses of new data were undertaken.

List Length and Presentation Rate

Some data that are suitable for this analysis may again be taken from the study by Harcum and Coppage (1969) of serial learning, using the method of serial anticipation with CVC trigrams. Their conditions, it may be remembered, included varied lengths of list and different rates of presentation.

The results for the two slowest-learning subjects under the 12-item paced (12P) condition of Harcum and Coppage (1969) are shown in Figure 10-1. In this figure, in order to increase the stability of the results, the order of accuracy for items is defined in terms of the middle-trial results. The TSC criterion increases the number of trials to the middle trial by at least 1, of course, since the TSC criterion would require more trials than the FCR criterion. The data of both subjects support the predictions since the NFE and TSC curves bend in opposite directions, tending to rectify the middle-trial data.

Figure 10-2 shows the TSC and NFE results for the two fastest learners under the 12-item paced condition of Harcum and Coppage (1969). Immediately apparent is the fact that the two functions for different criteria are almost entirely overlapping—the intercriterial range is almost absent. The one disparity between curves which does occur, for Subject 61 in the upper graph, appears at the sixth position, where the theory predicts that the intercriterial range would be broadest. The functions for

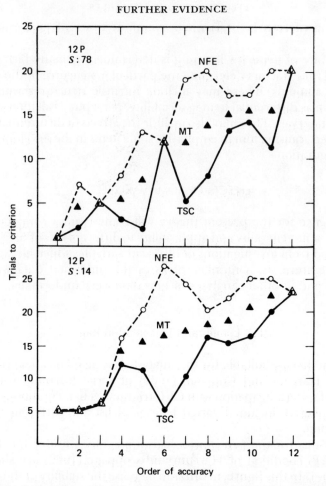

Figure 10-1   Trials to three criteria by two "slow" subjects for 12 items ranked by accuracy, after Harcum and Coppage (1969). Copyright © (1969) by the American Psychological Association. Reprinted by permission.

both subjects are basically linear, although the final point for Subject 71 is relatively high, as has been previously pointed out for this subject in the case of error data. For these fast learners the learning processes seem to have collapsed into a resultant that does in fact approximate a linear course of acquisition.

In Figure 10–3 the middle-trial results for 12-item paced presentation (Harcum & Coppage, 1969) can be compared to the error data. In this figure the abscissa gives the order of accuracy per individual item for the

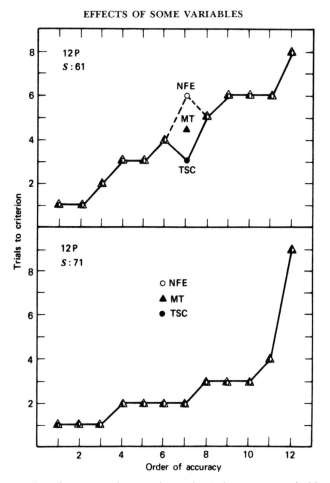

Figure 10-2 Trials to three criteria by two "fast" subjects for 12 items ranked by accuracy, after Harcum and Coppage (1969). Copyright © (1969) by the American Psychological Association. Reprinted by permission.

subject, and the ordinate represents the mean middle trial, or the mean of errors + 1, as appropriate. The middle trial is given separately for tabulations from the two early criteria of TSC and FCR. The middle trial is defined as the arithmetic mean of the lower criterion and the final NFE criterion for a given item—that is, midway through the interval of oscillation. Since the three sets of data are nearly parallel, one is tempted to conclude that the information in totals of errors for the various items is essentially nothing more than an indication of an intermediate criterion of learning between two extreme criteria. This argument would imply

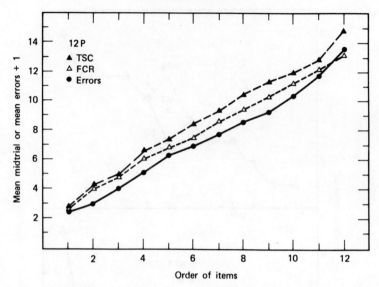

Figure 10-3   Comparison of middle trials to errors for 12 items ranked by accuracy, after Harcum and Coppage (1969). Copyright © (1969) by the American Psychological Association. Reprinted by permission.

that the remaining small absolute difference between middle-trial and mean-error curves is due to the inelegant method for establishing the middle trial. If the acquisition of an individual item mirrors the acquisition of the entire series, then one would expect that the distribution of errors within the envelope would be approximately rectangular, but a skew in either direction would be possible. Thus, the data in Figure 10–3 imply that the errors tend to cluster closer to the lower criterion than to the upper one—a reasonable presumption.

The ranks of a given item according to the middle trial and those in terms of number of errors are not perfectly correlated. It is not infrequent for an item to be acquired approximately midway through the series in terms of middle trial, but to reveal only one error after reaching the FCR criterion. Trials to criterion is not as sensitive a test of differences in learning performance as is totals of errors (Bahrick, 1967). Thus, one would not expect these two measures to be perfectly correlated.

Both the middle trial and error functions tend nevertheless to show the same minor variations from linearity; the points tend to fall above a linear progression at the beginning of the series, but drop below a linear progression as the end is approached. This is the result that would be predicted from the theoretical curves in Figure 9–17 shown by the dotted line in that

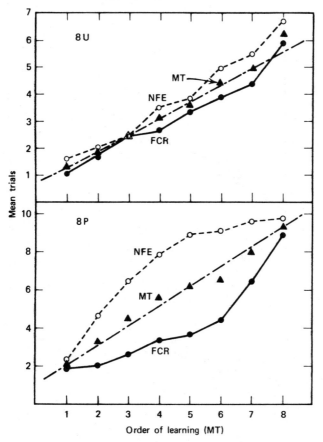

Figure 10-6   Trials to three criteria of learning for eight paced and unpaced items ranked by accuracy, after Harcum and Coppage (1969). Copyright © (1969) by the American Psychological Association. Reprinted by permission.

paced lists. The results for the 8-item paced condition are remarkably close to the prediction from the theoretical curves in Figure 9-17. These data show the opposite bowing of the FCR and the NFE functions, and the near-linearity in the progression of the middle-trial points. Moreover, the middle-trial results show the regular departures from the straight reference line—above at first and below at the end.

The 16-element data of Harcum and Coppage (1969) in Figure 10-7 ow an interesting difference from the data of the other conditions. The st few elements seem to fall on a different function from the rest of the a. This is the same result as that shown in Figure 2–4 for the error data

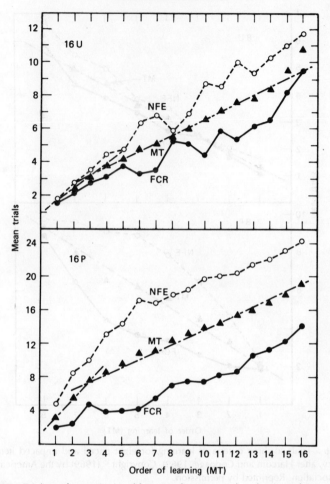

Figure 10-7   Trials to three criteria of learning for 16 paced and unpaced items ranked by accuracy, after Harcum and Coppage (1969). Copyright © (1969) by the American Psychological Association. Reprinted by permission.

under this condition. Therefore, the middle-trial data are described by two lines—one to represent the so-called anchor-learning phase at the beginning of learning, and a second one to describe the so-called serial learning per se (Harcum & Coppage, 1965b). The results for the serial learning phase, starting at the third position in the order of learning, f well with the theory, although again the unpaced data reveal less bowi

Again, also, the departures from linearity appear to be systematic for both paced and unpaced conditions, with deviations above early in the order and deviations below later.

Each set of data from the Harcum and Coppage (1969) experiment, therefore, tends to support the predictions from theory. Since these conditions include three lengths of list and several conditions for the rates of presentation, the generality would seem to be great. Nevertheless, additional evidence from serial-learning tasks that employ still other conditions should be helpful.

Practice

Harcum and Coppage (1965b) investigated the effect of prolonged practice on the distribution of errors in serial learning. Thirteen subjects learned by the anticipation method lists of ten nonsense syllables, one per day for 12 consecutive days, to a criterion of two perfect recitations. For two of the subjects, the experiment continued until, respectively, 34 and 42 lists were learned. The authors concluded that the subjects improved in the use of a strategy that employed the first serial item as an anchor item for directing learning. The analyses of trials to first, middle, and final criteria are shown in Figure 10-8 for the first and twelfth lists learned. The results for both the first trials (in the upper graph) and for the twelfth trials (in the lower graph) show the negative acceleration for the NFE curves, and the positive acceleration for the FCR curves. Also, both middle-trial curves show a generally linear function with the usual systematic departures from linearity.

The total number of trials to criteria are fewer after practice, of course, and the intercriterial envelope is narrower. Thus an effect of practice is to bring the first and last criteria closer together, particularly at the beginning of learning. Thus, the impression is of an intercriterial envelope that is wider earlier in the acquisition of a list before the subject is practiced, and then an envelope that is more open after practice at the end of the learning task. The learning appears to be more discontinuous for the practiced subjects.

The results for the two very highly practiced subjects are shown in Figure 10-9. For one subject (G.D.), in the upper graph, who continued the experiment for 42 days, the two criteria were reached on identical trials for the first five syllables learned, after which an intercriterial range appeared. The functions for the second subject (A.M.), who learned 34 lists, are shown in the lower graph of Figure 10-9. The intercriterial range is virtually absent, and each of the three functions is approximately linear.

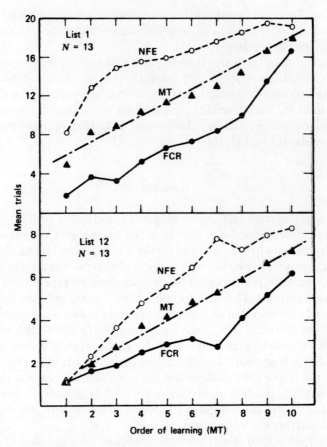

Figure 10-8   Trials to three criteria of learning for ranked items for naive and practiced subjects, after Harcum and Coppage (1965b). Reprinted with permission of publisher.

Thus, for these subjects many items seem to have been learned in "one" trial.

Continuous Presentation

The generality of the present analysis of the learning curves can be assessed by examination of a different serial-learning situation. In the condition of continuous presentation, the interstimulus interval and intertrial interval are set to be equal. Mitchell (1933a,b) was apparently first

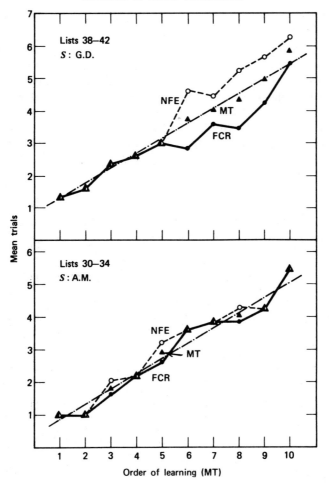

Figure 10-9   Trials to three criteria of learning for ranked items for two highly practiced subjects, after Harcum and Coppage (1965b). Reprinted with permission of publisher.

to use continuous presentation of nonsense syllable lists in serial learning, in which the intertrial interval is equal to the interstimulus interval. She discovered a serial-position curve organized around the syllable that had appeared temporally first. This result has been verified many times (e.g., Lippman & Denny, 1964; Glanzer & Dolinsky, 1965; Coppage & Harcum, 1967). The critical factor seems to be whether or not the temporal primacy, or some other basis of item differentiation, causes the subject to cognize that item as first (Lippman & Denny, 1964). Thus, merely beginning with a particular item distinguishes that item as the beginning of the series.

A study of Coppage and Harcum (1967), which employed a 3-second rate of continuous presentation of nonsense syllables, was discussed earlier. Under four different experimental conditions certain syllables were perceptually isolated by having them typed in a different color of ink. The data for both control and experimental conditions, shown in Figure 10-10, are based on the results of 20 subjects in each group. The two sets of NFE curves show the predicted bow downward toward the end, and each of the two FCR curves conforms to the present hypothesis.

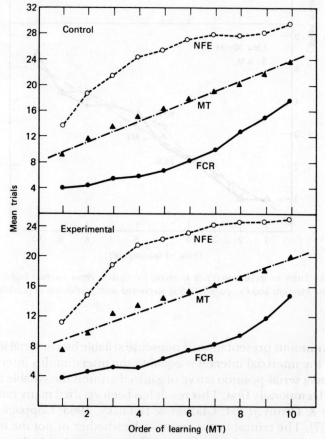

Figure 10-10   Trials to three criteria of learning for ranked items for two isolation conditions, after Coppage and Harcum (1967). Reprinted by permission of the Academic Press.

Harcum, Pschirrer, and Coppage (1968) also presented syllables for continuous serial learning with one of the items perceptually isolated in some lists. The isolation, again achieved by typing one item in red ink in contrast to the black type for the remaining items, occurred at first, third, fifth, seventh, and ninth temporal positions. The results for the control condition, in which no item was isolated, and for the one-isolated condition, in which the temporally first item was isolated, are shown in Figure 10–11. Both sets of data show a close approximation to the predictions from the theory. The midtrial data show the near-linearity, but again with the systematic departures that are now familiar.

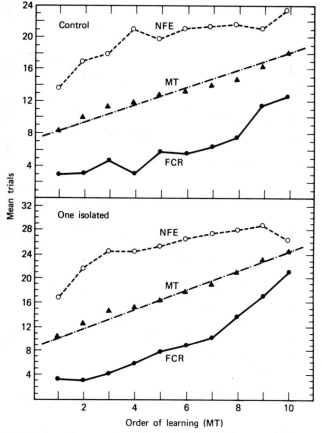

Figure 10-11 Trials to three criteria of learning for ranked items under control and one-isolated conditions, after Harcum, Pschirrer, and Coppage (1968). Reprinted with permission of the publisher.

The results from the Harcum, Pschirrer, and Coppage (1968) experiment for the condition in which the temporally third and fifth items were isolated are shown in Figure 10–12. These curves are similar to those for the control and one-isolated conditions, shown in Figure 10–11, except that the NFE and FCR curves tend to be somewhat straighter. Similar results for the seven- and nine-isolated conditions are shown in Figure 10-13. Although the nine-isolated data are very similar to the data that have previously been described, the seven-isolated results reveal one notable difference. That is, for the seven-isolated condition there is evi-

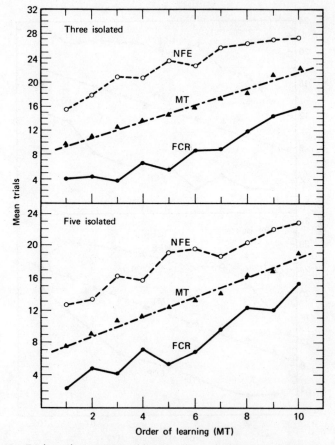

Figure 10-12 Trials to three criteria of learning for ranked items under three-isolated and five-isolated conditions, after Harcum, Pschirrer, and Coppage (1968). Reprinted with permission of the publisher.

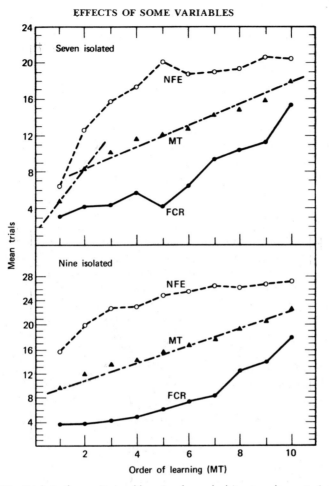

Figure 10-13 Trials to three criteria of learning for ranked items under seven-isolated and nine-isolated conditions, after Harcum, Pschirrer, and Coppage (1968). Reprinted with permission of the publisher.

dence for the slower anchor-learning phase in the acquisition of the first-learned item (Harcum & Coppage, 1965b). Nevertheless, the overall similarity of the learning curves for seven-isolated and other conditions is in contrast to the serial-position curves (Harcum, Pschirrer, & Coppage, 1968). These curves showed a greater primacy effect for the seventh temporal position under the seven-isolated condition, compared to the greater primacy effects at other temporal positions for the other conditions. Presumably, it was harder to form an anchor when the seventh position was isolated in a series of ten items.

Short Intertrial Interval

A study by Harcum (1973) employing an intertrial interval shorter than interstimulus interval was described in Chapter 7. Under several instructional conditions the serial-position curves were organized around the temporally first items as anchors. Nevertheless, this item revealed a marked peak of errors when it followed the shorter interstimulus interval. Harcum concluded that the subject needed more time before the "first" item to "re-set" the cognition of the list from "end" to "beginning." The Jensen plots of percentage of errors, as a function of order of accuracy, are shown in Figure 10-14. Each function, and especially the one for Experiment 3, shows the slight, but consistent, departures from the straight line that is visually fitted through the data.

The FCR, middle-trial, and NFE data combined for all groups in this study with shorter interstimulus interval are shown in Figure 10-15. The upper panel gives the results for the condition in which the shorter interval followed the fourteenth item (i.e., at the ends), and the lower panel gives the results for the condition in which the shorter interval followed the seventh item (i.e., in the middle). The data of both panels reflect obvious and excellent correspondence to the theoretical prediction.

In order to assess the possibility that the smooth sigmoidal curve of middle-trial data was not an artifact of differential weighting of fast and slow learners in different segments of the acquisition process, the data from shorter interstimulus interval were re-analyzed after all results were converted from trials-to-criterion to percentages-of-trials-to-criterion for each subject across all three instructional conditions, and then averaged. The results for the stimulus condition only, in which the shorter interstimulus interval appeared after the fourteenth temporal position, shown in Figure 10-16, give an even smoother appearance to the results. The middle-trial data, represented by the open triangles, is very nicely sigmoid. The error data are also illustrated in this figure for comparison to the middle-trial data. The closed triangles represent the mean of the percentage of trials on which the subject made an error, plus a constant of one to compensate for the fact that the subject could not make an error on the criterion trials. Not only is the ranking of the items identical for these two measures, the actual values of the individual pairs of data-points are very close.

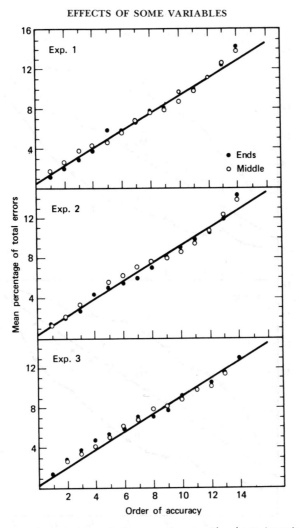

Figure 10-14   Errors for ranked items in three experiments with a shorter interstimulus interval, from Harcum (1973). Reprinted with permission of the publisher.

List Criterion

A question has been raised above about the effect of the criterion of learning the complete list on the measures of learning individual items—particularly on the NFE criterion—and thus on the intercriterial range at the end of learning. As the criterion for learning the complete list

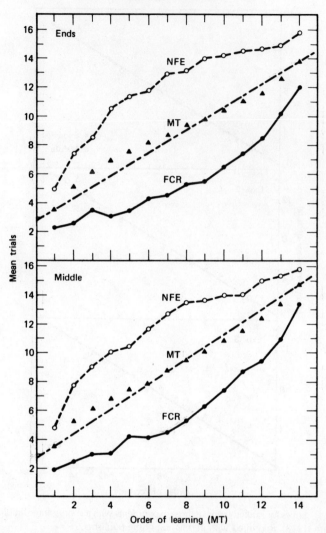

Figure 10-15   Trials to three criteria of learning for ranked items with a shorter interstimulus interval, after Harcum (1973). Reprinted with permission of the publisher.

is approached, the number of trials for which it is possible for the subject to make an error on a previously learned item is progressively reduced, as was mentioned above. Thus, a bending together of the FCR and NFE curves at the end of learning may result from the fact that the subject learned the complete list to a stringent criterion.

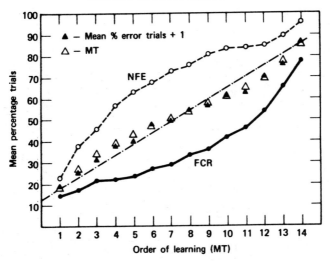

Figure 10-16 Comparison of trials to three criteria of learning with error data for ranked items with a shorter interstimulus interval, after Harcum (1973). Reprinted with permission of the publisher.

Evidence against this possibility is provided in Figure 10–17. The data in Figure 10–17 show the results of treating the data of 12-item lists with paced and unpaced presentation (Harcum & Coppage, 1969) for each subject as though the experiment were terminated after a selected number of trials. The larger the number of trials that are used, the greater the number of data-points, of course. Increasing the number of trials that are examined eventually leads, however, to the necessity for discarding the results for those faster-learning subjects who learned the list in fewer trials. The upper-left panel shows that when the data are treated as though learning were terminated after eight trials, the maximum number of points that could be used for all 12 subjects was five. The ordinate represents the means of errors for the individual items, and the abscissa represents the order of items in terms of accuracy, starting with the first item to produce at least one error, and ending with the last item for which the subject made at least one correct response. Thus, the shapes of the curves should be independent of whether the subject showed a memory span at the beginning of the list, or a ceiling effect that was related to complete failure of accurate performance.

Both functions in the upper-left panel of Figure 10–17 are sufficiently close to a linear progression to prove the point. So also are the functions in the upper-right and lower-left panels, in which the number of usable points has been increased at the cost of losing subjects. In the lower-right

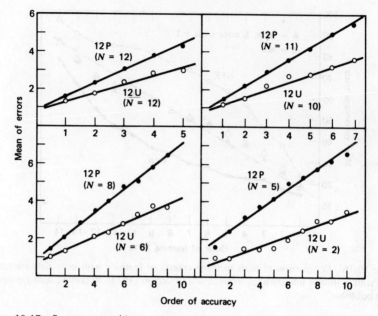

Figure 10-17   Errors to an arbitrary criterion of learning for 12 paced and unpaced items ranked by accuracy, after Harcum and Coppage (1969). Copyright © (1969) by the American Psychological Association. Reprinted by permission.

panel where the number of subjects has decreased to five and two, respectively, for the paced and unpaced conditions, the paced data reveal a definite downward bending at the end. Examination of the data for individual subjects shows that this bowing is due to the results for one subject. The apparent linearity for the data in the other panels occurred because the data of another subject, which showed the opposite direction of bowing and which could not be included in the final panel, had been compensating in the earlier analyses for the results of this subject. The data for the unpaced condition in the lower-right panel appear more or less linear, with any trend in these data toward an upward turning later.

The data of Figure 10–17 thus imply that the apparent linearity of the relationship between errors and order of accuracy for items is not an artifact of a fixed criterion for learning. That is, the general linearity of the progression for errors results from self-rectifying processes at each stage of acquisition. It is not the result of some artifact that was related to the fact that the subjects had learned to a stringent criterion for the complete list. The above analysis does suggest, however, that the relationship is not necessarily linear for each subject.

AN EXPERIMENTAL TEST

An unpublished experiment from this laboratory was designed to evaluate the effects on the FCR, middle-trial, and NFE curves of using a very stringent criterion of learning. This stringent criterion would permit the subject to make additional errors for the last-learned item, after its individual criterion had been reached. Other variables investigated were the associability and discriminability of the items.

The goal of the experiment was to examine the shapes of the respective learning curves, as predicted from the theory. A cautionary note is necessary, however, since the Jensen plot does not always yield a straight line. In an unpublished study, Jensen found that a series that is composed of a familiar, known population of items produces a positively accelerated curve.* Therefore, the shapes of the FCR and NFE curves would presumably be changed accordingly.

Method

There were four stimulus conditions in the experiment: Hi Tri: high-associability trigrams consisting of ten three-letter words with an associability rating of 100% on Archer's (1960) list of CVC trigrams; Lo Tri: low-associability trigrams consisting of ten CVC trigrams with an associability rating under 9%; Hi Vo: high-associability vowels consisting of the five vowels appearing once as a capital letter and once as a lower-case letter (the only list which consisted of one-letter items rather than trigrams); and Lo Vo: low-associability vowels consisting of the five vowels flanked once by Z's and once by Q's to make ten CVC trigrams.

Each list was preceded by a centered asterisk followed by a spare equal to the interitem space. All but the Hi Vo list were typed exclusively in capital letters. A list was presented in a memory drum at a 4-second rate with an intertrial interval of 16 seconds, until the subject learned it to a criterion of five consecutive errorless trials.

For both Hi Tri and Lo Tri lists the subjects were told that they were to learn a list of ten three-letter items, and given standard instructions for serial-anticipation learning. They spelled their responses. They were also told to keep doing the best they could, until they were told to stop, so that we could learn whether or not a perfect level of performance could be maintained.

The instructions for Hi Vo and Lo Vo included an exact explanation of the items to be learned. Also, with these two conditions each subject was

*Personal communication from Professor A.R. Jensen.

presented with a different order of the items than what he would learn immediately afterwards, and asked to guess what each item would be while the item before it was visible or, in the case of the first item, while the asterisk was visible. Then the drum was changed, and the list to be learned was presented with the same instructions as had been given to the subjects in the Hi Tri and Lo Tri conditions.

Results and Discussion

The FCR, midtrial, and NFE curves for 100% and 9% associability of syllables are shown in Figures 10-18 and 10-19, respectively. Whereas the low-associative items produced in Figure 10-19 the usual near-linear middle-trial plot, the high-association items in Figure 10-18 show a positive acceleration.

The results for the ten-item lists of vowels rendered to have high or low discriminability by the addition of flanking letters are shown in Figures 10-20 and 10-21, respectively. Again the items of low discriminability show the near-linear middle-trial curve, and the items of high discriminability show the middle-trial function with positive acceleration. These findings show that the middle-trial plot does not always produce

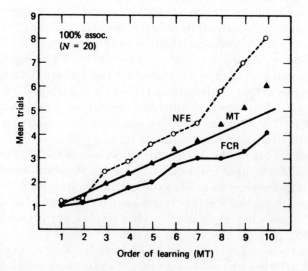

Figure 10-18   Trials to three criteria with high-meaningful items learned to a stringent criterion, ranked by accuracy.

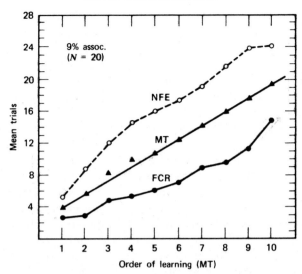

Figure 10-19   Trials to three criteria with low-meaningful items learned to a stringent criterion, ranked by accuracy.

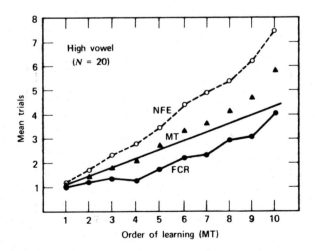

Figure 10-20   Trials to three criteria with high-discriminable vowels learned to a stringent criterion, ranked by accuracy.

the near-linear curve. Similarly, the Jensen plot for these data shows the positive acceleration for the items of high discriminability.

The size of the intercriterial range as a function of serial position of items is shown in Figures 10–22 and 10–23 for the vowels and trigrams, respectively. The tendency for each curve to bow up about the middle of the series is obvious. This range, therefore, is most likely a manifestation of the associative interference within the list (Harcum, 1969). Hovland (1938c) and Shipley (1939) suggest that the range-of-oscillation measure resembles the serial position of total errors and therefore is an indicator of the amount of interference. Although Shipley (1939) did not analyze his serial-position results in any detail, the results did indicate fewer oscillations of correct anticipation and failures of anticipation at the ends of the series than about the middle, for series of various lengths. Rehula (1960) also states that response oscillation from omission errors to correct responses is greater in the middle of the series, and least at the ends.

The Jensen plots for the first several items learned in the above study of learning to a stringent criterion are shown in Figures 10–24 and 10–25 for the high- and low-associative items, respectively. While no definitive statements can be made, no marked or consistent tendencies toward curvature are obvious.

The systematic departures from the straight line in the Jensen plot (errors) or the middle-trial curve in these studies represent the classical sigmoid curve of learning. The subjects are learning the easy items first

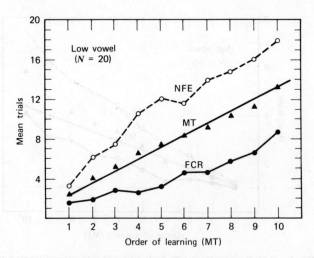

Figure 10-21   Trials to three criteria of learning with low-discriminable vowels learned to a stringent criterion, ranked by accuracy.

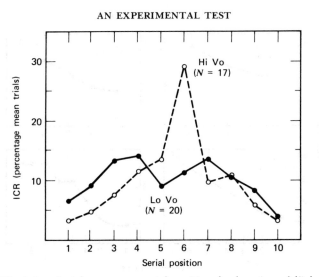

Figure 10-22 Intercriterial range per serial position for learning of high- and low-discriminable vowels.

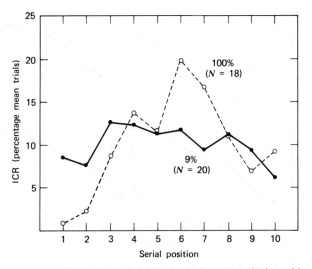

Figure 10-23 Intercriterial range per serial position for learning of high- and low-meaningful syllables.

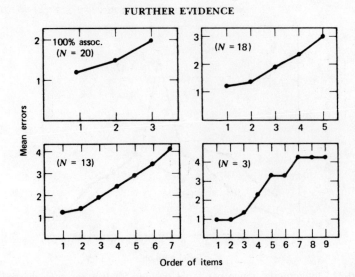

Figure 10-24   Errors for items ranked by accuracy to an arbitrary criterion with high-meaningful syllables learned to a stringent criterion.

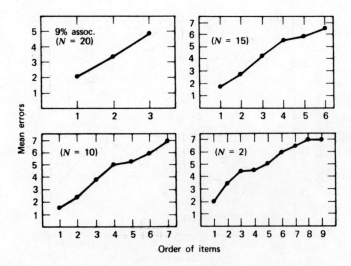

Figure 10-25   Errors for items ranked by accuracy to an arbitrary criterion with low-meaningful items learned to a stringent criterion.

and establishing an anchor. Toward the end they encounter the problem of achieving a criterion that is close to perfection.

A REPRESENTATIVE EXAMPLE

The data that have been analyzed to support the predicted shapes of FCR, middle-trial, and NFE curves have been obtained in this laboratory, and used because of their availability, of course. It should therefore be instructive to determine whether or not this analysis can be applied successfully to other serial-learning results. Fortunately, Deese (1958) supplied the data of an individual subject in order to illustrate the serial-position results. The data given by Deese (1958, p. 168) for an individual subject are reduced to TSC, NFE and middle-trial curves in Figure 10–26. Since the data represent the effort of only one subject, the curve for the lower criterion, particularly, is rather irregular. Nevertheless, the middle-trial curve is relatively straight; the visually-fitted line through the middle-trial points appears to be about as good a fit as any other simple function. Of great interest is the shape of the intercriterial envelope. Although for six items the upper and lower criteria were reached on the same trial, these

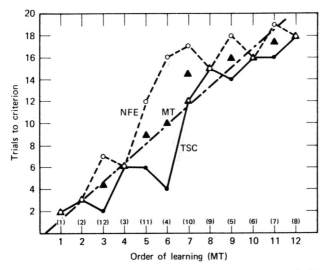

Figure 10-26   Trials to three criteria of learning by one subject for items ranked by accuracy. From *The Psychology of Learning* by James Deese. Copyright © (1958) by the McGraw-Hill Book Company, Inc. Used with permission of McGraw-Hill Book Company.

items tended to be the first or the last learned. The widest part of the intercriterial envelope is about the fifth, sixth, and seventh items learned, using the middle trials as the basis of ordering.

The middle-trial and mean-errors results, in terms of Jensen plots, for the Deese (1958, p. 168) data are given in Figure 10-27 in order to compare the performance in terms of errors and in terms of the middle-trial criterion. The solid circles represent the numbers of errors, with a constant of 1 added to compensate for the fact that an error is never possible when the criterion of learning an item is reached. The open circles represent the middle-trial data based on the FCR criterion. The order of accuracy is determined on the basis of ranking in terms of the errors, eliminating the possibility for inversions in the succession of solid points, of course. Nevertheless, the ranking of the middle-trial points is quite consistent with the error ranking, and shows only two inversions of minor degree. The absolute value of the points are also quite close in most cases, being identical in five instances. These data provide further evidence that the middle-trial curve is essentially equivalent to a Jensen plot of errors in serial-learning data. Also they show the generality of the shapes of curves for FCR and NFE criteria of plotting.

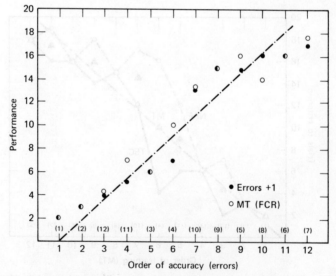

Figure 10-27 Comparison of errors and middle-trial criterion for items ranked by accuracy for one subject, after Deese (1958). Copyright © (1958) by the McGraw-Hill Book Company, Inc. Used with permission of McGraw-Hill Book Company.

Evidence for the oval shape of the intercriterial envelope can be drawn from the study of Malmo and Amsel (1948) who studied the "extratask" factor of clinical anxiety on rote serial learning, with emphasis on the relation to interference theory. On the basis of the hypothesis that frontal lobectomies increase susceptibility to associative interference, these researchers predicted that frontal-lobe patients would produce greater bowing of the curves. Although this prediction would seem to follow from the concept of competing intralist interference, as proposed by Harcum and Coppage (1969), Malmo and Amsel arrive at it differently but, ironically, with an assumption similar to one proposed by Harcum and Coppage (1969). They propose that "anxiety-produced interference" is a general characteristic of anxious patients, but that such interferences can be reduced by voluntary effort. The lobectomized patients were presumed to have more (residual) anxiety than a matched control group—primarily members of the hospital staff.

Apparently the interference caused by anxiety can at first be overcome by the increased motivation to learn the items at the beginning of the list, but this is effective only on the first trial for the patients. Therefore, the advantage of primacy is reduced for these subjects, producing a greater deficit for them at the beginning of the list. According to Malmo and Amsel, these greater initial failures cause an increase of motivation for the patients, accounting for the lack of deficit for the items at the end of the list. Lists of eight nonsense syllables were learned to a criterion of one perfect recitation. Results in terms of errors of anticipation conformed to predictions set forth by the researchers. The patients were significantly

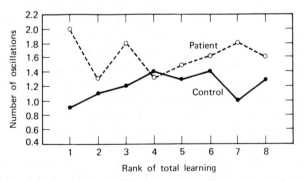

Figure 10-28   Oscillations per item ranked by accuracy for patients and control subjects, after Malmo and Amsel (1948). Copyright © (1948) by the American Psychological Association. Reprinted by permission.

inferior at the first temporal positions, but not at the last positions. Whereas the shape of the serial-position curve of errors was asymmetrically bowed, as is typical of the serial-position result, the curve for patients was more nearly symmetrical. Malmo and Amsel contrast this result with that of Hovland (1938c) for distributed and massed practice in which the largest absolute difference between curves occurred at about the sixt.. position in an eight-item series—where the difficulty in both conditions was greatest. These researchers argue that the differences in results for the different comparisons reflect differences between intraserial interference and anxiety-induced interference, respectively. Specifically, the massed practice increased intraserial interference where presumably this interference is greatest, whereas the clinical anxiety produced greater interferences at the beginning of the series. Malmo and Amsel further showed that the range of oscillations between first success and last failure was generally greater for the patients, greatest at first and second items. But Figure 10–28 shows most oscillations midway in order of learning.

Malmo and Amsel (1948) also showed that the relative primacy effect increased for the control subjects across the four lists, using as an index the number of errors at Position One relative to the average of Positions Four, Five, and Six. This value remained at about 50% for the clinical group, but dropped from about 30% to 14% for the control subjects. The authors conclude that this result indicates greater adaptation by control subjects to distraction in the experiment produced by their own anxiety.

The learning curves for the lobectomized and control subjects, plotted in the manner of Melton (1936), were essentially parallel with a slight superiority consistently favoring the control subjects. An exception to this occurred for the final criterion, however, in which the curves suddenly diverged. Malmo and Amsel (1948) conclude that this divergence was caused by a sudden increase in anxiety by the clinical patients with the realization that the task could be complete with good performance. This appears likely; also there appears to be a slight end-spurt for the control subjects, probably an artifact of the lax criterion of learning.

According to the theory of Harcum and Coppage (1969) the lobectomized patients of Malmo and Amsel (1948) were less organized in using the temporal structuring of the task, and therefore were less able to establish an anchor for the learning. Therefore, the linear-strategy component is less marked, and the shape of the curve determined more by the intralist interference component.

The presence of oscillation in item-retention is obviously a fact of serial learning. It is still an open question, however, whether or not this oscillation is caused by fluctuations in "habit strength," by field effects in stimulation, or by differential effectiveness of retrieval cues. These possibilities are certainly not mutually exclusive.

CONCLUSIONS

Evidence for the present argument has been obtained from re-analysis of data from this laboratory, from new studies designed to test these hypotheses, and from analysis of other, independent data. The evidence has been uniformly positive; the experimental situations have been sufficiently diverse so that the effects appear to be quite general.

Thus, the evidence gives substantial support to the present argument for an item-sequence strategy in serial acquisition. Although elegant curve-fitting procedures were not used to validate precise curve shape, better yet, there was a theoretical basis for predicting the general shape of the curves. Of even stronger thrust, however, is the consistent departure from the predicted linear Jensen plot, which was not expected initially, but that nevertheless emerged from the theoretical propositions.

SUMMARY

This chapter described the results of re-analyses of different sets of data to determine the shapes of the learning curves for different criteria of learning. The results consistently support the predictions. An experiment expressly designed to test the theory was described. The results of this experiment consistently supported the predictions, except for the special case when the population of items is already known to the subject and he must merely learn the serial order.

An initially unexpected result, but one that is a direct consequence of the theory, is that the learning curve of errors reveals a slight systematic departure from a straight line, taking the classical sigmoid shape.

CHAPTER

11

FINAL
INTERPRETATION

The first task of this chapter is to reconcile the learning curve, as conventionally plotted, with the "real" curve as proposed in Chapter 9. As Harcum and Coppage (1969) maintained, an adequate theory of serial learning must include a treatment of the fate of the different types of error over trials, as well as over serial positions.

A second goal is to integrate the discussion of learning curves into a general theory of serial acquisition. Such a general theory includes a treatment of the macroprocesses in terms of gross strategies of attack. It also includes the microprocesses that determine the associative and retrieval mechanisms of acquisition and retention.

CURVE OF SERIAL LEARNING

The shape of the serial-learning curve is at issue here. The previous evidence and discussion surely indicates that one shape of curve would not apply to all conditions, all criteria, and all types of response.

The Vincent plot of serial acquisition over trials, shown in Figure 9–2 from unpublished data of Jensen, was shown to reveal a near-linear

378

function. Nevertheless, there is evidence for a slight negative acceleration in that plot. Other evidence from this laboratory for nonlinearity of the Vincent plot of learning curves for errors creates a slight problem for the present theory, in view of the relatively linear "real" curves, as seen in Jensen plots and in the middle-trial plots of Chapter 9. Although the Jensen plots of serial acquisition are essentially linear, in a number of cases the last item or two revealed an ascending tail. This may be related to some artifact of reaching the criterion. The tendency is greater in the data from this laboratory, because the first criterion trial was included in the summation of the data. Moreover, learning curves for known populations of items were shown in Chapter 9 to have strong negative acceleration.

Vincent plots of serial learning for 12-item paced and unpaced lists of trigrams from the study of Harcum and Coppage (1969) are shown in Figure 11–1. Although the segments of the curve to the seventh tenth have only a slight bow with negative acceleration, the segments from seventh to last tenth show a marked flattening, so that the overall appearance of each curve is decidedly nonlinear. Vincent plots for serial learning of 16-item lists of trigrams with paced and unpaced presentation are shown in Figure 11–2. These plots show more consistent negative acceleration of the curves over each tenth of the learning process. This supports the results of Waugh (1963) for serial anticipation and serial recall. The negative acceleration is not great, of course, but its existence is undeniable.

The next objective is, then, to determine which factors tend to rectify

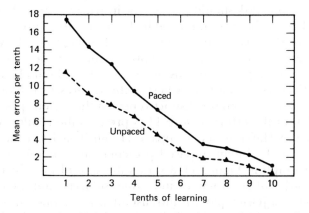

Figure 11-1   Vincent plots for learning 12 paced and unpaced trigrams, after Harcum and Coppage (1969). Copyright © (1969) by the American Psychological Association. Reprinted by permission.

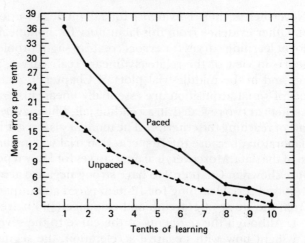

Figure 11-2   Vincent plots for learning 16 paced and unpaced trigrams, after Harcum and Coppage (1969). Copyright © (1969) by the American Psychological Association. Reprinted by permission.

the serial-learning data in terms of trials. Part of the solution, at least, seems to lie in an analysis of the different types of error.

TYPES OF ERRORS

An examination of the learning curves for the various types of errors in the serial-learning task should prove to be instructive, since these different types of errors have been related by Harcum and Coppage (1969) to the effects of the factors that are illustrated in Figure 5–3. Also these factors presumably determine the shape of the serial-learning curves. The errors resulting from intralist intrusions (ILI) should be related to the distinctiveness of position, whereas the failures to respond (FTR) should be related to both the distinctiveness of the various positions and the direction of the effort. Figure 11–3 presents the results of such an analysis of the Harcum and Coppage (1969) data for 12-item paced presentation and 12-item unpaced presentation of nonsense syllables. The upper graph in Figure 11–3 shows the sum of intralist intrusions ranked in order of accuracy for individual subjects, and then summed over subjects—a Jensen plot for intralist intrusions alone. Instead of the usual straight line for totals of all errors, both curves show negative acceleration of the learning. Intralist intrusions are few at the beginning of learning because the subject must learn to make errors of this

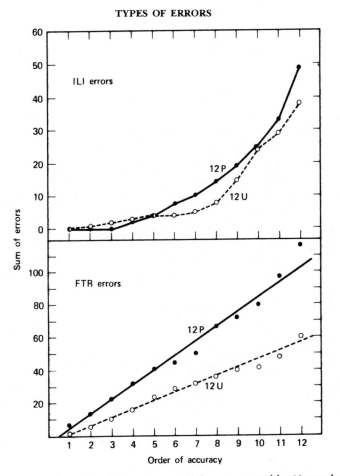

Figure 11-3 Jensen plots of intralist intrusions and failures to respond for 12 paced and un-paced trigrams, after Harcum and Coppage (1969). Copyright © (1969) by the American Psychological Association. Reprinted by permission.

type. Gibson (1940) postulated that a tendency to give an incorrect response tends to block the elicitation of the correct response. Thus, overt errors serve as an index of generalization during learning. Thus, she argues that generalization (overt error) increases at first during learning, reaches a maximum, and declines with further practice. This prediction was confirmed in Gibson's (1942) later study of paired-associate learning.

Since the items at first-learned positions are presumably the most distinctive, and less subject to associative interference, they tend to be free of errors both before and after the first-correct criterion is reached. The accelerated increase of intralist intrusions is consistent with the prediction for associative confusion drawn from the position curve in Figure 5–3, and described by the curve of first correct responses in Figure 9–17. As can be predicted from the theoretical plots in Figure 9–17, after the first-correct criterion is reached, most of the intralist intrusions occur for those items that are acquired about midway through the learning process. On the other hand, for those items that are acquired near the end of learning, most of the intralist intrusions occur before the first-correct criterion is reached. These conclusions vary somewhat, of course, depending upon the conditions of practice, task difficulty, and so forth.

The function of failures to respond in the lower graph of Figure 11–3 reveals Jensen plots that are equivalent to results from the totals of all types of error. The functions are essentially linear, but also show evidence for the usual minor variations from linearity. This supports the contention of Harcum and Coppage (1969) that the failures to respond reflect the overall strategy of the subject in terms of the sequence of attempting items.

The previous argument was supported by further analysis of data from a study reported in Chapter 7 (Harcum, 1975). Serial learning of a ten-item homogeneous list of trigrams was compared to the learning of ordered series of trigrams of varying association value. Jensen plots of the results for all errors under each condition are presented in Figure 11–4. The usual linear result for each group is obvious, along with the substantial difference in errors favoring the heterogeneous items arranged in

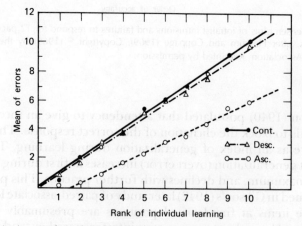

Figure 11-4   Jensen plots of total errors for homogeneous and organized heterogeneous trigrams, after Harcum (1975). Reprinted with permission of the publisher.

ascending (Asc.) order of difficulty. The omission errors of Harcum (1975) reveal the linear Jensen plots, in Figure 11–5, which is also consistent with the previous argument. Therefore, the failures to respond reflect the overall strategy—including both primattensity and end-segregation components. On the other hand, the results for commission errors reveal, as before, a bowed Jensen plot, as can be seen in Figure 11–6. Although the bowing is not as strong as for the Harcum and Coppage (1969) intralist intrusions, it is clearly present; the presence of any extralist intrusions would tend to reduce the bowing when all commission errors are plotted. Thus, the intruding errors increase at an ascending rate as the rank of accuracy is greater for items ranked in terms of intruding errors. The last item on this ranking is, however, not likely to be the last learned item, as examination of Figure 9–17 indicates; the intercriterial range is also small for this item.

Therefore, the order of items in terms of failures to respond is not highly correlated with the order for intralist intrusions. This result can be seen in Figure 11–7, in which the abscissa represents the order of accuracy for the particular subject for specific items according to failures to respond, and the ordinate represents the sums of intralist intrusions for these same items. For the 12-item paced condition, particularly, the number of intralist intrusions first increases and then decreases over the course of learning. This relation corresponds to the logical argument for this distribution of errors—the intralist intrusions should first increase as

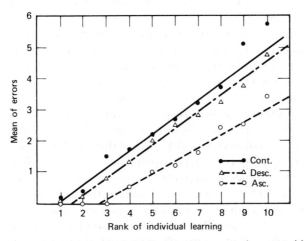

Figure 11-5   Jensen plots of omission errors for homogeneous and organized heterogenous trigrams, after Harcum (1975). Reprinted with permission of the publisher.

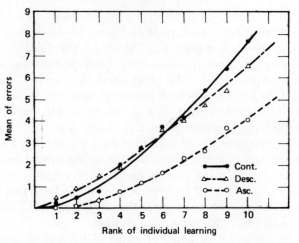

Figure 11-6   Jensen plots of commission errors for homogeneous and organized heterogeneous trigrams, after Harcum (1975). Reprinted with permission of the publisher.

the subject learns to differentiate items, and decrease as the total list approaches criterion. This function also conforms to the result of Slamecka (1964), except for the upward swing for the last several points on each curve, which is probably caused by the influence of the omission-error basis for the ranking of items. The true shape of the curve for intralist intrusions, with respect to the progress of learning, should be more clearly seen when plotted in terms of trials instead of the ascending order of errors.

Theoretical learning curves as a function of trials for errors of different types are illustrated in Figure 11–8. Here the curve of failures to respond shows an initial rapid drop and negative acceleration. This corresponds to the shape for the FCR curve in Figure 9–17, predicted from the theoretical factors in Figure 5–3. The curve in Figure 11–8 which is labeled EWR, referring to emitted wrong responses, represents the sum of intralist intrusions and extralist intrusions for each trial. This, of course, is the total of all commission errors. Addition of the failures-to-respond and the emitted-wrong-responses curves produces a virtually linear function. Nevertheless, it shows the departures from linearity that have been noted before for the middle-trial criterion and for the totals of errors in Jensen plots. Thus, the tendency toward rectification of the failure-to-respond curve of errors into the all-errors curve, is accomplished by the commission errors, which show a virtually symmetrical rise and fall as a function of trials.

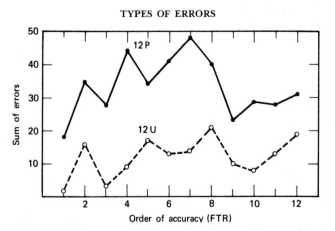

Figure 11-7 Intralist intrusion errors for 12 paced and unpaced items ranked by accuracy of omissions, after Harcum and Coppage (1969). Copyright © (1969) by the American Psychological Association. Reprinted by permission.

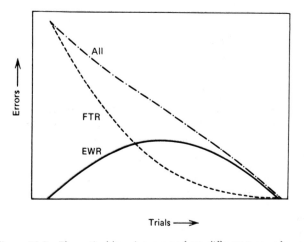

Figure 11-8 Theoretical learning curves from different types of errors.

The theoretical argument in Figure 11–8 can be tested against the available data in the Harcum and Coppage (1969) study. Empirical data for the two subjects who learned the list in fewer than ten trials are shown in Figure 11–9. Since these subjects learned the syllables very quickly there is no initial rise in emitted wrong responses. For Subject 61, in the upper graph of Figure 11–9, all three functions for the 12-item paced

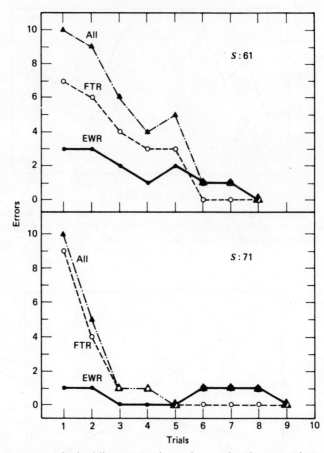

Figure 11-9   Learning for the different types of errors for two "fast" learners with 12 paced items, after Harcum and Coppage (1969). Copyright © (1969) by the American Psychological Association. Reprinted by permission.

condition are approximately linear. The results for Subject 71, in the lower graph, are nearly linear for three trials, but then performance falls just short of perfection for a number of trials, resulting in a decidedly nonlinear progression overall. These results for the two fast learners in the 12-item paced condition are consistent with the Jensen plots for these subjects, that were shown in Figures 9–11 and 9–12. The course of acquisition was represented by a generally linear progression, except for the last-learned syllable for Subject 71.

The two subjects who learned rapidly did not provide a very comprehensive view of the learning process because the acquisition was ac-

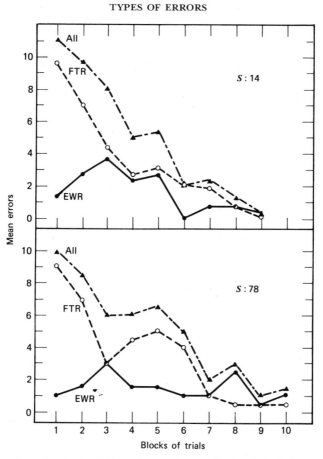

Figure 11-10   Learning for the different types of errors for two "slow" learners with 12
paced items, after Harcum and Coppage (1969). Copyright © (1969) by the American Psychological Association. Reprinted by permission.

complished too quickly; the slower learners should give a more complete
picture of the process. Such illustrations are seen in Figure 11–10 in the
results for the two slowest learners of Harcum and Coppage (1969) under
the 12-item paced condition. The abscissa for the upper graph represents
blocks of three trials, and the abscissa of the lower graph represents blocks
of two trials. Both ordinates represent means of errors per trial. The
results of both subjects conform generally to the predictions in Figure
11–8. The emitted wrong responses show the initial rise, and then fall to
about zero; there is a bit of a tail on the distribution before it finally

reaches zero. Since the failure-to-respond curves drop at ever decreasing rates, the curve for all errors is more nearly linear.

Although this analysis has been successful in handling the data of selected individuals, a broader test should be valuable. The results for all subjects who required ten or more trials to learn the 12-item paced list are shown in Figure 11-11. The abscissa represents Vincent tenths of the learning trials, and the ordinate represents the percentage of the total number of errors that were produced in each tenth of learning. The emitted wrong responses show the predicted increase and decrease, and the failures to respond show the negatively accelerated drop. These two curves tend to produce a curve for all errors that approaches linearity, but the rectification is not perfect. It should be noted, however, that the Jensen plot of the total errors did show relatively too many errors for the last item learned, relative to extrapolation from a linear progression. The Waugh (1963) study was also cited as showing near-linear curves, but with slight negative acceleration. Therefore, the results for the group of subjects supports the analyses of individual subjects.

Tulving's (1964) logarithmic learning curve for free recall of words would perhaps similarly be rectified if the possibility for position (commission) errors were present. This would seem to be a fundamental difference between free recall and serial recall.

MEANING OF MIDDLE-TRIAL CURVE

Although the middle-trial curve and the Jensen plot of errors produce essentially the same information, the two curves do not exhibit exactly the same ranking of items. Sometimes there is a wide intercriterial range between the FCR criterion and the point of NFE that produces a larger middle-trial value, but there are not many errors within the intercriterial range. In fact, after the trial of the FCR there may be no errors over several trials until the last trial before the NFE trial. It is possible that the FCR criterion reflects more faithfully a position-based strategy, whereas other factors (e.g., difficulty in encoding syllables) exert a greater effect on the NFE criterion. Evidence for this comes from the fact that the FCR curve corresponds to the shape of the Jensen plot for intralist intrusions, that seem to be more closely related to the confusion of location among items (Harcum & Coppage, 1969). Therefore, it is possible that the order of items on the NFE and middle-trial curve represents other bases of strategy in the acquisition process, whereas the FCR curve follows primarily the function of distinctiveness associated with serial-position. Thus, individual differences should be greater in the determination of the order of items by the NFE criterion.

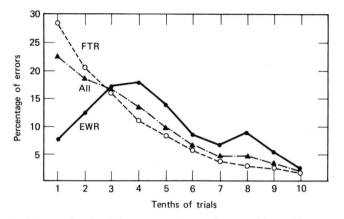

Figure 11-11 Vincent plots for different types of errors for ten subjects with 12 paced items, after Harcum and Coppage (1969). Copyright © (1969) by the American Psychological Association. Reprinted by permission.

The FCR curve of acquisition would predict an excessively peaked serial-position curve, even more than that of the strategy-based curve, if the subjects' strategies were perfectly consistent. The empirical data of Hovland (1940b) and of Postman and Schwartz (1964) for first-correct trials per serial position show curves of rather conventional shape, however. This is presumably due to departures from a consistent progressive sequence for individual subjects, and to variation in acquisition sequences among different subjects.

Oscillation

Whether or not associations are formed in a single trial there can be no doubt that trials of correct and incorrect responses are interleaved. This would be expected on the basis that the perceptual world is changing in a dynamic way. Stochastic considerations would suggest that the necessary stimulus events for a correct response may or may not occur on a given trial (for example, Atkinson, 1957).

The intercriterial range represents what Hull et al. (1940) called "behavioral oscillation." Hull et al., (1940) and Hovland (1940b) found that there were more oscillations at the center of lists. This would correspond generally, but not exactly, to the size of the intercriterial range. The range would be small at the beginning of learning, because these items tend to be near the ends of the series, and their positions are more salient. The apparent oscillation would be greater for the items about the middle of the series because there would be more confusion about location, although the item identities would be learned. This would be consistent with Slamecka's (1964) proposal of emitted, but mislocalized, responses.

Apparently different results were obtained by Workman (1951). He discovered that the oscillation interval (between first success and last failure) was greatest for the perceptually first items, and least for the last-learned items. This result is not given much weight by Workman because the subjects often became disturbed toward the end of the task, particularly those who had not learned by the fiftieth trial. Sometimes a subject would just cease trying for a trial or two, and then move on quickly to perfect performance. Therefore, the serial-position curve to last failures would be essentially a horizontal line.

The findings of Buxton and Ross (1949), however, argue against the notion of oscillation as mislocalization. They found more oscillation in retention for spelling of syllables. This indicates a more sensitive test of learning, rather than of position identification.

MACROPROCESSES OF ACQUISITION

As stated previously, for present purposes it is not critical whether or not Jensen plots of middle-trial curves are actually linear. It is, however, important to evaluate the importance of the exaggerated departures from linearity for the results of the last several items in the Jensen plots of different sets of data, and from the Vincentized learning curve of 12-item paced lists for which the data are given in Figure 11–11. The present argument is that this "tail" on the data in the acquisition process is due to the stringency of the learning criterion that was used in the collection of these data. Presumably, an increase in the stringency of the criterion for learning the complete list would add differentially more errors to the totals for last-learned items. Thus, the overall straightness of the functions would tend to break down as learning approached a criterion of mastery for the list. This reasoning implies that the usual apparent straightness of the acquisition functions is not an artifact of an arbitrary criterion for mastery of the series. On the contrary, it implies that learning to a criterion of mastery for the total series often adds a "tail" of errors at the end of learning, especially for the last-learned items. Therefore, when the subject requires a few extra trials to achieve perfection on the total task, the resulting errors often occur for the last-learned item—and the "true" serial-learning curve is consequently distorted.

Stimulus for Serial Learning

The present theoretical treatment transcends the issue of whether the process of serial learning is chaining (Ebbinghaus, 1913) or position learning (Young, 1968). The two mechanisms that are illustrated in Figure 5–3 correspond in a general way to the two proposed stimuli for association—on the basis of the one factor the position of the item determines the order for forming the associations, and on the basis of the second factor the preceding items are the stimulus for association.

The results of Battig, Brown, and Schild (1964) support the above conclusion. They found differential effects of position and sequence as a basis of association for end versus middle items. The use of position is greater for the end items, that are more easily discriminated, whereas the items at the middle of the series tend to be associated to "complex multiple-item associative units." This is consistent with the hierarchical-configuration hypothesis proposed in Chapter 4.

Relation to Perception

The foregoing discussion indicated that the acquisition of multiple-element arrays is affected by the subjects' strategy in organizing the material for storage in memory. The particular details of stimulus presentation or sensory capacity are less important (Harcum, 1957a; Broadbent, 1958). The case for the information-translation hypothesis (Harcum, 1967b) would be strengthened if it were now possible to explain how the present analysis of acquisition curves could be applied to the pattern-perception task. A demonstration of the relevance of the strategy mechanism to both the serial-learning and the pattern-perception tasks would indicate the general applicability of this approach. Unfortunately, there seems to be no way to perform for the perceptual task any operations paralleling the attainment of FCR and NFE criteria for serial-anticipation learning. The total information-processing operation is completed in a second, or fraction of a second, sometimes in a single tachistoscopic exposure, with a consequent speeding up and telescoping of the total process. Perhaps covert rehearsal duplicates the learning processes.

The primary evidence to date for the commonality of mechanisms in pattern perception and serial learning has come from the similar effects of manipulation of the same variables. For example, the left-right difference (skew in the distribution of errors) in the pattern-perception task increases with practice (e.g., Harcum, Filion, & Dyer, 1962), as does the skew in the serial-position curve (e.g., Harcum & Coppage, 1965b). The element-isolation variable seems to affect the distribution of errors in the same way (e.g., Harcum, 1965a, b; Jensen, 1962g). Unfortunately, these studies were not conducted on the same subjects.

Figures 11–12 and 11–13 illustrate data from free-recall learning and pattern perception obtained by McKenna and Harcum (1967) from the same nine elderly subjects. Of the nine subjects in the study, four were categorized as a low group on the basis of their poorer performance relative to a high group on the learning task. It is not surprising that these also differed similarly on the perceptual task, as can be seen in Figure 11–13.

The subject brings with him to the task learned tendencies for organizing the material to be learned. This strategy of organization may become modified as he practices in the situation. In the case of tachistoscopic pattern perception, Camp and Harcum (1964) found a change in the distribution of errors among elements of the spatial pattern after practice with a certain type of responding template. From this they inferred that the subjects were changing their strategy of perception in accordance with the requirements of the recording system. Thus, the central analysis mechanism can be affected by the particular attributes of the response. The response system may change even the original process of translation

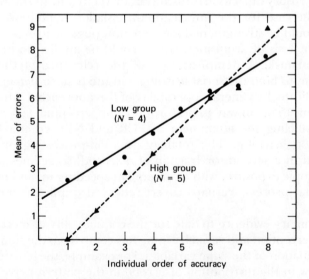

Figure 11-12   Jensen plots of learning by high- and low-performance aged subjects, after McKenna and Harcum (1967). Used by permission of the publisher.

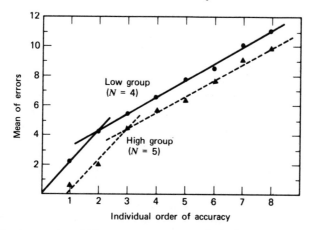

Figure 11-13   Jensen plots of binary-pattern perception by high- and low-performance aged subjects, after McKenna and Harcum (1967). Used by permission of the publisher.

from the stimulus into the conceptual system of the organism. That is, the codification would be consistent with the kind of response to be made. Harcum and Friedman (1963) found that presenting elements of binary patterns in sequence interfered with reproduction of the pattern, presumably because the differential strengths of traces of elements interfered with the mnemonic organization.

If a response configuration that was relatively incompatible with the stimulus configuration were required after stimulation, the information-translation process would be more difficult. The process would continue until an effective coding between stimulus and response configurations was reached, particularly if the subject were not instructed about the responding condition until after the exposure. A compatible stimulus-response relation (Fitts & Seeger, 1953) is one in which the organization of the stimulus configuration requires minimal transformation in order to fit into the response requirement.

If an appropriate code for the stimulus is not available to the subject, he would have difficulty in responding effectively. In such a case the organism would experience great difficulty in producing a quick and accurate response in learning or in perception. If responding conditions are not specified, then the subjects would reproduce the response in a habitual way—a way of least effort. The order of responses would follow the syntax of the language, for example, or some other meaningful organization.

Acquisition Strategy

A postulate for theories of serial learning in terms of a selective strategy of acquisition is that the subject ordinarily begins to form associations about the item that he perceives is the beginning of the series. This postulate of a paralearning factor is supported by a substantial amount of evidence.

General support for the strategy argument comes from studies that show that the subject's approach to the task can be manipulated by the experimenter, and that individual differences among subjects interact with various task parameters. For example, Underwood and Keppel (1963) showed that it was possible to exert some control over how the subject encoded a trigram for later recall. Spielberger and Smith (1966) showed that effects on serial-learning curves of the subject's basic anxiety type interacted with the difficulty of the words and the amount of induced stress in the learning situation.

Asch, Hay, and Diamond (1960), studying distributions of errors for learning items arranged in various spatial configurations, concluded that these distributions of errors are determined by the subject's cognition of which item constitutes the beginning of the series. Coppage and Harcum (1967) concurred with this conclusion on the basis of alleged primacy effects in serial learning with continuous presentation in which the inter-trial interval equals the interstimulus interval and the stimuli appear at the same spatial position. Perceptually isolated syllables were more likely to be learned first.

Harcum, Pschirrer, and Coppage (1968) employed continuous presentation of ten-syllable lists, and asked the subjects at the end of the experiment whether they had used any particular strategy or approach in learning. The subject's report of which syllable was subjectively first in the series frequently corresponded with the "primacy effect" in his distribution of errors. These data from subjective reports measured directly the variable that Harcum and Coppage (1965b) proposed is the critical intervening variable in the establishment of the serial-position curve of learning—namely, the subject's cognition of a "first" item. This independent measure of which item is cognitively first removes the circularity of a predicted correlation between an idiosyncratic cognitively-first item and an idiosyncratic location of an alleged primacy effect. The imperfect correlation between cognitive-first and first-learned was attributed primarily to the inherent unreliability of subjective reports.

Another finding in the Harcum and Coppage (1969) experiment, mentioned previously, was that the items in a paced 12-item list were learned by the subjects in a more consistent order, as defined by errors per item. For the unpaced series the serial-position curves of errors for all subjects showed an apparent greater irregularity. This may be due in part to the fewer overall number of errors, but probably it is due to the greater opportunity under the unpaced condition for a subject's strategy of learning to be influenced by differences in learnability of individual items.

Cognitive Coding

Neisser (1967) proposes "cognitive structures" or coding systems to account for memory. An item is recalled by reconstruction from these codes, with time and space dimensions. Thus, even rote learning is a constructive process. The executive mechanism for this construction is much like an executive routine in computer programming. Mandler (1968) and Shiffrin and Atkinson (1969) suggest similar models.

Because this book is concerned with temporal and spatial ordering of both input and responses, the present concern is primarily with spatial and temporal bases of coding. Clearly, the expectations of the subject about the required output conditions influence the way he will encode the stimuli; he will tend to use the code that will most facilitate the retrieval of the required information. For example, Hinrichs (1968) found that subjects informed about whether the serial order of recall for nine digits would be forward or backwards before stimulus presentation performed more accurately than when they did not have this information until after presentation. Presumably the prior information permitted a more advantageous organization of the learning. Also, Mandler and Anderson (1971) found that correspondence of the temporal and spatial ordering facilitates recall, and that prior knowledge of the type of information to be tested improves retention. Both of these circumstances would aid encoding of the stimuli.

A number of studies have demonstrated that encoding of stimuli takes time. Without sufficient time the subject must rely more upon short-term traces and less upon organization and codification into secondary memory. Jahnke (1968) found an interaction between the rate of presentation and the serial-position distribution of errors in serial recall; the slower rates differentially facilitated the initial items. One of the reasons for this was that the subjects tended to depart from the instructed serial order of report for the faster presentations. Thus, the trace strength both influences the subject's tendency to select a particular recall order, and also the required recall order influences the strength of the trace when it is to be retrieved from memory.

Aaronson (1968) showed that with serial recall the subjects revealed more bowing in the serial-position curves for the faster rates of aural presentation. But the results were virtually identical for the end items under the various rates. Also, small mislocation errors were more frequent than large ones, as would be expected. These data suggest a position-based retrieval code that was more effective for end items, and when the time for encoding was greater.

Bjork and Allen (1970) also concluded that spaced presentations exert an advantage over massed presentations because they allow more time for encoding of the first presentation. Moreover, a difficult task requires more time for encoding. Thus, the strength of the trace does not control its recall, but rather the encoding-retrieval process determines the probability of retention.

The subjects of Wilkes and Kennedy (1970) read strings of nine letters with temporal pauses corresponding to spatial breaks in the series. The pauses produced groups of 4–5, 5–4, or 3–3–3 items. Latencies of responses to a sequential probe revealed bowed curves with pronounced dips for the items that were the first in a group. Latencies of responses to indicate whether or not a probed item had been present in the series yielded less regular curves; in general, letters closer to reference pauses produced smaller latencies, except that the latencies for first and ninth letters were somewhat slower than for second and eighth items. Thus, as was concluded in Chapter 4, the temporal pauses are more important in terms of the effect on organizational and encoding processes than they are as providers of opportunities for decay or consolidation.

Other evidence for the encoding argument was provided by Denner (1966) who found that letter-strings were processed perceptually faster when they appeared in a structured context. Therefore, the advantage of context is not only in the retrieval, but also on the encoding side of the total process. Johnson (1969) also supported the information-encoding proposition. He found that the mnemonic information within an encoded chunk was recalled as a unit, in an all-or-none fashion.

In summary, encoding mechanisms mean active processing by the subject. In fact, Norman (1971) argues that an active construction and organization of sensory events is the key to memory. He asserts that learning is not a passive association of one event with another, nor is memory merely a passive reproduction of one event given another. Memory, as perception, is an active, problem-solving task of processing stored information to construct an "image of the past." Norman joins the list of those who propose that memory is like perception, a reconstruction rather than a remembrance of the past, as follows:

> The conclusion one reaches from the study of perception, of memory, of problem solving, and of thinking is that they all have much in common with

one another and, indeed, may not even be separable. There is more to the processing of information than simple passive analysis by the nervous system. There is more to memory than simple, rote intensification of memory traces (1971, p. 63).

THE MICROPROCESSES

It is obviously best to construct a general theory of behavior in terms of central mechanisms. Although Lashley (1950) failed to find the engrams of memory, they must be in the higher centers of the brain. Gibson (1966) suggests that Lashley's (1950) search for the engram of memory might never succeed because there is no engram as such. Gibson suggests that perceptual learning may be a process by which the nervous system comes to "resonate" to a dynamic pattern of stimulation. The present contextual and configurational approach also requires a dynamic conception of the memory trace.

Some brief speculations will now be offered about possible neurological mechanisms of serial acquisition. These speculations will follow along the lines suggested by Lashley (1951) and Hebb (1949), and more recently by Wickelgren (1969). Wickelgren argues that Lashley (1951) convincingly disposed of a context-free associative conception of memory, but that a context-sensitive conception of associative memory is still viable. Wickelgren (1969) argued that Lashley's (1951) apparent disproof of associative-chaining theory in serial ordering applied to only one version of the theory. Wickelgren proposes an alternative in terms of "context-sensitive coding" based on the configuration of the stimulus elements.

The EPAM III model of Simon and Feigenbaum (1964) obviates the necessity for postulating a separate associational process in learning. Instead they propose image-building and a discrimination-learning process that account for both the integration of responses and the association or hookup of responses (Underwood & Schulz, 1960). They suggest that a stimulus and response are associated in the same way that the letters within, for example, a trigram stimulus are formed. Namely, the subject learns to become familiar with and discriminate a new compound stimulus-response unit.

Postman (1955) also has defended the conception of perceptual learning in terms of associational mechanisms. Again, he emphasizes the relevance to verbal learning:

The psychological associationism of a stimulus-response formulation serves to emphasize the continuity between perceptual learning and other types of learning, with respect to both experimental operations and functional relationships. Descriptively, perceptual learning *is* the attachment of new responses, or a change in the frequency of responses, to particular configurations or sequences of stimuli (p. 441).

Postman (1955) suggests that eventually a physiological conception such as Hebb's (1949) might become appropriate, in which the activity of the central nervous system is modified by the repeated stimulation.

As Hebb (1949) suggests, the stimuli impinging on the organism produce traces that may include response as well as sensory components. The stimuli, fed into existing patterns of neural firing, produce an overt response according to innate structural characteristics of the organism and the past history of responses in similar patterns of stimulation. The pattern of neural activity, or cell assembly, has a certain unity about it such that the discrete distinction between stimulus-trace and incipient motor response is lost. This cell assembly can be thought of as one kind of scanning mechanism; it will be called a scanning cell assembly.

The effects of the scanning cell assembly should be less important in serial learning because of the time factors involved, since each stimulus item could be scanned many times in an exposure of several seconds. Therefore, the associations would be, relatively speaking, between dynamically changed traces in memory rather than between merely fading stimulus traces. In other words, the associations are formed between reduced versions of a number of different scanning cell assemblies. This scanning can occur at the storage stages (Harcum, 1967b) and at the secondary stages (Sternberg, 1966).

The stimulus impinges on continuously active central processes (Hebb, 1949), that are themselves continually being affected by sensory input (Hebb, 1963). The relevant factor is a dynamic organization or codification of serially-presented elements. Therefore, stimuli that are physically salient, or are more attense due to focal attention (Neisser, 1967) have an advantage in retention over "aggregated" or undifferentiated elements.

The coding process could proceed by a mechanism similar to the neural models of Milner (1957, 1961) and Hebb (1949). Also capable of communication with the scanning cell assembly are superordinate cell assemblies corresponding to concepts or codes. In Milner's model, cell assemblies come to represent the stimuli, and by being fired contiguously, become associated. Perceptual learning results when newly added cells are predominantly primed by sensory input, and associative learning occurs when they are primed by the firing of another cell assembly. The prevailing cell assemblies determine how the original scanning cell assembly is reduced in memory. These reduced cell assemblies, corresponding to conceptualizations or codes, may be activated by feedback from the responses as well as by stimulation from the central state, by contextual cues, by instructions, and by the nominal stimulus. Activation of other cell assemblies produces a different pattern of excitation converging on the final common path, adding ambiguity in the response.

The total network of firings, or facilitations toward certain patterns of firings as a result of subthreshold stimulations, is thus a selective mechanism determining which concepts and codes are likely to be activated, and which responses are likely to be given. New patterns of firing can continually replace previous ones. This may occur in the manner of the "priming" of neurons suggested by Milner (1957). A given assembly can also be re-excited by an appropriate constellation of primings. When a stable pattern of firing is reached, the organism may be said to have attained the concept represented by that cell assembly. This train of cell assemblies may be thought of as another kind of scanning or searching process—something like scanning the mnemonic storage system (e.g., Sternberg, 1966, 1967; Yntema & Trask, 1963). Therefore, the scanning of cell assemblies proceeds until a stable pattern of firing is reached. Such a stable cell assembly would be activated earlier than would less-well-established cell assemblies, with the degree of stability corresponding to a hierarchy of codes or concepts in the order of their availability to the subject. The most available codes would be like a lowest common denominator of assembly action, corresponding to the overlap of many lesser assemblies.

If there were no superordinate cell assembly that could be activated easily and consistently by the stimulus (i.e., a concept or code for the stimulus does not exist in the repertoire of the organism), the subject would have difficulty in producing an accurate response. Conversely, a stimulus would be more likely to activate a strong and well-defined code cell assembly if it contained distinctive features and if there was strong support from the contextual stimulation.

In neurological terms, the particular response by the observer is dependent upon which cell assemblies have been activated. These cell assemblies are, of course, determined by the instructions given to the observer and by the nature of the task. If an "incompatible" response were required and instructed after stimulation, an inverse scanning or translation process would occur in which the code cell assembly would become modified progressively until a code cell assembly that was associated with the appropriate response requirement was reached. If the responding conditions were not specified, then the cell assemblies of incipient motor responses that had been associated with the code cell assembly would be activated. In other words, the subject would respond as appropriate to his prevailing schema (Bartlett, 1932).

Hebb (1949) gives the following theoretical account of serial learning, using the example of a rat learning a maze. When the rat arrives at a given choice point the neura sequence is changing from moment to moment. This "phase sequence" is dominated by an expectancy of reaching food, and perception of the position within the maze. Each two conceptual complexes are linked by activity of the cortical motor system facilitating not only movements of the head, but also locomotion. When the latter facilitation is above threshold, the rat runs in the direction determined by the earlier movement of the head and eyes. If no alley leading to the goal appears, expectancy was not confirmed. If the controlling phase sequence is not strongly established, it is easily replaced by another that produces a different direction of movement. On a second trial the run may be toward a correct alley. If the expectancy of an alley toward the goal is now reinforced by the sensation of such an alley, that part of the phase sequence is facilitated by a sensory and a central component. Therefore, the probability is that on a subsequent trial the rat will take the correct, reinforced movement at that choice point.

CONCLUSION

The theoretical position offered here transcends the issues of whether learning implies the formation of associative bonds between or among items, or associations of items with relative position. Even the rote learner finds a hanger or hook to attach an item to an organizational framework for memory and later retrieval. He can use any clue to solve his problem, just as Beach's (1942) male rat could find the female rat in estrus, providing he had one usable sensory modality. Systematic elimination of each clue would prove that no one of them was essential. But at least one basis for selecting the correct response was necessary for the final solution. In serial learning the subject could use only one cue, but probably he uses the confluence or configuration of all available cues. This configuration changes from trial to trial in relatively predictable ways.

The present position also bypasses the issue of one-trial learning. One-trial learning can be found for some items under some conditions. The learning process seems to be discrete if the sensitivity of measurement afforded by a single trial is large with respect to the difficulty of item acquisition for the subject. For very intelligent or highly practiced subjects, or for very easy tasks, the learning is more likely to appear discontinuous than it is for a task that the subject finds difficult.

Broadbent (1963) describes interference or facilitation effects in memory in terms of converging or diverging causal lines within the nervous system. In longer-term memory, stimuli that are similar will be more likely to be placed in the same category, and thus produce ambiguity (interference) in the response. As is consistent with the evidence, more time will be required to place the items into separate categories if a differential response is to be required.

The subject must first learn the population of items (i.e., response learning) and then learn to fit the items into a configuration of stimuli (i.e., associative learning or serial learning per se). Since each item as it is learned becomes part of the stimulus configuration, the stimulus configuration changes dynamically during the course of learning in a predictable hierarchy. Therefore, the potential cues for retrieval would be different at different stages of learning. The early ones would not be unlearned, but superseded by presumably more effective cues. This would explain why probe devices yield less effective performance than the total context of the task can produce.

Using factor analysis, Detterman and Ellis (1970) consistently extracted two factors from short-term memory for visually exposed stimuli—primacy and recency factors. These were attributed to secondary and primary memory (Waugh & Norman, 1965), respectively. The discussion of Chapter 7 indicates that control processes are important in determining whether the subject chooses to retrieve the items in primary or secondary memory.

In serial recall the subject is forced to rely more on secondary memory. The items to be recalled first are more likely to have passed out of the primary stage. Therefore, Bruder (1970) found that serial recall produced fewer correct responses than free recall. This was attributed to "editing" of items and loss of items during output.

Thus, the retention of series of items involves multifarious processes, as described in Chapter 5, Figure 5–1. Mechanisms, such as those described in Figure 5–2, operate at various stages of the acquisition-retention tandem. In short, the subject in the acquisition stage actively seeks cues and codification rules that he thinks will aid him in retrieving the correct response in the retention test. The total process can be succinctly described as the translation of input information into a form that is retrievable by the subject on demand. A break in this flow of information processing at any point would thus produce a failure of learning or memory. The integrity of this flow depends not only on learning per se, but also on paralearning and paraperceptual factors.

SUMMARY

This chapter completes the interpretation of the serial-learning and paralearning phenomena. The course of serial acquisition was interpreted as an approximately linear process. The rectification of the data was attributed to paralearning strategies that resulted in acquisition of the easy (usually end) items first. Since these items were at salient locations, their position was learned about as quickly as their identity. Later, the identity of items were learned sooner than their location, so that the number of overt intruding errors for the items increased. For the last-learned items the spatial alternatives were reduced, so again the number of overt intrusions was reduced.

Some suggestions about the nature of the microprocesses of learning were given. These were along the lines suggested by Hebb (1949) and many others. Primary emphasis was placed on the mechanisms by which so-called learned items are retrieved from memory. The distinction between learning and paralearning factors becomes blurred when one recalls the previous definition of a learned association as an empirical change in the probability that a given stimulus will produce the response.

REFERENCES

Aaronson, D. Temporal course of perception in an immediate recall task. *Journal of Experimental Psychology*, 1968, **76**, 129–140.

Ahmed, M., & Voss, J. F. Serial acquisition as a function of stage of learning. *Journal of Experimental Psychology*, 1969, **82**, 398–400.

Amelang, M., & Scholl, R. Die Effekte semantischer isolation im intentionalen und inzidentellen Lernen. *Zeitschrift für experimentelle und angewandte Psychologie*, 1971, **18**, 367–385.

Anderson, J. R., & Bower, G. H. Configural properties in sentence memory. *Journal of Verbal Learning and Verbal Behavior*, 1972, **11**, 594–605.

Anderson, J. R. & Bower, G. H. (Eds.) *Human Associative Memory* Washington, D. C.: Winston, 1973.

Andrews, T. G., Shapiro, S. & Cofer, C. N. Transfer and generalization of the inhibitory potential developed in rote serial learning. *American Journal of Psychology*, 1954, **67**, 453–463.

Archer, E. J. Re-evaluation of the meaningfulness of all possible CVC trigrams. *Psychological Monographs*, 1960, Whole No. 497, **74**, 1–23.

Asch, S. E. The process of free recall. In C. Scheerer (Ed.), *Cognition: theory, research, promise*. New York: Harper & Row, 1964, 79–88.

Asch, S. E. The doctrinal tyranny of associationism: or what is wrong with rote learning. In T. R. Dixon & D. L. Horton (Eds.), *Verbal behavior and general behavior theory*. Englewood Cliffs, New Jersey: Prentice-Hall, 1968, 214–228.

Asch, S. E., & Ebenholtz, S. M. The principle of associative symmetry. *Proceedings of the American Philosophical Society*, 1962, **106**, 135–163.

Asch, S. E., Hay, J., & Diamond, R. M. Perceptual organization in serial rote-learning. *American Journal of Psychology*, 1960, **73**, 177–198.

Atkinson, R. C. A stochastic model for rote serial learning. *Psychometrika*, 1957, **22**, 87–95.

Atkinson, R. C., & Shiffrin, R. M. A proposed system and its control processes. In K. W. Spence & J. T. Spence (Eds.), *The psychology of learning and motivation: Advances in research and theory*. Vol. 2. New York: Academic Press, 1968, 89–195. (a)

Atkinson, R. C., & Shiffrin, R. M. Some speculations on storage and retrieval processes in long-term memory. Technical Report No. 127, Institute for Mathematical Studies in Social Sciences, Stanford, Calif.: Stanford University Press, 1968.(b)

Baddeley, A. D., & Patterson, K. Relations between long-term and short-term memory. *British Medical Bulletin,* 1971, **27,** 237–242.

Bahrick, H. P. Relearning and measurement of retention. *Journal of Verbal Learning and Verbal Behavior,* 1967, **6,** 89–94.

Bahrick, H. P., Fitts, P. M., & Briggs, G. E. Learning curves—facts or artifacts? *Psychological Bulletin,* 1957, **54,** 256–268.

Barnes, J. M. & Underwood, B. J. "Fate" of first-list associations in transfer theory. *Journal of Experimental Psychology,* 1959, **58,** 97–105.

Barnett, C. D., Ellis, N. R., & Pryer, M. W. Serial position effects in superior and retarded subjects. *Psychological Reports,* 1960, **7,** 111–113.

Bartlett, F. C. *Remembering.* Cambridge, Mass.: University Press, 1932.

Bartz, W. H., Lewis, M. Q., & Swinton, G. Serial position effects for repeated free recall: Negative recency or positive primacy? *Journal of Experimental Psychology,* 1972, **96,** 10–16.

Battig, W. F. Further evidence that strongest free-recall items are not recalled first. *Psychological Reports,* 1965, **17,** 745–746. (a)

Battig, W. F. Procedural problems in paired-associate learning research. *Psychonomic Monograph Supplements,* 1965, **1,** No. 1.(b)

Battig, W. F. Effect of sequential blocking of similar trigrams on free and serial recall. *Psychonomic Science,* 1966, **5,** 369–370.

Battig, W. F. Paired-associate learning. In T. R. Dixon & D. L. Horton (Eds.), *Verbal behavior and general behavior theory.* Englewood Cliffs, New Jersey: Prentice-Hall, 1968, 149–171.

Battig, W. F., & Koppenaal, R. J. Associative asymmetry in S-R vs. R-S recall of double-function lists. *Psychological Reports,* 1965, **16,** 287–293.

Battig, W. F., & Lawrence, P. S. The greater sensitivity of the serial recall than anticipation procedure to variations in serial order. *Journal of Experimental Psychology,* 1967, **73,** 172–178.

Battig, W. F., & Young, R. K. Simultaneous serial-recall learning of two serial orders of the same list. *Journal of Verbal Learning and Verbal Behavior,* 1969, **8,** 393–402.

Battig, W. F., Allen, M., & Jensen, A. R. Priority of free recall of newly learned items. *Journal of Verbal Learning and Verbal Behavior,* 1965, **4,** 175–179.

Battig, W. F., Brown, S. C., & Nelson, D. Constant vs. varied serial order in paired-associate learning. *Psychological Reports,* 1963, **12,** 695–721. (Monograph Supplement 6—V12)

Battig, W. F., Brown, S. C., & Schild, M. E. Serial position and sequential associations in serial learning. *Journal of Experimental Psychology,* 1964, **67,** 449–457.

Beach, F. A. Analysis of the stimuli adequate to elicit mating behavior in the sexually inexperienced male rat. *Journal of Comparative Psychology,* 1942, **33,** 163–207.

Beam, J. C. Serial learning and conditioning under real-life stress. *Journal of Abnormal and Social Psychology,* 1955, **51,** 543–551.

Bean, L. L., & McCroskery. J. H. Implications for associative processes of switching the middle of the list during serial rote learning. *Journal of Psychology,* 1973, **83,** 227–235.

Beecroft, R. S. Verbal learning and retention as a function of the number of competing associations. *Journal of Experimental Psychology,* 1956, **51,** 216–221.

Bernbach, H. A. Replication processes in human memory and learning. In G. H. Bower

& J. T. Spence (Eds.), *The psychology of learning and motivation: Advances in research and theory*. Vol. 3. New York: Academic Press, 1969, 201–239.

Bewley, W. L. The functional stimulus in serial learning. In R. F. Thompson & J. F. Voss (Eds.), *Topics in learning and performance*. New York: Academic Press, 1972, 187–214.

Bewley, W. L., Nelson, D. L., & Brogden, W. J. Single, alternate, and successive practice in the acquisition of two and three serial lists. *Journal of Experimental Psychology*, 1968, **76**, 376–386.

Bewley, W. L., Nelson, D. L., & Brogden, W. J. Effect of cue alteration for ordinal position on acquisition and serial position curve form. *Journal of Experimental Psychology*, 1969, **79**, 445–451.

Bilodeau, I. M., & Schlosberg, H. Similarity in stimulating conditions as a variable in retroactive inhibition. *Journal of Experimental Psychology*, 1951, **41**, 199–204.

Bjork, R. A., & Allen, T. W. The spacing effect: Consolidation or differential encoding? *Journal of Verbal Learning and Verbal Behavior*, 1970, **9**, 567–572.

Blick, K. A., & Waite, C. J. A survey of mnemonic techniques used by college students in free recall learning. *Psychological Reports*, 1971, **29**, 76–78.

Blick, K. A., Buonassissi, J. V., & Boltwood, C. E. Mnemonic techniques used by college students in serial learning. *Psychological Reports*, 1972, **31**, 983–986.

Bolles, R. C. The effect of altering the middle of the list during serial learning. *American Journal of Psychology*, 1959, **72**, 577–580.

Bone, R. N., & Goulet, L. R. Serial position and the von Restorff isolation effect. *Journal of Experimental Psychology*, 1968, **76**, 494–496.

Bousfield, W. A. The occurrence of clustering in the recall of randomly arranged associates. *Journal of General Psychology*, 1953, **49**, 229–240.

Bousfield, W. A., Whitmarsh, G. A., & Esterson, J. Serial position effects and the "Marbe Effect" in the free recall of meaningful words. *Journal of General Psychology*, 1958, **59**, 255–262.

Bower, G. H. Organizational factors in memory. *Cognitive Psychology*, 1970, **1**, 18–46.

Bower, G. H., & Bolton, L. S. Why are rhymes easy to learn? *Journal of Experimental Psychology*, 1969, **82**, 453–461.

Bower, G. H., & Clark, M. C., Narrative stories as mediators for serial learning. *Psychonomic Science*, 1969, **14**, 181–182.

Bower, G. H., & Springston, F. Pauses as recoding points in letter series. *Journal of Experimental Psychology*, 1970, **83**, 421–430.

Bowman, R. E., & Thurlow, W. R. Determinants of the effect of position in serial learning. *American Journal of Psychology*, 1963, **76**, 436–445.

Braun, H. W., & Heymann, S. P. Meaningfulness of material, distribution of practice, and serial position curves. *Journal of Experimental Psychology*, 1958, **56**, 146–150.

Breckenridge, R. L., & Dixon, T. R. Problem of the stimulus in serial learning. *Journal of Experimental Psychology*, 1970, **83**, 126–130.

Breckenridge, K., Hakes, D. T., & Young, R. K. Reply to Keppel. *Psychonomic Science*. 1965, **3**, 474, 476. (a)

Breckenridge, K., Hakes, D. T., & Young, R. K. Serial learning in a continuous serial list. *Psychonomic Science*, 1965, **3**, 139–140. (b)

Bredenkamp, K., & Bredenkamp, J. Eine Untersuchung zum funktionalen Reiz beim seriellen Lernen. *Archiv für Psychologie,* 1970, **122,** 249–258.

Brent, S. B. Linguistic unity, list length, and rate of presentation in serial anticipation learning. *Journal of Verbal Learning and Verbal Behavior,* 1969, **8,** 70–79.

Brewer, C. L. Presentation time, trials to criterion, and total time in verbal learning. *Journal of Experimental Psychology,* 1967, **73,** 159–162.

Broadbent, D. E. *Perception and communication.* New York: Pergamon Press, 1958.

Broadbent, D. E. Flow of information within the organism. *Journal of Verbal Learning and Verbal Behavior,* 1963, **2,** 34–39.

Brogden, W. J., & Schmidt, R. E. Effect of number of choices per unit of a verbal maze on learning and serial position errors. *Journal of Experimental Psychology,* 1954, **47,** 235–240. (a)

Brogden, W. J., & Schmidt, R. E. Acquisition of a 24-unit verbal maze as a function of number of alternate choices per unit. *Journal of Experimental Psychology,* 1954, **48,** 335–338. (b)

Brown, C. H. The relation of magnitude of galvanic skin responses and resistance levels to the rate of learning. *Journal of Experimental Psychology,* 1937, **20,** 262–278.

Brown, R., & McNeill, D. The "tip of the tongue" phenomenon. *Journal of Verbal Learning and Verbal Behavior,* 1966, **5,** 325–337.

Brown, S. C. Cognitive style, as preferential organizing tendency, in serial learning and free recall. Unpublished doctoral dissertation, Wayne State University, 1964.

Brown, S. C., & Rubin, E. D. Cue utilization in serial learning. *Journal of Experimental Psychology,* 1967, **74,** 550–555.

Bruce, A. J. Effects of age and stimulus structure on serial learning. *Developmental Psychology,* 1974, **10,** 29–32.

Bruce, D., & Papay, J. P. Primacy effect in single-trial free recall. *Journal of Verbal Learning and Verbal Behavior,* 1970, **9,** 473–486.

Bruce, R. W. Conditions of transfer of training. *Journal of Experimental Psychology,* 1933, **16,** 343–361.

Bruder, G. A. Analysis of differences between free and serial recall. *Journal of Experimental Psychology,* 1970, **83,** 232–237.

Bryden, M. P. A model for the sequential organization of behaviour. *Canadian Journal of Psychology,* 1967, **21,** 37–56.

Bugelski, B. R. The influence of the remote association gradient in determining the relative difficulty of items in serial rote learning. *American Psychologist,* 1948, **3,** 251–252.

Bugelski, B. R. A remote association explanation of the relative difficulty of learning nonsense syllables in a serial list. *Journal of Experimental Psychology,* 1950, **40,** 336–348.

Bugelski, B. R. *The psychology of learning.* New York: Holt, 1956.

Bugelski, B. R. In defense of remote association. *Psychological Review,* 1965, **72,** 169–174.

Bugelski, B. R. The image as mediator in one-trial paired-associate learning: III. Sequential functions in serial lists. *Journal of Experimental Psychology,* 1974, **103,** 298–303.

Buonassissi, J. V., Blick, K. A., & Kibler, J. L. III. Evaluation of experimenter-supplied and subject-originated descriptive-story mnemonics in a free-recall task. *Psychological Reports,* 1972, **30,** 648.

Burnstein, E., & Dorfman, D. Some effects of meprobamate on human learning. *Journal of Psychology,* 1959, **47,** 81–86.

Buschke, H., & Hinrichs, J. V. Controlled rehearsal and recall order in serial list retention. *Journal of Experimental Psychology,* 1968, **78,** 502–509.

Buxton, C. E. Repetition of two basic experiments on reminiscence in serial verbal learning. *Journal of Experimental Psychology,* 1949, **39,** 676–682.

Buxton, C. E., & Bakan, M. B. Correction vs. non-correction learning techniques as related to reminiscence in serial anticipation learning. *Journal of Experimental Psychology,* 1949, **39,** 338–341.

Buxton, C. E., & Ross, H. V. Relationships between reminiscence and type of learning technique in serial anticipation learning. *Journal of Experimental Psychology,* 1949, **39,** 41–46.

Calkins, M. W. Association: An essay analytic and experimental. *Psychological Monographs,* 1895-1897, **1,** 1–56.

Camp, D. S., & Harcum, E. R. Visual pattern perception with varied fixation locus and response recording. *Perceptual and Motor Skills,* 1964, **18,** 283–296.

Cason, H. Specific serial learning: A study of backward association. *Journal of Experimental Psychology,* 1926, **9,** 195–227. (a)

Cason, H. Specific serial learning: A study of remote forward association. *Journal of Experimental Psychology,* 1926, **9,** 299–324. (b)

Ceraso, J. The interference theory of forgetting. *Scientific American,* 1967, **217,** 117–124.

Cermak, L. S. Rehearsal strategy as a function of recall expectation. *Quarterly Journal of Experimental Psychology,* 1972, **24,** 378–385.

Chan, A., & Travers, R. M. W. Effect of sense modality switching on serial learning. *Perceptual and Motor Skills,* 1965, **20,** 1185–1191.

Chan, A., & Travers, R. M. W. Sense modality switching and serial learning. *Perception and Psychophysics,* 1970, **8,** 37–39.

Cimbalo, R. S., & Pelonero, K. C. The isolation effect and mechanisms in short- and long-term memory. *Psychonomic Science,* 1970, **21,** 69–70.

Cofer, C. N. Commentary. In C. N. Cofer (Ed.), *Verbal learning and verbal behavior.* New York: McGraw-Hill, 1961, 224–228. (a)

Cofer, C. N. (Ed.) *Verbal learning and verbal behavior,* New York: McGraw-Hill, 1961. (b)

Cofer, C. N. On some factors in the organizational characteristics of free recall. *American Psychologist,* 1965, **20,** 261–272.

Cofer, C. N. Problems, issues, and implications. In T. R. Dixon & D. L. Horton (Eds.), *Verbal behavior and general behavior theory.* Englewood Cliffs, New Jersey: Prentice-Hall, 1968, 522–537.

Cofer, C. N. Introduction, conceptions, methods, and a controversy. In M. H. Marx (Ed.), *Learning: Processes.* New York: MacMillan, 1969, 300–313.

Conrad, R. Accuracy of using Keyset and telephone dial, and the effects of a prefix digit. *Journal of Applied Psychology,* 1958, **42,** 285–288.

Conrad, R. Errors of immediate memory. *British Journal of Psychology,* 1959, **50,** 349–359.

Conrad, R. Serial order intrusions in immediate memory. *British Journal of Psychology,* 1960, **51,** 45–48.

Conrad, R. Order error in immediate recall of sequences. *Journal of Verbal Learning and Verbal Behavior,* 1965, **4,** 161–169.

Coppage, E. W., & Harcum, E. R. Temporal vs. structural determinants of primacy in strategies of serial learning. *Journal of Verbal Learning and Verbal Behavior,* 1967, **6,** 487–490.

Corballis, M. C. Patterns of rehearsal in immediate memory. *British Journal of Psychology,* 1969, **60,** 41–49.

Craik, F. I. M. Primary memory. *British Medical Bulletin,* 1971, **27,** 232–236.

Cramer, P., & Cofer, C. N. The role of forward and reverse association in transfer of training. *American Psychologist,* 1960, **15,** 463. (Abstract)

Crowder, R. G. Prefix effects in immediate memory. *Canadian Journal of Psychology,* 1967, **21,** 450–461.

Crowder, R. G. Evidence for the chaining hypothesis of serial verbal learning. *Journal of Experimental Psychology,* 1968, **76,** 497–500.

Crowder, R. G. Behavioral strategies in immediate memory. *Journal of Verbal Learning and Verbal Behavior,* 1969, **8,** 524–528.

Crowder, R. G., Chisholm, D. D., & Fell, D. A. Transfer from serial to continuous paired-associate learning. *Psychonomic Science,* 1966, **6,** 455–456.

Culler, E. A. Nature of the learning curve. *Psychological Bulletin,* 1928, **25,** 143–144.

Dallenbach, K. M. Position vs. intensity as a determinant of clearness. *American Journal of Psychology,* 1923, **34,** 282–286.

Dallett, K. M. Retention of remote associations. *Journal of Experimental Psychology,* 1959, **58,** 252–255.

Dallett, K. M. In defense of remote associates. *Psychological Review,* 1965, **72,** 164–168.

Dashiell, J. F. An organizing procedure in rote memorizing. *Psychological Bulletin,* 1942, **39,** 481.

Deese, J. Serial organization in the recall of disconnected items. *Psychological Reports,* 1957, **3,** 577–582.

Deese, J. *The psychology of learning.* New York: McGraw-Hill, 1958.

Deese, J. On the prediction of occurrence of particular verbal intrusions in immediate recall. *Journal of Experimental Psychology,* 1959, **58,** 17–22.

Deese, J. From the isolated verbal unit to connected discourse. In C. N. Cofer (Ed.), *Verbal learning and verbal behavior.* New York: McGraw-Hill, 1961, 11–31.

Deese, J. Association and memory. In T. R. Dixon & D. L. Horton (Eds.), *Verbal behavior and general behavior theory.* Englewood Cliffs, N. J.: Prentice-Hall, 1968, 97–108.

Deese, J., & Hardman, G. W. An analysis of errors in retroactive inhibition of rote verbal learning. *American Journal of Psychology,* 1954, **67,** 299–307.

Deese, J., & Kaufman, R. A. Serial effects in recall of unorganized and sequentially organized verbal material. *Journal of Experimental Psychology,* 1957, **54,** 180–187.

Deese, J., & Kresse, F. H. An experimental analysis of errors in rote serial learning. *Journal of Experimental Psychology,* 1952, **43,** 199–202.

Deese, J., & Marder, V. J. The pattern of errors in delayed recall of serial learning after interpolation. *American Journal of Psychology,* 1957, **70,** 594–599.

Deese, J., Lazarus, R. S., & Keenan, J. Anxiety, anxiety reduction, and stress in learning. *Journal of Experimental Psychology,* 1953, **46,** 55–60.

Delin, P. S. The effects of mnemonic instruction and list length on serial learning and retention. *Psychonomic Science,* 1969, **17,** 111–113. (a)

Delin, P. S. The learning to criterion of a serial list with and without mnemonic instructions. *Psychonomic Science,* 1969, **16,** 169–170. (b)

Delin, P. S. Learning and retention of English words with successive approximations to a complex mnemonic instruction. *Psychonomic Science,* 1969, **17,** 87–89. (c)

Denner, B. Perceptual processing of syntactically structured and unstructured strings. *Perceptual and Motor Skills,* 1966, **23,** 1310.

Derks, P. L. The length-difficulty relation in immediate serial recall. *Journal of Verbal Learning and Verbal Behavior*, 1974, **13**, 335–354.

De Soto, C. B., & Bosley, J. J. The cognitive structure of a social-structure. *Journal of Abnormal and Social Psychology*, 1962, **64**, 303–307.

Detterman, D. K., & Ellis, N. R. A factor analytic demonstration of two memory processes. *Quarterly Journal of Experimental Psychology*, 1970, **22**, 484–493.

Detterman, D. K., & Ellis, N. R. Distinctiveness in short-term memory. *Psychonomic Science*, 1971, **22**, 239–241.

Dey, M. K. Generalization of position association in rote serial learning. *American Journal of Psychology*, 1970, **83**, 248–255.

Diethorn, J. A., & Voss, J. F. Serial learning as a function of locus of chained associations. *Journal of Experimental Psychology*, 1967, **73**, 411–418.

Dolinsky, R., & Juska, J. J. Backward association in serial learning as a function of prior paired-associate training. *Psychonomic Science*, 1967, **8**, 241–242.

Dulsky, S. G. The effect of a change of background on recall and relearning. *Journal of Experimental Psychology*, 1935, **18**, 725–740.

Eagle, M. N. The effect of learning strategies upon free recall. *American Journal of Psychology*, 1967, **80**, 421–425.

Earhard, M. Subjective organization and list organization as determinants of free-recall and serial-recall memorization. *Journal of Verbal Learning and Verbal Behavior*, 1967, **6**, 501–507.

Ebbinghaus, H. *Grundzüge der Psychologie*. Leipzig: Veit und Companie, 1902, Erster Band.

Ebbinghaus, H. *Das Gedächtnis*, Trans. as *Memory: A contribution to experimental psychology*. by H. A. Rugen & C. E. Bussenius, New York: Teachers College, Columbia University, 1913.

Ebbinghaus, H. *Memory: A contribution to experimental psychology*. New York: Dover, 1964.

Ebenholtz, S. M. Position mediated transfer between serial learning and a spatial discrimination task. *Journal of Experimental Psychology*, 1963, **65**, 603–608. (a)

Ebenholtz, S. M. Serial learning: Position learning and sequential associations. *Journal of Experimental Psychology*, 1963, **66**, 353–362. (b)

Ebenholtz, S. M. Positional cues as mediators in discrimination learning. *Journal of Experimental Psychology*, 1965, **70**, 176–181.

Ebenholtz, S. M. Serial-list items as stimuli in paired-associate learning. *Journal of Experimental Psychology*, 1966, **72**, 154–155. (a)

Ebenholtz, S. M. Serial position effect of ordered stimulus dimensions in paired-associate learning. *Journal of Experimental Psychology*, 1966, **71**, 132–137. (b)

Ebenholtz, S. M. Serial learning and dimensional organization. In G. H. Bower (Ed.), *The psychology of learning and motivation: Advances in research and theory*. Vol. 5. New York: Academic Press, 1972, 267–314.

Eckstrand, G. A., & Wickens, D. D. Transfer of perceptual set. *Journal of Experimental Psychology*, 1954, **47**, 274–278.

Eisdorfer, C. Arousal and performance: Experiments in verbal learning and a tentative theory. In G. A. Talland (Ed.) *Human aging and behavior*. New York: Academic Press, 1968, 189–215.

Ekstrand, B. R. Backward associations. *Psychological Bulletin*, 1966, **65**, 50–64.

Ellis, H. C. Stimulus encoding processes in human learning and memory. In G. H. Bower

(Ed.), *The psychology of learning and motivation: Advances in research and theory*. Vol. 7. New York: Academic Press, 1973, 123–182.

Ellis, N. C. Serial task structure and the doctrine of remote associations. *Psychonomic Science*, 1970, **21**, 121–122.

Ellis, N. C., & Manning, W. H. Rote learning as a function of similarity structure and task sequence. *Journal of Experimental Psychology*, 1967, **73**, 292–297.

Ellis, N. R. Evidence for two storage processes in short-term memory. *Journal of Experimental Psychology*, 1969, **80**, 390–391.

Ellis, N. R., & Dugas, J. The serial-position effect in short-term memory under E- and S-paced conditions. *Psychonomic Science*, 1968, **12**, 55–56.

Ellis, N. R., & Hope, R. Memory processes and the serial position curve. *Journal of Experimental Psychology*, 1968, **77**, 613–619.

Ellis, N. R., Pryer, M. W., Distefano, M. K. Jr., & Pryer, R. S. Learning in mentally defective, normal, and superior subjects. *American Journal of Mental Deficiency*, 1960, **64**, 725–734.

Erickson, C. C., Ingram, R. D., & Young, R. K. Paired-associate learning as a function of rate of presentation and prior serial learning. *American Journal of Psychology*, 1963, **76**, 458–463.

Estes, W. K. The problem of inference from curves based on group data. *Psychological Bulletin*, 1956, **53**, 134–140.

Estes, W. K., The statistical approach to learning theory. In S. Koch, (Ed.), *Psychology: A study of a science*. New York: McGraw-Hill, 1959, Vol. 2, 380–491.

Estes, W. K. An associative basis for coding and organization in memory. In A. W. Melton, & E. Martin (Eds.), *Coding processes in human memory*. Washington: Winston, 1972, 161–190.

Eysenck, H. J. Serial position effects in nonsense syllable learning as a function of interlist rest pauses. *British Journal of Psychology*, 1959, **50**, 360–362.

Eysenck, H. J. *The Maudsley personality inventory*. San Diego: Educational & Industrial Testing Service, 1962.

Farber, I. E. The role of motivation in verbal learning and performance. *Psychological Bulletin*, 1955, **52**, 311–327.

Farber, I. E., & Spence, K. W. Complex learning and conditioning as a function of anxiety. *Journal of Experimental Psychology*, 1953, **45**, 120–125.

Farwell, B. A., & Vitz, P. C. A test of the Feigenbaum and Simon model of serial learning. *Journal of Experimental Psychology*, 1971, **91**, 240–244.

Feigenbaum, E. A. The simulation of verbal learning behavior. In E. A. Feigenbaum & J. Feldman (Eds.), *Computers and thought*. New York: McGraw-Hill, 1963.

Feigenbaum, E. A., & Simon, H. A. Comment: The distinctiveness of stimuli. *Psychological Review*, 1961, **68**, 285–288.

Feigenbaum, E. A., & Simon, H. A. A theory of the serial position effect. *British Journal of Psychology*, 1962, **53**, 307–320.

Feigenbaum, E. A., & Simon, H. A. Brief notes on the EPAM theory of verbal learning. In C. N. Cofer & B. S. Musgrave (Eds.), *Verbal behavior and learning: Problems and processes*. New York: McGraw-Hill, 1963, 333–335.

Feldman, S. M., & Underwood, B. J. Stimulus recall following paired-associate learning. *Journal of Experimental Psychology*, 1957, **53**, 11–15.

Fingeret, A. L., & Brogden, W. J. Part vs. whole practice in the acquisition of serial lists as a function of class and organization of material. *Journal of Experimental Psychology*, 1970, **83**, 406–414.

Fingeret, A. L., & Brogden, W. J. Item arrangement effects on transfer and serial position errors in part-whole learning of different materials. *Journal of Experimental Psychology*, 1972, **93**, 249–255.

Fingeret, A. L., & Brogden, W. J. Effect of pattern in display by letters and numerals upon acquisition of serial lists of numbers. *Journal of Experimental Psychology*, 1973, **98**, 339–343.

Fischer, G. J. Isolation and organizational effects in serial learning. *American Journal of Psychology*, 1964, **77**, 485–488.

Fischer, G. J. Isolation and perceptual organization in incidental learning. *Psychonomic Science*, 1966, **6**, 141–142. (a)

Fischer, G. J. Relation between stimulus presentation time, serial learning, and the serial-position effect. *Journal of Experimental Psychology*, 1966, **72**, 153–154. (b)

Fischer, G. J. Stimulus intensity effects on verbal learning. *Psychonomic Reports*, 1967, **20**, 75–78.

Fischer, G. J. On constant time to learn: A proposed modification of function. *Psychonomic Science*, 1968, **10**, 357–358.

Fischer, G. J., & Norton, J. A. A test of alternative hypotheses as to the nature of the serial learning curve. *Journal of General Psychology*, 1961, **64**, 219–224.

Fitts, P. M., & Seeger, C. M. S-R compatibility: Spatial characteristics of stimulus and response codes. *Journal of Experimental Psychology*, 1953, **46**, 199–210.

Foucault, M. Les inhibitions internes de fixation. *Année Psychologie*, 1928, **29**, 92–112.

Freeman, G. L. The role of context in associative formation. *American Journal of Psychology*, 1930, **42**, 173–212.

Friedrich, D. Comparison of intrusion errors and serial position curves on monaural and dichotic listening tasks. A developmental analysis. *Memory and Cognition*, 1974, **2**, 721–726.

Fudin, R. Critique of Heron's directional-reading conflict theory of scanning. *Perceptual and Motor Skills*, 1969, **29**, 271–276.

Gagné, R. M., & Foster, II. Transfer of training from practice on components in a motor skill. *Journal of Experimental Psychology*, 1949, **39**, 47–68.

Gallup, G. G. Jr., & Wollen, K. A., Asymmetry of S-R and R-S associations with the direction of recall equated. *Journal of Verbal Learning and Verbal Behavior*, 1968, **7**, 345–347.

Gamble, E. A. McC., & Wilson, L. A study of spatial associations in learning and in recall. *Psychological Monographs*, 1916, **22**, 41–97.

Gardner, R. M., Nappe, G. W., & Wallace, W. P. Order preference in serial learning. *Psychonomic Science*, 1968, **13**, 95–96.

Gardner, R. W., & Long, R. I. Leveling-sharpening and serial learning. *Perceptual and Motor Skills*, 1960, **10**, 179–185.

Garner, W. R., & Gottwald, R. L. Some perceptual factors in the learning of sequential patterns of binary events. *Journal of Verbal Learning and Verbal Behavior*, 1967, **6**, 582–584.

Garrett, H. E., & Hartman, G. W. An experiment on backward association in learning. *American Journal of Psychology*, 1926, **37**, 241–246.

Gibbons, D. E., & Leicht, K. L. Effects of meaningfulness and learning instructions on the isolation effect. *Psychonomic Science,* 1970, **18,** 353–354.

Gibson, E. J. A systematic application of the concepts of generalization and differentiation to verbal learning. *Psychological Review,* 1940, **47,** 196–229.

Gibson, E. J. Retroactive inhibition as a function of degree of generalization between tasks. *Journal of Experimental Psychology,* 1941, **28,** 93–115.

Gibson, E. J. Intra-list generalization as a factor in verbal learning. *Journal of Experimental Psychology,* 1942, **30,** 185–200.

Gibson, E. J. *Perceptual learning and development.* New York: Appleton-Century-Crofts, 1969.

Gibson, J. J. The problem of temporal order in stimulation and perception. *Journal of Psychology,* 1966, **62,** 141–149.

Gibson J. J., & Raffel. G. A technique for investigating retroactive and other inhibitory effects in immediate memory. *Journal of General Psychology,* 1936, **15,** 107–116.

Giurintano, S. L. Serial learning process: Test of chaining, position, and dual-process hypotheses. *Journal of Experimental Psychology,* 1973, **97,** 154–157.

Glanzer, M. Encoding in the perceptual (visual) serial position effect. *Journal of Verbal Learning and Verbal Behavior,* 1966, **5,** 92–97.

Glanzer, M. A note on the transformation of (visual) serial position curves. *Journal of Verbal Learning and Verbal Behavior,* 1968, **7,** 278.

Glanzer, M., & Clark, W. H. Accuracy of perceptual recall: An analysis of organization. *Journal of Verbal Learning and Verbal Behavior,* 1963, **1,** 289–299. (a)

Glanzer, M., & Clark, W. H. The verbal loop hypothesis: Binary numbers. *Journal of Verbal Learning and Verbal Behavior,* 1963, **2,** 301–309. (b)

Glanzer, M., & Cunitz, A. R. Two storage mechanisms in free recall. *Journal of Verbal Learning and Verbal Behavior,* 1966, **5,** 351–360.

Glanzer, M., & Dolinsky, R. The anchor for the serial position curve. *Journal of Verbal Learning and Verbal Behavior,* 1965, **4,** 267–273.

Glanzer, M., & Peters, S. C. Re-examination of the serial position effect. *Journal of Experimental Psychology,* 1962, **64,** 258–266.

Glaze, J. A. The association value of nonsense syllables. *Journal of Genetic Psychology,* 1928, **35,** 255–269.

Goggin, J. First-list recall as a function of second-list learning method. *Journal of Verbal Learning and Verbal Behavior,* 1967, **6,** 423–427.

Goulet, L. R., Bone, R. N., & Barker, D. D. Serial position, primacy and the von Restorff isolation effect. *Psychonomic Science,* 1967, **9,** 529–530.

Green, R. T. Surprise as a factor in the von Restorff effect. *Journal of Experimental Psychology,* 1956, **52,** 340–344.

Greeno, J. G., & Bjork, R. A. Mathematical learning theory and the new "mental forestry." In P. H. Mussen & M. R. Rosenzweig (Eds.) *Annual Review of Psychology,* 1973, **24,** 81–116.

Greeno, J. G., James, C. T., & DaPolito, F. J. A cognitive interpretation of negative transfer and forgetting of paired associates. *Journal of Verbal Learning and Verbal Behavior,* 1971, **10,** 331–345.

Greenspoon, J., & Ranyard, R. Stimulus conditions and retroactive inhibition. *Journal of Experimental Psychology,* 1957, **53,** 55–59.

Gregg, L. W. Simulation models of learning and memory. In L. W. Gregg (Ed.), *Cognition in learning and memory.* New York: Wiley, 1972, 1–17.

Gregg, L. W., & Simon, H. A. An information-processing explanation of one-trial and incremental learning. *Journal of Verbal Learning and Verbal Behavior*, 1967, **6,** 780–787.

Gross, P., & Cady, A. W. The effect of item difficulty and list length on the rate of paired associate learning. Paper presented at the meeting of the Southeastern Psychological Association, Louisville, Ky., April, 1970.

Gruneberg, M. M. The serial position curve and the distinction between short- and long-term memory. *Acta Psychologica*, 1972, **36,** 221–225.

Guilford, J. P. The role of form in learning. *Journal of Experimental Psychology*, 1927, **10,** 415–423.

Gumenik, W. E., & Slak, S. Is there an evaluative meaning isolation effect in serial learning? *Psychological Reports*, 1969, **25,** 606.

Haber, R. N., & Hershenson, M. The effects of repeated brief exposures on the growth of a percept. *Journal of Experimental Psychology*, 1965, **69,** 40–46.

Hakes, D. T., James, C. T., & Young, R. K. A re-examination of the Ebbinghaus derived-list paradigm. *Journal of Experimental Psychology*, 1964, **68,** 508–514.

Hakes, D. T., & Young, R. K. On remote associations and the interpretation of derived-list experiments. *Psychological Review*, 1966, **73,** 248–251.

Hall, M. E. Remote associative tendencies in serial learning. *Journal of Experimental Psychology*, 1928, **11,** 65–76.

Harcum, E. R. Verbal transfer of overlearned forward and backward associations. *American Journal of Psychology*, 1953, **66,** 622–625.

Harcum, E. R. Three inferred factors in the visual recognition of binary targets. In J. W. Wulfeck & J. H. Taylor (Ed.), Form discrimination as related to military problems. *National Academy of Sciences-National Research Council Publication 561*, 1957, 32–37. (a)

Harcum, E. R. Visual recognition along four meridians of the visual field: Preliminary experiments. *University of Michigan, Project MICHIGAN Report 2144-50-T*, 1957. (b)

Harcum, E. R. Interactive effects within visual patterns on the discriminability of individual elements. *Journal of Experimental Psychology*, 1964, **68,** 351–356. (a)

Harcum, E. R. Reproduction of linear visual patterns tachistoscopically exposed in various orientations. Williamsburg, Va.: College of William and Mary, 1964. (b)

Harcum, E. R. An isolation effect in pattern perception similar to that in serial learning. *Perceptual and Motor Skills*, 1965, **20,** 1121–1130. (a)

Harcum, E. R. Pre-knowledge of isolation as a prerequisite for the isolation-effect. *Psychonomic Science*, 1965, **3,** 443–444. (b)

Harcum, E. R. Mnemonic organization as a determinant of error-gradients in visual pattern perception. *Perceptual and Motor Skills*, 1966, **22,** 671–696. (Monograph Supplement 5-V22) (a)

Harcum, E. R. Visual hemifield differences as conflicts in direction of reading. *Journal of Experimental Psychology*, 1966, **72,** 479–480. (b)

Harcum, E. R. A note on "Encoding in the perceptual (visual) serial position effect". *Journal of Verbal Learning and Verbal Behavior*, 1967, **7,** 275–277. (a)

Harcum, E. R. Parallel functions of serial learning and tachistoscopic pattern perception. *Psychological Review*, 1967, **74,** 51–62. (b)

Harcum, E. R. Two possible mechanisms of differential set in tachistoscopic perception of multiple targets. *Perceptual and Motor Skills*, 1967, **25,** 289–304. (c)

Harcum, E. R. Perceptual serial-position curves with a frequently isolated element. *Ameri-*

can Journal of Psychology, 1968, **81,** 334–346.

Harcum, E. R. Cognitive anchoring of different errors in continuous serial learning. *Psychological Reports,* 1969, **25,** 79–82.

Harcum, E. R. Defining shape for perceptual element-position curves. *Psychological Bulletin,* 1970, **74,** 362–372. (a)

Harcum, E. R. Perceptibility gradients for tachistoscopic patterns: Sensitivity or salience? *Psychological Review,* 1970, **77,** 332–337. (b)

Harcum, E. R. Serial learning with shorter intertrial interval than interstimulus interval. *Psychological Reports,* 1973, **33,** 487–494.

Harcum, E. R. Serial of heterogeneous items in ordered and unordered sequences. *Psychological Reports,* 1975, **36,** 3–11.

Harcum, E. R., & Coppage, E. W. Serial learning without primacy or recency effects. *Psychonomic Science,* 1965, **3,** 571–572. (a)

Harcum, E. R., & Coppage, E. W. Serial-position curve of verbal learning after prolonged practice. *Psychological Reports,* 1965, **17,** 475–488. (b)

Harcum, E. R., & Coppage, E. W. Explanation of serial-learning errors within Deese-Kresse categories. *Journal of Experimental Psychology,* 1969, **81,** 489–496.

Harcum, E. R., & Friedman, S. M. Reproduction of binary visual patterns having different element-presentation sequences. *Journal of Experimental Psychology,* 1963, **66,** 300–307.

Harcum, E. R., & Shaw, M. R. Cognitive and sensory lateral masking of tachistoscopic patterns. *Journal of Experimental Psychology,* 1974, **103,** 663–667.

Harcum, E. R., & Smith, N. F. Stability of error distributions within tachistoscopic patterns. *Psychonomic Science,* 1966, **6,** 287–288.

Harcum, E. R., Filion, R. D. L., & Dyer, D. W. Distribution of errors in tachistoscopic reproduction of binary patterns after practice. *Perceptual and Motor Skills,* 1962, **15,** 83–89.

Harcum, E. R., Hartman, R., & Smith, N. F. Pre- vs. post-knowledge of required reproduction sequence for tachistoscopic patterns. *Canadian Journal of Psychology,* 1963, **17,** 263–273.

Harcum, E. R., Pschirrer, M. S., & Coppage, E. W. Determinants of primacy for items in continuous serial learning. *Psychological Reports,* 1968, **22,** 965–975.

Hayes, K. J. The backward curve: A method for the study of learning. *Psychological Review,* 1953, **60,** 269–275.

Hays, W. L. *Statistics for psychologists.* New York: Holt, 1963.

Heaps, R. S., Greene, W. A., & Cheney, C. D. Transfer from serial to paired-associate learning with two paired-associate rates. *Journal of Verbal Learning and Verbal Behavior,* 1968, **7,** 840–841.

Hebb, D. O. *The organization of behavior.* New York: Wiley, 1949.

Hebb, D. O. Alice in Wonderland or Psychology among the biological sciences. In H. F. Harlow & C. N. Woolsey (Eds.), *Biological and biochemical bases of behavior.* Madison: University of Wisconsin Press, 1958, 451–467.

Hebb, D. O. Distinctive features of learning in the higher animal. In J. F. Delafresnaye (Ed.), *Brain mechanisms and learning.* London: Oxford University Press, 1961, 37–46.

Hebb, D. O. The semiautonomous process: Its nature and nurture. *American Psychologist,* 1963, **18,** 16–27.

Hermans, T. G. A study of the relative amounts of forward and backward association of verbal material. *Journal of Experimental Psychology,* 1936, **19,** 769–775.

Heron, W. Perception as a function of retinal locus and attention. *American Journal of Psychology*, 1957, **70**, 38–48.

Hershenson, M. Perception of letter arrays as a function of absolute retinal locus. *Journal of Experimental Psychology*, 1969, **80**, 201–202.

Hertzman, M., & Neff, W. S. The development of intraserial relationships in rote learning. *Journal of Experimental Psychology*, 1939, **25**, 389–401.

Heslip, J. R. A methodological note on direct tests of the effectiveness of positional cues in serial learning. *Psychonomic Science*, 1968, **13**, 221–222.

Heslip, J. R. A cluster of preceding items as a cue in serial learning. Unpublished doctoral dissertation, University of Kansas, 1969. (a)

Heslip, J. R. Temporal contiguity and spatial separation of items in input as sources of serial order information. *Journal of Experimental Psychology*, 1969, **81**, 593–595. (b)

Heslip, J. R. A test of the cluster hypothesis of serial learning. *Psychonomic Science*, 1969, **14**, 273–274, 276. (c)

Heslip, J. R., & Englebrecht, L. R. Influence of four input conditions on serial output. *Psychonomic Science*, 1969, **16**, 309–310.

Heslip, J. R., & Epstein, W. Effectiveness of serial position and preceding-item cues in serial learning. *Journal of Experimental Psychology*, 1969, **80**, 64–68.

Hicks, R. Y., Hakes, D. T., & Young, R. K. Generalization of serial position in rote serial learning. *Journal of Experimental Psychology*, 1966, **71**, 916–917.

Hilgard, E. R., & Campbell, A. A. Vincent curves of conditioning. *Journal of Experimental Psychology*, 1937, **21**, 310–319.

Hilgard, E. R., & Marquis, D. G. *Conditioning and learning*. New York: Appleton-Century-Crofts, 1940.

Hinrichs, J. V. Prestimulus and poststimulus cuing of recall order in the memory span. *Psychonomic Science*, 1968, **12**, 261–262.

Hintzman, D. L., & Block, R. A. Repetition and memory: Evidence for a multiple-trace hypothesis. *Journal of Experimental Psychology*, 1971, **88**, 297–306.

Hintzman, D. L., Block, R. A., & Summers, J. J. Contextual associations and memory for serial position. *Journal of Experimental Psychology*, 1973, **97**, 220–229.

Horowitz, L. M. Free recall and ordering of trigrams. *Journal of Experimental Psychology*, 1961, **62**, 51–57.

Horowitz, L. M., & Izawa, C. Comparison of serial and paired-associate learning. *Journal of Experimental Psychology*, 1963, **65**, 352–361.

Horton, D. L., & Dixon, T. R. Traditions, trends, and innovations. In T. R. Dixon & D. L. Horton (Eds.), *Verbal behavior and general behavior theory*. Englewood Cliffs, New Jersey: Prentice-Hall, 1968, 572–580.

Horton, D. L., & Grover, D. E. Associative asymmetry in paired associate to serial transfer. *Psychonomic Science*, 1968, **10**, 133–134.

Horton, D. L., & Hartman, R. R. Verbal mediation as a function of associative directionality and exposure frequency. *Journal of Verbal Learning and Verbal Behavior*, 1963, **1**, 361–364.

Horton, D. L., & Turnage, T. W. Serial to paired-associate learning: Utilization of serial information. *Journal of Experimental Psychology*, 1970, **84**, 88–95.

Houck, R. L., & Mefferd, R. B. Jr. Perceptual categorization: A parallel between perceptual identification and serial learning. *Perceptual and Motor Skills*, 1971, **32**, 578. (a)

Houck, R. L., & Mefferd, R. B. Jr. Perceptual categorization: Factors influencing identification and reproduction of visual and auditory stimuli. *Perceptual and Motor Skills*, 1971, **32**, 519–522. (b)

Hovland, C. I. Experimental studies in rote-learning theory. I. Reminiscence following learning by massed and by distributed practice. *Journal of Experimental Psychology*. 1938, **22**, 201–224. (a)

Hovland, C. I. Experimental studies in rote-learning theory. II. Reminiscence with varying speeds of syllable presentation. *Journal of Experimental Psychology*, 1938, **22**, 338–353. (b)

Hovland, C. I. Experimental studies in rote-learning theory. III. Distribution of practice with varying speeds of syllable presentation. *Journal of Experimental Psychology*, 1938, **23**, 172–190. (c)

Hovland, C. I. Experimental studies in rote-learning theory. IV. Comparison of reminiscence in serial and paired-associate learning. *Journal of Experimental Psychology*, 1939, **24**, 466–484. (a)

Hovland, C. I. Experimental studies in rote-learning theory. V. Comparison of distribution of practice in serial and paired associate learning. *Journal of Experimental Psychology*, 1939, **25**, 622–633. (b)

Hovland, C. I. Experimental studies in rote-learning theory. VI. Comparison of retention following learning to same criterion by massed and distributed practice. *Journal of Experimental Psychology*, 1940, **26**, 568–587. (a)

Hovland, C. I. Experimental studies in rote-learning theory. VII. Distribution of practice with varying lengths of list. *Journal of Experimental Psychology*, 1940, **27**, 271–284. (b)

Hovland, C. I., & Kurtz, K. H. Experimental studies in rote-learning theory. X. Prelearning syllable familiarization and the length-difficulty relationship. *Journal of Experimental Psychology*, 1952, **44**, 31–39.

Huang, I., & Hynum, L. J. Degrees of isolation and the von Restorff effect in serial learning. *Psychonomic Science*, 1970, **21**, 357–359.

Hughes, J. B. II, Sprague, J. L., & Bendig, A. W. Anxiety level, response alternation, and performance in serial learning. *Journal of Psychology*, 1954, **38**, 421–426.

Hull, C. L. The factor of the conditioned reflex. In C. Murchison (Ed.), *Handbook of general experimental psychology*, Worcester, Mass.: Clarke University Press, 1934, 382–455.

Hull, C. L. The conflicting psychologies of learning—a way out. *Psychological Review*, 1935, **42**, 491–516. (a)

Hull, C. L. The influence of caffeine and other factors on certain phenomena of rote learning. *Journal of General Psychology*, 1935, **13**, 249–274. (b)

Hull, C. L. *Principles of behavior*. New York: Appleton-Century-Crofts, 1943.

Hull, C. L. *Essentials of behavior*. New Haven: Yale University Press, 1951.

Hull, C. L. *A behavior system: An introduction to behavior theory concerning the individual organism*. New Haven: Yale University Press, 1952.

Hull, C. L., Hovland, C. I., Ross, R. T., Hall, M., Perkins, D. T., & Fitch, F. B. *Mathematico-deductive theory of rote learning: A study in scientific methodology*. New Haven: Yale University Press, 1940.

Irion, A. L. Retroactive inhibition as a function of the relative serial positions of the original and interpolated items. *Journal of Experimental Psychology*, 1946, **36**, 262–270.

Irion, A. I. The relation of "set" to retention. *Psychological Review,* 1948, **55,** 336–341.

Jahnke, J. C. Serial position effects in immediate serial recall. *Journal of Verbal Learning and Verbal Behavior,* 1963, **2,** 284–287.

Jahnke, J. C. Primacy and recency effects in serial-position curves of immediate recall. *Journal of Experimental Psychology,* 1965, **70,** 130–132.

Jahnke, J. C. Presentation rate and the serial position effect of immediate serial recall. *Journal of Verbal Learning and Verbal Behavior,* 1968, **7,** 608–612.

Jahnke, J. C. Output interference and the Ranschburg effect. *Journal of Verbal Learning and Verbal Behavior,* 1969, **8,** 614–621. (a)

Jahnke, J. C. The Ranschburg effect. *Psychological Review,* 1969, **76,** 592–605. (b)

James, H. E. O. The problem of interference. *British Journal of Psychology,* 1931, **22,** 31–42.

Jantz, E. M., & Underwood, B. J. R-S learning as a function of meaningfulness and degree of S-R learning. *Journal of Experimental Psychology,* 1958, **56,** 174–179.

Jenkins, J. G., & Dallenbach, K. M. The effect of serial position upon recall. *American Journal of Psychology,* 1927, **38,** 285–291.

Jenkins, O., & Postman, L. Isolation and "spread of effect" in serial learning. *American Journal of Psychology,* 1948, **61,** 214–221.

Jensen, A. R. An empirical theory of the serial-position effect. *Journal of Psychology,* 1962, **53,** 127–142. (a)

Jensen, A. R. Extraversion, neuroticism, and serial learning. *Acta Psychologica,* 1962, **20,** 69–77. (b)

Jensen, A. R. Is the serial-position curve invariant? *British Journal of Psychology,* 1962, **53,** 159–166. (c)

Jensen, A. R. Spelling errors and the serial-position effect. *Journal of Educational Psychology,* 1962, **53,** 105–109. (d)

Jensen, A. R. Temporal and spatial effects of serial position. *American Journal of Psychology,* 1962, **75,** 390–400. (e)

Jensen, A. R. Transfer between paired-associate and serial learning. *Journal of Verbal Learning and Verbal Behavior,* 1962, **1,** 269–280. (f)

Jensen, A. R. The von Restorff isolation effect with minimal response learning. *Journal of Experimental Psychology,* 1962, **64,** 123–125. (g)

Jensen, A. R. Serial rote-learning: Incremental or all-or-none? *Quarterly Journal of Experimental Psychology,* 1963, **15,** 27–35.

Jensen, A. R. Individual differences in learning: Interference factor. *Cooperative Research Project No. 1867,* Berkeley, Calif.: University of California, Institute of Human Learning, 1964.

Jensen, A. R. Rote learning in retarded adults and normal children. *American Journal of Mental Deficiency,* 1965, **69,** 828–834.

Jensen, A. R., & Blank, S. S. Association with ordinal position in serial rote-learning. *Canadian Journal of Psychology,* 1962, **16,** 60–63.

Jensen, A. R., & Roden, A. Memory span and the skewness of the serial-position curve. *British Journal of Psychology,* 1963, **54,** 337–349.

Jensen, A. R., & Rohwer, W. D. Jr. Verbal mediation in paired-associate and serial learning. *Journal of Verbal Learning and Verbal Behavior,* 1963, **1,** 346–352.

Jensen, A. R., & Rohwer, W. D. Jr. What is learned in serial learning? *Journal of Verbal Learning and Verbal Behavior,* 1965, **4,** 62–72.

Johansson, B. S. Attention and the von Restorff effect. *British Journal of Psychology*, 1970, **61**, 163–170.

Johnson, G. J. Sequential and positional cues in serial to paired-associate transfer. *American Journal of Psychology*, 1972, **85**, 325–337.

Johnson, N. F. Sequential behavior. In T. R. Dixon & D. L. Horton (Eds.), *Verbal behavior and general behavior theory*. Englewood Cliffs, N. J.: Prentice-Hall, 1968, 421–450.

Johnson, N. F. Chunking: Associative chaining vs. coding. *Journal of Verbal Learning and Verbal Behavior*, 1969, **8**, 725–731.

Johnson, N. F. Organization and concept of a memory code. In A. W. Melton & E. Martin (Eds.), *Coding processes in human memory*, Washington: Winston, 1972, 125–159.

Johnson, R. E. Differential meaningfulness and isolation effects. *Journal of Experimental Psychology*, 1971, **88**, 376–379.

Johnson, R. E. Meaningfulness differentials, number of isolates, and isolation effects. *Journal of General Psychology*, 1972, **87**, 181–186.

Jones, H. G. Learning and abnormal behavior. In H. J. Eysenck (Ed.), *Handbook of abnormal psychology*, New York: Basic Books, 1961, 488–528.

Jones, F. N., & Jones, M. H. Vividness as a factor in learning lists of nonsense syllables. *American Journal of Psychology*, 1942, **55**, 96–101.

Jung, J. A. cumulative method of paired-associate and serial learning. *Journal of Verbal Learning and Verbal Behavior*, 1964, **3**, 290–299.

Kasschau, R. A. Polarization in serial and paired-associate learning. *American Journal of Psychology*, 1972, **85**, 43–55.

Katona, G. *Organizing and memorizing*. New York: Columbia University Press, 1940.

Kaufmann, H. The effects of experimenter-imposed temporal grouping upon serial learning. *Journal of Verbal Learning and Verbal Behavior*, 1967, **6**, 699–706.

Kausler, D. H. *Psychology of verbal learning and memory*. New York: Academic Press, 1974.

Kausler, D. H., & Trapp, E. P. Effects of incentive-set and task variables on relevant and irrelevant learning in serial verbal learning. *Psychological Reports*, 1962, **10**, 451–457.

Kausler, D. H., & Trapp, E. P. Irrelevant cues and serial learning effects. *Psychological Reports*, 1963, **12**, 798.

Kay, H., & Poulton, E. C. Anticipation in memorizing. *British Journal of Psychology*, 1951, **42**, 34–41.

Kayson, W. A. A study of strategies in serial learning. Unpublished doctoral dissertation, City University of New York, 1970.

Kayson, W. A., & Winnick, W. A. Instructional control of serial-learning strategies. *Journal of Experimental Psychology*, 1974, **102**, 670–677.

Keenan, V. C. Presentation method and learning-time constancy in serial learning. Unpublished doctoral dissertation, University of California, Berkeley, 1967.

Kendler, H. H. What is learned?—A theoretical blind alley. *Psychological Review*, 1952, **59**, 269–277.

Keppel, G. Retroactive inhibition of serial lists as a function of the presence or absence of positional cues. *Journal of Verbal Learning and Verbal Behavior*, 1964, **3**, 511–517.

Keppel, G. Comments on the hypothesis of implicit serial-position cues. *Psychonomic Science*, 1965, **3**, 471–472.

Keppel, G. Unlearning in serial learning. *Journal of Experimental Psychology*, 1966, **71**, 143–149.

Keppel, G. Retroactive and proactive inhibition. In T. R. Dixon & D. L. Horton (Eds.), *Verbal behavior and general behavior theory.* Englewood Cliffs, N. J.: Prentice-Hall, 1968, 172–213.

Keppel, G., & Rehula, R. J. Rate of presentation in serial learning. *Journal of Experimental Psychology,* 1965, **69,** 121–125.

Keppel, G., & Saufley, W. H. Jr. Serial position as a stimulus in serial learning. *Journal of Verbal Learning and Verbal Behavior,* 1964, **3,** 335–343.

Keppel, G., & Underwood, B. J. Proactive inhibition in short-term retention of single items. *Journal of Verbal Learning and Verbal Behavior,* 1962, **1,** 153–161. (a)

Keppel, G., & Underwood, B. J. Retroactive inhibition of R-S associations. *Journal of Experimental Psychology,* 1962, **64,** 400–404. (b)

Keppel, G., & Zavortink, B. Unlearning and competition in serial learning. *Journal of Verbal Learning and Verbal Behavior,* 1968, **7,** 142–147.

Kibler, J. L. III, & Blick, K. A. Evaluation of experimenter-supplied and subject-originated first-letter mnemonics in a free-recall task. *Psychological Reports,* 1972, **30,** 307–313.

Kimble, G. A., & Dufort, R. H. Meaningfulness and isolation as factors in verbal learning. *Journal of Experimental Psychology,* 1955, **50,** 361–368.

Kintz, B. L., Kirk, W. E., Miller, H. R., Regester, D. C., & Zupnick, S. M. Serial position as a factor in isolation. *Perceptual and Motor Skills,* 1965, **20,** 255–257.

Koffman, E. C., & Weinstock, R. B. Total time hypothesis in low-meaningful serial learning: Task, age, and verbalization instructions. *Journal of Experimental Psychology,* 1974, **103,** 1210–1213.

Köhler, W. *Gestalt psychology.* New York: Liveright, 1947.

Köhler, W. Perceptual organization and learning. *American Journal of Psychology,* 1958, **71,** 311–315.

Koustaal, C. W., Smith, O. W., & Panyard, C. Serial learning of CVCS with high and low effort ratings of CVCS. *Perceptual and Motor Skills,* 1972, **35,** 407–410.

Krishna, K. P., & Varma, C. R., Rote serial learning in high and low anxious groups. *Indian Journal of Experimental Psychology,* 1972, **6,** 35–37.

Krueger, W. C. F. Learning during directed attention. *Journal of Experimental Psychology,* 1932, **15,** 517–527.

Krueger, W. C. F. Rate of progress as related to difficulty of assignment. *Journal of Educational Psychology,* 1946, **37,** 247–249.

Krueger, W. C. F. Influence of difficulty of perceptual-motor task upon acceleration of curves of learning. *Journal of Educational Psychology,* 1947, **38,** 51–53.

Ladd, G. T., & Woodworth, R. S. *Elements of physiological psychology.* New York: Scribner, 1911.

Lashley, K. S. In search of the engram. *Symposium of the Society for Experimental Biology,* 1950, **4,** 454–482.

Lashley, K. S. The problem of serial order in behavior. In L. A. Jeffress (Ed.), *Cerebral mechanisms in behavior.* New York: Wiley, 1951, 112–136.

Lawrence, D. H. Acquired distinctiveness of cues: I. Transfer between discriminations on the basis of familiarity with the stimulus. *Journal of Experimental Psychology,* 1949, **39,** 770–784.

Lazarus, R. S., Deese, J., & Hamilton, R. Anxiety and stress in learning: The role of intraserial duplication. *Journal of Experimental Psychology,* 1954, **47,** 111–114.

Lazarus, R. S., Deese, J., & Osler, S. F. The effects of psychological stress upon performance. *Psychological Bulletin*, 1952, **49**, 293–317.

Leicht, K. L. Differential rehearsal and primacy effects. *Journal of Verbal Learning and Verbal Behavior*, 1968, **7**, 1115–1117.

Leonard, R. L. Jr., & Blick, K. A. A re-evaluation of the length-difficulty relationship. *Virginia Journal of Science*, 1970, **21**, 61–62.

Leonard, S. D., & Tangeman, P. A. Lack of effects of numbering on learning of serial lists. *Journal of Experimental Psychology*, 1973, **97**, 105–107.

Lepley, W. M. A theory of serial learning and forgetting based upon conditioned reflex principles. *Psychological Review*, 1932, **39**, 279–288.

Lepley, W. M. Serial reactions considered as conditioned reactions. *Psychological Monographs*, 1934, **46**, No. 205.

Lepley, W. M. Retention as a function of serial position. *Psychological Bulletin*, 1935, **32**, 730.

Lesgold, A. M., & Bower, G. H. Inefficiency of serial knowledge for associative responding. *Journal of Verbal Learning and Verbal Behavior*, 1970, **9**, 456–466.

Lester, O. P. Mental set in relation to retroactive inhibition. *Journal of Experimental Psychology*, 1932, **15**, 681–699.

Levin, J. R. The effect of verbal organizations on the location of subjects' errors in serial learning. *Psychonomic Science*, 1969, **16**, 61–63.

Levin, J. R., & Rohwer, W. D. Jr. Verbal organization and the facilitation of serial learning. *Journal of Educational Psychology*, 1968, **59**, 186–190.

Lieury, A. Facilitation, inhibition, and distortions of the serial curve in single-trial free recall as a function of prior within-word organization. *Journal of Experimental Psychology*, 1973, **98**, 91–94.

Lindley, R. H. Association value, familiarity, and pronunciability ratings as predictors of serial verbal learning. *Journal of Experimental Psychology*, 1963, **65**, 347–351.

Lippman, L. G. Cue utilization in serial learning. *Psychonomic Science*, 1968, **13**, 101–102.

Lippman, L. G. Compound stimuli in serial learning. *Journal of General Psychology*, 1971, **84**, 191–199. (a)

Lippman. L. G. Serial isolation effect as related to list-end demarcation. *Journal of Experimental Psychology*, 1971, **87**, 135–137. (b)

Lippman, L. G., & Denny, M. R. Serial position effect as a function of intertrial interval. *Journal of Verbal Learning and Verbal Behavior*, 1964, **3**, 496–501.

Lippman, L. G., & Lippman, M. Z. Serial reconstruction in third grade children. *Journal of General Psychology*, 1970, **82**, 81–85.

Lively, B. L. The von Restorff effect in short-term memory. *Journal of Experimental Psychology*, 1972, **93**, 361–366.

Lloyd, K. E., Reid, L. S., & Feallock, J. B. Short-term retention as a function of the average number of items presented. *Journal of Experimental Psychology*, 1960, **60**, 201–207.

Lucas, J. D. The interactive effects of anxiety, failure, and intra-serial duplication. *American Journal of Psychology*, 1952, **65**, 59–66.

Lumley, F. H. Anticipation as a factor in serial and maze learning. *Journal of Experimental Psychology*, 1932, **15**, 331–342. (a)

Lumley, F. H. Anticipation of correct responses as a source of error in the learning of serial responses. *Journal of Experimental Psychology*, 1932, **15**, 195–205. (b)

Lyon, D. O. The relation of length of material to time taken for learning and the optimum distribution of time. *Journal of Education Psychology*, 1914, **5**, 1–9; 85–91; 155–163.

Lyon, D. O. *Memory and the learning process.* Baltimore: Warwick & York, 1917.

Magne, O. *Perception and learning.* Uppsala: Appelbergs Boktryckeri Ab, 1952.

Maier, N. R. F., & Schneirla, T. C. *Principles of animal psychology.* New York: Dover, 1964.

Maisto, A. A., & Ward, L. C. Test of the ordinal position hypothesis using serial anticipation and serial recall procedures. *Journal of Experimental Psychology*, 1973, **101**, 232–236.

Malmo, R. B., & Amsel, A. Anxiety-produced interference in serial rote learning with observations on rote learning after partial frontal lobectomy. *Journal of Experimental Psychology*, 1948, **38**, 440–454.

Mandler, G. From association to structure. *Psychological Review*, 1962, **69**, 415–427.

Mandler, G. Organization and memory. In K. W. Spence & J. T. Spence (Eds.), *The psychology of learning and motivation: Advances in research and theory.* Vol. I. New York: Academic Press, 1967, 327–372. (a)

Mandler, G. Verbal learning. In G. Mandler, P. Mussen, N. Kogan, & M. A. Wallach, *New directions in psychology III.* New York: Holt, Rinehart and Winston, 1967, 3–50. (b)

Mandler, G. Association and organization: Facts, fancies, and theories. In T. R. Dixon & D. L. Horton (Eds.), *Verbal behavior and general behavior theory.* Englewood Cliffs, New Jersey: Prentice-Hall, 1968, 109–119.

Mandler, G., & Anderson, R. E. Temporal and spatial cues in seriation. *Journal of Experimental Psychology*, 1971, **90**, 128–135.

Mandler, G., & Earhard, B. Pseudomediation: Is chaining an artifact? *Psychonomic Science*, 1964, **1**, 247–248.

Mandler, G., & Mandler, J. M. Serial position effects in sentences. *Journal of Verbal Learning and Verbal Behavior*, 1964, **3**, 195–202.

Marshall, P. H., & Werder, P. R. The effects of the elimination of rehearsal on primacy and recency. *Journal of Verbal Learning and Verbal Behavior*, 1972, **11**, 649–653.

Martens, D. Spread of effect in verbal serial learning. *American Psychologist*, 1946, **1**, 448–449.

Martin, E. Verbal learning theory and independent retrieval phenomena, *Psychological Review*, 1971, **78**, 314–332.

Martin, C. J., & Saltz, E. Serial vs. random presentation of paired associates. *Journal of Experimental Psychology*, 1963, **65**, 609–615.

Martin, W. L., & Greene, W. A. Transfer of interitem associations from serial to paired-associate learning. *Psychonomic Science*, 1966, **4**, 295–296.

Masani, P. A. The attention mechanism and its relationship to post-perceptual short-term storage. *Papers in psychology*, 1967, **1**, No. 2.

Matarazzo, J. D., Ulett, G. A., & Saslow, G. Human maze performance as a function of increasing levels of anxiety. *Journal of General Psychology*, 1955, **53**, 79–95.

McCrary, J. W., & Hunter, W. S. Serial position curves in verbal learning. *Science*, 1953, **117**, 131–134.

McGeoch, J. A. The influence of associative value upon the difficulty of nonsense-syllable lists. *Journal of Genetic Psychology*, 1930, **37**, 421–426.

McGeoch, J. A. Forgetting and the law of disuse. *Psychological Review*, 1932, **39**, 352–370.

McGeoch, J. A. The direction and extent of intraserial associations at recall. *Psychological*

Bulletin, 1934, **31,** 717.

McGeoch, J. A. The direction and extent of intra-serial associations at recall. *American Journal of Psychology,* 1936, **48,** 221–245.

McGeoch, J. A. *The psychology of human learning: An introduction.* New York: Longmans, Green, 1942.

McGeoch, J. A., & Irion, A. L. *The psychology of human learning.* New York: Longmans, Green, 1952.

McGeoch, J. A., & McGeoch, G. O. Studies in retroactive inhibition. VI. The influence of the relative serial position of interpolated synonyms. *Journal of Experimental Psychology,* 1936, **19,** 1–23.

McGourty, M. C. Serial position effects in learning as a function of interfering associations. Unpublished master's thesis, University of Iowa, 1940.

McGovern, J. B. Extinction of associations in four transfer paradigms. *Psychological Monographs,* 1964, **78,** No. 16.

McHugh, A., Turnage, T. W., & Horton, D. L. Short-term serial recall as a function of similarity, serial position, and trials. *Journal of Experimental Psychology,* 1973, **97,** 204–209.

McKeever, B. The preceding item as a cue for a response in serial learning. *Psychonomic Science,* 1968, **11,** 51–52.

McKenna, V. V., & Harcum, E. R. Strategies in serial learning and tachistoscopic perception of aged subjects. *Virginia Journal of Science,* 1967, **18,** 210. (Abstract)

McLaughlin, J. P. The von Restorff effect in serial learning: Serial position of the isolate and length of list. *Journal of Experimental Psychology,* 1966, **72,** 603–609.

McLaughlin, J. P. Recall and recognition measures of the von Restorff effect in serial learning. *Journal of Experimental Psychology,* 1968, **78,** 99–102.

McLean, R. S., & Gregg, L. W. Effects of induced chunking on temporal aspects of serial recitation. *Journal of Experimental Psychology,* 1967, **74,** 455–459.

McManis, D. L. Position-cues in serial learning. *American Journal of Psychology,* 1965, **78,** 668–671.

McManis, D. L. Intralist differentiation and the isolation effect in serial learning: A test of the S-R competition hypothesis. *Journal of Verbal Learning and Verbal Behavior,* 1967, **6,** 714–720.

Mednick, S. A. *Learning,* Englewood Cliffs, N. J.: Prentice-Hall, 1964.

Mellgren, R. L. Position as a stimulus in verbal learning. *Psychonomic Science,* 1967, **8,** 73–74.

Melton, A. W. The end-spurt in memorization curves as an artifact of the averaging of individual curves. *Psychological Monographs,* 1936, No. 212.

Melton, A. W. Learning. In W. S. Monroe (Ed.), *Encyclopedia of educational research.* New York: Macmillan, 1941, 667–686.

Melton, A. W. Comments on Professor Peterson's paper. In C. N. Cofer & B. S. Musgrave (Eds.), *Verbal behavior and learning: Problems and processes.* New York: McGraw-Hill, 1963, 353–370. (a)

Melton, A. W. Implications of short-term memory for a general theory of memory. *Journal of Verbal Learning and Verbal Behavior,* 1963, **2,** 1–21. (b)

Melton, A. W. The taxonomy of human learning: Overview. In A. W. Melton (Ed.), *Categories of human learning,* New York: Academic Press, 1964, 325–339.

Melton, A. W. The concept of coding in learning-memory theory. *Memory and Cognition*, 1973, **1**, 508–512.

Melton, A. W., & Irwin, J. McQ. The influence of degree of interpolated learning on retroactive inhibition and the overt transfer of specific responses. *American Journal of Psychology*, 1940, **53**, 173–203.

Melton, A. W., & Martin, E. Preface. In A. W. Melton & E. Martin (Eds.), *Coding processes in human memory*. Washington: Winston, 1972, xi–xiv.

Melton, A. W., & Stone, G. R. Retention of serial lists of adjectives. *Journal of Experimental Psychology*, 1942, **30**, 295–310.

Melton, A. W., & von Lackum, W. J. Retroactive and proactive inhibition in retention: Evidence for a two-factor theory of retroactive inhibition. *American Journal of Psychology*, 1941, **54**, 157–173.

Mewhort, D. J. K. Familiarity of letter sequences, response uncertainty, and the tachistoscopic recognition experiment. *Canadian Journal of Psychology*, 1967, **21**, 309–321.

Meyer, G. Temporal organization and the initial reproductive tendency. *Journal of Psychology*, 1939, **7**, 269–282.

Miller, G. A. The magical number seven, plus or minus two: Some limits on our capacity for processing information. *Psychological Review*, 1956, **63**, 81–97.

Miller, G. A. Comments on Professor Postman's paper. In C. N. Cofer & B. S. Musgrave (Eds.), *Verbal behavior and learning: Problems and processes*. New York: McGraw-Hill, 1963, 321–329.

Miller, G. A., & Selfridge, J. A. Verbal context and the recall of meaningful material. *American Journal of Psychology*, 1950, **63**, 176–185.

Miller, G. A., Galanter, E., & Pribram, K. H. *Plans and the structure of behavior*. New York: Holt, Rinehart and Winston, 1960.

Miller, G. R. Intrinsic organization of serial lists. *Psychological Reports*, 1965, **16**, 47–50.

Milner, P. M. The cell assembly: Mark II. *Psychological Review*, 1957, **64**, 242–252.

Milner, P. M. A neural mechanism for the immediate recall of sequences. *Kybernetik*, 1961, **1**, 76–81.

Mitchell, M. B. The effect of serial position on the continuous memorization of numbers. *American Journal of Psychology*, 1933, **45**, 493–494. (a)

Mitchell, M. B. Errors in the memorization of numbers. *American Journal of Psychology*, 1933, **45**, 1–16. (b)

Montague, E. K. The role of anxiety in serial rote learning. *Journal of Experimental Psychology*, 1953, **45**, 91–98.

Montague, W. E. Elaborative strategies in verbal learning and memory. In G. H. Bower (Ed.), *The psychology of learning and motivation: Advances in research and theory*. Vol. 6. New York: Academic Press, 1972, 225–302.

Moore, J. H. The role of determining tendencies in learning. *American Journal of Psychology*, 1936, **48**, 559–571.

Mosher, D. L. The interfering effect of serial cognitive structures in long-term memory on word-order in short-term memory. *Psychonomic Science*, 1969, **16**, 317–319.

Mueller, J. H. Response properties of the position indicant in serial learning. *Journal of Experimental Psychology*, 1970, **84**, 35–39.

Mueller, J. H., & Jablonski, E. M. Transfer from serial to paired-associate learning. *Bulletin of the Psychonomic Society*, 1973, **2**, 285–286.

Muir, D., & Youssef, Z. I. The transfer of interitem associations in serial learning. *Psychonomic Science*, 1971, **25**, 69–70.

Müller, G. E., & Pilzecker, A. Experimentelle Beiträge zür Lehre vom Gedächtnis. *Zeitschrift für Psychologie*, 1900, **1**, 1–288.

Müller, G. E., & Schumann, F. Experimentelle Beiträge zür Untersuchung des Gedächtnisses. *Zeitschrift für Psychologie*, 1894, **6**, 81–190.

Murdock, B. B. Jr. Transfer designs and formulas. *Psychological Bulletin*, 1957, **54**, 313–326.

Murdock, B. B. Jr. "Backward" associations in transfer and learning. *Journal of Experimental Psychology*, 1958, **55**, 111–114.

Murdock, B. B. Jr. The distinctiveness of stimuli. *Psychological Review*, 1960, **67**, 16–31.

Murdock, B. B. Jr. Direction of recall in short-term memory. *Journal of Verbal Learning and Verbal Behavior*, 1962, **1**, 119–124. (a)

Murdock, B. B. Jr. The serial position effect of free recall. *Journal of Experimental Psychology*, 1962, **64**, 482–488. (b)

Murdock, B. B. Jr. Proactive inhibition in short-term memory. *Journal of Experimental Psychology*, 1964, **68**, 184–189.

Murdock, B. B. Jr. The criterion problem in short-term memory. *Journal of Experimental Psychology*, 1966, **72**, 317–324.

Murdock, B. B. Jr. Serial order effects in short-term memory. *Journal of Experimental Psychology*, 1968, **76**, 1–15.

Nachmias, J., Gleitman, H., & McKenna, V. V. The effect of isolation of stimuli and responses in paired associates. *American Journal of Psychology*, 1961, **74**, 452–456.

Nagel, F. Experimentelle Untersuchung über Grandfragen der Assoziationslehre. *Arkiv für der Gesellschaft Psychologie*, 1912, **23**, 156–253.

Nagge, J. W. An experimental test of the theory of associative interference. *Journal of Experimental Psychology*, 1935, **18**, 663–682.

Neisser, U. *Cognitive psychology.* New York: Appleton-Century-Crofts, 1967.

Neisser, U. The role of rhythm in active verbal memory: serial intrusions. *American Journal of Psychology*, 1969, **82**, 540–546.

Neisser, U., Hoenig, Y. J., & Goldstein, E. Perceptual organization in the prefix effect. *Journal of Verbal Learning and Verbal Behavior*, 1969, **8**, 424–429.

Newman, I. The learning of a long series. *Journal of Educational Psychology*, 1936, **27**, 253–257.

Newman, S. E. Serial position as a cue in learning: The effect of test rate. *Journal of Experimental Psychology*, 1966, **71**, 319–320.

Newman, S. E., & Saltz, E. Isolation effects: Stimulus and response generalization as explanatory concepts. *Journal of Experimental Psychology*, 1958, **55**, 467–472.

Newman, S. E., & Saltz, E. Serial position as a cue in learning. *American Journal of Psychology*, 1962, **75**, 102–108.

Noble, C. E. The role of stimulus meaning (*m*) in serial verbal learning. *Journal of Experimental Psychology*, 1952, **43**, 437–446. (a)

Noble, C. E. An analysis of meaning. *Psychological Review*, 1952, **59**, 421–430. (b)

Noble, C. E. The effect of familiarization upon serial verbal learning. *Journal of Experimental Psychology*, 1955, **49**, 333–338.

Noble, C. E. Verbal learning and individual differences. In C. N. Cofer (Ed.), *Verbal learning and verbal behavior,* New York: McGraw-Hill, 1961, 132–146.

Noble, C. E., & Fuchs, J. E. Serial errors in human learning: A test of the McCrary-Hunter hypothesis. *Science,* 1959, **129,** 570–571.

Norman, D. A. (Ed.) *Models of human memory.* New York: Academic Press, 1970.

Norman, D. A. Human information processing. *Bulletin of the School of Education, Indiana University,* 1971, **47,** 48–65.

Obrist, W. D. Skin resistance and electroencephalographic changes associated with learning. Unpublished doctoral dissertation, Northwestern University, 1950.

O'Connell, D. C., Stubbs, C. L., & Theby, M. A. Facilitation of recall by structure in serially presented nonsense strings. *Psychonomic Science,* 1968, **12,** 263–264.

Osgood, C. E. The similarity paradox in human learning: A resolution. *Psychological Review,* 1949, **56,** 132–143.

Osgood, C. E. *Method and theory in experimental psychology.* New York: Oxford, 1953.

Palmer, S. E., & Ornstein, P. A. Role of rehearsal strategy in serial probed recall. *Journal of Experimental Psychology,* 1971, **88,** 60–66.

Pash, J. R., & Blick, K. A. The effect of a mnemonic device on retention of verbal material. *Psychonomic Science,* 1970, **19,** 203–204.

Patten, E. F. The influence of distribution of repetitions on certain rote-learning phenomena. *Journal of Psychology,* 1938, **5,** 359–374.

Pavlov, I. P. *Conditioned reflexes. Translated by G. V. Anrep, Oxford: Oxford University Press,* 1927.

Peters, H. N. Mediate association. *Journal of Experimental Psychology,* 1935, **18,** 20–48.

Peterson, G. M. Negative acceleration with material of varying difficulty. *Journal of Experimental Psychology,* 1928, **11,** 40–44.

Peterson, L. R. Immediate memory: Data and theory. In C. N. Cofer & B. S. Musgrave (Eds.), *Verbal behavior and learning: Problems and processes.* New York: McGraw-Hill, 1963, 336–353.

Peterson, L. R., & Peterson, M. J. Short-term retention of individual verbal items. *Journal of Experimental Psychology,* 1959, **58,** 193–198.

Peterson, L. R., Brewer, C. L., & Bertucco, R. A guessing strategy with the anticipation technique. *Journal of Experimental Psychology,* 1963, **65,** 258–264.

Peterson, M. J., Meagher, R. B. Jr., & Ellsbury, S. W. Repetition effects in sensory memory. *Journal of Experimental Psychology,* 1970, **84,** 15–23.

Philip, B. R., & Peixotto, H. E. Generalization in the initial stages of learning nonsense syllables. I. Integral responses. *Journal of Experimental Psychology,* 1943, **33,** 50–63. (a)

Philip, B. R., & Peixotto, H. E. Generalization in the initial stages of learning nonsense syllables. II. Partial and inadequate responses. *Journal of Experimental Psychology,* 1943, **33,** 136–147. (b)

Phillips, J. L., Shiffrin, R. M., & Atkinson, R. C. Effects of list length on short-term memory. *Journal of Verbal Learning and Verbal Behavior,* 1967, **6,** 303–311.

Pillsbury, W. B., & Rausch, H. L. An extension of the Köhler-Restorff inhibition phenomenon. *American Journal of Psychology,* 1943, **56,** 293–298.

Pollack, I. Assimilation of sequentially encoded information. *American Journal of Psychology,* 1953, **66,** 421–435.

Pollack, I., Johnson, L. B., & Knaff, P. R. Running memory span. *Journal of Experimental Psychology*, 1959, **57**, 137–146.

Pollio, H. R. Associative structure and verbal behavior. In T. R. Dixon & D. L. Horton (Eds.), *Verbal behavior and general behavior theory*. Englewood Cliffs, New Jersey: Prentice-Hall, 1968, 37–66.

Pollio, H. R., & Deitchman, R. The activational characteristics of a serial cognitive structure having oppositional end points. Mimeo, University of Tennessee, 1964. (Cited by Pollio, H. R. Associative structure and verbal behavior. In T. R. Dixon & D. L. Horton (Eds.), *Verbal behavior and general behavior theory*. Englewood Cliffs, New Jersey: Prentice-Hall, 1968, 37–66.

Posnansky, C. J. Probing for the functional stimuli in serial learning. *Journal of Experimental Psychology*, 1972, **96**, 184–193.

Posnansky, C. J., Battig, W. F., & Voss, J. F. A new probe technique for the identification of serial learning processes. *Behavior Research Methods & Instrumentation*, 1972, **4**, 129–132.

Postman, L. Retroactive inhibition in recall and recognition. *Journal of Experimental Psychology*, 1952, **44**, 165–169.

Postman, L. Learned principles of organization in memory. *Psychological Monographs*, 1954, **68**, Whole No. 374, 1–24.

Postman, L. Association theory and perceptual learning. *Psychological Review*, 1955, **62**, 438–446.

Postman, L. Extra-experimental interference and the retention of words. *Journal of Experimental Psychology*, 1961, **61**, 97–110.

Postman, L. Does interference theory predict too much forgetting? *Journal of Verbal Learning and Verbal Behavior*, 1963, **2**, 40–48. (a)

Postman, L. One-trial learning. In C. N. Cofer & B. S. Musgrave (Eds.), *Verbal behavior and learning*. New York: McGraw-Hill, 1963, 295–321. (b)

Postman, L. Short-term memory and incidental learning. In A. W. Melton (Ed.), *Categories of human learning*. New York: Academic Press, 1964, 145–201.

Postman, L. The effect of interitem associative strength on the acquisition and retention of serial lists. *Journal of Verbal Learning and Verbal Behavior*, 1967, **6**, 721–728.

Postman, L. Association and performance in the analysis of verbal learning. In T. R. Dixon & D. L. Horton (Eds.) *Verbal behavior and general behavior theory*, Englewood Cliffs, New Jersey: Prentice-Hall, 1968. 550–571. (a)

Postman, L. Hermann Ebbinghaus. *American Psychologist*, 1968, **23**, 149–157. (b)

Postman, L. Experimental analysis of learning to learn. In G. H. Bower & J. T. Spence (Eds.), *The psychology of learning and motivation: Advances in research and theory*. Vol. 3. New York: Academic Press, 1969, 241–297.

Postman, L., & Adams, P. A. Studies in incidental learning. VI. Intraserial interference. *Journal of Experimental Psychology*, 1957, **54**, 153–167.

Postman, L., & Goggin, J. Whole vs. part learning of serial lists as a function of meaningfulness and intralist similarity. *Journal of Experimental Psychology*, 1964, **68**, 140–150.

Postman, L., & Jenkins, W. O. An experimental analysis of set in rote learning: The interaction of learning instruction and retention performance. *Journal of Experimental Psychology*, 1948, **38**, 683–689.

Postman, L., & Phillips, L. W. Studies in incidental learning. I. The effects of crowding and isolation. *Journal of Experimental Psychology*, 1954, **48**, 48–56.

Postman, L., & Phillips, L. W. Short-term temporal changes in free recall. *Quarterly Journal of Experimental Psychology*, 1965, **17**, 132–138.

Postman, L., & Riley, D. A. Degree of learning and interserial interference in retention. *University of California Publications in Psychology*, 1959, **8**, 271–396.

Postman, L., & Schwartz, M. Studies of learning to learn. I. Transfer as a function of method of practice and class of verbal materials. *Journal of Verbal Learning and Verbal Behavior*, 1964, **3**, 37–49.

Postman, L., & Stark, K. Studies of learning to learn. IV. Transfer from serial to paired-associate learning. *Journal of Verbal Learning and Verbal Behavior*, 1967, **6**, 339–353.

Postman, L., & Underwood, B. J. Critical issues in interference theory. *Memory and Cognition*, 1973, **1**, 19–40.

Postman, L., Adams, P. A., & Bohm, A. M. Studies in incidental learning. V. Recall for order and associative clustering. *Journal of Experimental Psychology*, 1956, **51**, 334–342.

Postman, L., Stark, K., & Fraser, J. Temporal changes in interference. *Journal of Verbal Learning and Verbal Behavior*, 1968, **7**, 672–694.

Primoff, E. Backward and forward association as an organizing act in serial and in paired associate learning. *Journal of Psychology*, 1938, **5**, 375–395.

Rabinowitz, F. M., & Andrews, S. R. Intentional and incidental learning in children and the von Restorff effect. *Journal of Experimental Psychology*, 1973, **100**, 315–318.

Raffel, G. Two determinants of the effect of primacy. *American Journal of Psychology*, 1936, **48**, 654–657.

Raskin, D. C., Hattle, M., & Rubel, E. W. The effects of electric shock isolation in serial learning. *Psychonomic Science*, 1967, **8**, 413–414.

Raskin, E., & Cook, S. W. The strength and direction of associations formed in the learning of nonsense syllables. *Journal of Experimental Psychology*, 1937, **20**, 381–395.

Ratliff, F. Inhibitory interaction and the detection and enhancement of contours. In W. A. Rosenblith (Ed.), *Sensory communication*. Cambridge, Mass.: M. I. T. Press, 1961.

Rehula, R. J. A test of two alternative hypotheses of the associations that develop in serial verbal learning. Unpublished doctoral dissertation, Northwestern University, 1960.

Reitman, W. What does it take to remember? In D. A. Norman (Ed.), *Models of human memory*. New York: Academic Press, 1970, 469–509.

Restle, F. The selection of strategies in cue learning. *Psychological Review*, 1962, **69**, 329–343.

Restle, F. Significance of all-or-none learning. *Psychological Bulletin*, 1965, **64**, 313–325.

Restle, F. Theory of serial pattern learning: Structural trees. *Psychological Review*, 1970, **77**, 481–495.

Restle, F. Serial patterns: The role of phrasing. *Journal of Experimental Psychology*, 1972, **92**, 385–390.

Restle, F. Coding of nonsense vs. the detection of patterns. *Memory and Cognition*, 1973, **1**, 499–502.

Restle, F., & Brown, E. Organization of serial pattern learning. In G. H. Bower (Ed.), *The psychology of learning and motivation: Advances in research and theory*. Vol. 4. New York: Academic Press, 1970, 249–331. (a)

Restle, F., & Brown, E. R. Serial pattern learning. *Journal of Experimental Psychology*, 1970, **83**, 120–125. (b)

Restorff, H. von. Über die Wirkung von Bereichsbildünge im Spurenfeld: Analyse von Vorgänge im Spurenfeld. *Psychologische Forschung,* 1933, **18,** 299–342.

Reynolds, J. H., & Houston, J. P. Rehearsal strategies and the primacy effect in serial learning. *Psychonomic Science,* 1964, **1,** 279–280.

Ribback, A., & Underwood, B. J. An empirical explanation of the skewness of the bowed serial position curve. *Journal of Experimental Psychology,* 1950, **40,** 329–335.

Riley, D. A., & Phillips, L. W. The effects of syllable familiarization on rote learning, association value, and reminiscence. *Journal of Experimental Psychology,* 1959, **57,** 372–379.

Roberts, D. M., & Lewis, L. Individual differences in memory and the serial position effect. *Psychonomic Science,* 1968, **12,** 77–78.

Roberts, W. A. A further test of the effect of isolation in serial learning. *American Journal of Psychology,* 1962, **75,** 134–139.

Robinson, E. S., & Brown, M. A. Effect of serial position upon memorization. *American Journal of Psychology,* 1926, **37,** 538–552.

Rock, I. The role of repetition in associative learning. *American Journal of Psychology,* 1957, **70,** 186–193.

Rosen, H., Richardson, D. H., & Saltz, E. Supplementary report: Meaningfulness as a differentiation variable in the von Restorff effect. *Journal of Experimental Psychology,* 1962, **64,** 327–328.

Rosenbaum, G. Stimulus generalization as a function of clinical anxiety. *Journal of Abnormal Psychology,* 1956, **53,** 281–285.

Rosner, S. R. Serial mediation: Effects of associative strength and structure in serial learning and transfer. *Journal of Experimental Psychology,* 1970, **84,** 370–372.

Rosner, S. R. Primacy in preschoolers' short term memory: The effects of repeated tests and shift-trials. *Journal of Experimental Child Psychology,* 1972, **13,** 220–230.

Rubin, E. D., & Brown, S. C. Constant vs. varied serial order in paired-associate learning: The effect of formal intralist similarity. *Journal of Experimental Psychology,* 1967, **73,** 257–262.

Russell, W. A., & Storms, L. H. Implicit verbal chaining in paired-associate learning. *Journal of Experimental Psychology,* 1955, **49,** 287–293.

Saltz, E. *The cognitive bases of human learning.* Homewood, Ill.: Dorsey, 1971.

Saltz, E., & Hoehn, A. J. A test of the Taylor-Spence theory of anxiety. *Journal of Abnormal and Social Psychology,* 1957, **54,** 114–117.

Saltz, E., & Newman, S. E. The von Restorff isolation effect: Test of the intralist association assumption. *Journal of Experimental Psychology,* 1959, **58,** 445–451.

Saltz, E., & Newman, S. E. Test of a "common sense" theory of the von Restorff effect. *American Psychologist,* 1960, **15,** 451. (Abstract)

Sampson, J. R. Influence of rehearsal on serial-position effects in immediate free recall. *Psychological Reports,* 1969, **25,** 893–894.

Sarason, I. G. Effect of anxiety, motivational instructions, and failure on serial learning. *Journal of Experimental Psychology,* 1956, **51,** 253–260.

Sarason, I. G. The effect of anxiety and two kinds of failure on serial learning. *Journal of Personality,* 1957, **25,** 383–392.

Saufley, W. H. Jr. An analysis of cues in serial learning. *Journal of Experimental Psychology,* 1967, **74,** 414–419.

Saul, E. V., & Osgood, C. E. Perceptual organization of materials as a factor influencing ease of learning and degree of retention. *Journal of Experimental Psychology,* 1950, **40,** 372–379.

Scheible, H., & Underwood, B. J. The role of overt errors in serial rote learning. *Journal of Experimental Psychology,* 1954, **47,** 160–162.

Schild, M. E., & Battig, W. F. Directionality in paired-associate learning. *Journal of Verbal Learning and Verbal Behavior,* 1966, **5,** 42–49.

Schlosberg, H. Time relations in serial visual perception. *Canadian Psychologist,* 1965, **6a,** 161–172.

Schmeck, R. R. The effect of intralist similarity on serial anticipation and free recall. *Psychonomic Science,* 1970, **20,** 371.

Schmeidler, G. R. Retroaction and proaction in serial learning. *American Journal of Psychology,* 1939, **52,** 592–600.

Schulz, R. W. Generalization of serial position in rote serial learning. *Journal of Experimental Psychology,* 1955, **49,** 267–272.

Schulz, R. W., & Kasschau, R. A. Serial learning as a function of meaningfulness and mode of presentation with audio and visual stimuli of equivalent duration. *Journal of Experimental Psychology,* 1966, **71,** 350–354.

Schumsky, D. A., Grasha, A. F., Trinder, J., & Richman, C. L. List length and single-trial short-term memory. *Journal of Experimental Psychology,* 1969, **82,** 238–241.

Schwartz, R. M. Confusion errors in serial learning. Unpublished master's thesis, The University of British Columbia, 1970. (a)

Schwartz, R. M. Dual process of serial learning. *Psychonomic Science,* 1970, **19,** 214–215. (b)

Seamon, J. G. Serial position effects in probe recall: Effect of rehearsal on reaction time. *Journal of Experimental Psychology,* 1972, **96,** 460–462.

Sen, A. K., Clarke, A. M., & Cooper, G. M. The effect of isolating items in serial learning in severely retarded subjects. *American Journal of Mental Deficiency,* 1968, **72,** 851–856.

Shebilske, W., & Ebenholtz, S. M. Ebbinghaus' derived-list experiments reconsidered. *Psychological Review,* 1971, **78,** 553–555.

Shephard, R. N. Comments on Professor Underwood's paper. In C. N. Cofer & B. S. Musgrave (Eds.), *Verbal behavior and learning: Problems and processes,* New York, McGraw-Hill, 1963, 48–70.

Shepard, R. N., Hovland, C. I., & Jenkins, H. M. Learning and memorization of classifications. *Psychological Monographs,* 1961, **75,** Whole No. 517.

Shiffrin, R. M. Memory search. In D. A. Norman (Ed.), *Models of Human Memory.* New York: Academic Press, 1970, 375–447.

Shiffrin, R. M., & Atkinson, R. C. Storage and retrieval processes in long-term memory. *Psychological Review,* 1969, **76,** 179–193.

Shipley, W. C. The effect of a short rest pause on retention in rote series of different lengths. *Journal of General Psychology,* 1939, **21,** 99–117.

Shuell, T. J., & Keppel, G. A further test of the chaining hypothesis of serial learning. *Journal of Verbal Learning and Verbal Behavior,* 1967, **6,** 439–445. (a)

Shuell, T. J., & Keppel, G. Retroactive inhibition as a function of learning method. *Journal of Experimental Psychology,* 1967, **75,** 457–463. (b)

Shurrager, H. C. The measurement of memory on an absolute scale. *Psychological Monographs,* 1940, **52,** 21–38.

Siegel, P. S. Structure effects within a memory series. *Journal of Experimental Psychology,* 1943, **33,** 311–316.

Siegel, S. *Nonparametric statistics.* New York: McGraw-Hill, 1956.

Silverman, R. E., & Blitz, B. Learning and two kinds of anxiety. *Journal of Abnormal and Social Psychology,* 1956, **52,** 301–303.

Simon, H. A., & Feigenbaum, E. A. An information-processing theory of some effects of similarity, familiarization, and meaningfulness in verbal learning. *Journal of Verbal Learning and Verbal Behavior,* 1964, **3,** 385–396.

Simpson, W. E. Effects of approximation to sentence word-order and grammatical class upon the serial learning of word lists. *Journal of Verbal Learning and Verbal Behavior,* 1965, **4,** 510–514.

Simpson, W. E. Errors vs. correct responses in the serial learning of word lists. *Psychonomic Science,* 1967, **7,** 213–214.

Sisson, E. D. Retroactive inhibition: Serial vs. random order of presentation of material. *Journal of Experimental Psychology,* 1938, **23,** 288–294.

Slamecka, N. J. An inquiry into the doctrine of remote associations. *Psychological Review,* 1964, **71,** 61–76.

Slamecka, N. J. In defense of a new approach to old phenomena. *Psychological Review,* 1965, **72,** 242–246.

Slamecka, N. J. Serial learning and order information. *Journal of Experimental Psychology,* 1967, **74,** 62–66.

Smith, M. H. Jr. Spread of the isolation effect in serial learning. *American Psychologist,* 1948, **3,** 235. (Abstract)

Smith, M. H. Jr. The influence of isolation on immediate memory. *American Journal of Psychology,* 1949, **62,** 405–411.

Smith, M. H., & McDougall, W. Some experiments in learning and retention. *British Journal of Psychology,* 1920, **10,** 199–209.

Smith, M. H., & Stearns, E. G. The influence of isolation on the learning of surrounding materials. *American Journal of Psychology,* 1949, **62,** 369–381.

Smith, R. K., & Brown, J. Serial acquisition as a function of the meaningfulness *(m)* of words chosen vs. mean *m* value of words learned. *Psychological Record,* 1968, **18,** 623–627.

Smith, R. K., & Noble, C. E. Effects of a mnemonic technique applied to verbal learning and memory. *Perceptual and Motor Skills,* 1965, **21,** 123–134.

Spear, N. E. Verbal learning and retention. In L. D'Amato, *Experimental psychology: Methodology, psychophysics and learning.* New York: McGraw-Hill, 1970.

Sperling, G. The information available in brief visual presentations. *Psychological Monographs,* 1960, **74,** No. 498.

Sperling, G. Successive approximations to a model for short-term memory. *Acta Psychologica,* 1967, **27,** 285–292.

Spielberger, C. D., & Smith, L. H. Anxiety (drive), stress, and serial-position effects in serial-verbal learning. *Journal of Experimental Psychology,* 1966, **72,** 589–595.

Stark, K. Transfer from serial to paired-associate learning: A reappraisal. *Journal of Verbal Learning and Verbal Behavior,* 1968, **7,** 20–30.

Steil, P., & Hynum, L. The von Restorff isolation effect employing one and three isolates. *Psychological Reports,* 1970, **27,** 963–966.

Sternberg, S. High-speed scanning in human memory. *Science,* 1966, **153,** 652–654.

Sternburg, S. Two operations in character recognition: Some evidence from reaction-time measurements. *Perception & Psychophysics,* 1967, **2,** 45–53.

Stevens, J. C., & Savin, H. B. On the form of learning curves. *Journal of the Experimental Analysis of Behavior,* 1962, **5,** 15–18.

Stone, G. R. The effect of negative incentives in serial learning: II. Response variability and incentive intensity. *American Psychologist,* 1946, **1,** 460.

Storms, L. H. Apparent backward association: A situational effect. *Journal of Experimental Psychology,* 1958, **55,** 390–395.

Swets, J. A., Tanner, W. P., & Birdsall, T. G. Decision processes in perception. *Psychological Review,* 1961, **68,** 301–340.

Taylor, J. A. The relationship of anxiety to the conditioned eyelid response. *Journal of Experimental Psychology,* 1951, **41,** 81–92.

Taylor, J. A., & Spence, K. W. The relationship of anxiety level to performance in serial learning. *Journal of Experimental Psychology,* 1952, **44,** 61–64.

Taylor, R. L., & Taub, H. A. Spatial coding of serial verbal input. *Perceptual and Motor Skills,* 1972, **34,** 919–922.

Teghtsoonian, R. One-trial learning directly observed. *Canadian Journal of Psychology,* 1964, **18,** 304–310.

Teghtsoonian, R., & Teghtsoonian, M. Discontinuities in recognition learning revealed by critical-trial analysis. *American Journal of Psychology,* 1971, **84,** 75–84.

Thieman, T. J. Levels of processing serial lists embedded in narratives. *Journal of Experimental Psychology,* 1973, **100,** 423–425.

Thomas, H. B. G. An information-theoretic model for the serial position effect. *Psychological Review,* 1968, **75,** 409–420.

Thomas, H. B. G. A serial position effect along a factor-analytic dimension. *Journal of Genetic Psychology,* 1971, **119,** 267–280.

Thompson, L. W., & Obrist, W. D. EEG correlates of verbal learning and overlearning. *Electroencephalography and Clinical Neurophysiology,* 1964, **16,** 332–342.

Thorndike, E. L. & Lorge, I. *The teacher's word book of 30,000 words.* New York: Teachers College, Columbia University, 1944.

Thurstone, L. L. The relation between learning time and length of task. *Psychological Review,* 1930, **37,** 44–53.

Tulving, E. Subjective organization in free recall of "unrelated" words. *Psychological Review,* 1962, **69,** 344–354.

Tulving, E. Intratrial and intertrial retention: Notes towards a theory of free recall verbal learning. *Psychological Review,* 1964, **71,** 219–237.

Tulving, E. The effect of order of presentation on learning of "unrelated" words. *Psychonomic Science,* 1965, **3,** 337–338.

Tulving, E. Theoretical issues in free recall. In T. R. Dixon & D. L. Horton (Eds.), *Verbal behavior and general behavior theory.* Englewood Cliffs, New Jersey: Prentice-Hall, 1968.

Tulving, E. Cue-dependent forgetting. *American Scientist,* 1974, **62,** 74–82.

Tulving, E., & Donaldson, W. (Eds.), *Organization of memory.* New York: Academic Press, 1972.

Tulving, E., & Madigan, S. A. Memory and verbal learning. *Annual Review of Psychology,* 1970, **21,** 437–484.

Tulving, E., & Patterson, R. D. Functional units and retrieval processes in free recall, *Journal of Experimental Psychology*, 1968, **77**, 239–248.

Tulving, E., & Pearlstone, Z. Availability vs. accessibility of information in memory for words. *Journal of Verbal Learning and Verbal Behavior*, 1966, **5**, 381–391.

Tulving, E., & Thomson, D. M. Retrieval processes in recognition memory: Effects of associative context. *Journal of Experimental Psychology*, 1971, **87**, 116–124.

Umemoto, T., & Hilgard, E. R. Paired-associate learning as a function of similarity: Common stimulus and response items within the list. *Journal of Experimental Psychology*, 1961, **62**, 97–104.

Underwood, B. J. The effects of punishment in serial learning. *Proceedings of the Iowa Academy of Science*, 1941, **48**, 349–352.

Underwood, B. J. *Experimental psychology*. New York: Appleton-Century-Crofts, 1949.

Underwood, B. J. Studies of distributed practice: VII. Learning and retention of serial nonsense lists as a function of intralist similarity. *Journal of Experimental Psychology*, 1952, **44**, 80–87. (a)

Underwood, B. J. Studies of distributed practice: VI. The influence of rest-interval activity in serial learning. *Journal of Experimental Psychology*, 1952, **43**, 329–340. (b)

Underwood, B. J. Studies of distributed practice: X. The influence of intralist similarity on learning and retention of serial adjective lists. *Journal of Experimental Psychology*, 1953, **45**, 253–259.

Underwood, B. J. Intralist similarity in verbal learning and retention. *Psychological Review*, 1954, **61**, 160–166.

Underwood, B. J. Interference and forgetting. *Psychological Review*, 1957, **64**, 49–60.

Underwood, B. J. An evaluation of Gibson's theory of verbal learning. In C. N. Cofer (Ed.), *Verbal learning and verbal behavior*. New York: McGraw-Hill, 1961, 197–217.

Underwood, B. J. Stimulus selection in verbal learning. In C. N. Cofer & B. S. Musgrave (Eds.), *Verbal behavior and learning: Problems and processes*. New York: McGraw-Hill, 1963.

Underwood, B. J. The representativeness of rote verbal learning. In A. W. Melton (Ed.), *Categories of human learning*. New York: Academic Press, 1964, 47–78.

Underwood, B. J. Individual and group predictions of item difficulty for free learning. *Journal of Experimental Psychology*, 1966, **71**, 673–679.

Underwood, B. J., & Goad, D. Studies of distributed practice: I. The influence of intralist similarity in serial learning. *Journal of Experimental Psychology*, 1951, **42**, 125–134.

Underwood, B. J., & Keppel, G. One-trial learning? *Journal of Verbal Learning and Verbal Behavior*, 1962, **1**, 1–13.

Underwood, B. J., & Keppel, G. Coding processes in verbal learning. *Journal of Verbal Learning and Verbal Behavior*, 1963, **1**, 250–257.

Underwood, B. J., & Richardson, J. Studies of distributed practice. XIII. Interlist interference and the retention of serial nonsense lists. *Journal of Experimental Psychology*, 1955, **50**, 39–46.

Underwood, B. J., & Richardson, J. The influence of meaningfulness, intralist similarity, and serial position on retention. *Journal of Experimental Psychology*, 1956, **52**, 119–126.

Underwood, B. J., & Richardson, J. Studies of distributed practice: XVIII. The influence of meaningfulness and intralist similarity of serial nonsense lists. *Journal of Experimental Psychology*, 1958, **56**, 213–219.

Underwood, B. J., & Schulz, R. W. *Meaningfulness and verbal learning.* Chicago: Lippincott, 1960.

Underwood, B. J., & Zimmerman, J. Serial retention as a function of hierarchical structure. *Journal of Experimental Psychology,* 1973, **99,** 236–242.

Underwood, B. J., Ham, M., & Ekstrand, B. Cue selection in paired-associate learning. *Journal of Experimental Psychology,* 1962, **64,** 405–409.

Underwood, B. J., Rundquist, W. N., & Schulz, R. W. Response learning in paired-associate lists as a function of intralist similarity. *Journal of Experimental Psychology,* 1959, **58,** 70–78.

Underwood, G. Response organization in attention control and a perceptual serial position effect. *Quarterly Journal of Experimental Psychology,* 1972, **24,** 340–351.

Underwood, G. Concerning the role of perceptual factors in the serial position effect. *Perception & Psychophysics,* 1973, **13,** 344–348.

Van Buskirk, W. L. An experimental study of vividness in learning and retention. *Journal of Experimental Psychology,* 1932, **15,** 563–573.

Vincent, S. B. The function of the vibrissae in the behavior of the white rat. *Behavior Monographs,* 1912, **1,** iv–81.

Voss, J. F. A comparison of motor and verbal serial learning with length of sequence and verbal material as parameters. Unpublished doctoral dissertation, University of Wisconsin, 1956.

Voss, J. F. Serial acquisition as a function of item probability and sequential probability. *Journal of Experimental Psychology,* 1966, **71,** 304–313.

Voss, J. F. Serial acquisition as a function of number of successively occurring list items. *Journal of Experimental Psychology,* 1968, **78,** 456–462.

Voss, J. F. Serial acquisition as a function of stage of learning. *Journal of Experimental Psychology,* 1969, **79,** 220–225.

Wagner, J. Experimentelle Beiträge zür Psychologie des Lesens. *Zeitschrift für Psychologie,* 1918, **80,** 1–75.

Wallace, W. P. Review of the historical, empirical, and theoretical status of the von Restorff phenomenon. *Psychological Bulletin,* 1965, **63,** 410–424.

Wapner, S., & Rand, G. Ontogenetic differences in the nature of organization underlying serial learning. *Human Development,* 1968, **11,** 249–259.

Ward, L. B. Reminiscence and rote learning. *Psychological Monographs,* 1937, **49,** No. 220.

Waters, R. H. Some comments on perceptual organization as the theoretical basis of learning. *American Psychologist,* 1948, **3,** 235.

Watts, G. H., & Royer, J. M. Stimulus context and retroactive inhibition in free recall. *Psychonomic Science,* 1969, **17,** 253–254.

Waugh, N. C. Serial position and the memory-span. *American Journal of Psychology,* 1960, **73,** 68–79.

Waugh, N. C. Free vs. serial recall. *Journal of Experimental Psychology,* 1961, **62,** 496–502.

Waugh, N. C. Length of series and the learning curve. *American Journal of Psychology,* 1962, **75,** 177–192.

Waugh, N. C. Two methods for testing serial memorization. *Journal of Experimental Psychology,* 1963, **65,** 215–216.

Waugh, N. C., & Norman, D. A. Primary memory. *Psychological Review,* 1965, **72,** 89–104.

Webster's third new international dictionary of the English language, unabridged. Springfield, Mass.: Merriam, 1968.

Weingartner, H. Associative structure and serial learning. *Journal of Verbal Learning and Verbal Behavior,* 1963, **2,** 476–479.

Weitz, J. Criteria for criteria. *American Psychologist,* 1961, **16,** 228–231.

Welch, G. B., & Burnett, C. T. Is primacy a factor in association-formation? *American Journal of Psychology,* 1924, **35,** 396–401.

Werner, H. Process and achievement: A basic problem in education and developmental psychology. *Harvard Educational Review,* 1937, **7,** 353–368.

White, M. J. Retinal locus and the letter-span error function. *Perception & Psychophysics,* 1970, **8,** 107–109.

Wickelgren, W. A. Associative intrusions in short-term recall. *Journal of Experimental Psychology,* 1966, **72,** 853–858.

Wickelgren, W. A. Context-sensitive coding, associative memory, and serial order in (speech) behavior. *Psychological Review,* 1969, **76,** 1–15.

Wickelgren, W. A. Multitrace strength theory. In D. A. Norman (Ed.), *Models of human memory.* New York: Academic Press, 1970, 65–102.

Wickens, D. D., Born, D. G., & Allen, C. K. Proactive inhibition and item similarity in short-term memory. *Journal of Verbal Learning and Verbal Behavior,* 1963, **2,** 440–445.

Wiener, Y. Rate of presentation as a factor in isolation. *Perceptual and Motor Skills,* 1970, **31,** 735–738.

Wilkes, A. L. Reading pauses during serial list learning with fixed or randomly changing groups. *Journal of Experimental Psychology,* 1972, **94,** 206–209.

Wilkes, A. L., & Kennedy, R. A. The relative accessibility of list items within different pause-defined groups. *Journal of Verbal Learning and Verbal Behavior,* 1970, **9,** 197–201.

Willet, R. A. The effect of a stimulant and a depressant drug on the serial rote learning of nonsense syllables. Unpublished paper, 1958. Cited by H. G. Jones in Eysenck, H. J. (Ed.), *Handbook of abnormal psychology,* New York: Basic Books, 1961, 488–528.

Williams, J. P. Supplementary report: A selection artifact in Rock's study of the role of repetition. *Journal of Experimental Psychology,* 1961, **62,** 627–628.

Williams, J. P. A test of the all-or-none hypothesis for verbal learning. *Journal of Experimental Psychology,* 1962, **64,** 158–165.

Wilson, J. T. Remote associations as a function of the length of interval between learning and recall. *Journal of Experimental Psychology,* 1943, **33,** 40–49.

Wilson, J. T. The formation and retention of remote associations in rote learning. *Journal of Experimental Psychology,* 1949, **39,** 830–838.

Wilson, M. E., & Hartman, R. R. Certain time relations in serial rote learning. *Virginia Journal of Science,* 1960, **11,** 217. (Abstract)

Wing, J. F. Effects of set on the serial-position curve for typographically-differentiated lists. *Perceptual and Motor Skills,* 1964, **19,** 515–519.

Wing, J. F. Stimulus-trace model of serial acquisition and retention. *Proceedings of the 75th Annual Convention, American Psychological Association,* 1967, 59–60.

Winnick, W. A., & Dornbush, R. L. Role of positional cues in serial rote learning. *Journal of Experimental Psychology,* 1963, **66,** 419–421.

Winnick, W. A., & Dornbush, R. L. Ordinal position in serial learning. *Journal of Experimental Psychology,* 1968, **78,** 536–538.

Winzenz, D. Group structure and coding in serial learning. *Journal of Experimental Psychology,* 1972, **92,** 8–19.

Wishner, J., Shipley, T. E., & Hurvich, M. S. The serial position curve as a function of organization. *American Journal of Psychology*, 1957, **70**, 258–262.

Wohlgemuth, A. On memory and the direction of associations. *British Journal of Psychology*, 1913, **5**, 447–465.

Wood, G. Whole-part transfer from free recall to serial learning. *Journal of Experimental Psychology*, 1969, **79**, 540–544.

Woods, S. C., & Epstein, M. I. Learning and recall differentiated in serial learning. *Psychonomic Science*, 1969, **15**, 297–299.

Woodward, A. Jr. A search for the stimulus in serial learning. Unpublished doctoral dissertation, University of Toronto, 1968.

Woodward, A. E. Continuity between serial memory and serial learning. *Journal of Experimental Psychology*, 1970, **85**, 90–94.

Woodward, A. E., & Murdock, B. B. Jr. Positional and sequential probes in serial learning. *Canadian Journal of Psychology*, 1968, **22**, 131–138.

Woodworth, R. S. *Experimental psychology.* New York: Holt, 1938.

Woodworth, R. S., & Poffenberger, A. T. A textbook of experimental psychology. Mimeographed, 1920. Cited by W. G. Workman, An experimental investigation of cognitive factors as contrasted with non-cognitive factors in rote serial learning. Unpublished doctoral dissertation, University of Chicago, 1951.

Woodworth, R. S., & Schlosberg, H. *Experimental psychology.* New York: Holt, Rinehart and Winston, 1954.

Workman, W. G. An experimental investigation of cognitive factors as contrasted with non-cognitive factors in rote serial learning. Unpublished doctoral dissertation, University of Chicago, 1951.

Wright, J. H., & Bernstein, D. A. Effects of conceptual grouping of adjacent items on serial-learning. *Psychological Reports*, 1965, **17**, 187–190.

Yerkes, R. M., & Dodson, J. D. The relation of strength of stimulus to rapidity of habit-formation. *Journal of Comparative Neurology and Psychology*, 1908, **18**, 459–482.

Yntema, D. B., & Trask, F. P. Recall as a search process. *Journal of Verbal Learning and Verbal Behavior*, 1963, **2**, 65–74.

Young, R. K. A comparison of two methods of learning serial associations. *American Journal of Psychology*, 1959, **72**, 554–559.

Young, R. K. The stimulus in serial verbal learning. *American Journal of Psychology*, 1961, **74**, 517–528.

Young, R. K. Tests of three hypotheses about the effective stimulus in serial learning. *Journal of Experimental Psychology*, 1962, **63**, 307–313.

Young, R. K. Serial learning. In T. R. Dixon & D. L. Horton (Eds.), *Verbal behavior and general behavior theory.* Englewood Cliffs, New Jersey: Prentice-Hall, 1968, 122–148.

Young, R. K., & Casey, M. Transfer from serial to paired-associate learning. *Journal of Experimental Psychology*, 1964, **67**, 594–595.

Young, R. K., & Clark, J. Compound-stimulus hypothesis in serial learning. *Journal of Experimental Psychology*, 1964, **67**, 301–302.

Young, R. K., & Jennings, P. C. Backward learning when the same items serve as stimuli and responses. *Journal of Experimental Psychology*, 1964, **68**, 64–70.

Young, R. K., & Parker, G. V. C. Serial learning as a function of experimentally induced meaningfulness. *Journal of Experimental Psychology*, 1970, **84**, 24–26.

Young, R. K., Hakes, D. T., & Hicks, R. Y. Effects of list length in the Ebbinghaus derived-list paradigm. *Journal of Experimental Psychology,* 1965, **70,** 338–341.

Young, R. K., Hakes, D. T., & Hicks, R. Y. Ordinal position number as a cue in serial learning. *Journal of Experimental Psychology,* 1967, **73,** 427–438.

Young, R. K., Milauckas, E. W., & Bryan, J. D. Serial learning as a function of prior paired-associate training. *American Journal of Psychology,* 1963, **76,** 82–88.

Young, R. K., Patterson, J., & Benson, W. M. Backward serial learning. *Journal of Verbal Learning and Verbal Behavior,* 1963, **1,** 335–338.

Youssef, Z. I. Association and integration in serial learning. *American Journal of Psychology,* 1967, **80,** 355–367.

Zaffiro, W. R. The relative roles of serial position and sequential association effects as related to levels of meaningfulness in a serial learning task. Unpublished doctoral dissertation, University of Southern Mississippi, 1969.

Zavortink, B., & Keppel, G. Retroactive inhibition of interitem associations for serial lists with constant or varied starting positions. *Journal of Verbal Learning and Verbal Behavior,* 1968, **7,** 771–775.

Zeigler, T. W. Forced and optional intervals of presentation in the serial learning of nonsense material. *Journal of General Psychology,* 1939, **21,** 277–306.

Zirkle, G. A. Success and failure in serial learning. II. Isolation and the Thorndike effect. *Journal of Experimental Psychology,* 1946, **36,** 302–315.

AUTHOR INDEX

SUBJECT INDEX